Adventure Planner

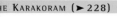

November colour in the Mastuj Valley, Hindu Kush

ADVENTURE TRAVELLERS

INDIA, PAKISTAN & THE HIMALAYA

AA World Travel Guides

ADVENTURE TRAVELLERS

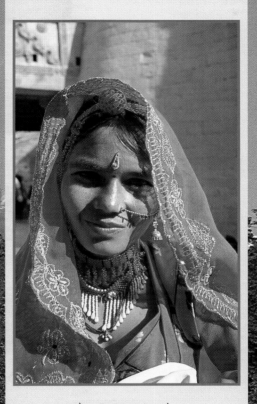

INDIA, PAKISTAN
& THE HIMALAYA

Produced by AA Publishing
© Automobile Association Developments Ltd 2001
Maps © Automobile Association Developments Ltd 2001
Coloured maps produced by the Cartographic Department,
The Automobile Association
Black and white maps produced by Advanced Illustration,
Congleton, Cheshire
A CIP catalogue record for this book is available from
the British Library
ISBN 0-7495-2358-1

The contents of this publication are believed correct at the time of
printing. Nevertheless, the publishers cannot be held responsible for any
errors or omissions or for changes in the details given in this guide or for
the consequences of any reliance on the information provided by the
same. Assessments of sights, accommodation, restaurants and so forth are
based upon the authors' own experience and, therefore, descriptions
given in this guide necessarily contain an element of subjective opinion
which may not reflect the publisher's opinion or dictate a reader's own
experience on another occasion.
We have tried to ensure accuracy in this guide, but things do change
and we would be grateful if readers would advise us of any inaccuracies
they may encounter.
The areas covered in this guide can be subject to political, economic,
and climatic upheaval, readers should consult tour operators, embassies
and consulates, airlines, e.t.c. for current requirements and advice before
travelling. The publishers and authors cannot accept responsibility for any
loss, injury, or inconvenience, however caused.

Published by AA Publishing, a trading name of Automobile Association
Developments Limited, whose registered office is Norfolk House, Priestley
Road, Basingstoke, Hampshire RG24 9NY.
Registered number 1878835.

Visit our website at www.theAA.com

Colour separation by Chroma Graphics (Overseas) Pte Ltd, Singapore
Printed and bound G Canale & C. s.p.a., Torino, Italy
Previous page: *The Annapurna range is glorious trekking country*
Inset: *Jaiselmer tribal woman in vibrantly coloured* odinis

4

CONTENTS

INTRODUCTION

Between the sultry heat of southern India and Pakistan and the rarefied air of the Himalayan countries far to the north, exists an extraordinary and exotic and sometimes bewildering concoction of landscapes, people, and cultures. Amongst boundless opportunities for adventurous souls, you can choose to go camel riding, tracking tigers, visiting ancient tribes, scuba diving, whitewater rafting, horseback-riding, and hiking. India alone is enough to keep you busy for a lifetime and Pakistan is still a relatively undiscovered destination for travellers. In Nepal the magnificent grandeur of the Himalayan Mountains awaits, and you get to see the age-old cultures of the mountain people, little changed in thousands of years. Tropical Sri Lanka offers a completely different kind of experience, with a motorbike being an excellent way to tour the island. From north to south, jungle, forest, dusty desert, hills and plains, and a myriad waterways all vie with each other to test the adventurer. There is no way these diverse locations can be summarized and do them any justice, save to say that if it is a truly extraordinary experience that you are after then this is the place to travel. The lure of the region is so strong that it demands at least one return visit, or you may join the other travellers who come back again and again throughout their lives.

Tibetan prayer wheels
Inset: *Local cyclists crossing the Rapti Khola River in Nepal*

About the Authors

JILL GOCHER

Australian travel photo-journalist Jill Gocher has spent much of her life

travelling starting some time ago as a 'military brat' when a family posting to Penang began her love affair with Asia. After specialising in Indonesia, for years and writing several books on that country, she now prefers to spend her time in the mountains where the cool air and cooler altitudes allow heightened perceptions on life. She writes for numerous magazines, books and guide books.

DES HANNIGAN

Des Hannigan was a professional fisherman for fifteen years before taking up what he mistakenly thought

might be an easier life as a journalist. He is now a freelance travel writer and photographer and has written over twenty books, including rock climbing guides and walking guides as well as general travel guides to Northern Europe, Greece and Spain.

SIMON RICHMOND

Simon Richmond's first brush with adventure was

on the Big Dipper rollercoaster in his hometown of Blackpool, England. He's been in search of the same adrenalin rush ever since. Now based in Sydney, Australia, he's worked as a journalist in London and Tokyo. His features have been published in many U.K. newspapers, the *Sydney Morning Herald*, and *The Australian*. He now spends most of his time travelling and writing guidebooks for the AA, Lonely Planet, and Rough Guides.

EMMA STANFORD

Emma Stanford was born on a Thursday and still

has far to go. Her travels have taken her around the world and she has written books and articles on far-flung adventures from volcano-watching in Hawaii and kit-car rallying in Morocco to horse riding in the Hindu Kush. For this guide she discovers rhinos and river dolphins in Assam.

LEE KAREN STOW

Lee Karen Stow is a full-

time travel journalist and photographer, based in Yorkshire, England. A member of the British Guild of Travel Writers, Lee's work has appeared in a number of publications, including *The Times*; the *Sunday Express*; *In Britain*; *Wanderlust*; *Travel Weekly* among others. Born with a wandering spirit, Lee travels whenever possible perhaps scuba diving, scrubbing floors, sailing a yacht or teaching English to schoolchildren.

HUGH TAYLOR

Hugh Taylor, compiler of

the A–Z section, is a freelance broadcaster, travel writer, and photographer working regularly for a variety of newspapers and magazines, guidebook publishers and the BBC. He is co-author of *AA Essential Scotland*, *AA Spiral Scotland* and part author of the *AA Book of Britain's Walks* and *AA Exploring Britain*.

STEVE WATKINS

Photographer and writer Steve Watkins specializes

in covering adventure travel, extreme sports and cultural issues, especially in his favourite destinations—Latin America and Australia. His work has featured in numerous publications, including *No Limits World*, *Traveller*, *Global Adventure*, *Wanderlust*, *Mountain Biking UK*, *Sunday Express* and various BBC publications, and his photographs have been widely exhibited, including at London's Barbican Gallery. Now based in south Wales, he has recently finished writing *Adventure Sports Europe* (Queensgate Publishing).

How to Use this Book

The book is divided into three distinct sections:

SECTION 1 — PAGES 6–17

This comprises the introductory material and some general practical advice to guide you on your travels. We have included an introduction to the writing team. Our authors come from all walks of life and cover a wide age range. What they do have in common, though, is a spirit of adventure and a wealth of travel experience.

The map on pages 10–11 shows the areas covered, and is colour-coded to highlight the regional divides. The 25 adventures are numbered for reference; the contents page will guide you straight to the relevant page numbers.

Pages 12–17 offer practical advice from experienced travellers, complementing information given later.

The seasonal calendar inside the cover gives a guide to the optimum time to visit the areas covered in the adventures. However, there are many factors affecting when you might like to go, and greater details of climate patterns and their effect on activities are given at the end of each chapter. When arranging your trip always seek advice about the conditions you are likely to encounter from a tour operator or country tourist information office.

SECTION 2 — PAGES 18–256

The main section of the book contains 25 adventures, chosen to give you a taste of a wide range of activities in a variety of places—some familiar, others not. The first page of each adventure carries a practical information box that gives you an idea of what to expect, plus a grade, numbered according to the relative difficulty of the activity or the level of skill required.

Going it Alone—Each adventure ends with a page of dedicated practical advice for planning that specific adventure yourself. This information should be used in conjunction with the "Blue Pages" at the end of the book (see below).

Any prices mentioned in the book are given in US dollars and were the approximate prices current at the time of the trip. Due to variations in inflation and exchange rates these are only meant as guidelines to give an idea of comparative cost.

 Challenge Rating: If you have even thought about booking the trip, you will manage

 Not too difficult but you may need some basic skills

 You will need to be fit, with lots of stamina and may need specialist qualifications

 You need to be fit and determined—not for the faint-hearted*

 This is for the serious adventurer— physically and mentally challenging!*

Sometimes only part of the trip is very hard and there may be an easier option

 Comfort rating: Indicates the degree of hardship you can expect, where 3 is comfort-able and 1 is uncomfortable. This category not only covers accommodation, but also factors such as climate and other conditions that may affect your journey.

 Specialist equipment: Advice on any equipment needed for the journey, covering specialist items like diving gear, and also clothing and photographic gear.

SECTION 3 — PAGES 257–320

"Blue Pages"—*Contacts* and *A–Z of Activities*—begin with selected contacts specific to the 25 main adventures. Here you'll find names referred to in the main stories, including tour operators, with addresses and contact numbers.

The A–Z lists a wide range of the best activities available in the region, with general information and full contact details of the outfits and organizations able to help you plan your journey. Finally, the book ends with a comprehensive index and gazetteer.

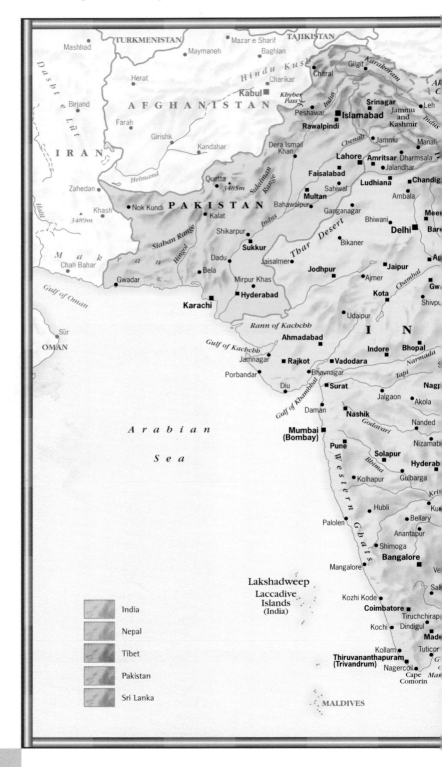

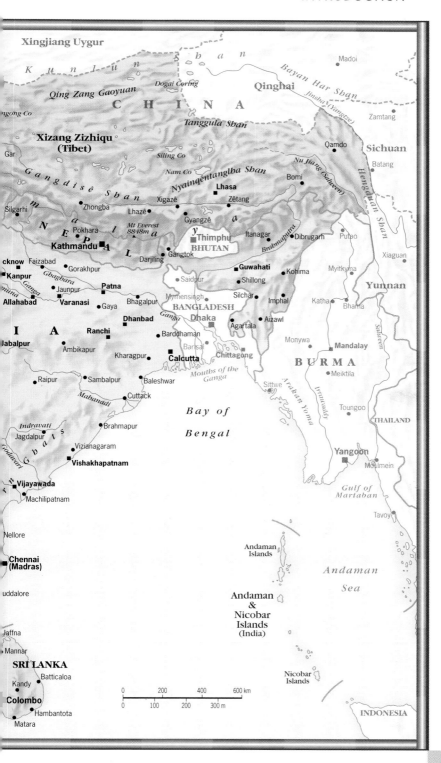

Practical Matters

TRAVEL DOCUMENTS

Although a passport is the first thing to be packed by most travellers, it is worth checking to ensure that it is valid for much longer than your stay, and there are enough blank pages left for visa stamps. Many immigration officials are reluctant to stamp previously used pages, no matter how much space is left on it. Of course, the more countries you visit the more blank pages you need. It is also important to carry several copies of the passport, especially the front cover, personal details page and those pages containing any essential visas. These copies can significantly speed up arranging a new passport should it be lost or stolen. It is also worth leaving copies at home with friends or relatives, in case you lose everything.

Be sure to check at least a couple of months before your intended departure date about the visa requirements for the countries you are visiting. Obtaining travel visas has become much easier in the last decade or so as governments have realized that tourism numbers increase with a reduction in red tape. Many countries now allow tourist visas to be issued on entry into the country, especially if you arrive by air, whilst others still require you to obtain a visa before travelling. If possible, get a visa for the longest duration possible and certainly for longer than you intend to be there. This allows the option to stay on if you like it too much to leave, and provides leeway for any problems with delays departing the country, such as cancelled flights or illness.

HEALTH MATTERS

Nothing can make such a difference to your enjoyment of an adventure as your health, so it is worth taking as many precautions as possible to maintain it. Necessary vaccinations vary with the country you are visiting and even which region of the country you go to, but ensuring your protection against tetanus is current is important wherever you travel. Give yourself plenty of time, at least six weeks, to get all the necessary vaccinations, as some require more than one visit to the doctor. Also, if you think you already have a full complement of inoculations then it is still worth checking with a doctor before travelling as situations change reasonably regularly and there can be sudden outbreaks of diseases. Polio and hepatitis A vaccinations are needed for travel outside of Europe,

" LANGUAGE

Although there are various languages spoken throughout this region, in the popular spots along the tourism routes English is understood too. There are some very basic phrases, such as "hello," "how are you," and "goodbye", that can be easily learnt in all the local languages. They are real icebreakers when meeting people so it is worth taking a phrasebook with you.

India	Hindi, English
Pakistan	Urdu, English
Nepal	Nepali
Sri Lanka	Sinhala, Tamil, English

LOCAL CURRENCY

India	Rupee = 100 paise
Pakistan	Pakistani Rupee = 100 paisa
Nepal	Nepalese Rupee = 100 paisa
Sri Lanka	Sri Lankan Rupee = 100 cents

North America, and Australasia. Other vaccinations that may be necessary are hepatitis B, cholera, typhoid, rabies, Japanese encephalitis, and yellow fever. A current yellow fever vaccination certificate may be demanded on entry to some countries if you have recently visited a potential risk area. Record your vaccinations on an International Health Certificate and carry it with you.

Do not ignore the dentist either in preparation for a trip. Get your teeth checked out at home as it can cost a surprisingly large amount of money to get dental work done in other countries, costs that may not be covered by your travel insurance. It is particularly important to have your teeth in good working order when visiting areas with very cold climates as the temperature can cause problems with fillings. A comprehensive travel insurance policy that covers substantial medical costs is absolutely essential on any trip.

INSURANCE

Unless you are fabulously wealthy or a big-time gambler then comprehensive travel insurance is essential. It may seem to cost a lot for something you are unlikely to use, but if things do go wrong then it could not only save your holiday but, in more serious cases, it could save you going bankrupt too. If you are not convinced then consider the cost of being airlifted from a mountain environment in the event of a serious injury and transferring you to a suitable hospital. Think in tens of thousands of US dollars and suddenly the insurance fee seems a bargain. If you want to ensure the best care then take out a good policy, one that includes cover for at least personal accident, medical and air ambulance, personal liability, legal expenses, cancellation, personal baggage and loss of passport. Ensure that the policy covers 'adventure' activities, which are usually excluded in ordinary policies. With the baggage cover, check the single item limits as expensive items, such as cameras, can fall outside of this. If you are lucky enough to travel a few times a year then consider taking out an annual policy as they can be cheaper than several individual trip policies.

Try to keep receipts for anything you buy to go away, or instead take a photograph of all your gear laid out. With more and more fraudulent claims taking place every year, insurance companies are even keener to prove ownership. Each insurance company has differing requirements for lodging a claim but the very least you will need to do for theft

✚ VACCINATIONS

For visits to any of the countries featured in this title then the following vaccinations are currently recommended: yellow fever (if coming from an infected area), cholera, typhoid, polio, and hepatitis A. Protection against malaria is also necessary. Check with your doctor for the latest information, as the situation can change.

→ CUSTOMS/ENTRY REQUIREMENTS ⚊

Passport photos are necessary for applying for the following visas:

India Visas are required by all foreign nationals and should be obtained prior to arriving in the country. Visas for India can be acquired from the Indian embassy in Kathmandu, Nepal, but the process takes at least one week. It is usually much quicker in your home country. Tourist visas are valid for six months from date of issue, not from date of entry.

Pakistan All foreign nationals require visas. They are valid for three months and must be used within six months of issue.

Nepal Tourist visas are required by all foreign nationals and can be applied for on arrival at Kathmandu airport. It is advisable though to acquire one from the Nepalese consulate in your home country before travelling as this saves time and hassle on arrival. It is essential to get a visa beforehand if you are arriving overland. There are several types of visa available from single-entry to multiple-entry. Single-entry visas are valid for 60 days and must be used within six months of date of issue.

Sri Lanka Tourist visas are issued free of charge on arrival at the international airport to E.U., U.S. and Canadian nationals for stay of up to 30 days. Australian passport holders can stay for up to 90 days.

cases is obtain a signed local police report detailing the incident and every item that was taken.

MONEY

There are several useful ways of getting access to money while travelling that reduce the risk of loss through theft. A very popular option is to take travellers' cheques, which can be converted into local currency at banks and larger hotels or even used to pay directly for goods and services. The most globally accepted

Below: *Turbaned Jaisalmer man showing off his moustaches*

travellers' cheques are Thomas Cook, American Express, and Visa in US dollars. Be aware though that on top of the commission fees most issuers charge to issue the cheques, you are often charged another commission fee to use them, which can result in significant loss of value (3 percent or more). However, if you keep track of where you use the cheques and they are subsequently lost or stolen, it is relatively straightforward to cancel them and have new ones sent to you in a matter of a few days at most.

With the spread of automatic bank teller machines (ATMs) to even remote areas, an increasingly easy way to access money is via a credit or debit card. If you have a Personal Identification Number (PIN) and a card that is linked to one of the international transaction systems, such as Link or Cirrus, then you can withdraw local currency up to your daily limit. Many machines detect the nationality of your card and provide instructions in your own language just to make things even easier. This is a very safe way of carrying money and can be very cost effective on debit cards. However, credit card companies treat

TIME DIFFERENCES

	London, noon = 0 hours (Greenwich Mean Time)	New York Noon local time	San Franicisco Noon local time
India	+5½	+10½	+13½
Pakistan	+5	+10	+13
Nepal	+5¾	+10¾	+13¾
Sri Lanka	+6	+11	+14

foreign currency withdrawals as cash advances and usually charge a commission fee and you incur interest charges from day of withdrawal. Wherever you travel, it is essential to carry some cash with you, but do not make it so much that losing it could spoil your trip. The more remote the area you are visiting the more important it is to carry smaller denominations, as sometimes change for large notes can be hard to come by if you are only buying a soft drink or snack.

There is no completely safe method of carrying your money, but a travel money belt or neck pouch are particularly popular as both are designed to be concealed under your clothing and are big enough to carry a passport too. It is wise to carry a small wallet with a little money in that is easily accessible so that you do not have to rummage under your

Above: The usual daily bustle at Darjeeling's Legship bazaar, one of the many busy bazaars below the Chowrasta

clothes to buy small things. It can also be a useful decoy if thieves accost you—giving up your lightly filled wallet may be enough to make them happy! Try to avoid revealing your main stash of cash in crowded places, such as markets. Do not leave money hanging around in hotel rooms, no matter how exclusive a place it is. We all bow to temptation at some time or another so avoid tempting room cleaners and hotel staff with stuffed wallets or expensive equipment. Use the hotel safe deposit box, making sure you are given a full receipt for all deposits. Many insurance policies do not cover valuables stolen from a room if there is a deposit box available at reception.

Travelling Safe

WHAT TO TAKE

While the majority of things you take with you when you are travelling are specific to each country, there is a core of travel gear that can be considered important on all trips.

BAG IT UP

Although travellers can be seen using all sorts of luggage carriers, some are just suckers for suffering. Unless every single aspect of your trip is sorted beforehand and you are doing everything from a base then forget about taking a hard suitcase. They are unwieldy and generally not suited to more adventurous trips. Hold-all bags, available from outdoor stores, are large, robust and have good handle options—some even have tuck-away backpack straps for short hikes to hotels or stations. However, if you plan on doing any lengthier walks with your luggage, then it is worth buying a suitcase-style travel backpack. Most have excellent harnesses for carrying heavy loads over a reasonable distance. The straps all pack away to make the luggage look smarter in hotels and prevent straps from snagging on conveyor belts. The main compartment opens up fully like a suitcase, so it is easier to keep clothes neat, and there are numerous extra pockets and storage areas for organizing your luggage. Top-loading backpacks, or expedition-style packs, are only really necessary if you envisage doing long hikes where you need to carry a lot of equipment.

In addition to your main baggage, a daypack is invaluable for use as hand luggage on aircraft and for carrying around towns or on day trips. If you can avoid taking more than two bags then you will find things a lot easier when taking public transport. Make sure you have some way of securing all bags, such as a lock or a strap.

CLOTHING

Clothing requirements will very much depend on what you intend doing and where you intend doing it. For flexibility in varying climate conditions, it is better to take a number of thin layers rather than one or two thick layers. Most trips require a lightweight waterproof jacket and a warm layer, such as a fleece jacket, to keep the chills at bay on cool evenings. Footwear is heavy and bulky. Seasoned travellers will take just one pair of shoes and maybe lightweight sandals or sand-shoes for relaxing times and visits to the beach. There is plenty of good travel footwear available these days, with shoes or boots that are okay for light hiking but still smart enough to wear out to a bar.

ACCESSORIZE

Useful accessories include a universal sink plug (you'll be amazed how many hotels do not have sink plugs!), a light-weight travel towel, a pocket knife, and some duct tape, which can be used for backpack repairs. A basic first aid kit is essential too.

FILM

For photographers it is wise to take as much film as you think you'll need for the entire trip (overestimate rather than run out of film when things get exciting). Film is generally available in major cities around the world but it is hard to ensure quality of storage conditions in some places, so play safe and take it with you. Keep the film in your hand luggage for all air travel and, except in airports in developed countries with "film safe" X-ray machines, insist on having it hand searched at X-ray machines. This is usually agreed to with little fuss. X-ray effects build up on film with each pass, through a machine so avoid taking left-over film from previous trips.

What to Avoid

A few simple precautions can make your trip a lot safer.

Drugs and Other Traps

It may seem obvious, but using or carrying illegal drugs of any kind whilst travelling is asking for trouble. If you're caught then it may not just be a fine or the drugs that you lose, but your freedom too, possibly for years. In countries that still operate the death penalty, drug smuggling is often one of the qualifying crimes.

Perhaps the easiest trap to fall into is purchasing souvenirs made from parts of endangered animals. Check your own country's customs regulations before travelling to ensure that you do not unwittingly contravene the laws. Penalties for smuggling endangered animals, dead or alive, can be as severe as those for drug smuggling in some countries. Never carry anything for anyone else through customs, no matter how friendly they may seem or how much they offer to pay.

Personal Safety

Whilst staying safe is very important on your travels, there is little point in becoming so obsessed with it that it spoils your holiday. Using the common sense that comes naturally to most people when visiting any big cities is really all you need on adventures in remote regions too. A healthy level of scepticism will help prevent you falling foul of the various tricks and scams that travellers encounter.

Travellers Tips

- Treat any stranger who approaches you with caution. The more eager the person, the more caution is necessary.

- Learn to say no with some conviction.

- Stay as calm and clear-headed as possible, though this can be hard in stressful, crowded situations.

- Take a second or two before answering any question from a stranger.

At Night

Talk to friendly locals that you have met, such as hotel owners and tour guides, and ask about safe and unsafe areas to visit. It is very much in their interest that you remain safe for the sake of the tourism business. If possible, when you arrive somewhere, take time to get to know the place before heading out for a big night of partying and don't drink too much. Avoiding getting very drunk is a major factor in staying safe.

Avoid wearing any signs of wealth. Even if your watch and jewellery are not that expensive in your own country, they are relatively valuable in many other countries where incomes are much lower. The majority of impromptu attacks are money related so keeping your valuables out of sight is a good idea. Use a money belt or pouch that fits under your clothing and avoid accessing it in public areas. When going out around town, leave any large sums of money in your hotel safe deposit box.

Dress Sense

Dress conservatively. Flashy or revealing clothes all attract the wrong sort of attention. For women, it is sensible not to expose too much of your body no matter how strongly you feel that your personal rights should allow you to wear whatever you want. This is particularly important in countries where it is culturally insensitive to wear such clothing.

Be Honest

On active adventures there is often an inherent but usually small risk of personal injury or worse involved. Be very honest with tour operators about your own abilities. There are often easier options available. Halfway down a big, wild rapid in a raft is not the time to divulge that you cannot swim. Take responsibility for your own actions, think on your feet rather than being led like a sheep and voice concerns over any safety issues that you are not happy or comfortable with. Any good operator won't take offence at such questions.

INDIA

I rritating, enthralling, vast, and teeming with life, India never fails to enchant. Mother India, as she is fondly known, is the cradle of uncountable cultures and ancient crafts. Hi-tech computer and industrial sites contrast with age-old villages where life carries on unchanged, and even in the midst of great change, things remain the same. Millennia-old buildings slowly crumble to dust as bright new hotels emerge in the big cities. The all-encompassing culture makes no distinction. All is embraced, all is accepted.

In India, travel itself can be an adventure, as this is one country that has not completely geared itself to the tourist. Self-absorbed India trundles on, regardless of visitors. From sleepy beaches to Himalayan hideaways, ancient architecture and traditional tribal villages, wildlife sanctuaries and desert fortresses, there is so much to see and experience that it could take years of wandering. But there is no need to rush. Timeless India will be there for a long time to come.

The Yamuna River, behind the Taj Mahal

1 Camel Safari in Jaisalmer

by Jill Gocher

Riding a camel in the Rajasthan desert and sleeping out under the stars can be an almost mystical experience—as long as you choose a reliable operator. The slow, rhythmic pace of the camels' walk allows time to attune to the pace of the desert, and there is plenty to enjoy, especially the rests in the shade of the trees at noon, the evening campfire, the sunsets, and sunrises.

Swaying slowly along on the back of the camel, my mind wandered to thoughts of the desert and its enormity. The Thar (meaning sandy ridges or dunes) is part of the Great Indian Desert. It marks the eastern extremities of the northern tropical desert belt, which sweeps from the Atlantic coast of Africa, through the Sahara and on through Arabia, Iran, and Pakistan, to India. The Great Indian Desert is the world's most thickly populated desert, averaging 83 people per square kilometre. While it is also the most ecologically disturbed, it manages to retain a stark grandeur, a large tribal population, some wildlife, and a surprising amount of birdlife.

Jaisalmer, in Rajasthan, is the preferred departure point for the majority of camel safaris. Pushkar and Bikaneer are two alternatives, but Jaisalmer, an ancient fort city on the edge of the desert, remains the acknowledged centre of the camel safari business. The town has years of experience conducting safaris and an abundance of tour companies. However, choosing a good one requires an amount of checking before you go (see box). Owing to circumstance and an innate ability to go with the flow, I ended up with possibly the worst safari company in town. When the safari I had booked was cancelled, my hotel put me in touch with another company. Although the price I paid was the equivalent of $20 a day— enough for a mid-range to luxurious safari—what I received was the very worst of the bottom end. While others were raving about fabulous food, great sights, and good accommodations, my own experience was somewhat less than spectacular.

Everyone has an opinion about riding a camel, and few seem to be positive. Sitting atop one of these quirky ships of the desert has been likened to being tossed about in a small boat in the middle of an ocean storm. Generally, any talk relating to camel riding includes such sterling advice as "take a pillow," bring sea sickness pills," or simply "don't bother." But there is a plus side. It is generally preferable to walking!

In fact I found it quite comfortable— for an hour or so. The comfort factor seemed to fade pretty fast after that. In the East, they say, camel riders sit cross-

1 There is little difficulty in riding a camel. All it needs is a strong constitution, a hard seat, and the ability to withstand long hours sitting under the hot sun.

★★ While sleeping under the stars has its charm, at the end of the day a shower and a cool drink are hard to beat. The quality of the experience is very dependent on who organizes the trek. Make plenty of inquiries about the food, the facilities, the journey, and the sights to ensure that it is a good one.

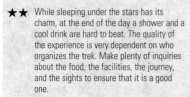 Sun protection and drinking water are the most obvious needs. It is better to do as the camel men do and cover up, rather than wearing bare backs or skimpy tops, which can lead to sunburn, sunstroke, and dehydration. Even in the autumn months (September–November) the days get to be quite hot, with temperatures reaching 30°C (85°F).

legged, but with all the baggage and lumps on our saddle, this was not an option. I found it was the feet that suffered most. The hard, thin, nylon rope of our makeshift stirrups cut into my legs and feet with the efficiency of a chain saw. Proper stirrups would have made a major difference. But you need something in order to hold on, so it was a choice between foot shredding or letting the legs hang loose—fine for a 10-minute break, but not really an all-day option.

GETTING TO THE CAMELS

My group was very small: just Astrid, a German girl, and me. We left town around 9am to drive into the desert. Traditionally, operators have headed towards Samm, a desert area where the rolling sand dunes are at their best. Increasingly, however, they are saving on fuel and heading to an area conveniently close to town, a stony desert populated with a number of villages and things to see. A 20-minute ride brought us to a small, dusty village where we stopped to await our "team" of helpers. After a short time, a Muslim man arrived with two camels and our guide—an 18-year-old Muslim boy wearing a long, dark robe and a surly expression. Salleh was to be our team: our cook, guide, assistant, and provider of entertainment rolled into one. Visions of an exotic Rajasthan experience dissolved in an instant.

Taking a deep breath and hoping that things would improve, I alighted from the jeep to examine the situation up close. It didn't look any better from the ground. Each camel had an enormous bag of grassy substance on his back—fuel for the journey. Our own supplies seemed suspiciously meagre. I could see one small bag of vegetables and not much else. What were we going to EAT? Having had previous experience of unscrupulous tour operators, my suspicions were strongly aroused and, as it turned out, with good reason.

Astrid, on the other hand, was delighted. She had her own camel, she

meant to learn to ride it, and she set about readying herself for her coming adventure. Perhaps it was that Teutonic nature, or maybe her youth, that made her so amenable to adversity.

SETTING OFF

We set off almost immediately, following the direction of the main road, but about 100 metres away from it. The land was stony and hot, with small scrubby bushes the only objects to relieve the visual boredom. I had been hoping for real desert, with sand, sandhills, and that kind of endless expanse of time and space that changes your consciousness. As we wandered along, we passed a couple of other groups returning to Jaisalmer, but they were too far away to speak to. The whole trip seemed to take on a slightly surreal air. Where were we going? What were we doing?

I had imagined sitting happily atop a camel for an hour or so, until we came to a local village, where we would stop for a while and look around, take pictures of the inhabitants, enjoy a cool drink and a chat, then wander on to the next one. Middays would be spent sitting under a shady tree enjoying a simple meal with a glass of wine, taking a little siesta, or reading a book. The possibility of stringing up a hammock and getting more comfortable was also quite attractive. We might do a spot of quiet birdwatching, in the cooler hours of the afternoon, then move on in time to stop and make camp before sunset. I was not expecting a survival course.

THE CAMELS

Another camel arrived, making three in total—Dangi, Babloo, and Sunya. Babloo, a three-year-old, was the baby, so he trailed behind the other two, learning the ropes of the camel business. After all I had read about these extraordinary-looking animals, I expected more temperament and more bad manners, but these were remarkably well behaved, even to the extent of allowing us to

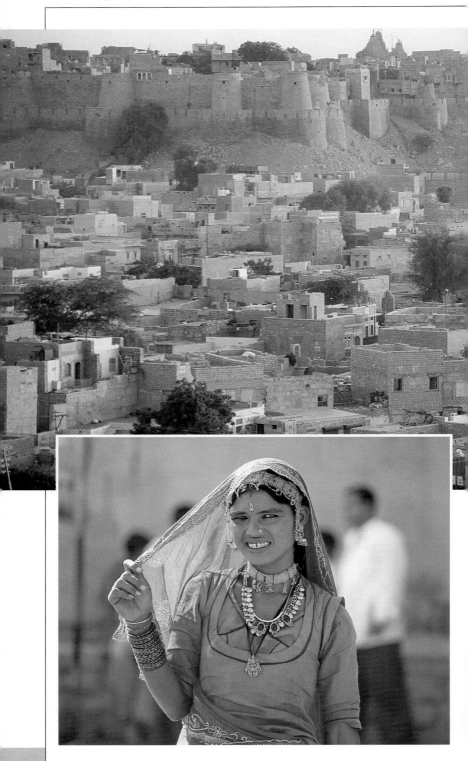

Left: *The sandstone city of Jaisalmer shimmers in the heat*
Below left: *Muslim tribal girl, Jaisalmer*
Below: *Camel safari operators enjoying a break*

mount and steer them without Salleh's guiding hand. But they were not interested in building personal relationships. They were there to do a job, and they did well. Being pampered and playing with the guests had no part in their agenda. They wanted to be left alone to eat as much feed as they could.

Getting on and off a camel is quite an adventure in itself. The camel has to kneel down; you clamber on; then he stands, back feet first (or is it the front feet?). Whichever way, it's dizzying, with a lot of leaning forward (or back), hoping that the saddle is well secured, and hanging on tight, as he sways up to a standing position. This is usually accompanied by a grunt and a groan or two—camels seem to be quite loquacious.

It is always worth checking the bindings that run around the camel's girth. Simply slip your fingers between the strap and the camel, and pull, making sure that it's tight. If you can move the strap around, or slip your fingers in easily, then it's too loose and you could fall off. Tell your guide to tighten it properly.

UNDER THE STARS

The minor excitement of arriving at a place to camp broke the ennui of the day's ride. At least it brought the aimless wandering to an end. The campsite was a small sand dune, mysteriously standing in the midst of scrubby desert. The Sahara of my dreams—the endless dunes with oases of date palms and mysterious black-eyed women—was not to be. But then reality only rarely comes up to expectations. For some reason, the Thar is short on oases. The best we managed was the occasional small lake. And there were no palms to be seen anywhere.

When we reached the campsite, the sun was already low on the horizon, colouring the dunes with gold. Only a few minutes later it set, in a blaze of glory, leaving the sky glowing a warm red. We unloaded the animals and began to prepare for the night. Salleh sat hunched over a minuscule fire, cooking our meagre meal. Astrid sat with the camels, watching them happily munching as they sat, grouped around the feed bag. I lay back on the sleeping gear, listening to the sounds of the desert and watching the first stars make their timid appearance.

As the sky darkened, a full galaxy appeared, blazing in the black sky. The moon was so bright it cast shadows across the sand.

Astrid had ordered a tent. It was a very small tent. She was a big girl, and it must have been cosy in there. For me, the stars and the cool night air were roof enough. By nine o'clock our little camp had settled into slumber. Nine o'clock is a late night in the desert. Away from the convenience of electric light and T.V., people sleep early, and rise with the sun.

My "mattress" was a thin layer of stitched cloth, but placed on the sand, which retains the heat, it was surprisingly warm. The cover was the quilt on which I had sat all day. Only a faint smell of camel entered my dreams that night.

THE NEXT DAY

We awoke next morning to a rising sun and a clear sky. While Salleh busied himself with breakfast, I watched the morning light, enjoying the faint chill of an approaching winter in the air. These heavenly mornings and evenings were what made the trip worthwhile. The camels were nowhere to be seen. Even with one leg bent back double and bound (an effective form of restraint to keep them from straying too far), they had hobbled off in the night, looking for feed.

Astrid clambered out of her low-slung tent to marvel at the morning. As we breakfasted on tea, biscuits, and squashed bananas, Salleh disappeared in

search of the animals. He finally caught up with them a kilometre or two away, where they had been helping themselves to a farmer's garden. Looking suitable chastened, they returned to camp, ready for the day's work.

We prepared to set off on our meanderings again. We were going to wander through more scrubby country and maybe visit a village or two.

TRACKS IN THE SAND

Although wildlife is not abundant in this region, it obviously exists. They say that the desert is alive with deer and antelope, desert fox, jackals, and black buck. Although the last lion was shot in 1876, and the last cheetah at the turn of the 19th century, desert cats, jungle cats, black-tailed mongeese, and chinkara (Indian gazelles) are still very much alive, even if they are rarely seen. Snakes include the sand boa and several varieties of krait. Our most exciting discovery was the dung beetle, a tiny creature that rolls enormous balls of dung, far bigger than itself, into its nest, to feed its young.

But other wildlife definitely exists. Each morning, I noticed the sand was covered with fresh tracks, especially all around my sleeping gear. Imprints of tiny little feet—the feet of rodents, desert mice, lizards and who knows what—were there in abundance. There were also the winding trails of small snakes. Fortunately, none went under my blanket line.

India is also remarkable for the extraordinary diversity of its birdlife. Over 300 species are reputed to live in the Thar. We missed the king vultures, the desert buzzards, the white-eyed buzzards, and the green bee-eaters. The Indian rollers, blue jays, and short-toed eagles were also in short supply. What we did see were a few small birds and the odd black crow, a British legacy that is almost impossible to escape anywhere on the sub-continent. Others I spoke to in Rajasthan reported seeing giant buzzards standing almost a metre (3ft) tall on the highway. It's good to know that they do exist.

PEOPLE OF THE DESERT

The Bhil, Meena, Gujar, Banjara, Girasia, the snake-charming Kalbelias, and the cattle breeding Rebaris are just some of the tribes who live in the desert. Their proud bearing, fine features, and exotic costumes and jewellery hold them apart from normal city dwellers. Typically, these tribal folk live in small and sheltered communities. Their houses are made behind thick mud walls that protect them from the strong desert winds, which can reach up to 130kph (80mph), and envelope the land in thick clouds of impenetrable dust. The people are naturally superstitious, living in a world populated by evil spirits and supernatural beings. Most groups practice ancestor worship, some revere snake gods, and some worship their own deities rather than the more commonly revered Hindu pantheon. Each February sees a huge gathering of Bhil tribal folk at Baneshwar (in Dungapur) where they congregate for the Kumbh Mela Festival.

VISITING A VILLAGE

After what seemed like several hours, but was probably only two, we approached a very small village. At last we had a chance to see how the locals lived. It was almost noon when we arrived and the village seemed deserted. The inhabitants, no doubt, were out working in the fields. We walked in (the law of the desert states that it's rude to arrive in a village mounted) and sat outside a thickly walled house. I smiled in a friendly manner, hoping to get a photograph of at least one person.

Astrid was bored and wandered off. Finally someone came along and invited me to their remarkable house. Made of manicured mud, smoothed to the consistency of plaster, it had a large, sheltering wall, providing privacy as well as protection from the strong winds and sandstorms that blow during the hot season. Within the compound were several rooms, one used for sleeping, one for cooking, another for storage. Broad white bands outlined doors and windows. In some areas, intricate patterns are painted, giving the appearance of fine lace work. We sat in the shade of a sheltered courtyard.

After much persuasion, a very young woman allowed me to take a few pictures of her and her baby. Then Salleh appeared and said it was time to go. We had to hurry off, but the day passed without further incident. We ate an indifferent lunch in a dry gully, before rushing off to do yet more camel sitting.

AN EVENING GET-TOGETHER

That night we camped in another small sand dune in the midst of the stony desert. The expanse of soft, grey sand was broken by a few short bushes. A couple of visitors from a nearby village dropped by—the local school teacher and his offsider, a businessman/trader. They sat down politely for tea and a chat.

We asked if they could find some local *rakshi*, a kind of rice wine. One man disappeared and after dinner reappeared bearing a bottle. Things were looking up. As we sat under the stars around a tiny campfire drinking *rakshi*, the charm of the desert began to reassert itself. Astrid had bought extra feed for the camels that day, so after eating their fill, they too sat contentedly, chewing their cud, providing happy background noise. They had no need to wander this night, and a feeling of peace descended over our little camp.

BACK TO JAISALMER BY BUS

By the third morning I had had enough. The plan for the day was another long ride of 6 or 7 hours through the semi-desert in the sun, possibly stopping at one small village. And for what? Another mediocre lunch? I decided to cut my losses. Salleh, knowing that this could be

Above: Shorter excursions by camel are often timed to take in sunset over the desert

old woman and the half-submerged body of a small boy, I managed to find a seat on a milk churn.

After stopping once more to pick up another 15 or so passengers, we were on our way. In 20 minutes we were back in Jaisalmer. It was a great and fitting end to the world's worst safari.

They say that riding a camel is the only true way to see the desert as the rider slows to the pace of his surroundings. Romantic as this may seem, it is also the most uncomfortable way to get around, and an hour or two is probably enough. From time to time on our journey, however, I could see the potential of the camel safari. I am convinced that with a bigger group and a reputable operator it could be a fantastic experience.

a long day, thoughtfully suggested that I take the bus back to town. It sounded good to me.

We waited in the scanty shade of a thorny bush for half an hour or so. When the bus came, it was filled to bursting with those turbaned men and bejewelled women that Astrid told me no longer exist. Shrouded with brilliant coloured veils and dripping with heavy silver Rajasthani jewellery, these were the vibrant tribal folk I had expected to encounter in our travels. What a visual treat.

The only problem was that the bus seemed to be somewhat full already. There were at least 30 men sitting on the roof and the inside was almost impossible to enter. Finally, squeezing in between an

Below: *Tombs with distinctive Mughal architecture*

OTHER SAFARI COMPANIES

This account should serve as a warning that you need to choose your travel company carefully. Shop around and be sure of what the company is providing. There are many excellent companies operating out of Jaisalmer and there is no need to suffer. Most of the better companies start their trek in the afternoon, with an introductory hour or two on a camel before stopping at the desert edge for sunset drinks and a great desert meal. Visiting villages also goes a long way to alleviate the boredom of looking at featureless landscapes. Choose a Rajasthani rather than a Muslim guide. Muslims (at least in our case) seem to be unable to enter many of the more interesting villages.

GOING IT ALONE

INTERNAL TRAVEL

There is little need to take a tour to Jaisalmer. If necessary, hotel bookings can be made in advance from Delhi or Jaipur. Travel companies are always keen to sell car tours, but bear in mind that the train service is excellent, and allows you to stop along the way. Many of the trains run at night, which allows you to sleep and arrive in the morning, without having had to spend endless hours gazing at the dust. It is always possible to hire a car for just a day or two rather than being tied to a car for a whole trip.

WHEN TO GO

The desert can get very cold in the winter months of December and January, with temperatures plunging to below 0°C (32°F) at night. By contrast, in the summer months of May to August, the mercury can rise above 50°C (120°F). January/ February sees the Jaisalmer desert festival, when a tented city accommodates the extra influx of visitors. March is also a good time to visit, before the desert heats up too much. From September to November the nights are cool and the days pleasantly warm. Basically, the desert is best avoided from April to August.

PLANNING

A trip to Jaisalmer need not be expensive. Hotels range from low-budget to luxury, from around $5 to over $100. Camel trek prices range from 250 rupees (about $6) per day upwards to about $20. Train fares are generally reasonable, and even first-class A/C is not prohibitive.

Guides abound in the old city, whether you look for a freelance guide or one from a reputable tour company, the choice is varied.

CAR/JEEP/CYCLE HIRE

Autorickshaws, cars, jeeps, bicycles are all available for hire in Jaisalmer. Bicycles are a popular option for getting around town and can be hired from your hotel or from the main gate of the fort. Prices are negligible (around 50 cents to $1 per day). Tour companies hire jeeps, with a driver, which is good for extended trips to the desert, or to visit surrounding villages. For local transport, the autorickshaws are fine. The drivers are often betel-chewing characters who provide a colourful and amusing accompaniment for local trips.

LOCAL CUSTOMS

Cultural mores in Jaisalmer, and in fact in much of Rajasthan, seem to have dissolved with the influx of tourists. The most noticeable custom is the tendency for some unscrupulous Rajasthanis to extract as much money as they can from tourists. Trickery and bluff tactics are the norm. Always check prices and keep your wits about you when shopping or paying for services rendered.

Women travelling alone are an easy target for the sometimes overwhelming attentions of Rajasthani men. Be aware that a high percentage of the local men working in the tourist trade have acquired Western "girl-friends" who send them´ money and generally help to improve their living conditions. It's a lucrative business.

HEALTH MATTERS

There are no serious health problems concerned with Jaisalmer. Take mosquito repellent, sunscreen, hats. Bottled water is available everywhere. Food is not a problem, with enough decent restaurants around to avoid stomach problems. Avoid ice and fresh fruit juices sold on the street (they may contain water).

WHAT TO TAKE

❑ Light cotton clothes, preferably khaki-coloured, to merge with the desert.
❑ High-factor sunblock.
❑ Shading hat.
❑ Long-sleeved shirt or Indian *kurta* (white helps to reflect the heat).
❑ Mosquito repellent.

Below: *If you've never ridden a ship of the desert before, keep it short and sweet*

2 Hunting Tigers in the Fortress Garden

by Jill Gocher

Once the hunting preserve and gardens of maharajas, Rajasthan's Ranthambhore National Park offers visitors to India their best chance of seeing a Bengal tiger in the wild. Here, beneath the ramparts of the imposing jungle fort, the animals roam with complete impunity, with little sense of danger—except from poachers who make the occasional raid.

The sun has not yet risen above the rocky escarpments as we pass through the giant gates that mark the entrance to Ranthambhore National Park, near Sawai Madhopur. Sitting in a big green truck known known as a *canter*, we are on a tiger hunt; a hunt to spot the tigers, that is, not to shoot them. Shooting tigers has long been out of fashion.

A hunting ground for privileged maharajas for eight centuries, Ranthambhore is one of 23 tiger reserves in India, and one of the best places to spot tigers in the wild.

Ironically, it was the maharajas' hunting that led to this park becoming a protected reserve. By virtue of the fact that these powerful rulers imposed draconian punishments on anyone daring to poach animals on their property, the park has always had an inbuilt tradition of conservation. The maharajas, for all their love of largesse, would shoot only during one short season. For the rest of the year, the reserve was left alone.

Having stopped to check in with the authorities and pay our 180 rupees entry fee, we are on our way. The *canter* is the largest of the vehicles used within the park, and certainly the noisiest. I have managed to arrive at Ranthambhore in the middle of the Indian festival of Deepavali. This means that accommodation is almost fully booked and that all the smaller vehicles (Gypsies and jeeps) are taken up by prior bookings.

The only park transport still available is this clumsy Canter, an open-backed truck filled with an assortment of sari-clad hopefuls and their families, all determined to enjoy their foray into the natural world. I am the only European aboard.

Making the most of things, I have commandeered the front seat of this unwieldy machine as the most likely position from which to take photographs.

TIGER SPOTTING

Almost immediately we enter the park confines, the guide and driver begin to watch the road for signs of tiger pug

Almost anyone can sit in the back of a jeep or a *canter* and get driven around the park. Patience and some degree of tolerance for bumpy roads are the only requirements.

★ Hours spent relaxing in natural surroundings are very pleasant, but luxury is not really part of the package. Food is basic, at even the best hotels, so don't expect high cuisine or great variety. Hotels are comfortable, but in the hot season you may feel the lack of swimming pools.

Things to do with the park are well organized. All forays inside are arranged by the state wildlife department so you don't have to deal with wily independent operators.

Bring a camera with at least a medium zoom lens (200–300mm) if you plan to photograph any wildlife. Take comfortable cotton clothing; neutral and khaki colours are best. A sunhat and sunglasses are indispensable.

marks (footprints). Their practised eyes are easily able to differentiate them from the host of other prints that litter the road. They quickly spot a line of tracks, and we keep driving, moving slowly along the bumpy track. Suddenly, ahead of us, monkeys start to scatter and deer look disturbed—a sure sign of danger in the bushes.

All noise ceases. The jungle is silent. Monkeys stop their chattering and the deer edge quietly away. Sure enough... lurking in the dim bushes, there she is: a large mature female, looking for breakfast. It is too dark to take photographs, and she is half hidden in the bushes, but she is very clearly visible. This is our first brief, but exciting, encounter, and we have been inside the park for only 10 minutes. The passengers are ecstatic. This is their first time out, and already they have had a sighting! Everyone is laughing and talking at once, thrilled to see a creature in the wild, and even though we are perfectly safe in our vehicle, that tiny element of danger adds an extra frisson.

We are very lucky today. Many visitors don't get to see a tiger at all. Unfortunately the tigress doesn't stay around to give us a demonstration of her hunting abilities, but melts quickly into deeper undergrowth.

While the noise of the vehicles rarely disturbs these magnificent creatures, it is uncanny to think that a noisy truckful of 20 or more animated tourists can come across a wild tiger with such ease.

FOILED!

Still shaded from the morning sun, which is just colouring the highest branches, we head up along another trail. The guide and the driver have their eyes glued to the road and the passengers are in a state of suspense. Surely we can't be lucky twice in one morning? Then, just a minute or two later, we pass a jeep full of Americans coming down the trail. They have just spotted another tiger further up.

The Canter bounces along the trail, making so much noise that I can't believe we will see any animals at all. But, as the engine splutters and the driver cranks the hefty truck around the corner, we pull up to watch the jeep ahead. There, stalking right down the middle of the road, completely oblivious to the people, the jeep, and our big green truck, is a mature male tiger.

Standing in the front seat, with my camera gear at the ready, I have high hopes of getting pictures. I am foiled in my attempts, however, as the jeep in front

MAHARAJA HUNTING PARTIES

A visit to the Sawai Madhopur Lodge will be rewarded with extraordinary photos of various maharajas and their hunting parties. Dressed lavishly in "hunting attire" the maharajas would entertain their guests in a style that only they could manage. Tented camps were set up in the elaborate gardens of the lodge and guests often included members of the British Raj.

Little hunting was actually involved. A team of 500 or more beaters would be sent into the forest making such a racket that the tigers would be forced to flee—right into the waiting guns of the maharaja and his party. When the shot was lined up, the bearers would hand their master his gun, he would take a potshot, and another trophy would be ready for stuffing.

INDIA

starts backing down the slope towards us, completely blocking our view of this splendid beast. With my blood pressure steadily rising, I am on the point of jumping out of the truck in pursuit, but the guide stops me.

There is nothing more irritating than having an incredible, perhaps unrepeatable, photo opportunity disappear before

your eyes. The closer the tiger comes, the more the jeep backs towards us. Whether it's because the people in the jeep are fearful of a close encounter, or whether they (understandably) want to keep him in their sights for as long as possible, I can't surmise. Whatever the reason, this is one of the most frustrating days of my life!

We stand watching for as long as possible until he disappears into the bushes and then we head on up the rough track. The forest looks beautiful in the morning light, but the excitement is over. We pass another truck and our passengers excitedly start to shout "tiger, tiger!" to the other, less lucky park visitors. We are all feeling pretty smug.

But as lucky as we are, we are not the luckiest. Later I speak with some American visitors who actually sat in their jeep watching a tiger for half an hour as she swam, played with her cubs, and went about her morning activities.

Above left: *Vijay, the cheerful driver on our* canter *trip into Ranthambhore*
Above: *The tigers of Ranthambhore are renowned for their indifference to humans, which makes the park a popular choice for tiger-spotting trips*
Right: *The audience hall of Ranthambhore Fort offers splendid views and is a great place for bird-watching*

NO MORE TIGERS

We spend the rest of our morning following the trail round the park, but we don't see any more tigers. The physical geography of the park changes radically within a mile or two, and other wildlife is there in plenty. Passing through the dry jungle terrain, we round a corner to be greeted

RANTHAMBHORE FORT—
A COLOURFUL HISTORY

The park is dominated by the enigmatic jungle fortress of Ranthambhore, which dates back to the 9th century. Standing atop an isolated and rocky outcrop, 481m (1,580ft) above sea level, the Ranasthambhapura, or Ranthambhore Fort, is one of Rajasthan's most evocative. From below, it appears deserted, half overgrown with jungle. White-faced langurs guard the heavy, cobblestoned ramparts, and it looks a fitting location for an *Indiana Jones* or *Jungle Book* movie.

The fort has always proved difficult to conquer. Narrow, zigzagging walkways and four heavy, spike-studded gateways were designed to deter charging elephant troops, or any other attempt at entry. The steep, high walls, which make a circumference of 7km (4 miles) appear, even today, unscalable. It is difficult to imagine how any marauding army could have ever invaded it successfully. The huge battlements and heavy stone walls are strengthened by towers and bastions that have lasted over a 1,000 years. Within the walls are the remains of palaces, temples, audience halls, barracks for the garrisons, water tanks, and gardens, some of which are still in remarkably good condition. The origins of the fort are obscure, although colourful stories abound. Legend has it that in 1301 10,000 women committed *johar* or suicide, hurling themselves from the battlements, rather than be taken by the victorious opposing army.

During its long and convoluted history, the rulers have changed several times. In 1192 it was taken by the Chauhans, Delhi's last Hindu rajas, and by the 14th century it was the centre of a Hindu kingdom. In 1569 the powerful Mughal emperor, Akbar the Great, laid a successful siege, using trickery to make his way inside. Later it passed back to the Rajput rulers of Jaipur

with open, savannah-like plains covered in the long, dry grasses that support herds of sambar deer. Another species of spotted deer (*chital*) graze nearby. Some of the males are sitting in the shade of stunted dhok trees, proudly brandishing their brand new sets of antlers. Other buck practise mock battles, all barely aware of their curious visitors.

It is quite a revelation to me that driving through countryside in an open truck, looking at animals in the wild, can bring so much pleasure. It has never been one of the activities high on my list of travel priorities, yet when I am here, actually involved in this low-risk, basically passive activity, it is mood-enhancing and soul-renewing. The trips are done in early morning and late afternoon, so you avoid the heat of the day.

After our 3-hour round is completed, we make our way back through the scrubby cattle land that circles the Ranthambhore National Park, and the Canter drops us off at our respective hotels.

RANTHAMBHORE'S FEARLESS TIGERS

The removal of villages from within the park's confines and a total ban on hunting seems to have bred new generations of tigers that know no fear. As they become accustomed to living in the park's danger-free environment, they are gradually relinquishing their natural nocturnal habits, preferring to hunt and mate in the daylight. This makes Ranthambhore perfect for observing these creatures in the wild, and a favourite with wildlife photographers and film-makers.

Visitors have been able to witness these normally reclusive creatures hunting and mating. Some have watched a

THE TRAIL LOTTERY

In Ranthambhore, the game wardens have a rather curious method of assigning trails. The four main trails within the park are allocated to vehicles and their drivers on a daily lottery system, as the vehicles cannot all follow the same path. Visitors have little say in the matter, as the vehicle driver is simply handed a card with a number on it (between 1 and 4) and away you go. This can be frustrating, as the tigers generally seem to prefer certain areas. However, that said, tigers have been spotted on all the paths.

started with nine separate reserves within India. The aim of the organization was clear: to rehabilitate the country's alarmingly decreasing tiger population.

Project Tiger helped to stop logging within the reserves and was instrumental in relocating villages away from tiger habitats. This led directly to an increase in the tiger population.

Under Project Tiger's guidance, Ranthambhore's tiger population increased from an all-time low of 11 in 1973 to an estimated 40 by the mid-1980s. In the late 1980s, however, as government support for the programme declined and Project Tiger lost its momentum, the numbers dropped drastically again. Successful poachers (including, apparently, some of the park wardens), succumbing to the unceasing Asian demand for tiger parts, brought the numbers down; today, with strict policing, the population in Ranthambhorehas has recovered to around 28.

tigress feeding her young or playing with her cubs; others have seen a mature male spraying out his territory, preying on herds of deer, and generally going about life without regard for observers. Even the rattling and creaking of the big Canter trucks doesn't seem to disturb them.

TIGER TRIALS

A tiger's life is not necessarily an easy one. Since the early days of the 20th century, when India's tiger population was estimated at around 40,000, the numbers have dwindled alarmingly owing to hunting and the gradual encroachment of natural habitat. The situation went from bad to worse, until by 1972 the estimated population was a low 1,800.

This was a time of rising awareness of the serious need for nature conservation in India, and 1972 saw the passing of strict new wildlife protection laws. Stern implementation of these laws backed by Indira Gandhi's government and the growth of new organizations such as Project Tiger, helped to stem the decline and even to reverse the fall in numbers.

PROJECT TIGER

Inaugurated in April, 1973, and backed by both the government and the World Wide Fund for Nature (WWF), Project Tiger

RANTHAMBHORE FOUNDATION AND OTHER ADDRESSES

Another organization that works towards the protection of tigers in the wild is the Ranthambhore Foundation. Registered in 1987, the Ranthambhore Foundation conducts and supports socio-economic surveys and scientific research around Ranthambhore National Park.

If you are interested, you can contact the Foundation through Valmik Thapar, Executive Director, Ranthambhore Foundation, 19 Kautilya Marg, Chanakyapura, New Delhi 110 021. Tel: (011) 301 6261; Fax: 011 301 9457.

The regional office is in Sawai Madhopur, at 10, Bal Mandir Colony, Mantown, Sawai Modhopur, Rajasthan 322 011. Tel: 07462 20286.

Above: *Langur monkeys playing on a banyan tree—a common sight in the park*

RANTHAMBHORE NATIONAL PARK

Located several miles from the railhead of Sawai Madhopur, Ranthambhore National Park is one of the most picturesque of all India's parks. A range of landforms and vegetation types exists within its 410sq km (158 square miles). Dry, deciduous forests and areas of peepul, mango, and banyan trees are complemented by high, stone escarpments, waterfalls, and open grasslands. Manmade lakes within the park boundaries support an abundant birdlife and attract many varieties of migratory birds during the winter months.

Since 1955, when it was first pronounced a sanctuary, Ranthambhore has provided a measure of security to its tiger population, although maharajas continued to exercise their traditional hunting

Below: *Recent heavy rain attracted some deer out into the open*

A CORNUCOPIA OF WILDLIFE

Many other animals live within the protected confines of Ranthambhore National Park. The 410sq km (158 square miles) are home to 272 species of birds and 30 mammals, including tigers, langurs, leopards, hares, sambar, boars, porcupines, gazelles, sloth bears, mongoose, striped hyenas, deer, foxes, mice, desert cats, and the blue bull. Several interesting reptile species can also be found here, including banded krait, common krait, cobra, freshwater crocodiles, saw-scaled viper, Russel's viper, Indian pythons, and Ganges soft-shelled turtle.

rights until 1972. In 1973, it became one of India's nine tiger sanctuaries run under the auspices of Project Tiger and in 1980 it was gazetted as a fully fledged national park. Recently, the reserve has been merged with the adjacent Sawai Man Singh Sanctuary. Only a narrow corridor runs between them, but there is now a much larger space in which to continue the important tiger conservation work.

The reserve is also well filled with other wildlife, including the rarely seen leopard, which tends to live on the outer areas of the tiger's territory, as well as many species of birds, antelope, sambar, spotted deer, and the startlingly attractive langurs.

GOING IT ALONE

INTERNAL TRAVEL

The park is near Sawai Madhopur. Finding your way is quite easy even without prior bookings.

Travel to Sawai Madhopur is best by train, as it lies on the main Delhi–Mumbai (Bombay) line, halfway between Bharatpur and Kota. Choice of seats is varied, depending on the train taken. Each train is met at the station by rickshaw and jeep drivers, who take passengers to the hotels. They can also help with booking arrangements.

Both the Project Tiger Office and Tourist Office are a 5-minute walk from the station. Staff can help with information and bookings for accommodation and park tours. They can also provide guided service. Tour companies meet passengers with prior bookings at the train.

WHEN TO GO

The park is open all year except during the hot summer months of July, August, and September. October and November are good months to go as the air has cooled enough to be bearable and the animals are fresh after a respite from the noise of tourists and their transport.

PLANNING

Most accommodation is in the lower to medium price range, with the exception of the high-end Sawai Madhopur Lodge, run by the Indian Taj Hotel Group.

Tours are not really necessary as local operators can arrange a car, guide and any other things needed,

but they may be booked from Delhi. Booking a hotel and perhaps a jeep in advance is really all that is needed.

Even a one-night visit can be quite a rewarding experience, but 3 to 5 days is probably the optimum time to spend to maximize your chance of seeing and observing tigers in the wild. This will also allow time to explore the fort, linger by the lake, do some bird-watching, and generally enjoy the area in a leisurely manner.

Try not to arrive during a major Indian festival, as I did. Unless confirmed bookings have been made, it means that instead of a private jeep that offers a degree of independence, you are forced to use a mini Canter, (a truck-like vehicle painted in desert camouflage, which holds eight passengers) or a big green Canter, which holds 20. It is also very noisy.

CAR/JEEP HIRE

Book your own jeep (including compulsory guide, driver, and jeep entrance fee), to allow greater flexibility. The alternative is to share seats in a larger vehicle known as a Gypsy (also with guide) or a 20-seater truck known as Canter. Both leave at fixed times of 7am and 2:30 in the afternoon (winter times) or 6:30am and 3:30pm (summer). Jeeps and seats on the larger Canter at the park can be booked at the booking office in the compound of the RTDC Vinayak Tourist Complex on Ranthambhore National Park Road, Tel: 91 7426 21 333.

RANTHAMBHORE NATIONAL PARK

The park is open between October and June each year. It then closes for a few months to allow revitalization of the park and its inhabitants.

You can book your rides, and a guide if necessary, through the park at the Tourist Reception Centre, at the RTDC Hotel Vinayak on the road to the park.

Prices are reasonable and the trips are well organized. However, with the big vehicles and a crowd of people, it is difficult to linger at any particular spot within the park.

FOOD AND DRINK

Food is available from the hotel restaurants that line the road to the park. Bottled water is readily available in the hotels and in the small shops of Sawai Madhopur.

HEALTH MATTERS

Eating at Ranthambhore hotels should present no problems for health. Malaria tablets can be taken on the advice of your doctor.

WHAT TO TAKE

- ❏ Sun hat.
- ❏ Sunblock.
- ❏ Sunglasses.
- ❏ Mosquito repellent.
- ❏ Water bottle.
- ❏ Camera with zoom lens.

SAFETY

Do not leave your vehicle when sighting a tiger, no matter how tempting the photo opportunity, even though holy men and villagers seem to walk through the park with complete disregard for any danger.

INDIA

3 Tracing the Mughals

by Jill Gocher

Braving hordes of rickshaw wallahs, tricky train touts, Agra poisoners, and too many tourists, we tracked down the architectural splendour of the Mughals—a legacy left by one of India's most powerful dynasties. Their love of grandeur and distinctive motifs were rendered in larger-than-life creations, designed to impress, leaving an enduring legacy of incredible architecture.

The great Muslim Mughals created a vast empire that, at its peak, stretched from beyond the Khyber Pass, through Afghanistan and Pakistan to India, far beyond Delhi to Bengal in the east, and as far south as Madras and Pondicherry. They left behind a legacy of magnificent architecture, culminating in the Taj Mahal, the epitome of the Mughal style. Many of the best architectural examples are concentrated around Delhi, Agra, and the deserted city of Fatepur Sikri, although the architectural influence spread far and wide.

Evocative memorials apart from the Taj abound, and while three days is almost enough to take in the main Mughal works, a week is better. In Delhi the impressive Red Fort and the truly awesome Jama Masjid are the most visited sites, while various other tombs and gates are dotted around the city. Agra has the Taj, the Agra Fort, the royal ghost town of Fatepur Sikri, as well as various evocative mosques and tombs outside the city proper.

JOURNEY TO AGRA

My own journey started grandly enough from the luxurious confines of Delhi's Imperial Hotel, which, although not quite Mughal style, is old enough and sufficiently colonial in style to conjure up an appropriately retrospective mood. Starting off early, at around 5:30am in time to catch the morning train to Agra, I arrived at Delhi Station, alone, to be accosted with touts demanding to see my ticket. Fancying myself as an experienced traveller, I brushed them away and with a trusty turbanned, red-coated porter in tow, carried on, only to be stopped again. The crack of dawn is not the best time of day for clear thinking and when a fellow in railway khakis, brandishing what looks like a pass, tries again, I finally succumb.

Needless to say, on examining my ticket, he assures me that it is not confirmed, and that I must follow him quickly. We dash across the already busy road to a subsidiary railway office as the main office is still closed. "Hurry, hurry," he urges, "there is no time to waste." He leads me up a dingy narrow staircase to a first floor office with a big "Indian Railways" logo behind the desk.

The fellow sitting examines my ticket, and looking serious, makes a quick phone call. Sure enough, "this ticket is not confirmed," he tells me. A few minutes of spirited haggling takes place. While the

Wandering about at your own pace admiring beautiful architecture is something that almost everyone can manage. The only advice here is avoid the hot summer months.

It really depends of your choice of transport and accommodation. Make the rounds in five star comfort or on a budget, it all depends on personal preference. Agra is well known for its aggressive rickshaw drivers and touts. Keep away from them. Book tours to keep the trip hassle-free.

A pair of walking shoes, a sun hat and sun block together with comfortable clothes, are all that's needed.

WHAT'S IN A NAME?

The name Mughal actually derives from Murghul, the Persian word for Mongol, the warlike ancestors of these great empire builders who derived from Mongolia. The Mughals descended from both the famous Mongols, Tamburlane (Timur the Lame) and Genghis Khan. In those earlier warlike times, the warriors spent their energies acquiring and losing kingdoms, rather than establishing great civilisations. They preferred to live in tents, making it easier to change location, although the early warriors, notably Tamburlane, established the Mughal love of formal gardens.

were accompanied with a flowering of the arts, and their miniature paintings created a style that was later adopted with great effect by Rajasthan's Rajputs.

While a good guide book adds details, architecture needs perspective and background; at least a brief outline of historical events is needed to give this jumble of impressive masonary some meaning.

The Mughals' story dates back to the times of the Mongol conquerors, Genghis Khan and Timur-I-Leng (Timur the Lame, who became known in the West as Tamburlane). The warlike Tamburlane successfully conquered Delhi in 1398, leaving in his wake carnage unprecedented in India's long history, and the bare beginnings of the empire that would follow. But this marauding Mongol didn't stay long. He returned triumphantly to his beloved Samarkand, his troops heavily laden with the easily picked spoils of war. They took with them elephants, gold, and many slaves, including craftsmen—notably the stonemasons whose descendants would later return to work the great monuments of the Mughals.

BABUR THE TIGER

In 1526, more than a hundred years after Tamburlane's conquest, the warrior

red-robed porter stands impatiently at the door, they try to sell me rail passes, hire cars, luxury coach trips, and all manner of absurdly expensive items, which I decline. I suggest that taking a later train may be a more reasonable option but he seems to think that all the trains for the next week are fully booked. My goodness.

Having failed to reduce me to a quivering state of anxiety, I suggest to them that as a travel writer, I must write something about the appalling state of Indian Railways. The first shadow of doubt starts to cross his face. "Do you have a card?" he asks cautiously. Of course I did. This was the right move. All right then. "Let me try and help you," he offers again. A second phone call brings a smile and a confirmation. "Your seat number is 23B (exactly the same number I started with)—but hurry—you have five minutes to catch the train." Ah! The power of the press. Making another mad dash across the road, luggage and porter in tow, I reach the air-conditioned comfort of the train with seconds to spare.

THE MUGHAL STORY

The powerful Mughals forged an empire that marks one of the high points in India's history. Architectural marvels

AN IMPERIAL STAY

It may not be Mughal, but the Imperial Hotel is definitely colonial, and with its century-long history makes a fine starting place for an historical architecture tour. Set out in spacious gardens, close to the centre of Connaught Place but insulated from the bustle, it is one of those hotels that induce instant feelings of well being—a quality that can't be bought. It has been carefully renovated with respect paid to tradition. With polished wooden floors and fresh cut flowers at every turn, the hotel exudes the general ambiance of a well loved club.

Babur, descended from both Tamburlane, and, on his mother's side, from Genghis Khan, returned to conquer Delhi. It was a massively successful campaign, but unfortunately for him, Babur was not to live long enough to enjoy the fruits of his new conquest or to make any significant architectural contributions to the newly created empire. At his death, four years later, Delhi and the newly founded empire was little more than a military occupation rather than a showcase of Mughal might.

Below: *Looking out from Masjid Jama to the Red Fort looming up through the mist*

HUMAYAN

While Babur secured the city, his son and successor Humayan continued the tradition. Less warlike than his ancestors, he found the pleasures of poetry, wine and opium more to his tastes. But he managed some advances, and, in 1533, laid the foundation for a new city in Delhi to be called Din Panah, or Asylum of Faith. Giving notice to the Muslim world that this liberal new capital would welcome philosophers and poets, no matter which Islamic sect they belonged to, he attracted scholars that contributed to the great flowering of the arts.

Hamayan's untimely death in 1556 left his work unfinished and all that remains today of his liberal empire are the crumbling walls of the Purana Qila, or Old Fort, in south Delhi. The standing buildings within were, ironically, built by an enemy

after his death. His magnificent tomb, a stylistic forerunner to the Taj, was built long after his death by his second wife, Haji Begum, in 1564–73. It is believed the architect was brought from Persia and the tomb was built in a style influenced by that of Tamburlane, who lay buried in Samarkand.

AKBAR

Humayan's son Akbar inherited all the strength of his forebears, and after ascending to the throne in 1556 at the tender age of 13 set about consolidating his position. By 1560 he had established his rule after annihilating his oppostion.

Realising that India had far too many Hindus to subjugate, Akbar adopted a liberal attitude towards both the Hindus and subjects of other religions. The large civil service he set up employed significant

numbers of Hindus as advisors and administrators. One effective way of integration was by marriage, and he accumulated more than 300 wives. Rajas of each state and petty kingdom in his empire each offered one of their daughters as a tribute; one even came from Tibet. He allowed the practice of Hindu rites within his harems and, with great foresight, integrated himself into Indian culture. The Mughal Empire began to flourish as never before.

Arrival in Agra

With all these characterful figures to ponder over, the journey to Agra passed by smoothly, enlivened by a vegetarian breakfast and a chat with my neighbours, air hostesses making a grand tour.

As almost every visitor to India visits the Taj, tourism in Agra is big business

Above: *The classic view of the Taj Mahal in its immaculate setting; come to see it at different times of day to marvel at the changes in colour*

and the train is met by a throng of hopeful rickshaw wallahs, while well-dressed tour guides stand by bearing placards printed with the names of their well-organized guests.

I allow the rickshaw wallahs an audience—a major mistake, as it turns out. Twenty drivers vie volubly trying to convince me that his rickshaw and his tour is superior. Sometimes I wonder why this doesn't seem to happen to other travellers. After 20 minutes of haggling and subterfuge, still in the station confines, I head for the safety of the tour desk. As I book the daily tour with Uttar Pradesh Tourism, the throng slowly melts away and a measure of peace is regained.

FATEPUR SIKRI—THE WORLD'S MOST PERFECT GHOST TOWN

The first stop is the monumental ghost town of Fatepur Sikri, about an hour's drive away from Agra. Our group, comprised of Indian and foreign tourist of assorted nationalities gets down and troops off to view the sights, shepherded by the guide and his assistants. I sneak off to take some pictures, although the sun is already high.

Between 1571 and 1585 this former stonecutter's village became the short-lived centre of Akbar's Mughal empire. According to the annals, Akbar, still childless at 26 in spite of his many wives, was inspired after visiting a holy Muslim seer, Shaikh Salim Christi, here at Sikri. The seer foretold of the coming birth of three sons. When the birth of his first son suggested the prophecy was coming true, Akbar took it as an omen and began work on his new capital on a hilltop above the village. Within 14 years, however, the palace/town was deserted, apparently due to water shortages. The almost perfectly preserved city remains a place of pilgrimage and a monument to Akbar, who set the grandiose style that would characterize Mughal building projects for the next century.

The architecture here is almost pure Hindu/Indian without the Persian/Arab influence that would characterize his later works. As the Mughal style developed, more use was made of inlay work and marble. Akbar's earlier sandstone buildings echo the intricate wood carving found in Hindu temples and palaces. It is believed that much of the inspiration came from the Rajput palace fort at Gwalior, which his grandfather Babur had found so inspiring 50 years earlier.

We stop at the tomb Akbar built for Shaikh Salim Christi, who died in 1572. One of the memorable buildings within the complex, the tomb's dome was originally built in sandstone, later faced with marble by Shan Jahan. The superb marble screens, also added later, lend this masterpiece a distinctive, almost ethereal quality.

We leave the imposing surroundings of Fatepur Sikri and head back to Agra for a quick lunch before making our way to India's greatest highlight.

JAHANGIR AND SHAH JAHAN

In 1605 Akbar's son Jahangir took the throne in Agra. While he left few architectural monuments, the arts, especially painting and portraiture, flowered under his benign rule. However, he devoted so much of his time and talents to the arts and the imbibing of opium and alcohol that the empire suffered.

By the time Jahangir's son Shah Jahan came to power in 1628, the Mughal coffers were less than full and the borders were under attack. But this didn't stop the latest emperor. While attempting to re-establish power in the northwest and extend Mughal territory to the south, he was also busy commissioning new artworks, literature, and an unprecedented spate of monument building. It was during his reign that most of the great buildings were created. New fort and mosque complexes were built in Delhi and Lahore, and, added to the existing structures in Agra, Shah Jahan replaced most of Akbar's red sandstone palaces of Agra's Red Fort with white marble. The crown of his achievements was the Taj Mahal, his memorial to his beloved wife Mumtaz Mahal.

EXPERIENCING THE TAJ

We arrive mid-afternoon and the place is packed. Queues of visitors are lined up, waiting for their turn to enter. The big gates tower above us and even with the crowds, the perfection of the inlay work is visible and the well-planned layout can be appreciated.

But for me, contemplating such architectural perfection at first hand is something of a letdown. Somehow seeing this long-cherished icon in reality can never live up to the expectations we develop. It seems smaller, and while the perfection is there, the less perfect structures of Fatepur Sikri and the raw boldness of Humayan's Tomb seem to hold more interest.

The best visit for me came the next day, when I returned to the Taj by the back door, down along the riverbanks. After the crowds of the previous day, the emptiness was blissful. A lone flat-bottomed ferry awaited customers and apart from a goatherder and another photographer, the place was deserted. I took the ferry across with Ahmed, my trusty rickshaw driver, and gazed in admiration at the smooth curves of the Taj glowing gold in the late afternoon sun.

AGRA FORT

By the time we reach the Agra Fort it is ten minutes to closing time, but our long-suffering guide continues his running monologue to anyone who can still listen.

The Agra Fort was one of Akbar's first creations. Established on the banks of the Yumana River in 1565 it took just five years to build. The red sandstone walls, designed to keep out all marauders, tower over 20m (70ft) in height, while the circumference measures 2.5km (1½ miles) in length. A moat once circled the ramparts, yet another way to discourage unwanted visitors.

Akbar's red sandstone palaces were placed along the top of the wall, positioned to enable him to watch his elephants fighting. Only one of his palaces, the Jahangiri Mahal, remains, the others were later demolished by his descendent Shan Jahan, to be replaced with elegant marble edifices.

Although we are pushed for time and miss some of the finer points of the huge complex, we rush to the Musamman Buri, or Octagonal Tower, where Shah Jahan was imprisoned by his son Aurangzeb for the last ten years of his life. Looking out through the marbled arches along the banks of the Yamuna River towards the Taj, it is easy to imagine how Shah Jahan spent his last years in sad contemplation of his masterpiece.

THE TAJ FROM ANOTHER ANGLE

For a different view of India's most famous monument, walk behind the Taj to the Yamuna River and take a small boat across to the opposite bank for an uncrowded view, especially nice at sunset and sunrise. Don't be led astray by the wily rickshaw drivers who will try to drive you the long way round and then leave you to walk for half a kilometre or more through the muddy river flats.

The next morning I arise before sunrise to photograph the Taj in the early light. Ahmed the rickshaw driver awaits, and we head off into the misty gloom. I have an idea for a location and we head towards the fort and the big railway bridge by the flat banks of the Yamuna. But the site is not perfect. Picturesque as it is, the banks are also the main bathroom for hundreds of local villagers and making one's way delicately through the debris, carrying camera gear and tripod, is an exercise requiring great dexterity.

We reach a suitable spot and I set up, awaiting the sun. The mist hovers delicately above the river and in the distance some early morning *dhobis* have already started work on the day's piles of laundry. A train crosses over the bridge, golden in the early morning glow. Finally the sun makes its appearance, but it is not quite the big red fireball of colour I am expecting. The mist is so thick that the Taj fails to materialize and only a faint outline of the onion domes can be discerned, floating through the thick, grey fog. However, the washing strung up along the river flats makes a rather evocative picture.

MONUMENTAL MANIA— SHAH JAHANABAD

It is time to return to Delhi, to catch up on the works of Shah Jahan, who in 1648 decided to relocate to the old capital. His plan was to build a whole new city that he

Above: *Delicate red sandstone archways in the audience hall of Delhi's Red Fort (Lal Qila)*

would name after himself—Shah Jahanabad, now the colourful area of Old Delhi. He created the Red Fort and the main streets and Chandi Chowk of Old Delhi, the city gates, and the Great Mosque.

While tours are available around Delhi, I found it better to spread the visits out over a few days to allow time to see each place properly and to explore the surrounding areas, especially the fabulous *chowks* of Old Delhi.

DELHI'S RED FORT

Probably the most visited monument after the Taj, Shah Jahan's Red Fort was started in 1638, taking 10 years to complete. Its imposing outlines, once overlooking the banks of the Yamuna River, echo those of Akbar's Red Fort in Agra, which was in turn influenced by the design of the Rajput Fort built in 1500 in Gwalior.

Where Agra's Fort is almost intact, the interior of Delhi's Red Fort has suffered so many changes over the decades that the layout makes little sense. After dispatching the last emperor, Bahadur Shah, the British built barracks within the Fort, using it as their own base of operations. Later, the Indians changed and replaced more of the original structure, using it as

an army barracks and administration centre. Only a few of the original halls and palaces remain, and that historical ambience, so strong in Agra, is missing here.

HUMAYAN'S TOMB

Later, I hire a taxi and head south to Humayan's Tomb. Built in 1565 by Humayan's widow, Bega Begam, popularly known as Haji Begam, the tomb was begun nine years after Humayan's death. It is the first substantial example of Mughal architecture in India. Its red sandstone and white marble inlay, the lofty arches, rounded domes, double domes, lacy fretwork of stone, pillared kiosks, and octagonal plan laid the foundation for many of the mausoleums and edifices that followed, culminating in the sublime perfection that is the Taj. It is also India's first example of the garden tomb concept, a legacy that had started with Tamburlane's tomb in Samarkand more than a century before.

The private garden, where wild peacocks strut by and the odd visitor takes time to sit, is a haven of peace—a place to relax and soak up the atmosphere as the tour groups rush by. Humayan's Tomb is just one of several tombs within the enclosure. Other less important tombs belong to petty rulers, princes and princesses, including Bega Begam.

GOING IT ALONE

INTERNAL TRAVEL

While it is possible to visit all the monuments without the services of either a guide or a tour, unless you have your own hired car, convenience dictates the use of a tour to visit Fatepur Sikri, which includes a preliminary introduction to the Taj.

This is one tour that can be done from the cheap to the chic. Four- and five-star accommodation is readily available in Delhi and Agra and luxury tours can arrange it all for you. At the other end of the scale, there is no reason for budget travellers to miss out, and you can see all the sights for US$100 or so.

PLANNING

Tours can be booked from the Delhi hotels, even one day tours are available, where guests are bussed by A/C coach to and around Agra or driven in the luxury of a white Ambassador car. Personally I found that the high speed morning train to Agra is the best option. With comfortable reclining A/C seats, breakfast, and good service, it gets you there in three hours, in time to pick up the daily tours run by UP Tourism. Tickets for this tour are available right on the platform of Agra Station where UP Tourism has an office.

If tours are not required, then there is a seething army of rickshaw wallahs, drivers, and taxi drivers awaiting passengers at Agra Station, also right there on the platform. Nothing much deters them, and each will try to shout over all his colleagues to convince you to take his transport.

Conversely you can book the taxi from Delhi through the Tourism India office and be picked up in a relaxed manner on arrival at Agra.

WHEN TO GO

While the buildings and monuments are there all year, it is wise to leave out the sweltering summer months of May to September, when it is far too hot to do a tour justice. After all, it is supposed to be enjoyable.

FINDING A GUIDE

In India finding a guide is not the problem, but finding a reputable one can take some work. Contact a good tour company or ask at the Government of India Tourist Office in the area.

CAR/JEEP/CYCLE HIRE

Bicycles are available in Agra, although in general I like to try my luck with the rickshaw drivers. A hire car insulates you from most of the travel hassles—and the real India.

HEALTH MATTERS

Buy bottled water and ensure that it is well sealed. It is not unknown for vendors to refill water bottles with tap water. Budget travellers should pick their accommodation with care in Agra, where a few unscrupulous guest houses intentionally poison their guests, then make a deal with the local medical resource to increase their profits.

WHAT TO TAKE

❏ Sunhat.
❏ Sunblock.
❏ Light clothing.
❏ Umbrella to shield pale skin from the hot sun.
❏ Comfortable walking shoes.
❏ A good insect repellent.

SAFETY TIPS

Indian people do not often carry out violent attacks on tourists. Bag-snatching and pickpocketing seem relatively rare although not unknown. However, there have been cases of serious attacks, mostly on visitors who take unlicensed taxis from the airport. Choose only booked taxis from the licensed depot just at the airport entrance. Cheating or tricking tourists is a popular pastime so keep the touts at bay—the sensible thing to do in any country. When taking autorickshaws, it is wise to fix the price before stepping in, rather than risk argument at the end of the ride.

LOCAL CUSTOMS

India and Delhi have been accustomed to visiting foreigners for centuries, but still dress modestly to avoid any unwanted attentions. As everywhere, politeness pays in most circumstances.

FOOD AND DRINK

For a capital city, Delhi is relatively short on good places to eat. The big hotels have generally good food and quite often delicious snacks can be bought at the street stalls. Freshly cooked potato cakes and other snacks appear in the afternoons. Small restaurants sell south Indian favourites like *marsala dosa* (potato and vegetable curry in a crispy pancake), almost a mandatory experience for any visitor to the country. On trains, I would recommend sticking with the vegetarian choices. Tea, *chai*, the Indian national drink, is available everywhere, and is usually very good.

INDIA

4 At Play in the Valley of the Gods

by Steve Watkins

Think of India and the last images to come to mind are probably snow and skiing. Yet the Himalaya mountains of the northwest are home to a fledgling ski industry that is growing in stature, especially for off-piste routes. I travelled to Manali, adventure capital of the region, to enjoy three days on the slopes.

Skiing – in India? If shock value plays any part in the choice of adventure, then I scored a good many points when I announced to friends that I was off to tackle the white stuff in the country famous for hot curries and even hotter weather. To be truthful, discovering that India had a fledgling ski industry at all came as a surprise to me too, and I had difficulty envisaging just what to expect. Snowploughing women in flowing saris? With my interest piqued, I set about planning how to get to the base town of the region's booming adventure travel industry, Manali, located amongst the western Himalaya mountains in the remote northwestern Indian state of Himachal Pradesh.

The travel options contrasted as starkly as the Himalayan peaks differ from the Ganges Plain. Road access to Manali from Delhi is limited to twisting, dramatic routes through a maze of deep valleys. The journey takes 16, body-jarring hours. By air, the same journey, with a brief stop at the old colonial hill town of Shimla, takes less than 2 hours and the flight promised to be scenically wonderful. Despite the excessive cost difference ($290 return to fly, compared to just $30 by bus), I chose to treat myself and, after an unavoidable overnight stay in manic Delhi, got an early morning taxi out to the domestic terminal to clamber aboard a cramped, 12-seater Indian Airlines plane.

There is something about the hum of propellers and feeling every gust of wind that makes flying in a small aircraft very much more adventurous than cruising in a big jet, but the small size meant I had to hunch down to see out of the window. It was a cloudless day and the snow-topped Himalayan peaks were capped by an expanse of dark blue sky. As dramatic as the view of the high mountains was, the most exciting part of the flight was the approach to Shimla airport. Shimla used to be the principal summer retreat for members of the British colonial government because of its mountaintop setting and the cooler summer temperatures. Our pilot manoeuvred the plane lower until he was literally slaloming between the hills, before landing in a hurry on the short runway that is built on an artificially flattened hilltop. A communal sigh of

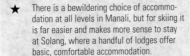
You need to be reasonably fit to undertake this ski tour (just getting up and down the slope is enough of a workout for most people) and you should be able to ski at good intermediate level if you plan to go ski touring.

★ There is a bewildering choice of accommodation at all levels in Manali, but for skiing it is far easier and makes more sense to stay at Solang, where a handful of lodges offer basic, comfortable accommodation.

All specialist ski equipment is available for hire in Manali, though it is not quite up to European or North American standards. However, you should take clothing suitable for cold conditions, including waterproof jacket and trousers, warm fleece-type jumpers, and thermal underwear.

relief drifted around the passenger cabin, though we soon realized that we still had to take off again. Some 30 minutes after departing Shimla, we came into land at Bhuntar airport, over 50km (31 miles) south of Manali, but the nearest airport.

The 1-hour taxi journey from the airport to Manali passed through the narrow streets of bustling Kullu town, the provincial capital, and then twisted along the bottom of the increasingly impressive Kullu Valley, home to a major apple-growing industry and the mighty Beas River. The Beas River winds its way south from the glaciers of the Himalaya before turning westward near Bhuntar to continue its journey across the Indian state of Punjab and on into Pakistan. We were heading against the flow through tiny, ancient villages and past more recent, temporary shacks, constructed by Tibetan Buddhist refugees who have fled the repressive Chinese regime in their own country. The further we travelled up the valley, the higher the roadside deposits of snow became. A heavy snowfall just a few days before had not only rescued an otherwise poor ski season, but also provided much needed water for the region's apple-growers.

A BED AT ANY PRICE

After the simplicity and natural beauty of the valley, Manali's heavily developed tourism infrastructure—heralded by a steady build-up of roadside advertising signs—came as quite a rude shock. It was dumbfounding to see just how many hotels there were. In fact, the town was virtually made up of hotels. Up until the 1970s Manali had been a peaceful, sleepy village that was virtually unknown to tourists save for occasional hippie-trail followers looking for a place to hang out. However, the boom in tourism in the area during the 1980s and early 1990s led to an uncontrolled frenzy of hotel building, mainly fuelled by opportunistic businessmen from Delhi and Bombay. There are now around 12,000 hotel beds in the town. This is three times the permanent

population level, and a recent slump in visitor numbers has left many hotel owners going broke. The good news for travellers is that there is usually a good deal to be had with very little bargaining and it is sometimes possible to get a very comfortable room at backpackers' prices. To avoid the modern high-rise places and to get a feel for how Manali used to be, I opted to stay few hundred metres north of the main street at John Bannon's Guest House, one of the town's original hotels. John, now in his 70s, came out to greet me himself and we both kicked our way through the snow to my spacious room, where I had great views down the valley.

Although there was plenty of snow in and around Manali, the skiing action all takes place from the tiny mountain village of Solang Nullah, a further 14km (9 miles) north of town. To help with the organization and to ensure that my guides for the ski touring were suitably experienced and qualified, I linked up with Manali-based operator Himalayan Journeys. Owned by renowned local mountain man, Iqbal, the company's ski operation is managed by his enthusiastic and supremely effective son Himanshu. It is rare to find someone so switched on, and within an hour or so he had my skiing tour organized, with plenty of time left over to enjoy a complimentary cup of lemon tea. Along with my two guides, Juna and Anand, I hoped to spend three days ski touring out of the Solang Valley, but a reliable satellite weather forecast (normally used by Himalayan Journeys to plan their heli-skiing operations) had warned of an impending large storm coming from the north. We would just have to go to Solang and see what fate brought, as ski touring in low visibility is not only unpleasant but extremely dangerous too.

After an early morning start, we crossed the Beas River out of Manali and initially drove up the contorted dirt road that eventually crosses the Rohtang Pass at 3,978m (13,051ft) and continues to Leh. Our track to Solang Nullah turned off the main road well before the pass and climbed through increasingly deep snow to the village of Palchan. Thankfully, soldiers from a local army base had cleared the route sufficiently for us to continue a little further, but eventually our jeep could no longer conquer the slippery conditions and we were forced to unload and begin hiking the rest of the way to Solang. It was hard going with all our equipment and skis in our backpacks, but the effort involved just to get to the ski area made it feel infinitely more adventurous than simply driving right up to a ski lift as is the norm in Europe or the U.S. Forty minutes later, the incredibly small ski "resort" of Solang Nullah appeared ahead. Instead of

Above: *The ski lift has not arrived yet—we had to carry all our equipment up the slope ourselves*
Left: *First time on skis for this Indian man*
Below: *Anand, one of my guides*
Right: *Venturing off piste into amazing scenery*

large hotels and fancy chalets, there were half a dozen or so small, simple lodges. The exception was a large and impressive new lodge that had been recently finished in preparation for the annual National Ski Championships that were due to be held at the resort. We were booked into one of the cosy, government-owned lodges that had basic, en suite rooms each with an old, wood-burning heater in the centre. With the cloudy weather and freezing temperatures outside, it was severely tempting to curl up in front of the heater for the afternoon. However, although the weather was poor, the snow conditions were excellent, so we changed into our ski gear and ventured out. It was still too dangerous for ski touring, so instead we clipped into our downhill skis and went to play on the short, pisted run below the lodge.

A COMEDY OF SKIERS

If you are used to extensive ski-lift systems and an endless choice of runs then the single, liftless slope at Solang Nullah will keep you entertained for less than a

few hours. However, for beginners it is a reasonable place to learn and I met Rob Johnston, a British cycle touring traveller, who had stopped off to take a one-week, basic ski course. One big benefit of joining a course is that you are allowed to use the rudimentary drag lift that takes novice skiers about halfway up the slope. For experienced skiers, the options for getting up the slope are limited, very limited! There is a modern tow lift at the resort but it hadn't been operational for a few months, so Juna, Anand, and I took off our skis and trudged for 15 minutes to the top of the ski run. The only problem with having to walk to the top of the slope was that the motivation for going back down again was minimal. Less than 2 minutes of downhill action would only result in another 15-minute hike back to the top. None the less, the boundless enthusiasm of my guides plus the obvious commitment of local skiers to overcome such minor obstacles inspired me and I swooped down the slope in big, swishing arcs.

Before setting off back up the hill, I paused to take in the comical scene of a group of visiting Indians from Bombay having their first experience of snow. All the way up the road to Solang Nullah I had seen little huts with racks of gaudy, tacky fur coats and black Wellington boots outside, but I had no idea what they were for. The answer was—to keep the Bombay visitors warm and dry while they tried their hand at skiing, took rides on a snowmobile, or hurtled down a nearby slope on overinflated tyre tubes. I watched them having a go at all three activities, but it was the skiing that was far and away the most entertaining. Clamped into a set of ski boots and skis, the visitors were ungracefully dragged and pushed across the flat snow section at the bottom of the main slope. Despite there being no danger, several of them were so terrified of moving on skis that they begged to be let off, while others were bent over double as if they were flying down the slopes at high speed. Their

full-length fur coats only added to the overall comedy value.

Finally, with a dozen runs under my belt, I called it a day as dusk set in and joined Juna and Anand for a hot tea at one of the tiny cafés at the base of the slope. After my initial baulking at the thought of having to work so hard for each ski run, I found that I had actually found it refreshing to ski without all the modern conveniences. Later that night we enjoyed a great Indian meal at the Silver Spoon Restaurant before heading to the Patalsu Guest House and bar which, with its blinking TV showing overly dramatic soap operas and a freely available collection of chessboards, is the entertainment centre in Solang.

The following morning, the weather had improved slightly, though the sun was still struggling to break through, and Anand felt that conditions were safe enough for us to venture up the mountain on the touring skis. To achieve the seemingly miraculous feat of walking uphill on skis we needed to fit "skins" to the base. Skins have fine hairs on them that lie flat in one direction to allow the ski to slide normally and rise up in the other direction to grip on the snow. To assist the walking action further, special ski bindings are fitted to allow the skier's heel to lift off the ski. It is a rather strange feeling and it took me some time to trust the skins' ability to stick on the steeper slopes. Once we had moved up above the pisted slope and climbed through a narrow gully surrounded by pine trees, I was beginning to feel comfortable on even the steepest slopes; the skins allowed us to climb gradients of 60 degrees or more.

Perhaps the biggest attraction of ski touring is that it allows you to explore areas that other skiers cannot get to. As my skis crunched a trail through the virgin snow just 20 minutes into the mountains, I felt as if we were already a long way from the downhill crowds. Our route took us up onto a ridge and we were due to continue up above the tree line, but the cloud base level began to drop

AVALANCHE SAFETY

No matter how experienced a skier you are, there is always a danger associated with skiing in remote areas. There are two types of avalanche: a loose snow avalanche, when it starts from a single point; or a slab avalanche, when a whole area of snow slides. Avalanche conditions are most likely to occur after heavy snowstorms, particularly if there is a period of rapid thaw after it. The upper, more recently deposited snow layers do not have time to bed down or become fixed to the lower layers. The pull of gravity or a trigger event, such as someone skiing on the slope, can break the bonds between the layers and cause a slide. Most large slab avalanches occur on slopes between 25 and 45 degrees (with 30–45 degrees being particularly vulnerable), and convex slopes are more prone than concave ones. Wind is also a factor, as avalanches are more likely to occur on slopes that face away from prevailing winds. To increase safety, do not travel alone in backcountry snow areas, carry and use avalanche transceivers, climb or descend a slope as directly as possible rather than traversing, and cross potential danger areas one at a time. If you are caught in an avalanche, try to move to the side of the slide or use a swimming motion (backstroke or front crawl depending on which way up you are) to attempt to stay near the surface of the avalanche. When the avalanche slows up, try to keep an airspace clear in front of your mouth and nose. Time is crucial; the more time you can buy yourself, the greater your chance of rescue. To ease your fears: statistically, 14 out of 15 people caught in avalanches survive.

again and Anand decided that it was wiser to traverse before beginning the descent back down to the resort. With the skins off and our heels locked back onto the skis, we were free to enjoy some great powder snow conditions amongst the trees. Skiing in powder is an art in itself and requires different techniques and attitudes from tackling on-piste runs. Despite my relative lack of powder experience, it was great fun carving long turns and occasionally crashing into the deep snow, which caused a fine icy spray to chill every exposed body part. When I tired, it was a treat to watch Juna and Anand tackle some of the most difficult sections with aplomb and even launch themselves off big boulder jumps.

Emerging from the forest back onto the piste was a real disappointment after so much back-country fun, so, with the sky finally clearing, I was already looking forward to our final day's trip up into a small valley below North Peak, a broad mountain behind the Solang resort. North Peak is one of a series of peaks known as the "Seven Sisters" with the highest being Hanuman Tibba at 5,932m (19,462ft). An 8km (5-mile) long glacier on this peak is the major source of water for the Beas River.

A PERFECT TRAIL

Next morning we were awake before dawn. The vast array of stars in the crystal-clear sky caused a surge of excitement, and our clothing and skis were quickly donned. Entry to the valley was from just behind our lodge, and it was a serene experience to hear the gentle crush of snow beneath our skis as the morning sky turned first pink and then orange. Having spent two days' wondering what lay beyond the clouds, I was staggered by the outstanding scenery that I had been missing. Vast, snow-clad mountain ridges dotted with sharp, angular peaks encircled the whole resort and it was easy to understand why this area is called the Valley of the Gods. With the sunrise came a brilliant blue sky and, as we walked further into the deep snows of the valley mouth, it was hard to imagine a more perfect day for exploring. Steadily

we wound our way past scores of smoothly contoured mounds, formed where snow had settled on underlying boulders. The terrain was not steep, so we had plenty of opportunities to admire the surroundings. Arcing around to the right to follow the valley floor, we were quickly out of sight of the resort and into a wilderness where it felt as if we were the only people on Earth.

We kept a steady rhythm and made good progress, and after 1½ hours we reached a climb that would take us back over a ridge and down to the resort area. Under the glaring sun, things got very hot and sweaty on the ascent and I took to voluntarily slumping into the snow to cool off. With so much experience of the varying mountain conditions, Juna and Anand simply took the temperature rise in their stride and encouraged me to keep moving upwards. The rewards for enduring the climb were magnificent. From the top we enjoyed panoramic views over the choppy sea of Himalayan peaks, while before us lay a thick carpet of powder snow—not fresh, but still inviting. It was time for the skins to come off the skis. With a whoop I launched into the run, and quickly caught an edge and face-planted the snow. Back up and with my level of concentration sharpened, I

Above: A welcome rest—hot tea at one of the tiny cafés at the base of the slope

snaked my way down the slope, slaloming between trees and always looking for any hidden ledges and drops. While I avoided these, Juna headed straight for them and took great pleasure in flying off them to an inevitable wipe-out in the deep snow below.

An hour or so later we re-entered the normal skiing world at Solang Nullah and couldn't help but feel a bit smug about our little adventure. The difficulty I had had imagining what skiing in India would be like now seemed all the more reasonable, given my contrasting experiences. The resort area pretty much lived up, or down, to my expectations of how basic things would be and it would be hard to recommend a stay of more than a day to anyone but the absolute beginner or most committed snow-lover. However, venture away from the resort on touring skis and there are snow conditions and landscapes to match the best locations of Europe and North America, without any of the crowds. By the time I got back to Manali I was already working out how I could save the money to come back and really escape to the wilds with a week of heli-skiing.

GOING IT ALONE

INTERNAL TRAVEL

You need to be quite committed to get to Manali and then up to Solang Nullah, but the rewards more than justify the effort. Daily buses leave from Delhi for the 16-hour journey to Manali, or you may prefer to take the old, narrow-gauge hill train to Shimla from Kalka (served from Delhi by the Himalayan Queen train service) and then take the bus to Manali from there. Indian Airlines and privately owned Jagson Airlines fly from Delhi to Kullu (Bhuntar), the nearest airport to Manali. Flight schedules on this route change regularly depending on demand, so check with the airlines for the latest information; at the time of writing both airlines were operating three return flights a week on alternate days, i.e. there was a service on 6 days of the week. This flight is also subject to disruption due to weather conditions, so don't plan things too tightly around it. From Bhuntar airport entrance, buses and taxis operate direct services to Manali, about a 1-hour journey. There are plenty of taxis willing to go on to Solang Nullah, including jeeps for when the road conditions prevent ordinary cars from getting there.

WHEN TO GO

Manali is a year-round destination, with summer months dominated by hiking. The ski season at Solang Nullah is a short one, lasting from January to March. I was there in January and the nights were extremely cold. Late February and early March are probably the optimal

times to be there, though snow conditions have become increasingly unpredictable over the last decade.

PLANNING

It is fairly easy to organize a basic ski course on arrival in Manali, but it is always a good idea to book ahead if possible, as some companies run courses on fixed dates. The 5- or 6-day long courses are the most popular for beginners. For experienced skiers, skiing equipment can be arranged on demand, along with guides for off-piste skiing and ski touring. The mountains around Manali offer some of the best heli-skiing opportunities in the world. Himalayan Journeys and other tour operators in Manali can organize these trips, but be prepared for the very high costs involved (think in thousands of US dollars). The government-run ski school offers a comprehensive 16-day introductory ski course, though some say it is a little ponderous and that you can learn almost as much on the shorter, private operator courses.

HEALTH MATTERS

Avoid quiet restaurants and do not drink the tap water. Up in the mountains, streams that are above the population line should be as fresh as water gets and naturally chilled too. However, stick to bottled water, hot drinks, or bottled soft drinks in the resort. Ensure that you take adequate protective clothing with you at all times when ski touring, even if it is gloriously sunny when you depart. The weather here changes in an instant and being caught

out in a storm without waterproof and warm clothing could have dire consequences. Look out for the signs of hypothermia in yourself and others in your group. Any signs of shivering, blurring of speech, slowing of movement, or disorientation should be treated as potentially serious. Warm up the individual with extra, dry clothing and by huddling together. Move out of the wind and sip hot drinks if you have them. There is a well-trained mountain rescue team in Manali, but help can be a long time coming if you are in a remote spot.

WHAT TO TAKE

❑ Waterproof jacket.
❑ Waterproof trousers.
❑ Plenty of layers of warm clothing (such as fleece jackets).
❑ Thermal underwear.
❑ Warm hat.
❑ Good gloves.
❑ Thick, long socks.
❑ High-factor sunblock.
❑ Sunglasses.

TRAVELLERS' TIPS

To get to Manali, it is almost certain that you will spend at least one night in Delhi. The airport there is renowned for the disreputable tactics of the taxi drivers, both privateers and the official, pre-paid service. The scams they employ are numerous and convincing, but almost all are tailored to taking you to a different hotel from the one you want to go to—one from which they earn commission. Basically, you need to have a very clear plan of action for when you arrive at the airport and be strong, even rude, to leave the taxi driver in no doubt about who is pulling the strings. It is best to reserve a hotel beforehand, as Delhi's hotels are often full.

5 Off the Rails in Darjeeling

by Jill Gocher

Sitting atop a high ridge in the eastern Himalaya, Darjeeling is a town in the clouds. Under the Raj, this preferred British hill station afforded the sweltering sahibs welcome relief from the torrid heat of the plains. I took a trip on a world-famous narrow-gauge steam train to see some of the crumbling relics that remain.

Hidden high in the Himalaya, Darjeeling—or Darjiling (the word is a loose transliteration of the Tibetan *Dorje Ling* or Place of the Thunderbolt)—is a long-established trading centre and home to a cosmopolitan mix of Indians, Tibetans, Nepalis, Bhutanese Bhotias, Sikkimese, and Bengalis. It is the home of the world-famous tea, and on clear mornings estate workers can be seen plucking the world's best tea leaves against a backdrop of the white-peaked Himalaya mountains. This Indian Shangri-La has always embodied the essence of romantic travel.

DERAILED ON THE TOY TRAIN

A ride on the miniature steam railway known as the Toy Train is one of the essential experiences of Darjeeling— even if the legend remains far better than the reality. The train's upright wooden seats give little comfort, and at times it is all so slow it can tax the patience, but for a ride on one of the world's most scenic narow-gauge railways, one has to make sacrifices. To be derailed, however, is a fairly unromantic introduction to a Himalayan journey. Fortunately, the incident bore no omen of things to come.

The train starts from the rail junction of New Jalpaiguri (NJP to the locals). The lower part of the ride is slow and not much happens until the first low-level tea estates appear after half an hour or so. After crossing a 210m (700ft) long bridge over the almost dry Mahanadi River, we soon enter the foothills of the Himalaya and the first water-stop, at Sukna, one of the many we make during the ascent.

The 88km (55-mile) line climbs from around 150m (500ft) above sea level at Siliguri to over 2,250m (7,400ft) at Ghoom, the highest point on the line. The train wheezes its way almost 2,200m (7,000ft) up the steep mountain slopes, using a series of switchbacks. This means that it seesaws its way upwards, backing up one section of the track to a higher level and then going forward again, thus giving an impression that the driver is making a series of wrong turns.

As the track gets steeper, clouds of steam issue forth from the overtaxed engine and then clouds of coal dust, resembling fallout from a heavy hail-storm. Grit the size of small marbles showers in through the open windows and soon everyone is covered in layers of black. It's all part of the authentic steam

1. If you want to walk, be prepared for hill-walking. If not, transport is readily available. The numerous treks around Darjeeling and nearby Sikkim range from easy walks to difficult climbs.

★★ Hotels range from very comfortable to basic, as do transport arrangements. Darjeeling and the surrounding areas are inhabited by mountain people, who tend to be far more relaxed than the people of the plains. It is a soothing and exceptionally pleasant place to visit.

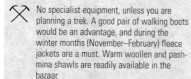

No specialist equipment, unless you are planning a trek. A good pair of walking boots would be an advantage, and during the winter months (November–February) fleece jackets are a must. Warm woollen and pashmina shawls are readily available in the bazaar.

train experience. And the views over the plains are fabulous.

Several slow hours pass, a ritual of zigzagging and seesawing, and stopping for water. As the coachload of 12 increasingly bored backpackers becomes more restive, we hit a smooth patch and suddenly we are bumping heavily along the track off the rails. Then, with an extra loud hissing of steam, the engine dies. The train comes to a grinding halt. Fortunately, we are on a level area, and not at the edge of a precipice. Everyone grabs their backpacks and jumps, and the carriage clears in less than a minute. Six hours along the line and we almost reached the halfway point of Kurseong!

Stranded in the middle of a small village, we are approached by several minivan drivers who have appeared almost instantaneously. Demanding extortionate rates to take us up the mountain, they are repelled without hesitation. Our newly formed group clings together until salvation comes in the form of a large flatbed truck filled with sand. We transship instantly. The friendly Tibetan driver gives us a truly memorable ride—a speedy drive with a panoramic view of steep mountainsides, verdant vegetation, and the distant Himalaya. Along the way, friendly villagers cheer and wave as we make our way up the mountainside. It is a ride to remember.

Now that I have made this journey once, I would recommend starting the rail trip at Kurseong Station, thus cutting out about 6 slow hours of travel. The views in second half of the trip are more exciting than the first. This section also includes the Batasia Loop, the most dramatic engineering feat of the line: the train describes a full circle (the best of five such circles it makes on the ascent), all against the spectacular backdrop of Kanchenjunga. The mountain appears to be so close you can almost touch it.

DARJEELING AT LAST

Finally we arrive at Darjeeling in the dark, to be greeted by a sea of touts all

By train to Darjeeling, then onward into Sikkim

brandishing hotel name cards. The touts are soon dispensed with, and everyone heads off to the hotel of their choice. In the morning there is another surprise. What the guidebooks don't mention is the 50 years of incredible growth and change since India achieved Independence. Once a quaint little hilltown, Darjeeling is now a sprawling metropolis, awash with white concrete. Block follows block of

THE TOY TRAIN—A HISTORY

Built in 1879 to circumvent the laborious horse-and-cart journey, the line was instigated by Franklyn Prestage of the East Bengal Railway. He formed the Darjeeling Himalaya Railway Company and built the 2ft (0.6m) gauge line. The original Class 8 engines were built in Scotland, from around 1889—well over 100 years ago. Remarkably, some of these originals are still in use. But, with the advent of group tours and minibuses, how much longer the line will keep going is a point of conjecture.

apartments, shops, and hotels, all clinging precariously to the steep mountain face.

But perseverance pays and the charm of the place soon begins to seep through. Most of this recent development stretches way beyond the ridge of the original British Chowrasta section, and this older part of town is still intact, albeit rather rundown.

When the East India Company was granted the hill of Darjeeling in 1835 from the Sikkim Rajah, it was a no more than a small, almost deserted Gurkha station on a jungle-covered mountain. The only access was on foot. With their usual indomitable spirit, the British set about taming the mountain. Development was rapid, and in just five years, the Hill Cart Road was opened, houses and a sanitorium were built, and the first hotel was operating. By 1857 the population had risen to over 10,000.

The British were quick to appreciate Darjeeling's potential. Its location, between Sikkim, Bhutan, Nepal, and the plains of India, was ideal for the development of trade. The altitude was perfect for growing tea. The first plantations were in operation by 1841, and by 1866 there were 40 tea gardens, covering 25,000ha (10,000 acres), with revenues totalling over £500,000 ($330,000).

Darjeeling's fortunes continued to rise and fall over the years, with various annexations and disagreements between the states. New treaties were made and broken until, in 1861, the British Indian Government forced the annexation of the Sikkim Terai and part of the Sikkim Hills, extending the Darjeeling territory to 1,660sq. km (640sq. miles). There was also an agreement to build a trade road through Sikkim to Tibet, to which access had long been denied.

The railway was fully opened in September 1881, by which time the jungle had given way to tea estates. Darjeeling was a fully fledged hill station, tea centre, and an important trans-Himalayan trading base.

IN PURSUIT OF THE RAJ

With India's laissez-faire attitude to architecture, (buildings are not pulled down—they just sink slowly to the ground) most of Darjeeling's famous old landmarks are still intact, if somewhat

Left: *Sunrise on Tiger Mountain: far in the distance, the snow-covered peaks change from gleaming white to orange to pink*
Below: *Our driver on one of the world's most scenic narrow-gauge rail routes*
Below inset: *The Toy Train on the Batasia Loop*

The centre of activity is a big square known as Chowrasta Chowk. In colonial times it was the main meeting place. On Sunday white-suited brass bands played in the decorative bandstand gazebo. The bandstand went soon after Independence and the Chowk has been taken over by rugged-looking mountain men hawking their horses for hire.

Wooden benches line the Chowk. From dawn till dusk a polyglot population takes up residence to watch the passing parade: Tibetans and tourists, Indians, loafers, the occasional hippie left over from another era, young backpackers, well-dressed tourists from the Windamere. Nothing much really happens—but, if it does, it is sure to happen here.

Below Chowrasta, the roads and paths descend steeply through a warren of small streets and alleyways. The bazaars are full of people, shops, and open-fronted stalls where vendors sit cross-legged, crammed into tiny spaces

neglected. The once snooty Planter's Club, around which the tea planters' social lives revolved, still presides over the Mall, despite looking a little worse for wear. In the tree-shaded streets round about are the hospital, the Windamere and New Elgin hotels, the Gymkhana Club, some churches, and some interesting shops dating from the turn of the 19th century.

RHODODENDRON SEASON

From mid-April to mid-May the valleys of Darjeeling and Sikkim are filled with the blossoms of rhododendrons and orchids. Over 40 rhododendron species and over 1,000 orchid species have been identified in the Darjeeling/Sikkim/Kalimpong area. Rhododendron treks take walkers on easy 2- or 3-day walks through lush valleys of rhododendron forests, in full bloom from late March until mid-May. Overnight stops can be made in trekkers' huts along the way.

hawking their wares. While exotic ethnic costumes have given way to the less romantic uniform of jeans and jackets, the trading activity is as frenetic as it ever was. The paths and roads lead to the town's main square, the market, the train station, and taxi stands.

THE WINDAMERE HOTEL

The first place on my itinerary was the Windamere—a short walk from Chowrasta. This 1930s hotel almost justifies a visit to Darjeeling in its own right. Situated in several buildings on top of Observatory Hill, guarded by men in strange hats, it enjoys a fabulous view of the Himalaya.

But it is the interior that makes it so special. The main building houses some of the guest rooms, the cosy bar, a room for evening soirées and cultural performances, and a card room. The timber walls are festooned with wonderful photographs of explorers, weather-tanned mountaineers with grappling irons, princes and kings, (the king of Sikkim, with his American wife, Hope Cooke, were there), a smiling Edmund Hillary in mountaineering gear, Tibetan traders, and other luminaries who have passed through these portals. Signed letters and pictures of the main market place below date back at least 50 years—and nothing appears to have changed.

Passing the reception, I enquired about the possibilities of getting dinner later that evening. The delightfully patronizing man behind the desk informed me that it needed to be booked ahead, preferably at least a day or so. However, on this occasion, as it was only a small booking, he would do me the great favour of squeezing me in. Feeling obliged for life, I left to explore some more.

MR. GURUNG AND THE GYMKHANA CLUB

I visited several other notable relics scattered around the top of Observatory Hill. Crowning the tree-shrouded hill is a Hindu temple dedicated to Shiva. Revered by both Hindus and Buddhists, the temple replaces a Tibetan monastery that was sacked by maurading Gurkhas in the 19th century. Lower down stands the Gymkhana Club, once a hub of Darjeeling social life. Today it is the empty haunt of the delightful Mr. Gurung, a retired Gurkha soldier who entertains visitors with his repertoire of stories. His picture album is filled with autographed photos of visitors new and old—a nostalgic picture of life in those good old days. Give him a chance, and he will take you on a guided tour of the empty clubrooms, the ballroom, and the billiard room. Refurbished guestrooms in a separate wing have been taken over by a management company.

Darjeeling is a town of contrasts. For some, it offers an escape from the heat of the plains; for others, a nostalgic journey, a foray into Tibetan Buddhism, an alternative trekking destination, or a jumping-off point to the Himalaya.

In the years before Nepal opened to tourism (and mountaineering), Darjeeling was the main gateway to the Himalaya. The town saw a continual procession of weatherbeaten mountain folk coming to make their attempt on surrounding peaks. When Sir Edmund Hillary and Tenzing Norgay made their ascent of Everest in 1953, they too came through Darjeeling.

The musty old Himalayan Mountaineering Institute opened in 1954 and from then until 1976 Tenzing Norgay was its director. He remained actively involved until he died in 1986. The Institute still offers training courses to aspiring mountaineers.

Its two exhibition rooms are filled with dusty exhibits that look as if they haven't been touched for at least 30 years. Relief models of the Himalaya, old mountaineering equipment, a set-up of a mountaineering tent, exhibits of flora and fauna all make for a fascinating hour or two, giving insights into a chilly world of crampons and ice axes that most of us know little about.

There is so much to do and visit in Darjeeling, it's difficult to leave. Days swim by in slow whirls of mist. I spent delightful, otherworldly hours wandering about the town, exploring *gompas* (Tibetan Buddhist monasteries), eating and talking in pleasant restaurants, and visiting the tea gardens. Bookshops and antiques shops filled a day or two. Then there is the zoo, with its baby red pandas, its yaks and tigers, and the snow leopard breeding programme. The Tibetan Refugee Self-Help Centre is another rewarding place to visit.

THE TIBETAN REFUGEE SELP-HELP CENTRE

The centre was established in the 1960s, not long after the Dalai Lama's flight from Tibet, to house some of the thousands of refugees who followed in his footsteps. Today, over 750 Tibetan refugees live in and around the centre—a people trying to make the best of an untenable situation. People of all ages are involved in the manufacture of a wide range goods and handicrafts, and quality is never sacrificed for greater production yields. Goods are exported to more than 36 countries around the world. There is a shop where visitors to the centre can make purchases, thereby helping these displaced people to help themselves. As well as products produced in the centre, it sells

goods from other Tibetan refugee centres scattered across India—carpets, hand-knitted goods, metalwork, silverwork, and various articles of clothing modified for Western tastes.

Everything is made to a high standard and training is considered to be very important. Any master craftsman who has managed to escape from Tibet is highly respected and given teaching work to ensure that knowledge and skills are passed on to new generations. Since its inception, the centre has trained over 1,600 people in various crafts. Of these, some 900–1,200 have left to establish their own businesses, integrating themselves into the Indian economy.

Everyone is made to feel useful. Many work at, and are paid for, making Tibetan carpets in traditional designs. The weaving is done by young people, while older folk are employed sorting and combing the yak's wool before it is spun and dyed.

I wanted to visit the nursery school. When I asked for directions, someone called out to an old woman who was huddled over a pile of yak's wool. She got up and came hobbling over to my side, taking my hand. Together we made our way up the steep steps to the school. Greeted with the utmost courtesy, I was led to the small staff room and given sweet tea and biscuits before being shown around the classrooms. The children were the dearest imaginable. One little boy came and

AMERICAN QUEEN, SIKKIM KING

Sikkim sprang to world attention in 1963 when American Hope Cooke married Sikkim's Crown Prince Palden Thondup. His coronation as King of Sikkim took place amid much celebration in 1965. But political change came after just ten years, when Sikkim became an Indian state. The Chogyul, or king, became no more than a figurehead. In 1981 Hope Cooke moved back to America with her children.

INDIA

wrapped his arms around my legs. I sat in as they worked at their books, sang songs, and played games under the kind gaze of their teachers. Once they have finished at the school, many of the youngsters are sponsored by foreigners and continue their education in one of the excellent higher schools for which Darjeeling is well known. It is a source of pride to the Tibetans that their students generally do extremely well.

SUNRISE AT TIGER MOUNTAIN

One of the things everybody does in Darjeeling is brave the cold morning air and drive to Tiger Hill to see Kanchenjunga at sunrise. As I left the

hotel at 4:30am, in the dark, with a group of other visitors, it was chillingly cold. On the 20-minute drive to the mountain, the sky began to lighten to the east. We were early, but quite a crowd had already gathered at this flat peak, high above the surrounding mountains. Wrapped in warm jackets and scarves, talking, laughing, sipping hot sweet coffee, we all watched as a pale line of pink appeared along the horizon. Far in the distance, the snow-covered peaks gleamed white. Then, as the sun rose higher, the colour changed to a deep orange, then pink. It was the morning of the world.

Even during the cloudy month of September, the skies often clear for sunrise, before the clouds resume their cover

Left: *The tea plantations around Darjeeling were planted by the British, but the area still produces the flavourful—and expensive—black tea today*
Below: *Young Tibetan monk at Pemayangtse*
Bottom: *Colonial church, Darjeeling*

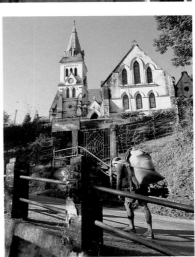

of grey. It is quite possible to walk the 12km (7½ miles) back to Darjeeling, and many people do. I asked my driver to drop me in Ghoom, and I stopped to visit several of the interesting Tibetan monasteries along the way back. There is always transport available if you get tired of walking.

A SIKKIM JOURNEY

As delightful as Darjeeling is, Sikkim was beckoning. I wanted to go to Pemayangtse, the country's second oldest and most revered monastery and the most important *gompa* of the Nyingmapa Sect, one of the four sects of Tibetan Buddhism. It lies near Pelling in West Sikkim, and is easily accessible from Darjeeling (if you can call a hair-raising ride down the mountain "easy"). Now that visiting restrictions to Sikkim have loosened, it is a simple, if time-consuming matter to get the necessary permit in Darjeeling. Foreigners are now free to go as they like, but visits are restricted to two weeks a year.

SHARING A JEEP

There are several ways to get to Sikkim, including bus and hired car, but I decided on a shared jeep. The 75km (47-mile) journey to Pelling starts around 8:30am from Darjeeling's main bazaar and is an experience in itself. Squeezed into a jeep (take the front seat if you can) that is packed to the rafters with passengers inside and piled high with luggage outside, we start a rollercoaster ride that loses a dramatic amount of elevation in less than an hour. Through one verdant tea plantation after another, the uneven track descends to Jorethang, with spectacular panoramas across to the Himalaya. My only advice is—don't look down.

Crossing the turbulent Rangeet River, we enter Sikkim and the border check-post, where a friendly guard looks at the papers of any foreigner on board. A short ride gets us to Naya Bazaar—possibly the least attractive town in the whole of Sikkim, with the desolate air of a typical border town. Here we are are thrown out of the jeep to hunt for transport to Pelling.

The ride to Pelling, in another jeep, took us through dramatic and largely untouched countryside of virgin forest and spectacular rice terraces. Sikkim has a policy of ecological conservation and one of the aims of the tourism department is to encourage ecotourism—and to promote the country as an attractive alternative trekking destination to Nepal.

The tiny township of Pelling has been discovered and the superb countryside is being desecrated with more stark white concrete and unsympathetic architecture. As it is the base for some of the country's oldest *gompas*, marvellous scenery, and the best trekking, it is enjoying a mild rush of popularity.

GOMPAS—AND LOTS OF LEECHES

For great views of the Himalaya and Kanchengjunga, don't go in September. I did, and in five days there was one morning when I saw the lower half of a mountain, coloured pink with the rising sun. For the rest of my stay, it was clouds all the way.

I took the 20-minute walk from Pelling to the Pemayangtse Gompa in the cool mountain mist one morning. As I approached the monastery I was greeted with the evocative sounds of drums, horns, and high chanting voices. When I entered the main prayer room, I was enchanted to see a group of young monks conducting a morning *puja*, or offering ceremony. I was politely ushered in to take a seat at the side while the young monks continued their devotions. Sheltered from the soft rain high up in the mountains, I knew this was an experience that would remain long in the memory.

The monastery, built in the early 18th century on the site of an older building, is close to the empty ruins of Rabdantse, former capital of Sikkim.

The most interesting monastery I visited was the Sanga Choeling Monastery. Even older than Pemayangtse, it is reputed to date from the late 17th century. An eventful walk up the mountainside—coloured by plentiful misty scenery and only a few leech attacks—brought us to the *gompa*, which stands alone on a mountainside. White prayer flags fluttered in the wet mist, the door was padlocked and the place seemed deserted. Eventually, however, a small boy appeared and after the requisite pantomime, disappeared to bring us the key.

We entered the main prayer hall, a room dominated by three imposing Buddha statues. Although the original monastery burned down, the statues, which are amongst Sikkim's oldest and certainly most powerful, were saved and restored. The upper level holds several forceful effigies of Guru Rimpoche/Padmasambhava, the sect's eighth-century founder. Monks of the Nyingmapa sect are allowed to marry, and consequently they spend their time out of the monastery, except for special festival dates. Although the monastery was empty, it was well worth a visit.

Pelling is beautiful, but it lacks the atmosphere of Darjeeling. With election rallies in the air, further excursions to Yuksam and beyond were impossible (all non-essential transport was requisitioned for the rallies) and I headed happily back to the town in the clouds.

GOING IT ALONE

GETTING THERE

The journey form Delhi to Darjeeling is a treat for train-lovers. From Delhi, the Radjani Express takes about 36 hours (two nights). It arrives in New Jalpaiguri (NJP) with more than an hour to spare before the Toy Train departs at 9am—just enough time to buy a ticket and have some breakfast at the station. Those in a hurry can fly to Bagdogra and take a taxi to the train station. It is possible to avoid the long queues at Indian railway stations by making confirmed bookings in London. Contact SD Enterprises, 103 Wembley Park Drive, London HA9 8HG (near the Wembley Park underground station. Tel: 020 8903 3411.

WHEN TO GO

For clear views, and to enjoy the rhododendron and orchid season at its best, visit in April. The monsoon months, from June till September, are cloudy, often misty, and rainy. Clear views return with the cold weather, which lasts from around October until past the Christmas season. White-water rafting is best in the months of September and October, when the Rangeet and Teesta rivers are high after the monsoon rains.

FINDING A GUIDE

For general sightseeing in Darjeeling, a guide is unnecessary, but trekking trips require a trekking guide.

Contact the Tourist Bureau in Darjeeling for advice on trekking and guides (they can be found in the Mall near Chowrasta). The Darjeeling Gorkha Hill Council (DGHC) is useful for information on adventure activities. In Sikkim, the Sikkim Tourist Information Council in Gangtok can help with information, maps, transport, and booking hotels.

VEHICLE HIRE

Hiring a car and driver in Darjeeling is simple, either through a tour company or from the taxi stand below the Planter's Club on Gandhi Road.

Shared jeeps operate to most destinations in Sikkim and make a colourful alternative to car hire, if you aren't overburdened with luggage. It is also possible to book a whole jeep, with driver, for yourself.

HEALTH MATTERS

The old rule of "don't drink the water" applies just as much in Darjeeling as anywhere else in India. Bottled water and tea are readily available and there is no need to take chances. Food is generally safe, but new travellers should probably be a little bit careful. As a general rule, it is always wise to go where there is a crowd.

WHAT TO TAKE

❑ Good walking or trekking shoes.
❑ Warm jacket.
❑ Raincoat or umbrella.
❑ Sweater (extra warm clothes are readily available in Darjeeling).

LOCAL CUSTOMS

Being a polyglot community and accustomed to foreign visitors, Darjeeling is not too culturally sensitive to the *faux pas* of Western visitors. Politeness is always appreciated and it is generally too cold to bare too much skin. Being less accustomed to foreign visitors, Sikkim folk are somewhat more sensitive. Always act with discretion when visiting sacred sites and monasteries. Try not to point your feet at a shrine, a person, or a cooking fire. Ask before you photograph someone; if they don't understand you, a friendly gesture and a smile usually suffice.

FOOD AND DRINK

Darjeeling is good for food, with Indian, Tibetan, and Western dishes on offer. The two small Tibetan restaurants opposite the taxi stand make a good introduction to Tibetan food. Glenary's Bakery in the Mall is the best for breakfast.

MOMOS—A TIBETAN FAVOURITE

Momos are almost the Tibetan national dish and are available in little Tibetan restaurants and teashops all over the Himalaya. These delicious dumplings come fried or steamed and are stuffed with pork, chicken, or vegetables. If you are driving down to Siliguri from Darjeeling, get your driver to stop at the *momo* shop halfway down the mountain. They have a continual trade from morning till night, so their *momos* are guaranteed fresh as well as being delicious.

6 Rhinos and River Dolphins in Assam

by Emma Stanford

It is famous for its tea gardens, but there is a lot more to Assam than a good cup of chai. At the heart of the state is the Kaziranga National Park, where I planned to encounter the rare, one-horned Indian rhino, which Marco Polo believed to be the origin of the legendary unicorn.

Glance at the map of India, and you might easily overlook the irregular spur of territory that is buried in the flanks of Myanmar (Burma) and Tibet. Here Assam and the other six northeastern hill states of Arunchal Pradesh, Nagaland, Meghalaya, Manipur, Mizoram, and Tripura gather in the shadow of the distant Himalaya. Tenuously linked to the main body of the subcontinent by the narrow Siliguri corridor between Nepal and Bangladesh, this is the most varied and least visited corner of India.

The whole region was once ruled by the Ahoms, an Indo-Chinese Shan tribe, who first migrated across the Patkoi Pass from upper Myanmar in the 13th century. Traditionally remote, both physically and culturally, today it remains India's main tribal area. The features, languages, and customs of its indigenous people have more in common with their neighbours in southeast Asia than the Indians who have gravitated to the region in huge numbers during the last 150 years.

Under the liberal Ahom dynasty, numerous small tribal kingdoms flourished and the incomers adopted Hinduism, successfully repelling a slew of attempted Muslim invasions and acting as a bulwark against the spread of Mohammadanism into southeast Asia. In 1826 the British annexed the region, naming it Assam and founding the world-famous tea industry that flourishes to this day. However, the creation of the state of Meghalaya at the demand of the rival Jaintia, Khasi, and Garo tribes led, in the 1970s and 1980s, to the break-up of old-style Assam.

Present-day Assam occupies the centre of the region traversed by the grandiose Brahmaputra River ("son of Brahma" and India's only male river). It is the largest, most developed, and most easily accessible of the "Seven Sisters," as the mini-states are often referred to. The Assamese countryside offers a landscape of striking diversity, from its impenetrable jungle-covered hills and orderly tea gardens to the paddies and swathes of 3-m (10ft) tall elephant grass that occupy the Brahmaputra's broad flood plains. Some 800-plus local plantations produce around 55 percent of India's tea (15 percent of the world's production). Oil is another important income earner and the

 This adventure is not physically demanding, but the bumpy jeep rides are not recommended for anyone who has back trouble.

 The government lodges at Kaziranga and the Eco-Camp tents at Nameri offer a fair degree of comfort, while accommodation at Wild Grass Resort verges on the luxurious as a base for an adventure travel. The sandbar camp at Tezpur is basic.

 Binoculars are essential for wildlife and bird watching, and it is well worth investing in the best pair you can afford. Keen photographers should bring a decent zoom lens and plenty of film. If you want to fish for mahseer at Nameri, bring a sturdy rod with a reel capable of holding at least 200m (650ft) of 0.35-mm line, 20–25g lures, and a few plugs.

rhino symbol of Assam Oil is a familiar sight along the roadside. A relative newcomer to tourism (until 1995 visitors required Restricted Area Permits), Assam lists as its top attraction the Kaziranga National Park. Home to a fantastic variety of birds and beasts including *Rhinoceros unicornis*, it also supports the highest density of wild tigers anywhere in the world.

NORTH BY NORTHEAST

The 10:30am flight from Calcutta to Guwahati left on time, rising quickly above a scud of puffy, white clouds and heading north by northeast across the feature- less hinterland of Bangladesh. Ensconced by a window on the left-hand side of the aircraft, I had a ringside view of the Himalayan ridge, where the

Top: *The colonial-style Wild Grass lodge at Kaziranga*
Above right: *Out on rhino patrol*
Right: *Kaziranga National Park bor- ders the south bank of the Brahmaputra River*

MAP OF KAZIRANGA NATIONAL PARK
AREA — 430 SQ.KM.

Notified as Reserved Forest in 1908.
as Game Sanctuary in 1916.
as Wildlife Sanctuary in 1950
as National Park in 1974

ENDANGERED SPECIES
Rhinoceros
Elephant
Royal Bengal Tiger
Wild Buffalo
Swamp Deer
Sambar
Hoolock Gibbon
Gangetic Dolphin
Florican
Great Indian Hornbill

63

INDIA

imposing snowy bulks of Everest and Kanchenjunga rose head and shoulders above serried ranks of spiky sisters on the horizon. My adventure was definitely under way.

The short plane hop ended in the mid-day heat of Guwahati, Assam's main city and the start point for my 5-hour road trip to Kaziranga. Just outside the airport, my guide, Rajan, pointed out a greyish lump off to the right. Gradually it came into focus as a group of wild elephants and their young, down from the hills to feast on water hyacinths in the flooded post-monsoon paddy fields. This is still a relatively rare sight so close to human habitation, but the large-scale destruction of local forests for timber and the expansion of the town has led to a dramatic increase in wild elephant incursions. Guwahati's official elephant-scarer—with his armoury of firecrackers and noisemak-ers—has a full-time job on his hands.

Beyond the city, the most instantly striking thing about Assam is the colour: blue forested hills, vivid green paddy fields punctuated by yellow mustard plots, and turquoise-painted villas set amongst more traditional dwellings constructed from sections of woven matting or smoothed mud and surrounded by yards swept spot-lessly clean. We reached the Wild Grass lodge on the borders of the national park at dusk, walking through the gardens and a wall of cicada song to a large, comfort-able room with mosquito screens and a reassuring reek of citronella. This would ward off blood-sucking winged predators, and I did not get a single bite during my stay. Over a generous curry dinner (notable for my introduction to *pura ben-gena pitika*, a delicious smoky aubergine dish made from aubergines baked over an open fire then mashed with garlic, chilli, mustard oil, ginger, and fresh coriander), I listened to fellow guests discussing their day's wildlife spotting. One couple visiting from the British High Commission in Bombay had chalked up Kaziranga's Big Three—wild elephants, rhinos, and tigers—all in the same visit, while the

THE GREAT INDIAN ONE-HORNED RHINOCEROS

The Indian rhinoceros is one of the largest of the existing rhinoceroses, bigger than the African black rhinoceros but smaller than the African white. The average height when full-grown is just under 180cm (6ft) at the shoulder with a girth of around 335cm (11ft). The rhino's chief predator is the poacher, whose sole objective is the 20cm (8in) fibrous horn. Highly prized in many Asian societies for its aphrodisiac and medicinal qualities, powdered rhino horn can fetch as much as US$40,000 a kilo on the open market.

ornithological contingent were marvelling at the quantity and variety of birdlife in and around the park.

KAZIRANGA AND THE VICEROY'S WIFE

A 6:45am wake-up call the following morning found me up and about and rar-ing to go. It was still distinctly chilly when, armed with binoculars and a gun-toting ranger, Maan Barua, the resort's eagle-eyed bird expert, and I arrived in the park just as the elephant safari pas-sengers were moseying gently back to base astride a handful of the park's 40 or so domestic elephants. The Kaziranga National Park spreads along the south bank of the Brahmaputra in a 430sq. km (170sq. mile) band bordered to the south by hills. The area has been a game reserve for almost a century, since Lady Curzon, wife of the then British Viceroy of India, made an unsuccessful visit to see the famous rhinos in 1904–5. Intrigued by British tea planters' tales of Assam's Indian rhinos, the viceroy's wife jour-neyed north, but by the time of her visit the rhino population had been hunted to the brink of extinction by colonial sports-men. She had to make do with hoof prints. On returning to Calcutta, Lady

Journey along the Brahmaputra

Curzon persuaded her husband to create a game reserve and thus almost single-handedly saved *Rhinoceros unicornis* from extinction.

ON THE PROWL

The jeep took us deep into the park's Central Range, making its way through the wavering sea of elephant grass on raised sandy tracks that disappear under water during the summer rainy season. Overhead, a magnificent Pallas's fish eagle swept across the sky and squadrons of noisy Alexandrine parrots ricocheted out of the tree tops in a streak of lime green tipped in red. At the edge of glassy still ox-bow lakes (known as *beels*), water buffaloes and deer grazed amongst egrets, herons, endangered greater adjutant storks, and dozens of other wading birds. Kaziranga boasts the world's largest population of both Asiatic water buffaloes and Eastern swamp deer, as well as 1,000-plus wild Indian elephants, more than 1,550 rhinos, and around 83 tigers (according to a 1998 census). Almost 200 resident and 300 migrating bird species have been sighted here also, many of them rare and globally endangered. As we trundled through the woodlands, where troops of macaque monkeys hide out, Maan pointed out all manner of cunningly concealed birds, including a handsome Brahminy kite, named for its red-ochre plumage the colour of the sandalwood *tikkas* (forehead marks) favoured by Brahmins. As the morning heated up, fish flopped in the *beels*, and rows of little tent turtles sunned themselves, squeezed nose-to-tail on branches poking out of the water—giving a new meaning to the word logjam. But no rhinos deigned to appear.

However, in the afternoon my luck changed. We had driven across to the Western Range and a watchtower beside a spreading *beel*. Across the water, on marshy grasslands, six rhinos browsed placidly, one of them a female with a small, stout two-month-old calf in tow. Magnified by binoculars, the rhinos were impressively prehistoric, massive and seemingly impregnable, with huge boat-shaped heads and three heavy folds of carbuncled skin arranged fore, centre, and aft, like armoured blankets. Though they look ponderous, rhinos are capable of amazing bursts of speed when on the attack. Maan told a cautionary tale of being chased by a nursing mother rhino that had been surprised. Rhinos will rarely take on an elephant, but in this case the mother charged a domestic elephant, bit it on the forehead, and then chased the panicked beast for some distance. Hence the no-walking policy in the park, and the need for an armed ranger (though his chief deterrent is blanks).

The rest of the afternoon was given over to birdwatching and as Maan's infectious enthusiasm rubbed off and my eyes became accustomed to searching for the best perches, I surprised myself by detecting the growing excitement of a latent "twitcher". One notable sight, perched in a copse near the watchtower, was a brown fish owl. Sporting an elegant jade-coloured beak to match its workmanlike talons, it observed us coolly between slow blinks of heavy red eyelids. As the last rays of sunlight tinged the snow-covered Himalayan peaks of Kangto (7,089m/23,252ft) and Tapkashir (6,816m/22,356ft) pink above the clouds,

INDIA

tiny wagtails and kingfishers darted past, rhinos grunted from the grasslands, and domestic elephants padded softly home along the path carrying their mahouts.

ELEPHANT SAFARI

The highlight of a trip to Kaziranga is the elephant safari. This necessitated a 4:45am wake-up call the next day. Shivering in the open jeep, a French-Austrian couple and I made our way back through the grey pre-dawn mist to the Central Range and joined a handful of Indian tourists from West Bengal. Our elephants had rings of oil painted like kohl around their eyes to ward off bugs and were fitted with howdahs (saddles). These we mounted easily from a purpose-built platform. The thick mist was discouraging, but 10 minutes later our swaying caravan stepped out of its embrace and into magical early morning sunshine. Beneath eggshell-blue skies,

the southern hills were striated with layer upon layer of mist and the golden light caught droplets of dew clinging to the tall grasses parted by our elephant's huge head and ears. The elephants fed as they walked, noisily tearing up tufts of grass with their trunks and chewing methodically while we spotted impressively horned buffalo and grazing deer. A startled doe hog deer stood uncertainly in our path and then bolted, leaving a tiny newborn curled on the ground. The elephants stepped around the tiny creature with exquisite care.

A few rhinos hove into view, hugging the borders of the long grass, but they quickly disappeared as our elephant caravan approached. Increasingly anxious that we might not manage to get close up to our quarry, we re-entered the mist and

Right: *Male Indian rhino—an unlikely candidate for the dainty unicorn*
Below: *Preparing for the elephant safari*

Above: *Morning activity on the streets of Kaziranga*
Right: *Vaishnavite monk, Majuli*
Far right: *A young Mising woman prepares fire-wood by stripping off the bark*

soon stumbled across a solo rhino, but it was snuffling away in a muddy bog where we couldn't approach. However, only minutes later we had a pair, a male and a female, browsing contentedly just ten paces away. Masticating thoughtfully, and apparently quite unconcerned at the appearance of five elephants loaded with humans eyeballing his every move, the male turned to give us a back view, poked his head around to ensure we admired his horned profile, and generally played to his breakfast audience like an old pro. It was an unforgettable encounter.

GETTING THE BIRD BUG

With another day-and-a-half in the park, I ventured out to the Eastern Range, where the magnificent wetlands land-scape is crowded with wading birds and ducks. At one point a small, rotund wild boar trotted across the track in front of the jeep, and in the shade of the creeper-draped woodlands jungle fowl and Kalij pheasants rootled beneath a carpet of ferns and the glossy fronds of cane plants. I spotted a wild ganesh, a one-tusked elephant named for the similarly one-tusked Hindu deity, and back at the

watchtower one afternoon we counted 24 rhinos. The tigers, however, continued to elude me, except for a viceroy's wife-style sighting of a pug mark.

Those early stirrings of amateur ornithological leanings had exploded into a full-blown case of addiction. Each evening found me carefully ticking off the day's sightings on the Kaziranga bird list and comparing notes with the Shuttleworths, a kindly (and patient) retired British couple who had once run a tea plantation in southern India.

Behind the lodge, I walked up into the tea gardens where "tea tribe" women in bright saris harvested the fresh green shoots, tossing them casually into woven panniers secured on their backs. In the 19th century, British planters found the native Assamese reluctant to work the plantations, so they introduced workers from Bihar and Orissa, the so-called "tea tribes" of today. There is also a small Karbi tribal village with neat, rectangular houses built of blonde mud. As I ambled by, grinning pre-school children played in spic-and-span yards and a few tiny, dainty women swayed gracefully down the path balancing rotund silver water vessels on their heads or huge wicker baskets supported by straps around their foreheads. Nearby, a flying fox colony exuded a distinctive musky scent. Dozens of these furry orchard raiders gather in the upper reaches of a bamboo break, hanging upside down as they squabble and preen, occasionally swooping off in a flap of leathery black wings (which span around 1.2m/4ft).

THE WORLD'S BIGGEST RIVER ISLAND

It was something of a wrench to leave the comforts of Wild Grass and its friendly and helpful staff, but I was anxious to see more of Assam. Rajan suggested a trip to Majuli, the world's biggest river island, which lies in the Brahmaputra. Currently its elongated mass covers around 875sq. km (340sq. miles), but its sand underpinnings are notoriously unstable and 35 villages have been washed away since 1991. Majuli's other claim to fame is its 22 Vaishnavite Hindu *satras* (monasteries), notable for religious dance dramas that depict stories from the *Mahabharata.*

An evening performance was scheduled, so at mid-morning Rajan and I joined a melee of fellow passengers, pilgrims, monks and stallholders at the Jorhat ferry ghat and set off downstream sandwiched between a hazy infinity of pale blue sky and water. A rickety wooden bus met the ferry and lurched creaking and straining like a ship on the high seas across the sand dunes to Majuli's main town, Garamur. Here, we left our sleeping bags in the rather grim guesthouse of Watun Kamalabaki Satra, and stepped out to explore. Watun Kamalabaki is one of the larger monasteries, with some 300 monks living in low, whitewashed cells around the modest temple building. Wandering through the peaceful compound, we sidestepped pairs of cattle threshing rice beneath their hooves as they walked slowly round

in tight circles; visited the simple, unadorned temple, and fielded countless polite enquiries about my origins.

Accompanied by a monk-translator, Rajan and I walked out to a Mising tribal village, where houses are built on stilts to escape the annual summer floods that cover most of the island in water. The Assamese say that where you find the Mising you'll find water, and where there is water there is bound to be Mising, who are renowned as boatmen and fishermen. Majuli's Mising women still practise traditional weaving and embroidery on stoops outside their homes. I was invited in to sample a beaker of homemade rice wine, a mild, milky-white, slightly sour-tasting but not unpleasant brew with the characteristic smoky flavour of local cooking.

From Garamur, a wild autorickshaw ride took us careening over a network of raised dykes to Auniati Satra and an audience with the *Satradhikar* (abbot). Auniati is the biggest monastery in Assam, founded in 1653—though the

SANKARADEVA AND VAISHNAVITE HINDUISM

The poet-saint Sankaradeva (1449–1568), also described as "the maker of Assamese nationality," is credited with developing the Vaishnavite doctrine that revolutionized the practice of Hinduism in Assam. Sankaradeva preached against the excessive ritualism and rigid caste system of the traditional Hindu faith, and encouraged his followers to strive for salvation through meditation and prayer rather than sacrifice. Vishnu is the leading deity in the Vaishnavite pantheon, but he is worshipped without form so Vaishnavite temples contain no idols. Young boys can join the celibate Vaishnavite orders from the age of six, but the *satras* have plenty of contact with the outside world and many monks work in the local community.

original buildings are now at the bottom of the Brahmaputra. The *Satradhikar* invited me to inspect the "museum," a dusty depository of antique Ahom swords, battered silver dishes, and a pair of huge sandals carved from ivory. But he had bad news on the dance front: the evening's performance was cancelled as the monks needed extra time to study for upcoming exams. Instead, as night fell, I stood mesmerized by the door of the temple while a clutch of tiny child monks lent their reedy voices to a cacophany of clashing cymbals, drums, and bells in the glow from the candlelit inner sanctum where a white-clad Brahmin made his obeisances.

RAFTING AND FISHING

After our trip to Majuli, the itinerary allowed for another night at Kaziranga and the opportunity to grab a final, early morning birding trip to the tea gardens. I managed to add a pair of great hornbills, assorted woodpeckers, drongos, and a glorious green magpie to my tally—now numbering over 100 species—before breakfast. Inordinately satisfied, I helped Rajan load our kit into an Ambassador (the backbone of the Indian automotive industry modelled on a 1950s Morris Oxford), and we headed west, crossing the Brahmaputra at Tezpur to arrive at the Nameri National Park in time for lunch. In the afternoon, I hoped to do some fishing.

The Jia-Bhoroli River, which runs through the park, is a breeding ground for golden mahseer, a mighty freshwater fish that attracts anglers from around the world. Contrary to reports, there was no fishing tackle for hire, so the very acceptable alternative was a gentle raft trip downstream with views off to the eastern Himalaya foothills where the snow-fed river rises. Back at the tented Eco-Camp, there was time for a stroll into the mustard fields before getting caught up in a dusty stream of cattle being driven home from the fields at *godhuli*, or "cattle dust," the descriptive Assamese word for dusk.

Our pre-dawn preparations for sunrise at the wildlife-viewing platform were thwarted by the non-appearance of the park ranger, who had overslept. But although we saw nothing more dramatic than the fast-disappearing scut of a sambar deer and a flock of little black and scarlet minivets flitting around in the trees, the crisp, clear morning was perfect for a dewy hike into the forest. On the way back, we took a cup of tea with the elephant vet as he dosed up the working elephants with antibiotics from an assortment of monumental syringes.

SANDBAR CAMPING

After a late breakfast we drove south to Tezpur, a tea town on the banks of the Brahmaputra. I have to admit my enthusiasm for the next item on itinerary waned dramatically as we stood beside the river gazing out to a barren sandbar shimmering like a mirage in the oven-like midday heat. Rajan's plan was to camp there overnight with local fishermen, but I rather hoped it was a mirage and would conveniently disappear while we toured Tezpur's historic temples. First stop was the Mahabhairava Temple, renowned for its 9th-century Shiva linga. The entrance was flanked by carved reliefs of Ganesh and Hanuman, the monkey god, coated in a gory-looking mixture of vermilion and mustard oil. Rajan made an offering of hibiscus flowers, joss sticks, sweets, and wood apple leaves and received a dribbling, yellow *tikka* mark in return. Crunching on a handful of hard little sugar sweets, we proceeded to the remains of the Da-Parbatia Temple along a country road lined by palm trees and fully occupied cricket pitches. Little remains of the Gupta-era temple save the elaborately carved 6th-century stone entrance, which features images of the river goddesses Ganga and Yumuna symbolically cleansing worshippers (who are supposed to bathe before entering the holy precincts).

At the end of the day, the five-strong camping party piled into a traditional flat-

INDIA

bottomed wooden boat loaded with provisions and rowed out into a river of molten gold as the huge orange ball of the sun sank onto the horizon. Suddenly, it all seemed a brilliant idea and ridiculously romantic. Rushing to set up camp in the dwindling light under the direction of Dharmeswar Das, our local host, we discovered the tent poles had got left behind in the trusty Ambassador. However, with a little ingenuity and twine, my tent was soon rigged up around a pair of upended oars. Meanwhile, driftwood fires were built and the cook, Jogot, assisted by his Number Two, Ashok, bent over the supper preparations. I was bidden to watch from my especially imported chair, presiding rather grandly over the proceedings in the manner of Queen Victoria. Piles of vegetables, limes, chillies, pastes, and a huge bunch of coriander were laid out on bamboo mats, chopped with lethal-looking curved knives, and tipped into a *kerahi* (similar to a wok) with spookily translucent river prawns. Dhal bubbled, rice boiled, tiny fish were tossed into the embers to bake, and we ate like kings toasting our toes on the fire beneath the stars before bed.

A muezzin call echoing across the water from Tezpur announced the imminent arrival of a new day and allowed me to perform my ablutions before the rest of the camp awoke. Jogot was out fishing early and returned carrying his nets over his shoulder speckled with small fish caught in the fine mesh. Dharmeswar and Ashok joined him on the foreshore for the painstaking task of extricating the catch by hand before we rowed across to the riverbank fish auction. In his official capacity as the fishing leaseholder for this portion of the river, Dhameswar carefully jotted down the day's prices and collected fees based on each boat's catch.

RIVER DOLPHINS

A brace of bicycle rickshaws transported Rajan, Dharmeswar, and me back to the Ambassador and a rendezvous with another boat for the trip upstream to see the river dolphins. From a *ghat* near the two dozen spans of the river crossing (one of only three bridges across the Brahmaputra in Assam), we embarked on the loudest and most shuddery boat ride of my life to the lively confluence of the Brahmaputra and the Bhordi rivers. Almost immediately, I spotted the first dolphin leap, a quicksilver glistening grey arc in the eye-scrunchingly bright water. Then another, and another, revealing distinctive long beak-like snouts. Gangetic dolphins are found in certain parts of the Ganges and Indus, as well as in the Brahmaputra. They are said to be untrainable and show no interest in playing with boats, so you can only sit and wait for their unpredictable appearances. However, there is plenty of action, and dolphin-watching on a sunny sandbank is a wonderful form of relaxation, though mildly frustrating if you are trying to capture a dolphin on film with a stills camera (I failed dismally).

SACRIFICES AND SILK

My Assamese adventure was coming to an end, but Guwahati offered a couple more diversions. The city was once known as Pragjyotishpura (The City of Eastern Light), and its Kamakhya Temple is one of the most important shrines in Assam. The temple is a centre of Tantric Hinduism, based on the belief that the *yoni* (vulva) of Parvati (or Shakti), Shiva's first wife, fell to earth here after

Left: *The bright red Chinaman's hat flower*
Right: *Jogot, Dharmeswar and Ashok tease the morning's catch from the finely meshed net*
Inset: *Sought-after* muga *silk is naturally golden*

her dead body was cut into 51 pieces by Vishnu's discus. Rajan and I joined a swarm of labouring autorickshaws packed with pilgrims climbing up Nilacha Hill, and then continued on foot up the temple steps amidst a press of saffron-robed priests, stalls covered with garlands and offerings, and excited families dragging bleating sacrificial goats on a one-way trip. (I was comforted by the news that some are set free to roam the hillside.) Lengthy queues wound around the entrance, but we found a friendly monk happy to arrange fast-track admittance for a couple of rupees, and entered the upper level of the temple, where figures of Shiva and Parvati showered in flowers are worshipped before the descent to the *yoni*. In the crowded, hot, dark and foetid atmosphere, thick with the sickly sweet smell of joss sticks, the *yoni* is convincingly womb-like. Offerings lie piled around a trickling natural spring that was a place of worship for the hill tribe Khasis long before the arrival of Hinduism. The current temple, founded in 1665 after Muslims destroyed the original, was constructed around the *yoni*, which dates from the 10th century.

It was a relief to be back in the fresh air, and we decided to continue our cultural tour with a trip to the Assam State Museum. The sculpture galleries and hill-tribe section with its dioramas depicting village life came highly recommended, but they proved rather difficult to survey by torchlight in the middle of a power cut, so the expedition adjourned to the Government Emporium next door. This is a good place to pick up Assamese silk and tribal crafts.

Assamese silk is some of the finest in the world, and if you are serious about silk you should take a side trip to Sualkuchi, 24km (15 miles) northwest of Guwahati on the north bank of the river. The main street of this bustling silk centre is one long seam of silk shops, and every house has a loom clattering away behind open windows and a pile of silkworm cocoons drying in the sunny yard.

In a factory (a dozen handlooms squeezed into an upstairs room), I watched skilled weavers transforming silken threads finer than the filaments of a spider's web into bolts of delicate cloth. Shuttles flew as patterns were dictated by a system of punched cardboard cards, which transferred their instructions to the warp through a fantastically intricate rigging of threads. Of the three locally produced silk varieties—*muga*, *endi*, and *pat*—the most expensive and sought-after is *muga*, a shimmering fine golden cloth made from the cocoon of the *muga* silkworm, which is endemic to Assam. The colour is natural, and silk buyers should make sure they are buying *muga*, not a cheaper, dyed gold product.

My choice was a huge, soft, warm and hardwearing *endi* wrap because I was not quite finished with the northeast. It was time to head for the hills in the neighbouring state of Meghalaya, where I had heard you could visit the Wettest Spot on Earth and gamble on archery competitions (the official state sport) in Shillong, the former capital of Assam. I would need to rug up against the freezing nights and build a log fire in my room at the old colonial Pinewood Hotel, where the likes of Lady Curzon once retreated from the summer heat. No, the adventure wasn't over just yet.

GOING IT ALONE

INTERNAL TRAVEL

Guwahati's Borjhar Airport (25km/15 miles from the city centre) is served by daily flights from Calcutta (1 hour 10 minutes) and Delhi (2½ hours). International passengers should make sure they clear luggage through customs at their gateway destination even if it has been checked through to Guwahati. Onward travel to Kaziranga National Park is by road (223km/140 miles, or 5 hours approximately). There are also several flights a week from Calcutta to Jorhat (97km/60 miles, or 2½ hours from Kaziranga).

Trains are a slower but cheaper option. The Kamrup Express from Calcutta-Howrah takes 22 hours 40 minutes. The thrice-weekly Rajdhani Express from New Delhi takes 28 hours.

Assam has a fairly efficient bus network linking major towns, the main entrance to Kaziranga National Park at Kohora, and other destinations in neighbouring states. Tourist class buses, which offer such luxuries as air con, are well worth the slightly higher fares.

WHEN TO GO

Kaziranga National Park is open from November to April, during the winter dry season. The early part of the season (Nov–Jan) probably offers the best weather with bright, cloudless sunny days and temperatures averaging 32.2°C (90°F) at midday, yet cool enough in the evenings to warrant a sweater. The rains can start in February–March, when Assam's characteristic humidity begins build up. However, areas of grassland in the park are burned off at around this time, so wildlife spotting gets easier. The height of the summer monsoon season is June–July.

PLANNING

Independent travel is not difficult in Assam if you have plenty of time to make the necessary arrangements when you get there. Guwahati is the state's main transport hub, with regular bus connections to Kaziranga, Jorhat (for Majuli), and Tezpur (for Nameri). Car hire is also available, but note that driving can be something of a challenge as you dodge potholes, wandering livestock, and suicidal truck drivers along the obstacle course known as the highway.

Kaziranga National Park is Assam's top tourist attraction, so there are plenty of tour options available from Guwahati. However, many of the organized excursions offered by local operators (and through some larger hotels) are really too short at two to three days including travel time. It is preferable to spend at least 4 nights at Kaziranga so that there is plenty of time both to explore the park and to relax. Government-run Assam Tourism operates tours to Kaziranga, and has three lodges near the park office in Kohora. Arrangements for jeep and elephant safaris can be made through the information office at Bonani Lodge or the park office (where daily camera fees are collected). Private cars may also enter the park, but walking or hiking is not permitted.

There is no doubt that exploring beyond Kaziranga is best done with a guide whose local knowledge and ground-handling skills can add greatly to the experience, taking the hassle out of making arrangements and offering valuable insights. For the determinedly independent traveller, taxis, rickshaws and auto-rickshaws, (motorized three-wheelers) take over where the bus routes run out. Always agree the price in advance.

HEALTH MATTERS

Travellers to India should take medical advice for cholera, hepatitis, and typhoid vaccines. Assam is a malarial zone, but there is little problem in winter. Do not drink tap water. Bottled water is readily available (always check the cap seal is unbroken). Otherwise, stick to boiled water (minimum four minutes) or use purifying tablets.Pack a basic first-aid kit.

WHAT TO TAKE

❑ Comfortable, light, cotton clothing for the day; extra layers, including socks and a warm sweater for the evening.
❑ Camera film and spare batteries.
❑ All basic toiletries. Shopping for even the simplest items is difficult in the park, so make sure you bring everything you need.
❑ Sleeping bag for the sandbar camp.
❑ Mosquito repellent.
❑ Anglers should bring their own fishing tackle for Nameri (see p000).
❑ Bills are best settled in rupees, though with advance notification arrangements can be made for payment in US dollars or pounds Sterling.

7 Life and Death on the Ganga

by Steve Watkins

Strikingly set on a bank of the holy Ganga River in northern India, Varanasi is known as the "City of Light" and is a microcosm of all that makes India a captivating and challenging destination. Utilizing local transport and my own legs, I explored the mystery and beauty of this ancient city and the Ganga's spiritual role in Hinduism.

Throughout history, the world's major rivers, such as the Nile and the Amazon, have captured the imagination and their waters have been subject to wondrous claims of spiritual powers. Yet few, if any, have retained the reverence still lavished on India's most holy stretch of water, the Ganga River, otherwise known as the Ganges. Coursing for 2,525km (1,569 miles) from the foothills of the Indian Himalaya all the way to Bangladesh, the Ganga reaches its

spiritual high point at the age-old city of Varanasi, in the northern Indian state of Uttar Pradesh. One of the principal pilgrimage destinations for Hindus, the city is a complex web of narrow alleyways, riverside *ghats* (ritual bathing places) and elaborate temples. It is filled to overflowing with an incalculable number of people, cows, rickshaws, and holy men. To get there, I decided to follow the popular overland route from Kathmandu in Nepal and then spent a couple of days exploring the

city and the river to see why they inspire such devotion.

With numerous travellers' tales of hassle fresh in my mind and a bone-jarring, sleepless 10-hour bus journey from Kathmandu already behind me, I crossed the Nepal–India border at Sunauli and braced myself for an onslaught of street sellers, rickshaw drivers, and kids hawking for travel agents. I was slightly disappointed when only a handful turned up. Even they were rather half-hearted in their efforts to fleece me of rupees. Maybe the "real" India lay in wait. From the border, a further 3-hour, nighttime journey on a naturally air-conditioned bus—the windows fitted so badly that the cold night air simply poured in—took me to Gorakphur, from where I caught an overnight train for Varanasi. It all seemed stress-free thus far.

Around 3am next morning, in a dark and dingy station roughly halfway to Varanasi, a barely audible tannoy announcement, in English, mentioned "delays of several hours." The train ahead of us had derailed (a common occurrence on the old, poorly maintained railway lines of India) and evidently our train was not going any further. The quickest solution, according to locals, was to return, on a different train, to Gorakphur, wait another three hours, and then get a bus to Varanasi, a further 10-hour trip. By the time I arrived in the holy city, some 27 hours after leaving Kathmandu, no street sellers or taxi hawkers dared approach me for fear of being singed by my manic, bug-eyed stare! As much as I wanted to get out and explore straight away, the bed at the peaceful Hotel Surya proved too alluring, and I slept for a couple of hours.

Varanasi has something in common with the cities of Banaras and Kashi; in fact, they are one and the same! Each name is still widely used (with Banaras being the more common), and each

Left: Residents and pilgrims gather daily on the stone steps for their ritual ablutions
Top right: *A riverside barber*
Above right: *A sari stretched out on the steps to dry*

 It may not be overly physically demanding, but exploring Varanasi is mentally very stimulating and you should be prepared to feel completely exhausted at the end of the day.

 There is a very wide range of accommodation available in Varanasi, from incredibly cheap backpacker lodges to top-end luxury hotels. Travel and life in the city assaults all the senses, all the time, so you need a flexible approach if you are to enjoy it to the full.

 No special gear is required for this trip.

INDIA

comes with its own story, or stories, of origin. Varanasi is now the official name, originally used around the first century A.D. in both Buddhist and Hindu texts. The popular local story of its derivation is simply that the city is located between the Varana and Asi rivers. However, it was only in later years that the city expanded towards the Asi River and it is more likely that the word comes from an earlier name—Varanasi—for the Varana River, which flows into the Ganga at the city's original location. Banaras is probably a corruption of the name Varanasi while Kashi, meaning "Luminous City" or "City of Light," is the oldest name, dating back some 3,000 years and first used to describe the kingdom of which Varanasi formed the capital. No matter what name it has adopted, the city has in many respects changed little from the one first described in the famous Hindu tale, the *Mahabharata*.

WILD RIDE

It was time for me to venture out. From the gathering of pushy autorickshaw drivers lying in wait at the hotel entrance, it was Nandu, a kind-faced man, who offered the most reasonable price for a journey around the northern *ghats* and the old city alleys. Adventure comes in many forms, but riding in an autorickshaw was an unexpected addition to the list. These three-wheeled motorbikes, with engines that seem to have been stolen from lawnmowers, have an open-sided passenger cabin that sits two at a squeeze—or four or five, if you're travelling local-style. Twisting and swerving, beeping and braking, Nandu expertly manoeuvred through the utterly chaotic streets. The obstacles were varied and usually appeared from nowhere, like those stiff-looking bad guys in shoot 'em up video games at arcades. People carrying huge bundles of wood on their heads, passengers hanging from the sides of buses, mangy dogs scouring for scraps in street-corner rubbish piles, and the ever-present and wholly unpredictable sacred

cows all came within a sliver of ending our journey and possibly their lives too. The ride was both mesmerizing and overwhelming, and it seemed the only way to stay sane was to act like the locals—relax and leave our progress to fate.

It was obviously my lucky day, as half an hour later we arrived safely, though a little ruffled, at Raj Ghat, the most northerly *ghat* in Varanasi and one that few travellers visit. Buddha himself was said to have forded the Ganga here in the sixth century B.C. on his way to preach his first-ever sermon, at nearby Sarnarth. Crossing the water is far easier these days. Dominating the river is the multi-arched Malaviya Bridge, an impressive two-tiered, steel-girder construction that carries vehicles on the top deck and trains on the lower. Built by the British during the colonial days, it is so long that the far end faded away into the afternoon haze of smog caused by the incessant traffic. Beyond the bridge lies the Rajghat Plateau, location of Varanasi's urban centre throughout much of its early history. Below the bridge, a stark scene of people striving to make a living or simply carrying out chores looked as if it had barely changed since Buddha's days. Stringy-muscled boys and men, wearing only dirty white wraps around their waists, shouldered big bundles of gnarly wood, destined for the Ganga funeral pyres, down the mud slope to awaiting rowboats. At the water's edge, men and women stood in the water washing clothes and linen by swinging them over their heads and slapping them against specially raised stone blocks on the bank. Laid out to dry, the washing cloaked the entire bank and only delicate footwork prevented the wood carriers from treading on them. Half submerged in front of one of the bridge's tall pillars, a middle-aged man thoroughly scrubbed his herd of water buffaloes with all the pride of a car enthusiast polishing his collection of Ferraris. It was awe-inspiring to contemplate how many centuries this kind of daily scene had been acted out.

EPIC TICKET TO HEAVEN

Two ancient stories dominate the history of Hinduism in India. The *Mahabharata* poem is possibly the longest of all the world's epic tales and tells of a holy war between the Kauravas and the Pandavas, two powerful Indian dynasties, during the Iron Age (actual dates given by scholars for this war vary widely and are hotly debated). Amongst the cut and thrust and intrigue of the battle, the main purpose of the story remains very clear; to give people a moral basis for living, and an insight into right and wrong action, truth and untruth. Part of the *Mahabharata* tale is the *Baghvad Gita*, a conversation between the god Krishna and Arjuna, who represents man, which explains the Hindu doctrine.

The other epic poem, the *Ramayana*, is thought to have been scribed by the sage Valmiki and originally contained 24,000 couplets (two lines of rhyming verse). Like the *Mahabharata*, this poem contains an amazing cast of characters and centres on Prince Rama, upholder of correct action and duty, going off to save his abducted wife, Sita, who had fallen into the hands of the ten-headed demon king Ravana. With the aid of Hanuman, leader of the monkey tribe and holder of magical powers, Prince Rama overcomes evil and espouses the virtues of love and devotion along the way. If you fancy reading it, consider going a step further and learning it by heart—being able to recite it all from memory is said to guarantee breaking the cycle of birth and rebirth.

TWISTED CITY

For Hindus, Varanasi is such a powerful, sacred place that they believe simply dying there grants release from the cycle of rebirth and ensures transcendence. The rituals of death in the city are focused around two burning *ghats* (cremation sites), Harischandra Ghat and Manikarnika Ghat, on the banks of the Ganga. It is impossible to drive to either because the extremely narrow streets of the old city are barely wide enough for

two people, let alone an autorickshaw. Instead, Nandu drove me as close as possible and then pointed me in the right direction to walk the final kilometre (half mile) or so. Nandu's advice seemed simple enough, but negotiating the intimidating maze of dark alleys proved to be a navigational challenge that would test the wits of even the city's own planners. The cobbled passageways weave past ancient, looming three-storey buildings where traders sit in tiny, gloomy shops selling

HINDUISM—THE ABRIDGED VERSION

It is not easy to sum up any religion in one paragraph, but the complexities of Hinduism, with its millions of god images, is particularly challenging. Briefly, it is based on the ritual practice of Dharma, or the code of life, and the philosophy of Vedanta (as expounded in the four holy books known as the *Vedas*), which centres on Brahman, the universal soul and impersonal god, being the absolute truth. Hindus believe in reincarnation and that this cycle of life, death, and rebirth is

only broken through maintaining good karma, or actions, during life in order to achieve *moksha*, or spiritual salvation, something that is supposedly guaranteed to all those who die in Varanasi, regardless of their sins. If this sounds an attractive way of life, you're out of luck. You must be born a Hindu and cannot become one, no matter how religiously you practise Dharma. Such a restrictive entry policy should mean that there are few members, but there are in fact over 700 million Hindus in the world, principally in India, but also in Nepal and parts of Indonesia.

a stone arch and light appeared at the end of the alley. I scampered down steep steps to emerge at Manikarnika Ghat.

Originally built around A.D. 1300, Manikarnika is dominated by three conical-shaped and elaborately sculpted temples, one of which collapsed slightly into the river during construction of the neighbouring Scindia Ghat and now resembles Italy's Leaning Tower of Pisa. For both locals and pilgrims, bathing at the *ghat* is considered to be more auspicious than bathing anywhere else in the city. Indeed, Manikarnika's mythical powers are deemed to be so great that the other *tirthas*—bathing *ghats* included on the principal pilgrimage routes—are said to come here to bathe at midday to wash away all the sins they have acquired from worshippers. As I wandered along the upper steps, boatmen persistently offered me trips on the river, some at just $2 per hour. In between the boatmen's sales pitches, pretty young girls with smiles to die for used their charm and the mantra "No buy, just look, costs nothing to look," to sell me dreary postcards of the city and river. Although the *ghat* has such spiritual standing, the name Manikarnika is these days more synonymous with the cremation rituals that take place alongside the bathing ghat.

Beyond huge piles of sandalwood logs at the edge of the burning ground, greyish

spices, *lhassi* (a yogurt-style drink that is best avoided here as it is mixed with Ganga water), and an array of vegetables and fruits. Knowing that I needed to find my way back out again later, I consciously tried to pick out a few landmarks, whilst attempting to avoid looking like a lost and hapless tourist. The more I twisted and turned, the more I just had to rely on gut instinct when I came to a junction. At one particularly narrow part, a cow feeding on spoiled vegetables that had tumbled from a broken carrier bag blocked my path. The impasse, fuelled by my reluctance to upset a sacred cow, looked set to last well past the main course until a local man came along and unflinchingly shooed the cow aside. Eventually, I turned left under

Above: *Houseboat on the Ganga River*
Below: *A pilgrim perched by the riverside to pray*

smoke meandered skyward from the dozen or so funeral pyres blazing away on a charcoal-blackened platform above the river. On steps that dissected the platform, corpses wrapped in colourful cloth and adorned with garlands lay on bamboo stretchers, awaiting their turn to make the final journey to liberation (a recent snap of cold weather had apparently caused a spate of deaths among the city's elderly population). All around the fires, crowds of families, friends, and bystanders with solemn faces watched the elaborate rituals. It was a dark, forbidding, and moving scene—one that is very strictly prohibited to photographers and videographers.

In among the holy ones

With the sun dipping behind the city skyline, I headed upriver past Scindia Ghat, the place where mourners go to bathe after a funeral, to observe some of the sadhus who had emerged from their temple accommodation to meditate. Sadhus, or "holy men," come from all walks of life and renounce their worldly possessions and relationships, including businesses and families, to go on long and meandering journeys in search of spiritual truth.

Easily recognizable from their minimal clothing and long, bedraggled hair, the sadhus rely entirely on the generosity of other people for food and money, neither of which are they supposed to receive directly. Instead, they carry a small stainless steel bucket around with them to receive the donations (a tip for differentiating between genuine sadhus and "fakes," who are simply beggars, is to see whether they eagerly grasp money that

you offer them!). The peace of dusk settled on the river and the holy men sat on riverside platforms in quiet contemplation, perhaps edging ever closer to heaven. Around them, worshippers stood in the Ganga, uttering entrancing mantras to their gods—"Aum mani Shiva aum, aum mani Vishnu aum"—interspersed with sudden plunges deep into the less-than-inviting muddy brown water to wash away their sins.

For an insight into the nightlife of the temples, I returned through the old city to Nandu and his autorickshaw, and we drove to Kedar Ghat, one of the oldest ghats in the city. It is home to a special temple dedicated to Lord Shiva, one of Hinduism's principal manifestations of god and the main deity of Varanasi. Fortunately, Nandu showed me the way to the *ghat*, for the entrance was an easily missed enclosed alley behind a rough wooden door. There was so little light, it was difficult to avoid stepping on the blanketed beggars that lined the pathway. Kedar Ghat is visually striking, with the steps on its steep, long stairway painted alternately pale red and white. At the top of the stairs, several small shrines herald Kedar Temple. The original Kedar Temple is actually high up in the Himalaya on one of the Ganga's tributary rivers, and is the place where Shiva lived before coming to Varanasi. This made the original Kedar such an auspicious place that it has been replicated at the major Hindu centres throughout India. A few minutes after our arrival, a crackling tannoy sparked into life with evening prayers, whilst, in a small side room of the temple, five holy men began to ring bells and play hand-held, simple drums. The deep rhythm was infectious and reverberated through my body. Beyond the bell ringers and drummers, a priest moved back and forth in the elaborate inner temple, swinging his incense carrier and sprinkling a statue of Shiva and wife, Parvati, with water collected from the Ganga. For a moment at least, I was entranced and couldn't help but feel the power of Shiva.

Shiva is one of Hinduism's holy trinity of gods (the others are Brahma and Vishnu) and he has the power to destroy as well as to re-create. When the Ganga fell from Heaven to Earth, flowing from Vishnu's toe, there were concerns that the deluge of water would devastate the country. Shiva agreed to allow the river to run first through his long, dreadlocked hair in order to mitigate the flow. Normally depicted grasping a trident and weapons in his many hands, Shiva is patently Varanasi's most revered god. The city and temple walls are said to be infused with him, the Ganga flows through his locks, and it is said that Shiva himself delivers the city's dying to Heaven. With the sounds of bells and drums still strong in the cool night air, I clambered back into the autorickshaw for the ride back to the hotel.

FOOLISH JOY

If the evening activity on the Ganga is inspiring, then dawn is supposed to be even more so. It is the most popular time for visitors to take boat trips as it is often possible to witness a serene sunrise over the river, bathing the city in golden light. Next morning before dawn, one step out onto my balcony confirmed that my run of good luck had ended. The low-lying lands of northern India are prone to suffer from dense fog, especially in December and January, and I couldn't even see the hotel grounds. Disappointed, I decided to venture back to Kedar Ghat anyway, in the hope of at least witnessing the morning bathing rituals of the holy men. Having thought that I had come to terms with the insanity of Varanasi's roads, it was a shock to become a gibbering wreck once more as Nandu zipped through the streets despite being unable to see anything beyond the windscreen. Somehow we made it through, and I stood at the top of the Kedar steps staring into the murky nothingness. Behind me, an old holy man with a long grey beard and skinny legs emerged from the temple and immediately broke into a manic, jolly laughing fit.

I turned around to see what the joke was and realized it was me! Hopping with joy from foot to foot, the old man blurted "A camera! Ha! Ha! Ha!" and I could only laugh along with him as I stood waiting to take a picture of the invisible river. I was not alone in my foolishness, however. Wandering down to the river's edge, I could vaguely make out the silhouetted image of tourists on a "sightseeing" rowboat tour. The boatmen must have been offering ridiculously cheap deals that morning.

By midday the fog had lifted and I ventured with Nandu downriver to Asi Ghat, the most southerly *ghat* in the city and the start point for the popular Panchatirthi pilgrimage route that later takes in the *ghats* at Dasaswamedh, Adi Keshava, Panchaganga, and Manikarnika. It was Sunday and the ghat was positively throbbing with pilgrims. Following the path they were on, I hiked back up the river for an hour or so. Past the impressive high walls of Shivala Ghat, home to the palace of 17th-century king Chet Singh, I came across two male pilgrims performing swallow dives into the river from a lofty platform. Athletic endeavour has a long history in Varanasi and although many of the city's famous gymnasiums have closed down it is still possible to see men working out and wrestling at various riverside spots. One unusual gymnastic activity is the swinging of the *gada*, a stone dumbbell. Watching one youngster swing this weight high over his shoulder and around his back, I wondered what his joints would be like in 20 years' time. On the steps of one smaller *ghat*, I spotted an old, wise-looking sadhu deep in meditation. With his trident in hand, this follower of Shiva didn't twitch a muscle for the ten minutes or so that I stayed to observe him. Eventually my hike took me back to Kedar Ghat and I finally decided to give in to one of the boatmen.

Earlier in the day I had been impressed with the less-than-pushy approach of Babu, a young boatman operating from Mansrowar Ghat, a short walk from Kedar and a hundred metres or so away from the boat trip frenzy at Dasaswamedh Ghat, where most tourists arrive at the river. Babu's father was a boatman and so he too became one for the Indian caste system categorizes people and prescribes set paths for their working lives. Having spent a decent amount of time exploring the *ghats* from the land, I had wondered if it was really worth getting a view from the river. How glad I was that I chose to go. The perspective of both the people and the city is totally different from the water, and a river trip is an absolutely essential part of any visit to the city. Being on this holy, serene stretch of water, with the oars gently breaking the surface as Babu rowed past the latest funeral pyres at Manikarnika, I began to get a wider, more relaxed appreciation of the magnitude and majesty of Varanasi. It is an entire

FURTHER READING

Banaras—City of Light by Diana L. Eck (Penguin (India) 1993; ISBN 0-14-019079-1). This superb, in-depth, accessible look at life and religion in Varanasi is useful both as a reference book and as a holiday read for those travellers with more than just a passing interest in the city. This book is probably available only in India or Nepal.

The Ganges by Raghubir Singh (Thames & Hudson, 1992; ISBN 0-50-001509-0). Principally a photographic book, this features a journey along the entire length of the Ganges, from the Himalayan foothills to Bangladesh. Raghubir Singh's work has appeared in *National Geographic*. His beautifully composed and insightful images result from a deep understanding and love of the river and the people that both live along it and worship at it. The narrative text section gives a good history of the river and information on the daily rituals witnessed by the author.

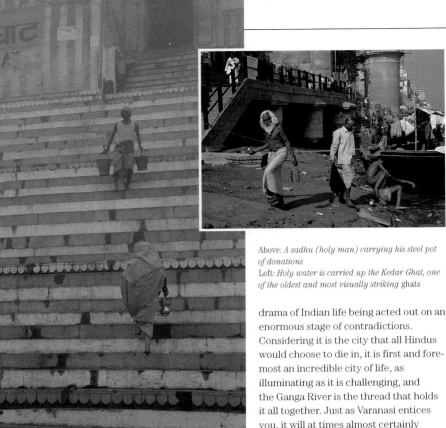

Above: *A sadhu (holy man) carrying his steel pot of donations*
Left: *Holy water is carried up the Kedar Ghat, one of the oldest and most visually striking* ghats

drama of Indian life being acted out on an enormous stage of contradictions. Considering it is the city that all Hindus would choose to die in, it is first and foremost an incredible city of life, as illuminating as it is challenging, and the Ganga River is the thread that holds it all together. Just as Varanasi entices you, it will at times almost certainly repulse you too, but I challenge any traveller to venture here without being affected by it.

HOLY WATER, POLLUTED RIVER

The Ganga River begins at the confluence of the Bhagirati River and the Alaknanda River at the town of Devprayag in the Himalaya. There, high up in the Himalaya foothills, the river is pure and wholly deserving of its life-giving and sin-cleansing status. However, all is not well with the holy river. As it courses through the Ganga Plain, the levels of pollution in the water grow, and they are now reaching critical levels. The sources of pollution are manifold and complex. Sewage and industrial waste from the riverside cities and towns pours in at an alarming rate, with some factories dumping over one quarter of a million litres (55,000 gallons) of waste every day, while several tanneries pump toxic chrome straight into the river. Added to these problems are those caused by the cremation and disposal of bodies in the river. Rising wood prices for funeral pyres has resulted in bodies being only half-cremated before they are cast into the water, and some of the deceased, including holy men, children, and pregnant women, are not cremated at all and simply float off downriver. How does this affect you, the traveller? You may not be planning a swim there, but you should be aware that the tea and coffee sellers along the *ghats* all use Ganga water for their brews. You have been warned!

GOING IT ALONE

INTERNAL TRAVEL

Varanasi is very well served by all major forms of transport, though there are no international flights to the city except for a daily flight from Kathmandu. Indian Airlines run daily flights between Varanasi and Delhi, Bombay, Agra, and Lucknow. However, flights to and from Varanasi can sometimes be delayed or cancelled during the winter owing to fog. There are several major express train services that link the city to Delhi, Calcutta (both served by the Poorva Express), and other major towns and cities throughout India. If there are no suitable trains to Varanasi itself, another option is to take a train (such as the fast Rajdhani Express from Delhi) to Mughalserai, just 12km (7.5 miles) south of Varanasi, and then catch a bus or autorickshaw. Flight and train tickets should be booked as far in advance as possible as they are extremely popular, especially the higher-class train tickets. Daily buses link the city with nearby towns and cities and other parts of India. Regular daily buses also link Varanasi with the Nepalese border, at Sunauli; but there are NO through buses to/from Nepal, so beware of buying packages.

TRAIN TICKETS

Booking a train ticket in India can seem like trying to apply for permanent residency in the country, as there are so many rules. There are different classes of travel, though not all are available on all trains. Avoid the basic second-class standard, as seats cannot be reserved and trying to secure one is mayhem. For long journeys, it is advisable to take one of the sleeper options. Sleeper class (six basic bunks in an open, dingy cabin) is bearable, but keep an eye on your possessions (buy a chain and padlock and use it at all times). The air-conditioned options are far more comfortable; food is cooked on board for you, too. Many trains have foreign tourist quotas, for tickets bought with foreign currency, so be sure to ask about these if the train is supposedly full. Make sure that your ticket is confirmed, as there is a standby system. Lists of confirmed passengers are posted at stations a few hours before departure. For further details, check out the Indian Railways website at www.indianrailway.com.

WHEN TO GO

Varanasi is a year-round destination, though the most popular time to visit is October to March, when the daytime temperatures are lower. The summer months are hot and humid, and the monsoon can lead to localized flooding. There are numerous major festivals in Varanasi, though few have fixed dates. In October/November on the night of a new moon the "Row of Lights" festival sees millions of oil lamps and, more recently, electric Christmas-style lights hung up all over the city to celebrate the end of the monsoon.

HEALTH MATTERS

Food and water hygiene have to be top of your list of concerns for travel here. There are no hard and fast rules for finding good restaurants, but generally you should avoid quiet places. Do not eat food from street sellers unless you are convinced of their hygiene standards. Meat is rarely stored properly, so stick to vegetarian dishes. Drink only bottled water and check the seal on the bottle before buying it. Mosquitoes are prevalent, so consult your doctor about an anti-malarial regime, and sleep under a mosquito net at night.

WHAT TO TAKE

- ❑ Good walking shoes.
- ❑ Sun hat.
- ❑ Sunblock.
- ❑ Mosquito repellent.
- ❑ Mosquito net.
- ❑ Long pants and long-sleeved shirts for entering temples.

TRAVELLERS' TIPS

Hassle and hard-nosed bargaining is all part of exploring Varanasi. Be mentally prepared for it. Even the remotest interest shown in an offered souvenir will lead to a persistent attempt to win your business. Be firm if you are not interested. Ask as many locals as possible about the going rates for local transport. This is to protect against paying either too high or too low a price for the service. Very low prices often mean that the driver will lead you on a merry chase around carpet, sari, or souvenir stores. I find it is always useful to claim to have been to the city many times before when the inevitable "Is this your first time in Varanasi?" question arises from drivers. On arrival in the city, taxi and rickshaw hawkers will harass you even before you get out of the airport or station. Keep walking and deal with the actual drivers. Know your hotel beforehand and have an idea of the route to get there.

8 Tales from the Orissan Tribal Lands

by Steve Watkins

Sprawling inland from the Bay of Bengal, the agricultural state of Orissa is one of India's richest cultural regions. In the state's southern hills, over 60 tribes live a life that has changed little in thousands of years. I took an enthralling four-day tour to visit a handful of tribal villages and markets.

India is a country that inspires travellers to return countless times, yet many of the addicts whom I have met have somehow managed to omit the eastern coastal state of Orissa. It certainly is one of the country's least publicized states and has very little tourism infrastructure. Perhaps it is not surprising that travellers pass it by. Personally, I enjoy exploring places that others ignore and it has often led to some of the most rewarding travel experiences of my life. After discovering that Orissa had a relatively inaccessible southern area that was home to a plethora of ancient and distinct tribes, all it needed to spark another adventure was a chance link-up with a local operator. I was surfing the web in a Kathmandu cybercafé when I discovered a travel company called Dove Adventures in Bhubaneshwar, the capital of Orissa. The company's affable and knowledgeable owner, Gagan Sarangi, assured me, via email, that they could organize a trip to the tribal areas and that the cyclone that had recently devastated much of the state's coastal area had had little or no impact inland.

I had travelled from Kathmandu to Varanasi in northern India, and from there the only reasonable option for travelling on to Bhubaneshwar was to take a 22-hour train journey. I had already experienced a second-class sleeper trip and felt that for such a lengthy journey I would like a bit more comfort. So I booked, at three times the cost of second class, a berth in the relative luxury of a two-tier air-conditioned sleeper car. As with most of my trips around India, the journey did not get off to a good start; in fact, it didn't even get out of the blocks. It was a cold night at crowded Varanasi Station and I struggled to comprehend the garbled announcements of numerous serious delays due to heavy fog. Eventually, I deciphered that my train, the Neelanchal Express, had been delayed for 10 hours! Not relishing an entire night on the platform, I gathered my luggage and took an autorickshaw back to the hotel to get some sleep. Up again before dawn, I arrived at the station just as the sun was rising over the Ganga River. The Neelanchal Express finally arrived just after 7am. The extra fare I paid was certainly worth it. With a very comfortable bed, space to move around, and the entertaining Vikash Sehgal, a sari

This tour is not strenuous, though there are several short walks to get to the villages.

Orissa's tourism infrastructure is not as developed as those of other Indian states, so accommodation levels in the major towns and cities are predominantly suited to the needs of locals rather than tourists. The best hotels are comfortable enough, however, and very reasonably priced. The tribal areas of Orissa are underdeveloped, and you need to have a flexible attitude towards where you stay. There are simply no hotels in many villages, so accommodation is sometimes in government worker huts or camping.

You will not need any special gear for this tour.

textile business owner, for company, the 22 hours heading east across the Ganga Plain and south to Bhubaneshwar was one of the most relaxing experiences of my stay in India. Fortunately, when I finally arrived at my destination, the travel plans started to fall into place and Gagan was there to meet me. The train delay meant that the tour was starting just 4 hours after I arrived, so Gagan had booked me into a nearby hotel to grab a few hours more sleep before the 10-hour drive south.

A lingering reminder of the colonial days in India is the very British-looking Ambassador car, a model that is still in production. It can be seen in use throughout the country and is particularly popular with politicians and other high-ranking officials. Our route south took us past the vast, watery expanse of Chilka Lake, a popular stop-off point for hundreds of species of migratory birds. On longer tours, Gagan often includes a boat trip to some of the island's lakes. However, we were on a mission to reach the town of Rayagada before nightfall and we turned inland, at Berhampur, shortly after passing the lake. The road began to climb into the beautiful, forested hills of the Eastern Ghats range, with the gain in altitude providing welcome relief from the heat of the lowlands.

EMERGENCE OF TRIBES

There had been no great wealth or industry to be seen down on the coast but even so there was a noticeable change in living standards in the hills. The tribal people of the hills live a simple, self-sufficient life that has yet to be drastically affected by modern world economics, and theirs is a more agreeable poverty than that of the city-dwelling poor.

Nearing Taptapani, a small town most noted for its natural hot springs, we began to see the first obvious signs of the region's largest tribe, the Kandha. In these tribal border areas, the influence of modern Indian dress standards, accelerated by the spread of Hinduism to the tribes, has made many Kandha people indistinguishable from other Indians. As is often the case with indigenous peoples around the world, however, it is the women of the Kandha tribe who have better held on to traditional ways. Amongst the colourful modern saris, it was still possible to spot a few women dressed in woven wraps and adorned with many bangles, earrings, and nose-rings. We didn't have time to stop and explore, but the scenery en route to Rayagada was enchanting. My expectations of rural India were more than matched by the gorgeous lush forests and the gentle sweep of the hills. By the time we reached Rayagada, it was dark and after a tasty meal at the Hotel Swagath restaurant, I was more than happy to get to bed to sleep off a bout of travel exhaustion.

The following morning, a gloriously sunny Wednesday, we set off early for the 40km (25-mile) journey to the weekly Dongria Kandha tribal market at Chatikana village, in Koraput District. En route, we picked up Mr. Sanjay Kumar Sahoo, head of the Dongria Kandha Development Agency, who had agreed to guide us through the market. The Dongria Kandha tribe is one of the major sub-groups of the Kandha tribe, though there are only around 5,000 of them remaining and their numbers are declining. *Dongria* means hill dwellers, and they are found principally in this area of the Niyamgiri Hills. One of the most astounding features of Orissan tribal society is that although the tribes all live relatively close to each other, they generally speak distinct languages; the Dongria language is called Kuvi.

The market was in the throes of setting up when we arrived, so we took the opportunity to walk out along a dusty track towards a nearby village. To get to the track we walked through Bhissamcuttack railway station and I watched, fascinated, as women and young girls, boys and old men carried their wares in large baskets balanced delicately on their heads across the four sets

Left: *Women returning home to Chatikana village*
Below: *Bondo girls buying bangles in Onukudelli market*

of tracks. The main platform area was abuzz with activity and it seemed some people couldn't wait for the market to start and instead traded right there on the platform. Presiding over baskets full of, amongst other goods, turmeric and tomatoes, the Dongria Kandha women looked spectacular with their multitudes of nose-rings, earrings, and neck-rings and colourful combs left in their hair. Although some women were wearing brightly coloured saris, others who had walked from more isolated villages, such as Khombesi, 14km (9 miles) away, still wore traditional, handwoven waist wraps and loosely slung fabric over their chests.

The Orissan people cover huge distances on foot as most of the villages have no road access, a situation that has fuelled the growing numbers of mysteries, tales, and myths associated with the tribes. They have a strong belief in magic, witchcraft, and sorcery and they worship a number of spirits and deities. Naturally suspicious of outsiders, the Dongria Kandha have been known to react aggressively when uninvited guests have wandered into their villages. They are not overtly violent, just protective of their endangered lifestyle and culture. Government efforts to convert the Orissan tribes to Hinduism and modern Indian dress standards have generally failed to make a significant impact in the remotest areas and even Gagan was wary of trying to visit the most isolated villages. In fact, special permits are required to enter the Orissan tribal areas and there are many villages you are strictly forbidden to enter.

UNTOUCHABLE FRIENDS

The Dongria Kandha is one of the most primitive groups of the Kandha tribe but they have a reputation for being successful agriculturists. In the fertile soils of the Eastern Ghats, they grow cotton, pineapples, tomatoes, apples, and turmeric. However, many families are trapped in a cycle of borrowing money at extortionate interest rates to buy crops which they then sell to non-Kandha middlemen, usually scheduled caste people otherwise known as Dombs, for little profit. The relationship between the Kandha people and the Dombs is a remarkable one. Dombs belong to the lowest group, or caste, of people in India and are also referred to as the "untouchables." They act as messengers within the tribal villages, buy fresh produce from the tribe and sell it on, herd cattle, and sweep the streets in return for the use of a patch of workable land. Because they tend to have more contact with non-Kandha society, their views on social and political matters hold some weight within the tribal community. One of the Dongria Kandha Development Agency's primary tasks is to lend money at a more affordable rate of interest, around 12 percent, and on a one-year term to allow the tribal families to escape from a virtual subsistence existence. Mr. Sahoo claimed that for every 1,000 rupees borrowed by the tribe to grow crops they would make 10,000 rupees on selling the resulting produce.

On the way back to the market we passed women bent double planting rice in the water-logged paddies while men worked the buffaloes and ploughs. The market was now in full swing and although the bright colours of the saris on sale and the jumbles of plastic bangles and hair combs in themselves enlivened the scene, the tribal people went about their business with little fuss or drama. Any haggling over price was low-key and short-lived. Women picked up clay pots and tapped them with their fingers as if the sound of the pot was in itself the only way to ascertain quality, while young girls, dressed in their finest outfits and on the lookout for potential suitors, browsed the kaleidoscopic arrays of bangles.

One of the most extraordinary customs of the Dongria Kandha (and other

Above: *A spectacularly adorned Bondo woman*
Right: *Sunrise over the tribal village of Hanumal*

BRIEF GUIDE TO OTHER TRIBES

Paroja – One of the best-known tribes in Orissa, the Paroja number 200,000 and live mainly in the Koraput and Kalahandi districts. '*Paroja*' derives from a word meaning common people. They are a strong, shy, and hard-working tribe.

Kotia A numerically small tribe found in Koraput, Kalahandi, and Phulbani districts.

Bhuyan Another primitive tribe, found in the remote Keonjhar district. Its people make a living from shifting cultivation and they are known for collecting flowers, seeds, mushrooms, and edible roots from the forests.

Birhors A semi-nomadic tribe whose people are renowned for their monkey-catching skills and for making ropes from the bark of the Siali creepers. They are among the most primitive of Orissan tribes.

Ho A major tribe in Orissa. The Ho people are short and dark and have flat, broad noses. They live in mixed villages throughout the state and are experts at making ropes and baskets.

Juang This tribe is only found in Orissa and inhabits the hills of Pallahara and Keonjhar. The Juang believe that they were the first humans to be born on Earth, and they are great lovers of dance and music.

Saora One of the oldest tribes in the state, the Saora are found throughout the state. Its people are famous for their wall paintings, called *ikons*, depicting humans, horses, elephants, aeroplanes, and the sun and moon. They are strong believers in shamanism.

Orissan tribes) is the way in which girls and boys meet and find their partners. Each community has a dormitory, which could be a special building or simply a room at one of the leader's houses, where girls and boys can meet, learn about the ways of life, and choose or coerce potential life partners into marriage. The boys do this by placing or trying to force bangles onto the girls' wrists. If a girl accepts, then the deal is done; if she rejects the gift, then it may be a signal of indifference or she may just be making him work hard for his reward! The dormitory is a fun and carefree place where the future sense of tribal identity is reinforced. To ensure that bloodlines are kept separate in the matchmaking process, it is strictly forbidden for boys to visit the dormitory at their own village.

By midday the market was beginning to ebb. Clans of women gathered under a large tree with their new possessions and their empty produce baskets, waiting until the entire group of women and girls from their extended families were together before setting off for the long trek home. The strong sense of unity and

community was remarkable and it was easy to understand how the Donghria Kandha tribe had purposefully resisted the onslaught of modern life for so long. During a brief stop at the main Chatikana village, where the houses were lined up on opposite sides of a straight street—the traditional setup for Donghria Kandha villages—I had a chance to buy some handmade crafts. The necklaces were beautiful and, as starting prices were only a few dollars, I didn't bargain with the sellers too hard.

We dropped off Mr. Sahoo, and our afternoon and evening were then taken up by another long drive, via Jeypore, to the village of Machhkund, set on the shore of the beautiful Lake Machhkund. The lake was formed by the building of a massive, but visually low-key, hydroelectric scheme in the valley. There is no formal accommodation in Machhkund, so we bedded down at a basic but comfortable cottage, which is usually reserved for workers from the government-run hydroelectric plant. The cottage was located on a hill above the village so, having arrived in the dark, it was a pleasant surprise to wake up to a spectacular sunrise view across the entire valley and down to the village and mist-clad river. The Bondo tribal market village of Onukudelli (various spellings of this and other Orissan village names abound—it is the sound that is important!) was about an hour's drive away. Our route initially skirted the shore of the lake before climbing into the Bondo Hills.

ARROWS AT DAWN

The Bondo people are perhaps the best-known but least visited tribe in Orissa. More than almost any other tribe, they have retained their traditional ways, culture, and lifestyle, partly due to their geographical isolation and partly because they have a fierce independent spirit. The tribe lives in a scattered group of 30 or so villages with almost no road access to any of them. To reach the market at Onukudelli, some of the Bondos have to travel on foot for up to 50km (30 miles), and that's just one way. At the end of the day, they pack up and head home. Interacting with the Bondo is notoriously difficult for outsiders, so we employed the services of an excellent local guide called Babuli. His links with the Bondo are so strong and well recognized that several documentary filmmakers have used him to smooth access to the tribe. His bright, smiling face and friendly, playful disposition made it easy to like and trust him. Before the market got under way, we all took a short stroll out along the dirt road that many of the Bondo use to reach Onukudelli. Near a causeway that crosses several large rice paddies, we sat and watched the remarkable procession of Bondo people. Under very strict instructions not to photograph the men, I did not need telling twice when the first long line of men jogging in perfect unison came past. Each of them had a rudimentary but well-crafted bow and a quiver of metal or wood tipped arrows. Babuli informed me that Bondo men have fiery tempers, particularly after they have been drinking a palm wine called *salap*,

FURTHER READING

It is almost impossible to find books on the tribes of Orissa, so I am eternally grateful to the amazing Dr. A. C. Sahoo, head of the Tribal Research Centre in Bhubaneshwar for most of the information on the tribes contained in the feature. Dr. A. C. Sahoo has been working with the tribes for over 20 years and is one of the leading experts on tribal life. There is a book called *Guide to Orissa Tribes*, usually available locally but currently out of print and almost impossible to find. The Tribal Research Centre is open to visitors but there are no displays— just people, like Dr. Sahoo, who know a great deal. If you are very interested in learning more about the tribes then it is worth making a visit (phone first to make an appointment).

and that they never go anywhere without their bow and arrows—which they are not averse to using.

Whilst the Bondo men were both impressive in their unity and slightly intimidating with their dispassionate faces and ever-ready weapons, the Bondo women were simply magnificent. They wore only tiny black waist wraps, called ringas, on their lower body, instead of clothing, they were spectacularly adorned with layer upon layer of long, multicoloured bead-and-brass necklaces. To provide some warmth on this cold and clear morning, they wore a blue wrap around their shoulders. Piled around their necks were up to one dozen or so aluminium and brass rings, and from their ears dangled elaborate and large brass earrings. Their forearms were covered in bangles and their fingers were full of rings. Some of the women wore nothing on their heads, which are completely shaved when they marry and remain so for the rest of their lives, while others wore pretty, multicoloured bead headpieces. There was no doubting the

strength of the Bondo peoples' spirit of independence—and what a breathtaking way to show it. Babuli had a lovely way with the women and would remove the loads from their heads to ensure they stopped for a photograph! After a bout of mock anger, the women would soon be laughing and joking with him, calling his name in vain and offering him a gourd of *salap* to drink as an act of friendship. Always playing hardball when it came to business, the women would playfully haggle over the photographic payments Babuli offered, but his long experience in dealing with the Bondo meant that he knew just what the going rate was and eventually both parties happily settled for it. It was a great privilege to be able to meet up with these people on such a personal basis and I was honoured when one group of women offered me a taste of *salap*. This very strong, cloudy white wine

is made from the sap of the sago palm and tastes a little like bitter lemonade.

SALAP ATTACK

Back at Onukudelli, the large and sprawling market was well under way. Stalls completely filled the main street, side streets, and central square. The square, which was surrounded by tall palms, hosted the *salap* market and groups of men and women sat on their haunches pouring wine from gourds straight into their mouths. The gradual rise in levels of inebriation was giving Gagan and Babuli cause for concern and they suggested that I should stay clear of the *salap*-selling area. Alcohol, arrows, and immense pride are certainly a recipe for potential trouble, and later in the afternoon a frantic fight broke out between two brothers. Arguing over ownership of a palm tree used for making *salap*, the brothers

Left: *Rainbow bus stopping off at the market*
Below: *Onukudelli market*
Bottom: *There was no accommodation available in Hanumal village so we shared a floor with the local schoolchildren*

INDIA

dashed around the square with bows drawn while friends, family, and community elders tried to calm them and disarm them. No harm came to either brother and the crowds eventually dispersed, but Gagan revealed that only a few weeks before in the same place a man had been shot with an arrow and killed. It was startling reminder that, despite the worldwide boom in tours to places off the beaten track, venturing into isolated, tribal areas still needs to be done with humble respect and an awareness that parts of such tours are not always controllable.

Our final night was to be spent at the tiny village of Hanumal, a short drive out along the track where Babuli had been playing and joking with the women that morning. Set at the base of rounded hills in an idyllic valley, Hanumal is a mixed tribal village where Bondo people live alongside members of the Gadaba tribe, another of the most primitive groups in the region. Nearing the village, the pace of life noticeably dropped a few gears. With no accommodation on offer, we were to share floor space in the school along with

SOCIETY AND WEDDINGS

The Bondo have a number of different social groups ranging from the family at one end to the tribe at the other. Clans are organized into *kudas*, a patrilineal grouping of several families connected by blood, and all Bondos use their *kuda* title as part of their own name. A wider grouping is the Soru-bhai, which comprises all the people in 12 Bondo villages. All the members of the Soru-bhai are treated as brothers and sisters and so are not allowed to marry. The Bondo, like the Dongria Kandha, have a dormitory system for boys and girls to meet up and choose their life partners. On a wedding day, the bride and her friends form an elaborate dancing procession to the groom's house for the ceremony. Women generally choose to marry younger men, as they will be more able to work when the woman gets older, so when Babuli found out that I was 34, he ruled out my chances of finding a Bondo bride. I was devastated.

20 or so excited young pupils who stay at the school during the week because their home villages are so far away. As the sun was setting, I took a stroll up a nearby hill to soak up the beauty of a village that has changed little for centuries. Smoke from kitchen fires drifted over the thatched huts and through the trees while stragglers from the Onukudelli market returned along the winding track.

Before heading off to bed, we visited a small group of houses belonging to one clan to enjoy a demonstration of traditional dancing by the village women. Drummers warmed their instruments around the sparking fire while the women discussed what dances they wanted to do. With a decision made, they all linked up in a snaking line, the drums rumbled into life, and the women began a mesmerizing series of synchronized, lunging steps whilst chanting and singing. If the drummers made a mistake, the women would joyously point it out whilst their own mistakes often led to the whole group breaking down into fits of laughter. I have visited a number of tribal areas during my travelling life, but I could not recall encountering tribes that made me feel as uplifted as those in Orissa. Eventually, the tribes will almost inevitably succumb to a more modern way of life, but until then there are still many, many years for travellers to go there and meet these beautiful, proud, and inspirational people.

KONARK SUN TEMPLE

Although the different tribes are a major reason for visiting Orissa, most people also come to see the state's incredible collection of temples. Top of the temple list is the majestic Sun Temple at Konark, a small town 64km (40 miles) southeast of Bhubaneshwar on the coast. The temple was built in the 13th century by one of Orissa's most successful kings, Narashimhadev I, to mark a great victory over the Muslim invaders, and originally it stood on the seashore. For many centuries the temple was abandoned, and it wasn't until the turn of the 20th century that excavation work revealed the stunning 24 chariot wheels sculpted from stone around the base of the temple. The façade is a breathtaking array of sculpted figures, including many erotic images of couples and dancers, along with carved elephants. The main stairway to the temple is guarded by two massive and impressive, if a bit weatherworn, stone lions. The site is a very popular place for pilgrims—not to mention a raucous and cheeky bunch of monkeys, too.

GOING IT ALONE

INTERNAL TRAVEL

Indian railways have a daily service, the Neelanchal Express, from Delhi to Bhubaneshwar, calling at Varanasi en route. The entire journey takes 30 hours, so splash out and book at least a two-tier air-conditioned sleeper berth. Indian Airlines operate a daily flight from Delhi to Bhubaneshwar, which takes only 2 hours. Getting to the south of Orissa from Bhubaneshwar can be done only by bus, and it is a long and tiring journey. Getting around in the hill areas is even slower, so it is advisable to take a tour unless you have unlimited time.

WHEN TO GO

The cooler, drier time of year is between November and March, so this is the best time to visit. It can get oppressively hot in the summer months.

PLANNING

Although it is theoretically possible to travel to some of the tribal areas independently, most are either out of bounds or require special permits. The area is also very sensitive and communicating with tribal leaders would be so difficult without speaking the local language that in practice the only option is to go on an organized tour. There are quite a few operators in Bhubaneshwar, but only a couple, including Gagan Sarangi's Dove Adventures, can be easily contacted from overseas. The distances and travelling times involved in getting from Bhubaneshwar to the tribal area and between villages are so great that short trips,

of 2, 3, or 4 days, would barely be worth it (though you can join tours from Jeypur in the south to save on travel time). The most popular duration is 1 week, but 10 or 12 days would be preferable to get to some rarely visited villages. Book the trip as far in advance as possible because there are no telephones in many of the villages and the tour operator has to send someone to the area beforehand to arrange accommodation and permits.

HEALTH MATTERS

You should be on an anti-malarial course of tablets while visiting Orissa and you should always use a mosquito net to sleep under. Consult your doctor for the latest information. Stick to drinking bottled water and use common sense when eating food in restaurants. Avoid eating salads or anything that isn't cooked or peeled. If a restaurant is full of locals, then there is a reasonable chance that the food will be all right for you too. It does get hot during the day in Orissa, so carry a bottle of water at all times, especially on walks to the villages.

WHAT TO TAKE

❑ Long trousers and long-sleeved shirts to visit villages.
❑ Comfortable walking shoes or boots.
❑ Insect repellent.
❑ Mosquito net.
❑ Sleeping bag.
❑ Torch.
❑ Plenty of small denomination rupees.
❑ Sunhat.
❑ Sunblock.
❑ Sunglasses.

TRAVELLERS' TIPS

❑ It is of utmost importance that you do not to take photographs of the Bondo men. They carry their bows and arrows with them at all times and have occasionally been known to react aggressively to tourists when under the influence of palm wine.

❑ With the assistance of your guide, it may be possible to photograph the women for a small fee. Do not take pictures if you are not willing to pay for them, as the women are well versed in creating a scene. Whilst it is not an overtly dangerous place for travellers, it is very remote, and the local police are reluctant to get involved in violent disputes.

❑ Try to buy handicrafts from the tribal people because this is a legitimate way for them to benefit directly from you being there and there are some lovely beads, bangles, and woven products.

❑ Remember that some of the tribal people have had very little contact with tourists, so be humble and attempt to make it a pleasant and rewarding encounter for both parties. The tribal people are on the whole friendly and welcoming, especially if you take a genuine interest in their lives. Drinking the potent palm wine with them will win you instant friends, but maybe at the cost of an upset stomach or a hangover!

INDIA

9 Travels in Temple Land

by Simon Richmond

From riotous Madurai, home of Meenakshi, the fish-eyed goddess, to the stone carvers of Mamallapuram, Tamil Nadu's sacred temple towns provide an insight into the subcontinent's millennia-old Hindu culture—not to mention a crash course in modern Indian life.

It's 7am and kaleidoscopic Madurai—epicentre of Tamil Nadu's 2,000-year-old Dravidian culture—is gearing up for another day of ear-thumping activity, as hectic as the 12 *gopuram* of its most famous temple, Sri Meenakshi. From the roof of my hotel, I can see the tallest of these sacred gateways, soaring heavenward above the patchwork of concrete buildings and painted billboards.

In the style of *gopuram* all over south India, every inch of its tapering surface is plastered with a stucco menagerie of colourfully painted gods, gyrating dancers, leering demons, celestial angels, and fabulous animals. I mop up the dregs of the sambar curry sauce with a feather-light idli rice cake (southern India's favourite breakfast), settle the bill, and head in the temple's direction.

The aroma of milky coffee mingles in the air with other pungent smells as I hurry past the sari shops, the persistent guides, and the rickshaw wallahs, already jostling for business. "Five rupees to the temple," they cry, but I prefer to walk the short distance, in the company of a family from the neighbouring state of Kerala. They, like tens of thousands of others daily, have come to pay their respects to Meenakshi, goddess of fertility and consort of Sundareshvara, or Shiva, creator and destroyer.

Just inside the temple's west gate, a musical cacophony spills out from the cowshed. Beside nonchalant cattle, a crowd of young men and children are stripped to the waist, their torsos smeared in mustard yellow sandalwood paste, their necks hung with garlands of jasmine. All are wailing in front of a shrine to Ganesh, the jubilant elephant-headed god, to the jazzy accompaniment of musicians on *tavil* drums, *talam* cymbals, and *nagaswaram* flutes.

Suddenly, the paste-smeared worshippers take up small silver urns of milk,

1 If you can buy a bus or train ticket, you can do this trip. Give yourself plenty of time at each location and be selective in what you see. If the crowded public transport gets too much, hire a taxi. Part of the fun is putting together your own pilgrimage, but if this sounds daunting, use one of the travel agents in Chennai and Madurai. There are also fully organized bus tours that take care of all accommodation, travel, and guides.

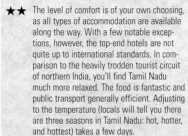
★★ The level of comfort is of your own choosing, as all types of accommodation are available along the way. With a few notable exceptions, however, the top-end hotels are not quite up to international standards. In comparison to the heavily trodden tourist circuit of northern India, you'll find Tamil Nadu much more relaxed. The food is fantastic and public transport generally efficient. Adjusting to the temperature (locals will tell you there are three seasons in Tamil Nadu: hot, hotter, and hottest) takes a few days.

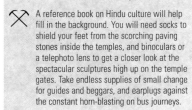
A reference book on Hindu culture will help fill in the background. You will need socks to shield your feet from the scorching paving stones inside the temples, and binoculars or a telephoto lens to get a closer look at the spectacular sculptures high up on the temple gates. Take endless supplies of small change for guides and beggars, and earplugs against the constant horn-blasting on bus journeys.

Right: *The temple of Sri Meenakshi, the greatest man-made spectacle in the south of India*
Inset: *Detail of the temple's intricately painted ceiling*

balance them on their heads, and proceed out into the street. The band leads the way, family and friends hurry alongside. Regal parasols shade the mini-procession from the already fierce sun. Shopkeepers explode firecrackers as the parade winds around the temple walls. My visit to Madurai, the last stop on a tour of Tamil Nadu's top temple towns, was literally starting off with a bang.

A SPLENDID PROVINCE

Marco Polo called it "the most noble and splendid province in the world." Tamil Nadu, at the southern tip of India, is made up of fertile rice-growing plains sandwiched between the Bay of Bengal and the verdant hills of the Western Ghats. Here you'll find some of the most sacred and architecturally impressive Hindu temples in India. Many date from between the Pallava dynasty of the seventh and eighth centuries and the Chola dynasty of the tenth to fourteenth centuries, but their cultural roots stretch back much further, to the Dravidians, one of subcontinent's earliest civilizations.

The rich history of these temples is displayed not only in their exotic and precise design, but in the rituals and practices that take place within and around them. Each is dedicated to one or several of Hinduism's pantheon of 330 million devas, or gods, their legends, and ceremonies. Between the unadorned bas relief rock carvings of Mamallapuram and the sumptuous painted murals of Madurai's Sri Meenakshi Temple, lies a fascinating and, to Western eyes, frequently bizarre world, where you can be blessed by elephants and inanimate effigies are treated like divine beings.

The start of my personal pilgrimage was Tamil Nadu's sprawling capital Chennai, better known by its former name of Madras. I had opted to ease myself gently into India's chaotic street life, by hiring a taxi for a couple of days to visit the nearby towns of Kanchipuram, famous for its temples and fine silks, and Mamallapuram, seaside capital of the

Pallava kings. From here I would travel by bus to the former French colony of Pondicherry, home of the Aurobindo Ashram; Chidambaram, where the venerable Nataraja Temple is run by a hereditary priesthood; Thanjavur with its beautiful Brihadishwara Temple, a World Heritage Site; and Tiruchirappalli (better known as Trichy), site of the striking Rock Fort and huge temple complex Srirangam. Finally I would take the train to Madurai, the star attraction of southern India's temple circuit.

FRESCOES AND MANGOS

At the appointed hour Jaishankur, my amiable driver, is waiting outside my Chennai hotel, beside a pristine white Ambassador, a car modelled on a 1950s British Morris Oxford and ubiquitous on India's roads. Fresh jasmine buds perfumed its plush interior. Overnight rain had cooled the air and the atmosphere immediately felt fresher as we abandoned the concrete, dust, and incessant noise of the city for the lush paddy fields and tamarind tree-lined roads en route to one of India's seven most sacred cities.

Once called "the golden city of a thousand temples," Kanchipuram is these days a bustling commercial centre for high-quality silk production. I'm stopping overnight so I have time to visit four of the 200 remaining temples, a silk factory, a home where cotton is woven, and a restored merchant's house. At the Kamakshi Aman Temple, I'm blessed by one of the many elephants found in southern Indian temples, trained to tap you on the head with its trunk after you have made an offering of a small sum of money. And at the Devarajaswami Temple, dedicated to Vishnu, the preserver, my young guide and sari-seller, Krishnamoorthy, points out *Karma Sutra* carving amid the florid decoration of the *mandapam* hall.

The most important of Kanchi's temples is Sri Ekambaranathar, dedicated to Shiva. Arriving outside the 59m (190ft) high *gopuram*, I'm mobbed by trinket-

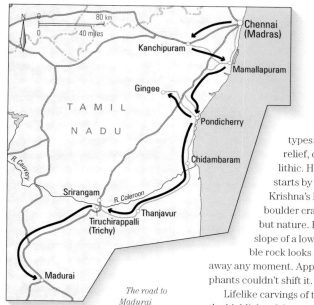

*The road to
Madurai*

sellers and guides, confirming the temple's reputation as a hotspot for hustlers. Gurana, a raffish guide on the lookout to extract as many rupees from visitors as possible, leads me round the ruins at the rear of the 12ha (30-acre) complex for a fine prospect across the temple roof.

Beyond the so-called 1,000-pillared hall (it has only 540), I'm shown a courtyard in which stands a sprawling mango tree, reputedly to be 3,500 years old. Two of the tree's four main branches broke off during a cyclone, but a shrine to fertility nestles under the trunk and from the remaining branches dangle offerings from the faithful—crudely painted toy wooden cradles.

SEASIDE ROCK CARVERS

Village life spills on to the highway early the following day as we drive past the sugar cane and rice fields towards Mamallapuram. Whole communities work together to clean 20m (65ft) long sari looms, strung out along the road. Across the bitumen, carpets of grains are spread out to be milled by the passing traffic. On the edge of town, Jaishankur pauses to

pick up Kumar, a gentle soul who will be my guide for the day.

Mamallapuram is famous for its exquisite rock carvings, of which there are four types: architectural, bas relief, cave, and monolithic. However, Kumar starts by showing me Krishna's Butterball, a huge boulder crafted not by man, but nature. Perched on the slope of a low hill, this incredible rock looks as if it might roll away any moment. Apparently seven elephants couldn't shift it.

Lifelike carvings of two elephants are the highlight of the nearby bas relief sculpture (the largest in the world) Arjuna's Penance, an intensely detailed depiction of Hindu fables. I run the gauntlet of souvenir sellers to admire this remarkable piece of art, the carvings of deities, animals, and humans as striking and unpretentious today as they were when the sculpture's completion was halted by war in the 7th century.

Rock carving still thrives in Mamallapuram, and the streets reverberate to the taps of hundreds of chisels on stone. At one workshop on the way to the Five Rathas—five temples sculpted from solid rocks in the style of chariots and weathered into dreamlike blurriness—the owner has had a bright idea for attracting customers. Outside, in front of serried ranks of Ganeshes, Parvatis, and Lakshimis, stands a life-size statue of a modern-day goddess, Princess Diana.

Best viewed from the beach, where fishermen squat unpicking debris from their nets, the beautiful Shore Temple is the last of seven that once lined Mamallapuram's sandy coast. The sharpness of the complex's detailed carvings have been softened by the elements, leaving two wedding-cake tiered sanctums

Above: Ornately painted elephants are a common sight at southern Indian temples

Having parted company with Jaishankur and the Ambassador, I make the journey by public bus, which arrives in Mamallapuram from Chennai already overflowing with passengers. While most disembark for tiffin (light lunch), I secure a spot on the floor near the driver. Here I squat for the next 3 hours, getting a first-hand lesson in the anarchic rules of the road as the kamikaze driver swerves recklessly around potholes and keeps me fully alert with regular blasts of the horn.

Thoroughly rattled, I'm more than ready for Pondicherry's soothing byways, particularly the elegant parks and restored mansions of the boulevards between the old canal and the breezy promenade. In the flower-decked court-yard of the Sri Aurobindo Ashram, I join devotees sitting in quiet contemplation beside the tomb of Aurobindo and his successor, a Frenchwoman known as Mother. In such a serene atmosphere it's easy to see the appeal of this popular sect, founded in 1926 and now so wealthy through donations and cottage industries that it owns a large part of Pondy.

The best reason for coming here, however, is to make a day trip to Gingee (pronounced Shingee), some 70km (45 miles) inland, to explore the vast, cinematic ruins of the 16th-century fort, rightly considered to be one of the most extraordinary in India. Some 5km (3 miles) of thick battlements link up citadels on three hills, seemingly com-posed from piles of giant boulders. Within the fort grounds are several temples, a gra-nary, stables, a mosque, and the Kalyana Mahal audience hall, partly restored and incorporating a tower that you can climb for an overview of the complex.

The most commanding panorama is from Rajagiri, highest of the citadels, reached by climbing over 1,000 steps. As I sweat my way up the hill in the punishing midday sun, I wish I'd arrived earlier. The bus had taken too long to get here, and I'd have been better off hiring a taxi for the day (800–1,000 rupees for the round trip). From the roof of the seemingly

containing shrines to Shiva and Vishnu, surrounded by walls topped with 52 stat-ues of the bull guardian, Nandi. Although this is now an archaeological site rather than a functioning temple, visitors still leave frangipani and marigolds as offer-ings, around Shiva's thick, black *lingam* (phallus) and the reposing, 2.5m (8ft) long statue of Vishnu.

ASHRAMS AND FORTS

It's difficult to move on from such an appealing place as Mamallapuram, but Pondicherry, some 95km (150 miles) down the Coromandel coast, has its attractions too. A French colonial enclave in British India, Pondy (as it's affection-ately known) is distinctly different from other towns in Tamil Nadu. One reason is that it's a separate Union Territory, and so does not impose the same high taxes on hotel and alcohol prices as Tamil Nadu (although this is more than made up for in the cost of its excellent, but expensive French restaurants). Another is that Pondy's lingering Gallic charms provide a break from the temple circuit.

impregnable clock tower, it's easy to image myself a maharaja looking down on my kingdom below. The best part is that, aside from a handful of workmen, and the occasional local tourist, I have the entire fort to myself.

LORD OF THE DANCE

I'm back at Pondy's bus station early the next day heading to Chidambaram, 60km (38 miles) south, where Nataraja, the greatest of the Shiva temples, dedicated by the Chola dynasty to the god's incarnation as lord of the cosmic dance, dominates the town. The 22ha (55-acre) compound is administered by the Dikshitas, a group of hereditary priests, who successfully fought the government to keep financial control of the temple with which they have been connected since the sixth century. Hence, while you wander around Nataraja's precincts you'll frequently be asked by the priests—who wear their long black hair wound up a bun, with their foreheads shaved—for contributions to the temple. Whether you give or not, there's no obligation to sign their account books, as you will inevitably be asked to do.

I'm initially underwhelmed by the comparatively shabby state of Nataraja; paint is fading on the *gopuram*, the interiors are gloomy. But as pilgrims begin drifting into the spacious compound during the late afternoon, the temple starts to come alive. My knowledgeable guide, Paneer, takes me first past the Nandi

pavilion to the small Ganesh shrine. Here a young priest has me remove my shirt before he incants a prayer in front of the god and dabs my forehead with two downward strokes of white and one of red—the mark of Vishnu. I'm given some of this holy ash to take away, assured it's good for medication.

The rising moon over the eastern *gopuram* is reflected in Nataraja's large sunken Sivaganga tank where sadhus (the wandering ascetics) and other faithful bathe before entering the Chit Sabha inner shrine. The roof of this holy of holies is covered, according to Paneer, with 21,600 gold tiles, pinned down by 72,000 gold nails. "The number of tiles is the same as the number of times we breathe each day," he explains, "and the number of nails, the same as the times that our hearts beat."

Guaranteed to set the heart beating faster is the thrilling *puja*, or worshipping ceremony, held daily at 6pm in the dark corridors around the Chit Sabha. Amid clashing of cymbals and ringing of bells, the Dikshitar priests chant and wave plates of fire before the image of Shiva. The tightly crushed crowd fervently press their hands together in prayer. The atmosphere is electric, and it becomes even wilder as people surge forward to perform *darshana*, passing their hands over the sacred flames held by the priests to receive Shiva's blessing.

THE CHOLA MASTERPIECE

The calm of Thanjavur's Brihadisvara Temple couldn't be more of a contrast. I had travelled the 110km (68 miles) to the one-time capital of the Chola empire during the relative cool of the night, surviving another life-threatening bus trip. The old town and the jumble of buildings (many crying out for restoration) that used to be Thanjavur's palace are worth exploring, but I head first to the World Heritage-listed temple. In the cloisters—on the walls of which are frescoes that depict corporal and mythical scenes—boys sit sketching, old men are gossiping, and sadhus are praying.

Built during the 10th century by the Chola king Rajaraja I, Bridhashwara, which translates as big temple of god, is a remarkable achievement. The 62m (200ft) *vimana* tower above the central shrine to Shiva is the tallest in India, and is topped by an 83-tonne granite dome. The ancient technology that shifted this mammoth block of stone into place was also used to transport a 6m (19ft, 25-tonne) block of granite, eventually carved into the guardian bull Nandi. This, the second largest Nandi in India, sits under an ornate stone canopy whose ceiling is painted with heavenly patterns, angels, and birds.

Sensuous sculptures abound, many recording the principal poses of classical dance. The central shrine, where four

TEMPLE ARCHITECTURE

South India's Hindu temples all have a similar design. The overall complex will be contained within a square, which is considered to be the most perfect shape. Entry to the temple is through the *gopuram*, a pyramid tower over the gateway. Their multicoloured facades are a relatively recent trend.

Within the temple precincts, before reaching the *garbhariha*, or inner shrine, you will pass *mandapam*, or halls, often supported by many ornately carved pillars. These are convenient spaces where pilgrims can rest after their journeys; some are open only on festival days.

If the temple is dedicated to Shiva, there will be a *nandi*, a statue of a white bull guarding the main shrine. Inside the shrine is a *lingam*, a phallic symbol worshipped as a form of the deity. The lingam is often found arising from the vulva-shaped *yoni*, the symbol of female energy. Over the central shrine will be the *vimana*, a stepped roof.

priests are in attendance to conduct the *puja*, has a giant *lingam*, above which rears the statue of a cobra with five golden heads. The platform is draped with ring upon ring of yellow, white, and pink garlands. An Indian doctor visiting from New York gives me flowers and a banana to leave as an offering. While Shiva gets the jasmine, I decide Kundavi, the elephant, would better appreciate the fruit.

THE GATE TO PARADISE

Tiruchirappalli, better known as Trichy, is 54km (34 miles) west of Thanjavur and stands on the banks of the sacred Cauvery River, revered by Tamils as the "Lady of Gold," nourishing the land and people. From my vantage point at the top of the 84m (275ft)-high Rock Fort, I have a dreamy view of the river, flowing languidly past a patchwork of rooftops and paddy-fields. It has to be said that this panorama is the best thing about climbing the 437 steps up the rock—the Vicayaka Temple at the summit, dedicated to Ganesh, is tiny, modern, and quite plain.

The vast temple complex of Srirangam, one of India's largest, occupies an island in the Cauvery, 3km (1¾ miles) from the Rock Fort. It's more a town than a temple, with seven concentric walls and 21 *gopuram*. The outer compounds are filled with the bazaar and the homes of the priests, an area in which you can wander freely and soak up the buzzing atmosphere. Beyond the fourth *gopuram* the main temple begins, where you'll need to remove your shoes, and for which you'll certainly need a guide.

The temple's genesis is lost in the mists of time, but virtually every ruling dynasty of the Tamil Nadu area has had a hand in its construction. The result is in a rich tapestry of sculptures and a rather erratic design. At its heart lies a shrine to Vishnu, closed to non-Hindus. First I climb on to the roof near the main entrance, and observe artisans beating out new golden panels for the central shrine's *vimana*. The nearest *gopuram*

TEMPLE ETIQUETTE

- ❏ Shoes are never worn inside the temple. There's always somewhere to leave them outside. Pay the small fee when you reclaim them.
- ❏ Avoid wearing shorts and sleeveless tops, and generally act respectfully within the temple.
- ❏ It is traditional to move clockwise around the temple, towards the main shrine.
- ❏ Don't enter the inner shrine, where only Hindus are allowed. At some temples entry may be allowed on payment of a small donation to the priests.
- ❏ In the temple precincts and surroundings you will find sellers of flower garlands, coconut husks, or baskets filled with fruit, clay pots of ghee, or cubes of camphor—all offerings for the gods.
- ❏ After prayer, it is traditional to mark the forehead with a dab of powder or ash, the colour and shape of the mark depending on the deity prayed to.

is swathed in tarpaulin and a rickety wooden scaffold, while it is in the process of being tarted up in gaudy colours, paid for by a rich local merchant.

Sundar, my guide, leads me through the labyrinth, to a spot where I can contort my body to catch a glimpse of the gate to paradise, past a stunning painting at the north gate of Vishnu reclining, and on the east side to the Sesayuni Rao *mandapa* where the roof is held up by columns carved into fabulous warrior horses. Here too are depictions of the ten incarnations of Vishnu, including the one yet to come: the horseman of the apocalypse. "Could be five years," says Sundar, when I ask him when this final, terrible version of Vishnu will arrive, "could be five minutes."

Above: *The Gandhi statue, Pondicherry*
Right: *A splash of colour in Pondicherry*

MEENAKSHI, THE SEDUCTRESS

The end of the world being potentially just around the corner, I waste no time in heading to Madurai. The manager of my hotel knows the right people at the station, so I am suddenly off the waiting list and am secured a first-class seat on the Vaigai Express. The carriage's shabby interior doesn't conform to any standard of first-class other than its own. But it's less crowded and has softer seats than the bus, the air conditioning works, I don't feel I'm about to meet my death in a hideous road crash, and I can chat with my neighbour without being interrupted every other minute by the deafening horn.

There's so much to experience within Sri Meenakshi temple that several visits are necessary. There are blessing elephants, daily rituals and musical performances, the shambolic, intriguing museum in the 1,000-pillared hall, and innumerable arresting images—from wall paintings of the gods, dappled with the reflected light of the Golden Lotus water tank, to the carved teak roof of Kalyan Manadpam, where the marriage of Shiva and Meenakshi is celebrated in an annual festival. You can't take it all in one go.

So having started the day at Sri Meenakshi with the fire-cracker parade, I return at 9pm to attend the most charming of the temple's daily rituals: the bedtime of the gods. A palanquin is brought forth from Sundaresvarar's shrine, carrying the image of the deity. Bells are rung, trumpets are blown, and a priest sings softly as we all move by candlelight through the temple's darkened corridors to the Vambuthurar Gopuram, the gateway to Meenakshi's womb-like shrine.

Before disappearing inside for the night, the palanquin is briefly laid to rest outside while the faithful strain to touch its silken covers, falling to the ground in worship. A band of flute, cymbal, drum, and harmonium players strikes up a droning lullaby, steadily increasing in tempo. The priests sprinkle holy water and waft flaming plates of camphor. Bare-chested attendants flap plumed fans, like extras in a production of the Hindu epic, the *Mahabharata*. It's a wonderful climax to my journey through the land of temples.

GOING IT ALONE

INTERNAL TRAVEL

Buses and/or taxis are the way to get around. The best opportunity to use the train would be between Chennai and Madurai on the Viagai Express, which goes via Trichy.

For train tickets, go to the booking office as far in advance of the date you wish travel as possible. Fill out a form with details of the service you want and then stand patiently in line. Pay the full amount for the ticket, even if you are put on a waiting list for the more expensive tickets; if a seat doesn't become available (check on the day of travel at the same ticket office), you will be given a refund. To save trouble, it is worth paying a travel agent the small premium for buying a ticket. Alternatively, buy the cheapest ticket and see if you can upgrade on the train.

For buses, it is usually just a case of turning up and waiting for the next service. Don't sit near the front if you can't handle the breakneck speeding and hornbashing ways of the driver. On some buses, the sexes may be segregated, with men sitting at the rear.

It is tempting to consider a motorbike or moped tour of southern India, but be prepared for chaotic traffic in the cities, potholed roads everywhere, and dangerous drivers. Chennai is home to India's Enfield factory (open for visits if you call in advance, tel: 044 543300); a new model sets you back around 50,000 rupees.

Within the towns, the best way of getting around is by autorickshaw, cheaper than

taxis, and more of a thrill ride.

WHEN TO GO

Avoid travel during the monsoon season, October and November. The coolest temperatures and the best chance of clear weather come in January and February.

Although it is great fun to be in a temple town during a special festival, you will have to take a chance on accommodation, and share street space with thousands of pilgrims and tourists. Madurai's Teppam festival can easily attract over a million people.

PLANNING

Allow at least a week to see the best of Tamil Nadu's temples, especially if you're going to be travelling by public transport. Hiring a taxi for the week will allow you to get to more off-the-beaten track places.

Both Kanchipuram and Mamallapuram can be visited in day trips from Chennai. Mamallapuram is the more pleasant place to stay overnight. There are frequent onward buses to Pondicherry, taking 3 hours. To visit Gingee, it is best to hire a taxi from Pondicherry. A day each is needed for Chidambaram, Thanjavur, and Trichy; there are plenty of buses between these towns, each taking no more than 4 hours. Madurai is also 4 hours by bus from Trichy. The fastest train covers the journey in little over half the time.

Entrance to temples is generally free; exceptions are Mamallapuram's Shore Temple and Five Rathas,

where a 5-rupee ticket allows entry to both. At Trichy's temples and in Sri Meenakshi in Madurai you will also be charged a camera fee (10–30 rupees). The best times to visit are early morning and evening, when people gather to say prayers; some inner sanctums and temples (such as Thanjavur's Brihadishwara Temple) are closed between noon and 4pm. Take socks to wear inside.

Hiring a guide to show you around is the best way to make sense of what's going on. There might be only one guide hanging around at the entrance, but if you don't fancy him (or occasionally her), then politely decline their services and move on; you'll almost certainly be approached by someone else. In fact, to stop being pestered incessantly, it sometimes pays to use a guide even if you don't want one. Chat to a guide before you start a tour to check if they know their stuff, and make sure that you can understand them. Make clear what it is that you would like to see and find out about. Also, you might want to agree a fee up-front, although it is advisable to wait till the end of the tour before handing over any cash. The average fee I paid during my trip was 200 rupees (around $5).

HEALTH MATTERS

The heat is the main enemy in southern India. Drink plenty of water, and always wear a wide-brimmed hat. Don't overexert yourself and avoid doing anything in the middle of the day. There is no need to be too paranoid about where and what you eat, but steer clear of uncooked food, especially salads, and drink bottled water.

10 Sailing through the Spice Kingdom

by Simon Richmond

INDIA

Between old Cochin and the tiger-patrolled jungles of Periyar lies a maze of canals, lakes, rivers, and streams. Floating through these tranquil backwaters is the best way to discover the true heart of Kerala.

The Malabar Coast, the Kuttanadu Backwaters, the Cardamom Hills: names so tantalizing they set the imagination spinning. These are among the prize facets of Kerala, the emerald slither of a state at the southwest tip of India that down the centuries has been seducing traders and travellers with its lush landscapes, fragrant spices, and genial atmosphere.

Backpackers and honeymooners flock

1 Home to an educated, relatively prosperous, and genial population, Kerala is one of the easiest and most pleasant places in India in which to travel. A night on a houseboat is a wonderful way to experience the backwaters, but making the trip by ferry between Alappuzha and Kollam, or taking a tour on a punt through the narrowest canals, will allow you to see more of daily life. If you want a more challenging adventure, try jungle trekking around the Periyar Wildlife Sanctuary or the hill station of Munnar.

★★ Some of India's best hotels and tastiest food are to be found in Kerala. Exploring the backwaters by boat is one of the most relaxing and pampered adventures you could have. Even trekking need not be difficult, with the day-hike routes through Periyar Wildlife Sanctuary easily negotiable. You need to watch out for leeches and insects, however. Heading off into the deepest forests of the Western Ghats will mean roughing it and requires patience while dealing with park bureaucracy.

Bring binoculars for spotting birds and wildlife in the nature reserves and along the backwaters. For protection here and on the coast, you will need a broad hat and sunscreen. If you plan to go trekking, bring hiking boots and leech-proof socks. For the cooler Cardamom Hills, you will need a sweater and rain jacket.

to the soft beaches around Kovalam and Varkala in the south of Kerala. Antiques buyers and history buffs scour the Byzantine streets of Fort Cochin. And avid readers come clutching copies of *The God of Small Things*, hoping to find something of the tropical sensuousness that suffuses Arundhati Roy's prize-winning novel. Few are disappointed.

In a week of travel through what the tourist literature calls, with only slight hyperbole, "God's own country," I was searching for the more intrepid options. My first stop was in the highlands of the Western Ghats at Periyar Wildlife Sanctuary, southern India's largest haven for wild elephants. My goal was the enigmatic port of Kochi, better known as Cochin, whose rich maritime history dates back a couple of thousand years.

In between, I took to the backwaters that spread through Kerala's verdant body like veins and arteries, feeding paddy fields and groves of coconut and exotic fruits and spices. I would travel by all manner of craft, but the most memorable trip was in a *kettuvallam*, a traditional rice barge converted into a houseboat, from which I discovered what previous guests called "Eden on earth." They weren't far wrong.

JOURNEY TO PERIYAR

From the Tamil Nadu temple city of Madurai (see Chapter 9), I opted for a taxi, rather than a bus, to travel the 134km (84 miles) to Kumily, the bustling town just across the state border that serves as the jumping-off point for the

Exploring Kerala, from Kumily to the coast

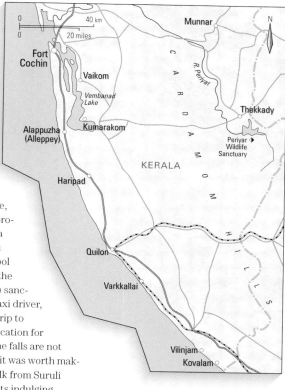

Periyar Wildlife Sanctuary, which lies some 3km (2 miles) further down the road at Thekkady. This way I could stop and enjoy the scenery along the route.

This fecund farming country, yielding rice, potatoes, and sugar, is broken by rocky outcrops, a foretaste of the Western Ghats, which rise to a cool 900m (3,000ft) around the 777sq. km (300sq.-mile) sanctuary. Manimaran, the taxi driver, suggested a quick side-trip to Suruli Falls, a popular location for filming Tamil movies. The falls are not particularly special, but it was worth making the 1km (½-mile) walk from Suruli village to see local tourists indulging enthusiastically in a communal shower—the men down to their underpants, the women soaping themselves while fully clothed in saris.

From here the road up to Kumily rises steeply, snaking past four thick, black pipes carrying water from the dammed Periyar River. Buses squeezed narrowly past each other around the tight corners, their poor passengers' only distraction being the stunning views across the plains below. By noon I was at the border, being bundled out of the taxi and into a jeep for a fast, expensive transfer to my hotel, the Spice Village. Kumily—where every other shop seems to sell packets of spices and/or Kashmiri handicrafts—is so small I could have easily walked.

ON THE LAKE

Periyar Lake was created in 1885, when the river was dammed by the British and diverted into Tamil Nadu for irrigation.

The hills surrounding the 26sq. km (10sq.-mile) body of water—home to some 900 elephants and 34 other species of animals, including tigers, and a diverse range of flora—are softly rounded and forested. It is easy to see why Periyar, set in such attractive landscape, draws a quarter of a million tourists a year.

Most visitors head directly to the jetty at the tip of Thekkady peninsula, from which the Tourist and Forest Department run cruises across the lake. There are five trips on chugging double-decker boats each day; the best trips for wildlife-spotting are the first and last, at 7am and 4pm.

Despite the glassy beauty of the lake and the dreamy landscape, these cruises are not for those seeking a tranquil experience. The racket of the boat engine is matched only by that of Indian tourists squealing in pleasure at the sight of any animal on the distant banks. Amazingly,

the commotion doesn't totally scare all wildlife away.

From the relative calm of the small boat chartered for the Spice Village's guests, I spotted sambar deer, wild pigs, and giant guar (bison-like cows) grazing on the grassy levees. Long-dead tree trunks, poking out of the water like a Salvador Dali painting, have become perches for cormorants, one of the sanctuary's 266 species of birds. Others are Malabar hornbills, kingfishers, and grey herons.

The Lake Palace hotel, former summer residence of the Maharaja of Travancore, commands a prime position overlooking the water. On its manicured lawns you can sip afternoon tea from china cups while keeping a eye out for elephants, deer, and, if you're extremely lucky, a tiger, on the open grasslands opposite. Even those on a tight budget can enjoy this view by arranging to spend time at one of the park's rustic observation towers close by the palace. It is possible to trek here

Left: *Negotiating the wide, calm waterways around Vaikom in a dugout punt*
Below: *Brightly coloured hisbiscus grows everywhere*
Below left: *Fish market at Nanjiarkulangara*

with a guide or, for 100 rupees, to stay overnight (bringing all your own food and bedding).

FEEDING TIME

Trekking in the sanctuary is not permitted without a guide, but you won't have to wait long either in Kumily or at Thekkady to be approached by someone offering their services. Not all guides are officially authorized and you will have to weigh up whether to risk a trek with someone who might not be qualified to deal with dangerous animals.

The Wildlife Information Centre runs a 4-hour trek (10 rupees) along the eastern side of the lake for the first ten people to turn up at the centre before 7:30am each day. For 125 rupees the Spice Village arranged a private guide for me, trained by the Forest Department. I hoped that with fewer people on the trek, I would have a better chance of encountering wildlife. I dressed in dark colours to blend in with the foliage, and borrowed some canvas, anti-leech socks from the hotel.

Shaji, a young-looking 21-year-old from the Mannam tribe, was waiting for me at the guides' hut beside the entrance gate to the sanctuary. The Mannam, along with the Muduan and Paliyan tribes, used to live within the sanctuary, and Shaji grew up spending the monsoons in a tree house, above the damp ground. His well-trained eye soon spotted a sambar deer camouflaged in the bushes. It was easier for me to hear, rather than see, the Nilgiri langur monkeys swinging through the trees. I also caught the warbling of the appropriately named racket-tailed drongo bird.

As for finding elephants, all Shaji had to do was sniff. Sensing fresh dung in the air, he set off to locate these grand animals, who munch through 25kg (55lb) of grass a day. Sadly they remained hidden in the dense jungle, but maybe this was just as well since a riled elephant can be even more dangerous than a tiger. But out on the plains we did witness a pack of wild dogs, with black, bushy fox-like tails, breakfasting on the carcass of a deer.

BEAST OF VEMBANAD

Early the next morning a car, arranged through the Cochin-based agent Clipper Holidays, was waiting to transfer me from

Periyar to Vembanad Lake, the starting point for my *kettuvallam* cruise through the backwaters. The dizzy drive through the Cardamom Hills is spectacular, even if I did feel a bit queasy as we hurtled along the twisting road. Shrouded in mist, the hills are plastered with tea bushes in their upper reaches and rubber trees on the lower, steamier slopes. In the villages and towns en route, I noticed churches and plaster saints and saviours in ornate, roadside shrines, evidence of Kerala's diverse cultural heritage.

Christianity is said to have been introduced to Kerala in the first century, when Thomas the Apostle dropped by the Malabar coast. About the same time Jews are believed to have arrived (Cochin has India's oldest Jewish community), and Syrian Christians followed a century later. Mix in the Muslims, Sikhs, and Buddhists, not to mention the majority Hindu population, and you have perhaps India's headiest and most tolerant religious brew.

"Welcome to Coconut Lagoon," said the receptionist, dressed in a graceful sari. She dabbed my forehead gently with sandalwood paste and offered a posy of marigolds, while another assistant presented me with a freshly chopped coconut, ready to drink from. It was such a pleasant welcome that I was very tempted to stay at this idyllic lakeside resort (reached by boat from the village of Kumarakom). But my night's accommodation was already taken care of: a houseboat which, with its hardwood bark stained black with pitch and woven palm leaf shades flying out to the sides, looked like some enormous beast of Vembanad.

The *kettuvallam* had a crew of three: captain Gobi, first mate Sajeev, and cook Kunjappan. I sat on the broad, sheltered deck, picking at a plate of banana and pineapple, while Gobi punted off and Sajeev started up the outboard motor that would propel us slowly across the lake. Behind me was a cabin with a double bed, mosquito net, and attached bathroom. The shower was a bit tricky to use, but all else was perfect.

FLOATING THROUGH PARADISE

Across the lake there was plenty to distract me, should I wish it, from a life of pampered indolence on the *kettuvallam*. Fishermen flung nets from boats, while the gentle breeze filled the ragged sheet sails. A dredger hauled up shells for cement. A public ferry chugged past on its way from Vembanad's bulbous end towards the cluster of islands and isthmuses that comprise the port of Cochin, 64km (40 miles) north.

Across the surface of the lake and

SNAKEBOAT AND ELEPHANT FESTIVALS

Alappuzha's Nehru Cup Snakeboat Race is held annually on the second Saturday of August. As many as 70 crews of up to a 100 rowers race 30m (100ft)-long *chundan vallams* (snakeboats), with magnificently carved prows, down the 1.6km (1-mile) course. The regatta attracts a huge crowd, and you'll need a ticket (available through KTDC offices) to secure a good spot: a space on the lawn costs 10 rupees, lake view 50 rupees, and the pavilions near the end of the race 150–300 rupees. The Rajiv Ghandi Boat Race is held on the second Saturday in September.

Kerala is also renowned for its parades of decorated elephants. The grandest are held in Trichur (also called Thrissur) about 70km (45 miles) north of Cochin. The four-day Great Elephant March takes place in January, when a hundred or so elephants from temples and plantations around the state are dressed in ornate regalia and ridden by mahouts carrying gilded parasols. During the Trissur Pooram, usually held in late April, teams of elephants and musicians compete for the crowd's approval in Vadakkumnathan Temple.

DARJEELING OF THE SOUTH

At 1,524m (5,000ft), the colonial hill station of Munnar is a good base for exploring the high ranges of the Western Ghats. The small town is little more than a pit stop for trucks on their way back and forth from Tamil Nadu. The surrounding slopes, however, have extensive tea plantations, cottages dating from the Raj, tropical forests, exotic fauna, including the Nilgiri tahr, a species of ibex, and Kerala's tallest mountain, the 2,695m (8,842ft) Anamudi.

Take an autorickshaw or bus 17km (11 miles) from Munnar to Erivakulam National Park, a 97sq. km (37sq.-mile) safe haven for the endangered Nilgiri tahr. Without a special permit (which can take a month to arrange) and an authorized guide, it is safest to restrict yourself to day walks on the edge of the reserve. If you wish to trek overnight, contact Clipper Holidays in Cochin, who can organize trips, including all camping gear and guides, for around $35 per day. In Munnar, you can hire bikes to tour the area for around 30 rupees a day.

down the canals floated a thick carpet of water hyacinth, dotted with mauve flowers. It may look pretty, but this weed, also known as African Moss, is the bane of the backwaters, quickly clogging up the narrower waterways. At one point the captain was forced to turn the boat around because of such a blockage.

As the sun sank towards the horizon, we moored across from a line of simple cottages built in the shade of coconut palms and reflected in the dark waters. By the light of storm lanterns I tucked into a dinner of chicken, vegetables, and chapattis, while radio music and voices in the cottages drifted across the canal. By the time I slipped under the net into my bed, the only sounds were the gentle lapping of ripples of water against the boat and the buzz of insects reclaiming the night.

THE SNAKE TEMPLE

The next morning I was up with the dawn. The sun breaking over the clouds and through the palm fronds was an even more beautiful sight than sunset the night before. While I breakfasted on an omelette and toast, I watched women shuttle their husbands and sons in rowing boats across the canal to the fields. Others waited for the ferry into the coastal town of Alappuzha, also known as Alleppey—which was where I too was headed.

As we sailed closer to Alappuzha, village life alongside the backwaters became more conspicuous. People waved from the front porches of houses daubed with the hammer and sickle (Kerala has the world's first freely elected Communist government). Children on their way to school shouted "Pen, pen," the chant of kids all over India when they see foreigners. Women washed clothes, and called out to boatmen selling fish and vegetables.

Near the end of the cruise, Captain Gobi pointed out the starting point of the town's famous snakeboat race. The reek of sewage and dead fish brought back the reality of daily life beyond the backwaters, and we pulled into the dock alongside ranks of other *kettuvallam*. Varkey Kurian from Clipper Holidays was waiting to drive me to Cochin. On the way we had checked out some of the sights around Alappuzha, a small town of canals and shops selling coir (rope made from coconut fibres), which is rather fancifully dubbed the Venice of the East.

Serpent worship is part of Kerala's Hindu tradition, and Mannavasala Nagaraja Temple in Haripad, 40km (25 miles) south of Alappuzha, is dedicated to the snake; stone cobras slither up its columns. Presided over by a female priestess it is a squat, wooden complex with broad eaves, looking more like a

Left: *The view out of my house-boat on Coconut Lagoon*
Below: *Lake Periyar, looking deceptively tranquil*

was lined with trucks spilling over with ice, fast melting in the searing noon sun. This was the outer perimeter of the fish market. On the sand, deals were feverishly hammered out in Malayalam, the local language—believed to be one of the world's fastest spoken. I picked my way through the crowds to the water's edge, where scores of men, women, and children relayed the morning's catch in coir baskets from boats to the shore. I'd arrived at the Arabian Sea.

Japanese Shinto shrine than the towering, ornate Hindu temples of neighbouring Tamil Nadu.

Outside the inner sanctum I noticed a large pair of scales for weighing offerings. The list is intriguing: please donate your body weight in turmeric for protection against poison; in pepper and mustard for good health; in silk and grain for education, prosperity, and fame; in gold for wealth; and in ghee for long life.

On the Arabian Sea

At Nangiarkulangara, some 30km (20 miles) south of Cochin the beachside road

With the exception of the trucks and ice, the essentials of this lively scene have been the same since long before Vasco da Gama arrived on this coast in 1502 and declared it Portuguese territory. A year later the first wooden version of St. Francis Church was erected in Fort Cochin, and the tombstone of da Gama's original grave (his body was returned to Portugal in 1538, 14 years after his death) is still there, one of the fragments of history that makes Cochin one of the most fascinating places in India to explore.

"If China is where you make your money, then Cochin is surely the place to

Above: *At the heart of Kerala lies a tranquil maze of canals, rivers, lakes, and streams*
Right: *Kathkali dancer in flamboyant costume*

spend it," said the 14th-century Italian traveller Nicolas Conti. On the narrow streets of Mattancherry, where warehouses packed with antiques rub shoulders with handicraft shops and spice trading houses, Conti's remark still holds true. Shopping is not the only reason, however, to explore this colourful neighbourhood next to Fort Cochin.

Here you'll find the splendid 17th-century Cochin Synagogue, for example; its floor is decorated with hand-painted tiles from Canton, China, and its ceiling is hung with multicoloured glass lamps from Belgium. In the nearby Mattancherry Palace, built by the Portuguese in 1555 for the Raja of Cochin, gorgeous murals remain—look out for highly provocative detailing of the Hindu gods at play.

DANCING FOR THE GODS

Back in Fort Cochin, I walked past the Chinese fishing nets—giant bamboo and rope contraptions—that line the harbour. Ducking into a palm-leaf hut on the water's edge, I watched two young men apply broad strokes of green, yellow, red, and black make-up to their faces in front of an enthralled audience. A third man

entered to assist one of the others fix a paper beard, or *chutti*, around his chin.

This is the fascinating overture to Kathkali, the Kerala dance form that depicts stories of the gods from the Hindu classics. Traditional Kathkali performances in temples last all night, but there are a handful of places in Cochin (including the See India Foundation, near Ernakulam Junction Station, and the Kerala Kathkali Centre, on River Road in Fort Cochin—where I was sitting) at which you can get an edited taste of this dazzling art form.

The make-up sessions begin around 5:30pm and last up to an hour and a half, during which time you are welcome to

111

DIVING DETAILS

On the Lakshadweep Islands there are only two places open to foreign visitors. The luxury resort on Bangaram Island is part of the Casino Hotels group. Bookings can be made in Kochi (Tel: 0484 666821; Fax: 668001; email: casino@giasmd01.vsnl.net.in). Single dive packages here start from $120 with an open-water certification course costing $250.

On Kadmat, Lacadives, a Mumbai-based dive school (Tel: 022-494 2723; Fax: 495 1644; email: lacadives@hotmail.com), offer 7-day packages including full-board accommoda-

tion and two dives a day for $800.

Indian Airlines has flights to the islands from Cochin for around $300; you will need to add on transfers by boat or helicopter to either Bangaram or Kadmat and you must keep your luggage to under 10kg (22lb). There is also the option of taking a 5-day cruise from Cochin, with three nights spent on Kadmat (from 8000 rupees). For details contact the main Lakshadweep tourist office, IG Rd., Willingdon Island, Cochin, Tel: 0484 666387; Fax: 0484 668155.

take photographs. The narrator and one of the dancers will then run through an explanation of Kathkali, demonstrating the language of gestures and facial movements. Finally, the dancers emerge fully dressed in the flamboyant costumes of hooped skirts and enormous, carved wooden crowns and begin energetically whirling to the beat to the drums. The effect is stunning.

LAND OF COCONUTS

I could not resist returning to the backwaters for one last cruise. Spending over an hour in a minivan weaving through heavy traffic to get out of the city was far from the most relaxing way to start the tour. But from the moment I climbed into the narrow dugout punt, made from jackfruit wood stitched together with coir rope, I could tell this was going to be another delightful excursion.

With a French and a Belgian couple for company, I was on a 3-hour tour of the labyrinthine canals around the village of Vaikom, some 40km (25 miles) south of Cochin. Such half- and full-day (including lunch) trips are a good way of exploring the backwaters if you are based in Cochin and don't have time for the longer, busier, and noisier ferry journey between Alappuzha and Kollam. They are also ideal if you want to get off the boat and see more of village life.

Sharing the punting duties were Pannappan and Uthaman, and our local guide was Reina. The shallow, slim channels we floated along were crowded in by trees drooping with red hibiscus, heady honeysuckle, and wild pineapple. At the first stop Reina pointed out a stagnant pool studded with lotuses. Hindus believe these are the first flower created by the gods, and their temples are decorated with lotus patterns.

The village is thinly spread and we occasionally passed the house beside the waterways. Near one we stopped to drink from freshly chopped coconuts. Standing by a pile of coconut shells, Reina explains how the shells are broken down so that the fibres can be turned into coir and the remaining husks into firewood or ornaments. From the fermented coconut juices comes toddy, an alcoholic tipple. It is easy to see why Kerala is sometimes known as the land of coconuts.

Was this Eden? Well, the bloated corpse of a rat floating past signalled that not all was ideal. But the villagers' back garden had mango, papaya, ginger, coffee, and a cornucopia of other fruits and spices on tap. Brilliant turquoise and brown kingfishers darted among the vines and creepers while cicadas chirped merrily. And traffic-clogged roads had been replaced by tranquil waterways. No wonder everyone we saw was smiling.

GOING IT ALONE

INTERNAL TRAVEL

Cochin's new airport is 40km (25 miles) north of the city. There may be international flights in the future, but for the time being you will be flying here from Bangalore, Delhi, Goa, Mumbai (Bombay), or Chennai (Madras). Expect to pay around 200 rupees for a taxi into the city.

From Ernakulam Town railway station there are services to Bangalore, Chennai, Delhi, Mangalore, and Thiruvananthapuram. Go to Ernakulam Junction for services north to Kozhikode, Mumbai, and Coimbatore (for the Nilgiri Hills).

From Ernakulam's public bus stand, at the end of Ammankovil Rd., there are services all over Kerala. Many will have originated elsewhere, so you can't make reservations for them. Fast private buses depart from other parts of town—check when buying a ticket. At least three buses daily head for Madurai, stopping at Kumily for the Periyar Wildlife Sanctuary (6 hours). You can also reach the sanctuary by bus from Madurai (4–5 hours).

Cochin's public ferries run from 6am to 9:10pm daily, from Ernakulam to Fort Cochin; the last one back to Ernakulam is at 9:30pm. If you miss this, an autorickshaw is likely to cost over 150 rupees. It is a good idea to hire an autorickshaw for the evening if you are travelling around Fort Cochin, since they almost totally disappear after dark.

WHEN TO GO

High season in Kerala is from October to April,

when hotel rates can increase by anything up to 50 percent. It can still be rainy in October, so wait until December if you want guaranteed sun.

The monsoon season lasts from June to September. During this time you can see the famous snakeboat races in Alappuzha and experience the four-day harvest festival of Onam with its pageants, dance performances, and spectacular elephant processions.

PLANNING

You need at least a week to tour Kerala. Allow a couple of days at Periyar or Munnar, and longer if you are planning an overnight trek. Most visitors find a day or overnight on a houseboat in the backwaters is sufficient, delightful as they are. Cochin, on the other hand, is so fascinating that you will undoubtedly want to linger.

A three-day admission ticket to Periyar Wildlife Sanctuary costs 50 rupees ($2); these are purchased at the Wildlife Information Centre beside the Thekkady jetty. This is also where you can book boat trips on Periyar Lake, the daily 7:30am jungle treks (10 rupees), and accommodation in the sanctuary's observation towers and resthouses.

Backwater boat trips and houseboat cruises can be arranged via agents in Cochin, Alappuzha, Kollam, and Thiruvananthapuram (Trivandrum). For houseboats, expect to pay at least 3000 rupees for a day cruise, and more for an overnight trip. You can cut

costs by negotiating directly with boat owners at Alappuzha and Kollam.

The Alappuzha Tourism Development Co-op (ATDC) and District Tourism Promotion Council (DTPC) run daily boat services (150 rupees) leaving Alappuzha or Kollam at 10:30am and arriving at the other end at 6:30pm. On the way south from Alappuzha you'll first pass Karumadi, where there's an 11th-century statue of Buddha. Lunch is at the villages of Thrikkunnapuzha or Ayiramthengu. There is also the chance to visit, and stay over at, the ashram of Matha Amrithanandamayi (Tel: 0476 621279), home of a revered female guru.

Refreshments can be bought on board the cruise boat, but it is a good idea to bring some of your own. Make sure you have plenty of sunscreen and a hat for shade.

HEALTH MATTERS

The heat is the main enemy in southern India. Drink plenty of water to avoid dehydration and always wear a wide-brimmed hat to shade against the unrelenting sunlight. Don't overexert yourself and avoid doing anything in the middle of the day.

There is no need to be too paranoid about where and what you eat, but always use common sense. Steer clear of uncooked food, especially salads, and drink bottled water.

WHAT TO TAKE

❑ Sun hat.
❑ Sunblock.
❑ Leek-proof socks.
❑ Sweater.
❑ Rain-proof jacket.
❑ Binoculars.

INDIA

11 A Passage to Ooty

by Simon Richmond

The rolling plateau of the Nilgiri Hills was made for trekking. Journey up to these damp, cool, sylvan highlands on a chugging Raj-era steam train and then, when you need to warm up, descend to the Mudumalai Wildlife Sanctuary to ride elephants through the jungle.

Like microcosms of the subcontinent, major Indian railway stations are invariably chaotic, a seething mass of people on their way to or from somewhere, stepping over and around others who have made where they stand, sit, or sleep their home. But even by these standards, Coimbatore at 8pm on a stormy October night was exceptionally frantic. One glance outside explained why: the roads were totally flooded, awash with a downpour that the drought-ridden state of Tamil Nadu had long been praying for. No wonder the mustachioed police captain was cracking his leather stick on the table and calling for order.

A quick word with the captain's female sidekick and a taxi driver was summoned. Could I make it to Mettupalayam tonight, I wondered, in order to catch the early morning train up to the Nilgiri Hills? No problem, claimed the plucky driver and, before I knew it, I was wading through the waterlogged forecourt to the taxi, and then being driven through the rain-lashed streets of industrial Coimbatore towards the market town of Mettupalayam at the foothills of the Nilgiris, or Blue Mountains.

At 6:30am the next morning, the atmosphere at Mettupalayam Station couldn't have been more different. The rain had ceased and there was no one else in line at the ticket office. I calmly secured a first-class seat to the hill station of Udhagamandalam, better known by its colonial name, Ootacamund or Ooty for short. Completed in 1898, this 46km (29-mile) track, rising over 1,800m (5,900ft) into the Nilgiri Hills, was an engineering marvel, using a rack-and-pinion system on the steepest gradients. Riding in the wooden carriages, being hauled most of the way by a magnificent steam engine, I realized it is still a splendid means of reaching the prime trekking country that surrounds the town once called Queen of the Hill Stations.

STEAMING AHEAD

I am sharing the tiny first-class compartment, at the front of the train, with two couples from Germany and one from India. The engine shunts from behind, so we have an unobstructed view of village

 The Blue Mountains Railway is an easy adventure, open to all. Once up in the hills there are treks to suit all capabilities, from day strolls around Ooty to overnight trips to rugged Mukurthi Peak. Trekking is not allowed in Mudumalai, but you can go on an elephant-ride safari and hike just outside the park. While it is possible to learn to paraglide in the Nilgiris from scratch, it is better if you already have some experience of this aerial sport.

 Many find the cool highlands a blessed relief from the heat of India's lowlands, but you should take warm clothes and rainwear because it does get quite chilly. Outside of a handful of hotels, be prepared for poor accommodation conditions in Ooty, where damp walls, musty carpets, frigid rooms, and infrequently hot water are the norm (for some places, however, this is part of their charm!).

 There is no specialist equipment required other than a good pair of hiking boots. You should take warm clothing and a raincoat for the highlands.

Below left: *The Nilgiri rack and pinion train is steam-powered as far as Conoor*
Below: *Flower sellers wait at the stations*
Inset: *Nilgiri Mountain Railway sign*

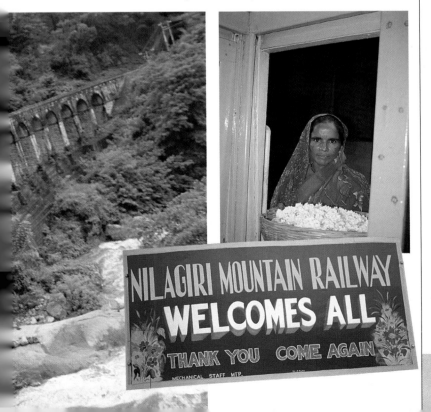

FLYING OVER THE NILGIRIS

Between September and May, depending on the monsoons, the South India Aerosports Co. runs paragliding, hang-gliding, and powered hang-gliding courses in the Nilgiris. Four-day courses can be organized for beginners, including all equipment, the history and technical theory of the sport, and how to rig and handle a glider on the ground. Launch spots covered in 2-week programmes for experienced gliders include a precipitous bluff crowned by a ruined fortress overlooking the Coimbatore plains; the highest vertical descent here is 1,590m (5,200ft) from take-off to the bottom landing area. Another launch site is Kalatti, which overlooks the jungle villages of Mavanhalla and Bokkapuram about 800m (2,500ft) below. The company has permission to launch from these sites, which are in otherwise protected reserve forests.

life—women washing clothes, a mother plaiting her daughter's hair—as we pass out of Mettupalayam. Ahead are the jungle and hills rising steeply into the clouds.

As we leave the level ground, the rack-and-pinion system clicks in and the train shudders up, scattering squirrels and monkeys as we go. In the first of the line's 16 tunnels, whoops and whistles rise from the crowded carriages behind. It's like being on a funfair ride—and it gets even more thrilling as we cross the tallest of the 252 bridges and I look back out of the window at the deep drop and the blue-and-cream painted train swinging round in a graceful arc.

THE CHILLY TROPICS

Now we are rising higher and I can see waterfalls tumbling down sheer cliffs into dense jungle. We pause at Hillgrove station at 10:30am while the engine is refilled with water. There's a refreshments counter here and a couple of opportunistic monkeys are waiting to be fed on bananas and dregs of sweet tea by the entranced passengers who stretch their legs in the fresh mountain air.

An hour later the forests have largely been replaced by cultivated hills and tea plantations established in the mid-19th century, when the Nilgiris began to be developed into a summer retreat by the British. By noon the train pulls into Conoor, the first of the three main Nilgiri hill stations, where the steam engine is uncoupled and replaced by a diesel one.

As the train comes closer to Ooty, Australian blackwood, eucalyptus, and wattle become more evident. All were introduced by the British to replace the native trees cut down by Badagas, one of the Nilgiri's main tribal groups and originally from the state of Karnataka. Where the landscape opens up and is not cultivated, it resembles the Highlands of Scotland. It's grey and chilly as we round Ooty Lake—unlike a Scottish loch, it's clogged with water hyacinths—and pull into the station, where a reassuring scrum of hotel touts and autorickshaw drivers are waiting on the platform.

THE CRUMBLING PALACE

For a taste of Ooty as it was in the days of the Raj, I take up temporary residence in the Regency Villa, part of the Maharaja of Mysore's Fernhill Palace estate, about 5 minutes south of the centre by autorickshaw. With rose bushes trailing around its front door, sepia-tinted photos of the Wadiyar dynasty (the current Maharaja is a member of India's parliament), white-tiled Victorian bathrooms, and teak and walnut furniture, the villa cuts a colonial dash, if tinged by decrepitude. But this is nothing compared to the gone-to-seed grandeur of the palace itself. Although it has been undergoing renovation for years, Fernhill Palace clearly is not going to reopen as a hotel for quite some time yet. When it does, what a place it promises to be! The highlight of this rambling, crumbling mansion is the Durbar Hall and its soaring, vaulted ceiling, enormous glass chandeliers, and ornately carved wooden fittings. If you're not staying at the Regency, the staff will happily show you around the palace for a small consideration.

I enjoy the palace, the flourishing, neatly clipped Botanical Gardens, and the Gothic-style St. Stephen's Church and its graveyard—an evocative roll-call of colonial identities—but I'm initially disappointed by Ooty's shabby, polluted centre. However, in the company of the lanky, curly haired R. Seniappan, better known as Sini, one of the best guides in Ooty, it all becomes more appealing. He leads me around the lively bazaar (the best place to stock up on provisions before a trek) showing me gems such as National Bakery, renowned for its cakes and biscuits, and Quetta Stores, a grocers-cum-department store squeezed into a box and selling everything from tins of baked beans to fishing rods.

INVITATION TO A WEDDING

Sini takes me to the Jain Tea Stall, tucked away on an alley off Main Bazaar Road, where the Rajasthani jewellers and pawnbrokers trade. Over a fragrant mug of masala tea he outlines the options for trekking around the Nilgiris. We decide on day trips out of Ooty, to Avalanche (pronounced Avalanchi) and Pykara Lake. For these places I won't need trekking permits from the District Forest Office. But first, Sini invites me to the wedding the next day of two young couples from the oldest and most important of the hill tribes, the Todas.

There are about 1,000 Toda people, spread across the Nilgiris in hamlets known as *munds*. Todas can be identified by their voluminous *puthukuli*—shawls of cream-coloured cotton, embroidered with black, red, and blue wool. At Mutinadu Mund, the village that is hosting the wedding reception, I see hundreds of these striking garments as

the Todas gather and greet each other in their traditional manner: one person kneeling and bringing their head into contact with the other's extended foot.

Together with Sini and fellow guide Shariff, a sad-eyed Muslim, I had taken the bus to Thalaikunda, about 10km (6 miles) west of Ooty, and from here I had walked 1km (½ mile) uphill towards the village. The wedding is a full-day affair, and while we wait for the brides to get ready and the rest of the guests to arrive, I am shown the village's two temples, or *boa*, where the Toda worship their god, the buffalo. One is built like a traditional Toda house, with an arched, thatched roof and tiny door at the bottom of the flat, decorated front. The other is much more unusual and has a roof like a giant upturned ice-cream cone.

In the afternoon we walk out of the village down into a dell, towards the sacred Naga tree before which the marriage will be blessed. Presents are laid at the foot of the tree, and the men start dancing and singing in a big circle, followed by the women. Meanwhile, the grooms are taken into the forest to make bows and arrows, which they will present to their brides. When they accept this offering and stare at a flame lit in a carved niche of the tree for one minute, the marriage is official.

HIKING AROUND AVALANCHE

The next morning, rather than waiting for the bus, Sini and I hire a taxi (600 rupees) for the 50km (30-mile) round trip to Avalanche, so-called because of a landslide in the area in 1823. The bus would have taken at least 2 hours to reach the hamlet of Lawrence, and from there we would probably have had to hike 5km (3 miles) to the hydroelectric power station at Avalanche (only one bus a day comes through to here). In the taxi, it takes half the time and we can stop along the route to admire the views across the abundant terraced fields, towards Emerald Lake.

Sini takes me to Mudi Mund, a nearby Toda village of some six families on the crest of a hill. The people—some of whom

Above: *Toda guests arriving for the wedding*

were at the wedding—are very welcoming, invite us into their homes for coffee, and show me their photo albums. It is possible to stay the night here, but the delightful Forest Resthouse, closer to Avalanche Lake, would be more comfortable. This lovingly maintained English-style country cottage has rooms with fireplaces, a garden full of rose trellises and bright gladioli, and a genial warden who will cook you dinner.

THE HILLS ARE ALIVE

The following day, we are hiking through the eucalyptus forests around Glenmorgan when we notice that the birdsong and tinkling of cow bells has been replaced by a livelier, amplified syncopation. It's hardly *The Sound of Music*, but on the open grasslands above the Toda village of Tharnadu Mund, we come across a film crew and team of dancers, dressed in royal purple and gold silks, gyrating around a movie star couple. The commotion has brought work in the fields to a standstill while the villagers enjoy this preview of what is, I'm told by the lead actress, a scene from a tale of a garage owner and the inspector she falls for.

The rolling Nilgiri hills, with their leafy forests, and rippling waterfalls are a favourite location for Tamil moviemakers; there are even tours (called Filmy Chakkar) from Ooty to the main shooting spots. Sini and I, however, have come to Tharnadu Mund at the invitation of the village headman, whom we met at the wedding. In his respected company, we planned to take the electricity company cable car (off-limits to the public) down the precipitous 1,000m (3,300ft) drop from Glenmorgan to Bokkapurma, on the fringe of Mudumulai Wildlife Sanctuary.

The problem is that the headman is not at home. In fact, his wife tells us she hasn't seen him since the wedding, two days ago.

Not to be put off, we set off past the village's three temples and buffalo pen, treading carefully along the narrow tracks between the terraced fields of carrots and sweet peas. Amongst the verdant, waist-high bushes of the Glenmorgan tea estate, sure-footed tea pickers balance

heaped baskets of the best leaves on their backs. Then, turning a bend in the road, I see the hilly plateau end abruptly in sheer cliffs, shooting down to the plains. It is topography like this that has made the Nilgiris a favourite spot in which to try out paragliding and hang-gliding.

Glenmorgan, the lakeside village for the workers at the hydroelectricity scheme, is a pretty place. The public rose garden is ringed by a fence of plaster ducks. The cook at the Electricity Department Inspectors' bungalow provides us with a tasty lunch and, after safely depositing my backpack and camera with the police, I'm allowed to see the cable car, if not actually ride it. Sini and I wait for the clouds to clear to catch the view down to Mudumalai, then return along the road towards Tharnadu Mund.

Above: The meandering streams and grassy slopes are a long way from the popular image of India as the land of heat and dust

Even though it's now dusk, the film-makers are still at work on another scene while we wait for the bus back to Ooty.

ACROSS PYKARA LAKE

The next day we set off for Pykara. Give a miss to the low, cascading Pykara Falls, another popular Tamil movie location, reached by a muddy, rubbish-strewn path, and head instead towards Pykara Lake. Here, you can hire pedalos and row boats (with rowers), to potter around on the murky green waters.

Sini arranges for us to be rowed across to the opposite side of the lake so that we can trek along an old logging truck route,

ECO-FRIENDLY HIKING

- ❏ Use only a fuel stove for cooking.
- ❏ Pack all non-biodegradable rubbish.
- ❏ If there are no toilets, dig a hole 15cm (6in) deep and bury your waste.
- ❏ If you use soap, toothpaste, or detergents make sure you do so at least 50 paces away from the water source.
- ❏ Purify your own water, rather than using bottled water.

now disbanded and fast being colonized by sapling acacias. We eventually emerge on undulating grasslands, grazed by buffalo and spiked by outcrops of rock. In the distance is Mukurthi Peak, another day's hike away through some of the most beautiful scenery in the Nilgiris.

ELEPHANTS GALORE

I eventually make it to Mudumalai. In a hired jeep I hurtle down the twisting, vertiginous Sighur Ghat Road, with sweeping views of the plains. This is a much more thrilling and direct ride than the longer bus route via Pykara and Gudalur, which are hemmed in by forests. On a mountain bike with sturdy brakes, it would be a blast, and there are also good hiking routes, for which you'll need a guide, either from Ooty or around Mudumalai.

The centre of the 321sq. km (124sq.-mile) wildlife sanctuary is Theppakadu, a junction on the road to Mysore beside the Moyar River, where you will find the park's reception centre, accommodation, and elephant camp. I had arranged to stay at the rustic Sylvan Lodge overlooking the river. Sadly, the tranquillity of this spot has been ruined by a new road that is being constructed so heavy machinery can be transported into the area to build a new hydroelectric plant. There is plenty of other accommodation around the village of Masinagudi, just outside the park, and, better still, in Bokkapuram, which has several appealing mini eco-resorts.

The sanctuary is home to gaur, sambar deer, wild boars, monkeys, and flying squirrels (as well as rarely spotted tigers, panthers, and bears), but it is to see the 27 domesticated elephants, including around ten tuskers, that you should come here. Many of these magnificent animals used to work in the area's logging camps, but since logging was stopped in 1972, they have been taken care of within the park, which has since gained a reputation as one of the best facilities in the world for training wild elephants.

PRAYING TO GANESH

Each elephant has its own keeper, or mahout. To appreciate the relationship between elephant and mahout, take one of short elephant-ride safaris held daily at 6:30am and 4pm. Although wildlife is not scared away by the elephants, the trails do stick close to Theppakadu, so don't expect to see much. None the less, these are enjoyable rides, especially in the cool of morning, and they provide an elephant's eye perspective on the jungle.

The evening wash and feed, on the other hand, should not be missed. In the Moyar River around 5pm, the mahouts scrub and rinse off the elephants and then march them back to the camp where giant cubes of their supplementary feed—flour, grain, salt, jaggery, coconut, and rice—are laid out for the 6pm supper. A chart on the wall lists each elephant's vital statistics (the oldest is 68) and what it needs to be fed, depending on its work. The mahouts knead all the ingredients together and pop the balls of the mixture straight into the elephants' mouths.

As the sun sets, two of the elephants are led to the nearby shrine to Ganesh, the Hindu god, to perform *puja*, or prayer. The animals kneel in front of the deity, as a priest incants prayers, and then circle the shrine three times, ringing handbells clasped in their trunks. Elephants praying to an elephant-headed god: it's the kind of surreal scene that makes travelling in South India so rewarding.

GOING IT ALONE

INTERNAL TRAVEL

The nearest airport to the Nilgiris is at Coimbatore, with flights to Mumbai (Bombay), Chennai, Cochin, and Bangalore.

The steam train to Ooty runs daily at around 7:45am from Mettupalayam. The journey takes 4½ hours, and tickets cost 30 rupees, or 90 rupees in first class. The Nilgiri Express from Chennai via Coimbatore is timed to arrive in Mettupalayam to connect with the steam train. From March to mid-June there is an extra service at 9:30am, reaching Ooty around 2pm. Tickets for the Blue Mountains service cannot be booked in advance, so if you want to be sure of a seat, get to Mettupalayam well in advance.

Frequent buses to Ooty depart from Coimbatore (3 hours) and Mettupalayam (2 hours). They are faster than the train, but not as fun. There are daily long-distance bus connections with Bangalore, Chennai, Kodaikanal, Mysore, and Thanjavur. The private services offer speed and comfort for little extra cost.

One-hour jeep rides from Ooty bus station to Mudumalai cost around 300–400 rupees. There are plenty of buses to the wildlife park, but they take about double the time, and you won't be able to stop along the way.

The centre of Ooty sprawls over a long valley; hop in an autorickshaw to save the hike between Charing Cross and the Botanical Gardens and the bus and train stations (around 20 rupees). Scooter and motorbikes can be hired from Hotel Sapphire, just off Ettines Road near the Hotel Khems, for around 400 rupees a day.

WHEN TO GO

From April to June, the Nilgiris' cool climes are a blessed relief from the heat of the plains. This is also when hotel prices double. Be prepared for rain at all times; the clearest weather is from November to March, the best period for trekking.

PLANNING

If you want to explore the wilderness areas around Ooty properly, checking out tribal villages or trekking overnight into the hills it is essential that you hire a guide. The best place to start looking—assuming they don't find you first—is the Ooty Tourist Guide Association, in a hut beside the bus station (or at the nearby Hotel Ravi Kiran, Tel: 0423 44449). Guides usually wear blue shirts and black trousers, have been trained by the government, and should have card identification. You can also contact the knowledgeable and dependable Sini by email (sini@hotmail.com) or via his co-guide, Sharrif, on 0423 40559.

The guides charge 250 rupees per day; you will also be expected to cover all the costs for transport, whether by bus, taxi, or jeep, and food. Before starting on a trek, get the guide to outline exactly where you will be going, what the terrain will be like and what you will need to take. Check whether you need a permit or accommodation in a forest guesthouse. Agents, such as Clipper Holidays in Bangalore, can put together tailor-made trekking packages for you.

To obtain permission to trek in the area, visit the Wildlife Warden's Office (WWO) in Ooty, tel: 0423 44098, open Mon–Fri 10:30am–5:30pm, and/or the District Forest Office (North), Tel: 0423 43968 and District Forest Office (South), Tel: 0423 44083, all located close to each other on Mount Stewart Hill, a short walk uphill from Charing Cross. Bookings for the lodges in Mudumalai Wildlife Sanctuary, as well as the elephant safari rides (120 rupees for 1–4 people), should also be made at the WWO. There are charges of 5 rupees for visitors to Mudulmalai, and 5 rupees for use of a camera (50 rupees for a video camera).

The tourist office hires out equipment for overnight treks including canvas rucksacks, heavy canvas tents, lightweight sleeping bags, and waterproof jackets. You must show any necessary District Forest Office permit and leave a deposit of 50 percent of the total rental cost.

HEALTH MATTERS

Drink plenty of water to avoid dehydration and always wear a wide-brimmed hat. Don't overexert yourself and avoid doing anything in the middle of the day.

There is no need to be too paranoid about eating, but always use common sense. Steer clear of uncooked food, especially salads, and drink bottled water.

WHAT TO TAKE

- ❑ Hiking boots.
- ❑ Raincoat.
- ❑ Binoculars.
- ❑ Warm clothing.

INDIA

12 Adrift in the Andamans

by Simon Richmond

Time, patience, and perseverance are essential if you plan to explore even a small fraction of the Andaman Islands. The rewards—magnificent marine life, pristine beaches, dense jungles, a fascinating history—are well worth the effort.

Verdant, sparsely inhabited peaks of land, ringed by halos of bleached yellow sand and enticing coral reefs set amid a vivid turquoise sea: the Andaman Islands, remnants of a drowned mountain range isolated in the Bay of Bengal, 1,200km (750 miles) east off the coast of mainland India, may look the part, but they are far from a run-of-the-mill paradise.

For starters, the first island I can see out of the window as our plane comes in to land is more a no-go area than nirvana. North Sentinel is the home of the Sentinelese, one of the six original tribal peoples of the Andaman and Nicobar Islands, and possibly the last Stone Age society left on Earth. Their population could be between 40 and 400—nobody really knows, since the Sentinelese have long had the habit of greeting visitors with a volley of arrows.

The welcome at Port Blair's banana-republic style airport is more congenial. I am promptly issued with an entry permit that allows me 30 days in which to visit some 14 of the 200-odd islands in the archipelago. Outside, across a building site (the airport is being expanded to accommodate the planned arrival of international flights), a ramshackle courtesy bus waits to transfer me the short distance to my hotel, the Peerless Resort at Corbyn's Cove.

This crescent of soft sand, rolling waves, and lolling palms is almost textbook tropical heaven. But this is still India, even though Port Blair, the administrative heart of the islands and the only gateway for all visitors, is much closer to Rangoon than New Dehli. So, as I stroll along the beach, a sacred white cow ambles past among the palms and a priest sits cross-legged by an impromptu altar of coconuts, bananas, and incense sticks, conducting *puja* (prayers) for a man mourning the death of his father.

DIVING POSSIBILITIES

I had arrived on the islands at the start of the ten-day Dusshera or Dasara festival, which celebrates the fierce goddess Durga's slaying of the buffalo demon Mahishasura. This is one of India's most popular events and the influx of

Left: *The boat to Jolly Buoy*

mainlanders was noticeably straining the tourist infrastructure of Port Blair, a small town that tumbles over hills at the southern end of South Andaman Island. Some backpackers were having problems finding decent places to stay. I, on the other hand, was looking for someone to arrange a dive trip with.

The Andamans are a diving and snorkelling dream. The reefs and lagoons round many of the islands are home to an abundance of marine life, including hammerhead sharks, turtles, manta rays, parrotfish, clownfish, and soldierfish, as well as hundreds of species of coral. Visibility in the unpolluted seas is excellent, and from late November to April there are at least two reputable P.A.D.I.-registered operators with whom to arrange diving trips (Sumudra at the Sinclair Bay View Hotel and Andaman Divers at the Peerless Resort).

But it was mid-October, and these diving operations had yet to open. On top of

Above: *Idyllic beach No. 5 on Havelock Island*

this, a cyclone was brewing north, in the Bay of Bengal, bringing rain and unsettled seas to the Andamans. According to the tourist office, the only chance of sorting out a trip now would be to keep my fingers crossed that the weather would improve and to visit the Water Sports Complex, beside Aberdeen Jetty, and ask for Faizel or Rustam Ali. It was worth a shot.

TRAVELLER CAMARADERIE

The Water Sports Complex—an overly grandiose title for a strip of concrete promenade and a *chai* stall, near a small aquarium displaying some of the fish I hoped to see while diving—is where you go if you want to zip around the bay in a speed boat (for 60 rupees) or on a jetski (25 rupees). You can also practise waterskiing (50 rupees) or windsurfing (30 rupees) and mess around in a variety of other boats. What I can't do is arrange a dive, at least not until around

Right: *Fish for sale at Port Blair*

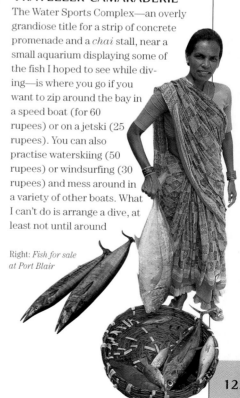

4 Outside of December to March, it is hard to find a reliable diving operator in the Andamans. P.A.D.I. open-water courses are offered, but it is really a location for experienced divers rather than novices. Snorkelling is very pleasant in the tropical waters, but you need to watch out for strong currents and sunburn. For more intrepid adventures, away from virtually all tourist comforts, head north to the settlements of Mayabunder and Diglipur, or south to Cinque Island.

★ Don't come expecting luxury; apart from a handful of hotels, accommodation is at best described as charmingly rustic. The government-run guesthouses are the best bet, but are often booked up well ahead. Away from Port Blair and Havelock Island, expect to rough it, sleeping on beaches or at shabby, mosquito-ridden lodges. Bus and ferry journeys between the islands are long and uncomfortable, and services are erratic. Credit cards are almost useless: bring plenty of currency from the mainland, where the exchange rate will be better.

✂ It is best to bring your own snorkel, mask, and flippers as those for rent are often in poor condition. Bring binoculars for wildlife and bird spotting. For the most remote islands you will need camping equipment, and you may want anti-nausea tablets for the long inter-island boat crossings.

THE FINAL FRONTIER

The 28 Nicobar Islands are currently off limits to all foreign visitors (Indians are allowed to visit Car Nicobar if they have a special permit), but the situation may change. I met a couple of Brazilian surfers who had been on an unofficial trip to the islands organized by South East Asia Liveaboards, a diving and adventure travel company based in Phuket, Thailand. Official tours may run in the future. If you do make it down past the deep, and at times, savage seas of the Ten Degree Channel that separates the Andamans from the Nicobar Islands, you will find the Asian-looking Nicobari tribal people. Their large round huts are raised on stilts, have thatched domes, and are entered up a ladder through the floor. While the surf was far from exceptional, the surfers reported being treated with great hospitality by the villagers, who love singing and dancing.

6pm when, I am told, Faizel might be around.

Back at Corbyn's Cove, I meet Vincent from Belgium, who has also been searching around for a chance to go diving. And I chat with Tom, a British backpacker with whom I had flown into the islands. He had met a couple of "crazy Dutch guys" who had heard about the possibility of diving with elephants and even crocodiles! (I later discover that the swimming elephants do exist, but that you need to go to Interview Island, off the west coast of Middle Andaman, to see them.)

The Andamans are like that. Accurate information is in short supply. Everything needs to be double checked, even infor-

mation from the tourist offices. A camaraderie develops quickly among visitors as everyone tries to make sense of the mysterious ways of this almost-paradise. For example, the Andamans run on Delhi time, so that the sun rises ridiculously early and has set by the time by the time I hop on my rented scooter and head back to the Water Sports Complex.

The assignation with Faizel and Rustam Ali plays like a scene in a spy movie. Under the beam of a street lamp on the promenade we discuss the options, none of which, given the deteriorating weather, look possible for several days. I am not shown any equipment and, although they claim to be P.A.D.I.-qualified dive masters, neither has cards on them to prove it. If you were to go out with these guys (or any others you met like them) you would have to be a highly experienced diver, capable of looking after yourself.

HAVELOCK BY NUMBERS

With diving on hold, I decided to catch the ferry to Havelock, the largest island tagged for tourism in Ritchie's Archipelago, on the east side of the Andamans. There are two ways of getting a ticket for the 6:15am ferry to Havelock: either jostle with the crowds at the ticket office the day before, or jostle with the crowds on the quayside on the day of the journey. I opt for the latter course and am joined by Vincent. With the ferry fast

CORAL REEF DOS AND DON'TS

❑ Use lead weights on your diving belt sparingly to avoid sinking too rapidly and crashing into a reef.

❑ Look, but don't touch: corals are easily damaged. And never take away shells or corals as souvenirs.

❑ Watch your fins: the vibrations caused by flapping around can stir up the sea and result in damage.

❑ Swim parallel to the seabed looking ahead or down. Keep a good distance between yourself and the reef and other divers.

filling up with the Dusshera holiday visitors, boarding looks dicey, so when a guy shows up flourishing tickets we are quick to hand over the exorbitant 30 rupees that he requests. We need not have panicked, because everyone squeezes on board eventually.

Immediately we leave Phoenix Bay the sea becomes choppy, and heavy rain means that the tarpaulins have to be pulled down, blotting out all views for the tedious 4-hour voyage. In good weather we might have spotted dolphins and flying fish—which I do get to see on the return journey.

Fortunately, when we reach the calmer waters of Tadma Bay at the north end of Havelock Island, the rain stops and the sun puts in a welcome appearance. We dock at No. 1 jetty and beach, beside which is Havelock's main village, a tiny settlement of wooden houses and a gaggle of unpushy Mr Fixits offering accommodation or scooter hire.

Most visitors head straight to the two main beaches—Radhnagar, otherwise known as beach No. 7, and beach No. 5, location of the Dolphin Yatri Niwas guesthouse, run by the Directorate of Tourism. There are buses and autorickshaws, but a scooter is the most convenient way to get around, so Vincent and I join one of the Mr Fixits in an autorickshaw ride to village No. 3. Here we cut a deal for a machine that we later discover splutters to a crawl on the slightest incline and whose lights fizzle come nightfall.

PARADISE'S BLUEPRINT

Dodgy scooters aside, Havelock comes close to the common blueprint for paradise. Dazzling green paddy fields and farmlands, where cockerels crow and pigs wallow, fringe an undulating, thickly forested landscape. Apart from the unobtrusive guesthouse at beach No. 5—where collapsed tree trunks lie in the sand like contemporary sculptures—there is hardly any tourist development.

Such is the charm of Havelock that, at the secluded Jungle Resort beach huts at

TOP DIVE SPOTS

To reach islands such as Narcondium and Barren, the easiest option is to arrange a liveaboard diving expedition, such as those offered by South East Asia Liveaboards in Phuket.

❑ Cinque Island: this is actually two islands joined by a sand bar at low tide, surrounded by emerald green waters. Visibility is up to 30 metres/yards. The reefs nearest the island are badly damaged, but further out there are good hard and soft corals, and there's the chance of sighting hawksbill turtles and schools of sharks.

❑ Rutland Island: just off Chidiya Tapu, this is used as a site for open-water training dives. The shallow waters and the reef has a good range of the area's smaller fish and colourful corals.

❑ Snake Island: just off Corbyn's Cove, this is known for its picturesque, submerged rock faces and unusual dive landscape. Trigger fish, grunts, goatfish, rays and schools of silver-jacks can all be seen here.

❑ Narcondium Island: the Andaman's most remote island, 259km (162 miles) from Port Blair, is an extinct volcano and bird sanctuary, home to the Narcondium hornbill. You might be able to arrange a boat here from Aerial Bay on North Andaman.

❑ Barren Island: India's only active volcano, which last erupted in 1995, is 139km (87 miles) east of Port Blair. Landing on the 3km (2-mile) wide, uninhabited island is not permitted. As you swim beside frozen lava flows, you are likely to see tuna and barracuda.

Above: *Saying prayers at Corbyn's Cove*
Left: *You can spot flying fish and dolphins off Phoenix Bay*
Inset: *Snorkelling is a joy in these unspoilt waters*
Below: *Ruined church on Ross Island*

Radhnagar where I stop for the night, Johnny from Ireland has just proposed to Pip from Australia. They could hardly have chosen a more romantic spot than Radhnagar, rightly celebrated as one of the most stunning stretches of sand in the Andamans. The local tourists cluster around the spot where the bus drops them, but the rest of the lengthy sugar soft beach, backed by dense forest, is empty save for shells and driftwood thrown up by the waves—which are ideal for body surfing.

After sunset, sleepy Havelock No. 1 bursts into life for the Dusshera festival. The small square fills with market stalls, bright lights, and pounding music. In the centre, a model of the goddess Durga is illuminated by flaming coals in coconut husks whirled around in the palms of young men who are dancing like possessed dervishes. The celebrations continue deep into the night, with back-to-back screenings of screechy musicals.

Hindi music is still blaring out across the empty village square, as I walk towards a stall by the jetty for a fine breakfast of chapattis, spicy curry, and omelette. The ferry back to Port Blair is delayed because of the bad weather, giving the coconut seller an ideal opportunity to shift a few dozen more husks.

This time the ferry sails round the east coast of Havelock towards Neil Island, where it makes a brief stop. There is one government-run guesthouse here; bookings should be made at the Port Blair tourist office. A few locals and tourists disembark to enjoy this small island's quiet, white sand beaches and snorkelling spots and nine braying goats are chucked on board, then tethered at the prow.

Flying fish, shooting out of the waves like silver rockets and skimming the surface for incredible distances, provide the main distraction during the 5-hour voyage. The biggest splash, however, is caused by a brief and graceful appearance of a school of dolphins.

PARADISE FOUND

The threatening heavens, having held their breath, break with vengeance on arrival back at Phoenix Bay. So it comes as little surprise (and something of a reassurance of good practice) when Rustam Ali confirms that diving is still off the agenda. But all is not lost as far as snorkelling is concerned. In fact, the snorkelling in the Mahatma Ghandi National Marine Park, reached from the jetty at Wandoor, some 30km (20 miles) southwest of Port Blair, is so good that I go twice.

On the first visit, I join one of the crowded passenger cruises to Jolly Buoy. This and Red Skin are the two islands within the park that are open to day-tripping tourists. Most cruises allow you 3 hours on one or both of the islands, plus an hour's voyage through the mangroves on the way to and from Wandoor.

Jolly Buoy is the more popular of the two islands, and even though patches of its delicate reefs are in a terrible state (because of tourists ignoring signs about not standing on the coral), it should definitely feature on your itinerary. The tiny island has soft sand beaches strewn with giant shells, an inpenetrable jungle with towering palms, and reefs teeming with fish so close to the shore that you can wade up to them. The beach is kept clean by the boatmen, who collect up packed-lunch rubbish and cart it back to Wandoor.

What's more, I get to see some incredible marine life: white-and orange-banded clownfish darting in and out of their golden anemone home; shoals of silver-jacks, parrotfish and soldierfish, mauve staghorn coral and lemon brain coral. Best of all, I spot a manta ray resting in the sandy seabed and follow it for several minutes as it swims away, long tail swishing, winged pectoral fins flapping.

So I have little difficulty in persuading five other travellers to join me the next day in chartering a boat to both Jolly Buoy Island and Red Skin Island. This is a much more relaxing trip, allowing us to arrive on Jolly Buoy at least an hour before all other visitors and leave when we feel like it. The reefs around the larger, Red Skin Island have a wider variety of coral, including some that unfurl like roses, studded with black spiky sea urchins, fat sea cucumbers, and giant clams.

With the sun finally shining and the island's quiet, sheltered beach to ourselves, we all agree that, at last, we have found paradise in the Andamans.

GOING UP ISLAND

The 194km (120-mile) journey to Aerial Bay on North Andaman, by both ferry and bus, is the most intrepid trip you could make during your visit to the Andamans. Travelling up the Andaman Trunk Road by bus, you could reach the village of Mayabunder (9 hours) at the top of Middle Andaman. From here you need to catch a ferry to Kalighat (2½ hours) on North Andaman to continue the road journey to Diglipur. Alternatively, stop in Mayabunder and arrange a boat to Interview Island, home of swimming elephants and one of the best places for viewing wildlife in the archipelago. There is also a ferry, taking 13 hours, from Port Blair to Diglipur, from where it is best to head straight to the fishing village of Aerial Bay. Here there is a wildlife department rest house and, 1km (½ mile) further away at Kalipur, the spacious and modern Turtle Resort Yatri Niwas. Both can be booked in Port Blair.

Once you've got this far, you could charter a boat to go snorkelling around nearby Smith Island where there are corals, barracuda, and angel, butterfly, and parrot fish. Alternatively, get permission from the ranger in Aerial Bay to climb Saddle Peak, which at 737m (2,148ft) is the highest point in the islands. The track is difficult, so take a guide and allow plenty of time for the climb.

GOING IT ALONE

GETTING THERE

There are two to four sailings a month from Chennai and Calcutta (fewer from Vishakhapatnam) to Port Blair. Get details on schedules and ticket availability from Shipping Corporation of India offices in Calcutta (Shipping House, 13 Strand Rd., Tel: 033 248 2354; Fax: 033 248 2035) and Chennai (Jawahar Building, Rajaji Salai, Tel: 044 523 1401; Fax: 044 523 1218). Prices range from around 3,500 rupees for a deluxe two-berth cabin to 1,000 rupees for bunk class. Take plenty to distract you during the monotonous three-day voyage and dreary rations (the same food is served up morning, noon, and night).

Jet Airways has daily flights to Port Blair from Chennai on modern, comfortable planes with excellent service. Air India flies four times a week from Calcutta and three times a week from Chennai. Expect to pay around 16,000 rupees ($400), and book well in advance.

INTERNAL TRAVEL

A scooter or motorbike is the best way to tour hilly Port Blair and South Andaman. A few autorickshaws putter around Port Blair, and you can hire a taxi for longer journeys. Chidiya Tapu is around 600 rupees return, Wandoor 500 rupees.

Ferries to the other islands depart from Phoenix Bay Jetty. Check the local papers for timetables and book tickets at the jetty early in the morning the day before you wish to go. Expect chaos at the ticket office.

Private boats to Cinque Island can be chartered at Chidiya (or Chiriya) Tapu and Wandoor for around 6,000 rupees.

WHEN TO GO

Late November to the end of April is the best time for diving and snorkelling. The monsoon is from mid-May to mid-September, but it can be rainy through October. Temperatures range between 20°C (68°F) and 32°C (90°F), with the heat and humidity tempered by sea breezes.

PLANNING

It invariably takes longer than expected to travel anywhere in the Andamans. If you are looking for a tranquil experience, head straight to Havelock and explore the less developed island of Ritchie's Archipelago. For rugged adventure, aim north, to Middle and North Andaman.

All foreign visitors need a permit, in addition to their regular India visa, obtained free from immigration officials on arrival at the port or airport.

In high season and around holidays there is often a shortage of accommodation. Government guesthouses are booked up for months ahead by Indian officials. If you are heading to any of the smaller islands, or up north, take camping gear, a water purification system, and food supplies.

DIVING AND SNORKELLING DETAILS

The dive operators all have similar charges. The cheapest dives are around Port Blair, which cost 2,500

rupees with all equipment included (except wetsuits, which cost 300 rupees extra). Longer trips cost 3,800 rupees. A 2-day trip is around 9,000 rupees, including food, camping gear, and four dives. Open Water Class is 15,000–16,000 rupees, including certification fees, equipment, and all course materials; advanced Open Water Class 10,000–11,000 rupees.

There is no decompression chamber on the islands, so practice safe diving and go no deeper than 25m. Make sure you have sufficient travel insurance to deal with emergencies. Be aware of strong currents, and use a wetsuit to keep warm and protect against sunburn.

You can hire snorkelling gear from the Water Sports Complex in Port Blair, cafés at Wandoor and Chidiya Tapu, and from the Jungle Lodge and Dolphin Yatri Niwas on Havelock, but the quality varies. Bring your own if you don't want a leaking mask.

All visitors to the marine park must to buy entry permits from the kiosk at Wandoor (10 rupees; 25 rupees for a camera; 1,000 rupees to dive). The passenger boat to Jolly Buoy costs 125 rupees; get to the jetty before 9am to ensure a ticket, especially in peak season.

If you are chartering a boat for up to 10 people, expect to pay 1,250 rupees to Jolly Buoy, 900 rupees to Red Skin, and around 2,000 rupees to both islands on one trip.

HEALTH MATTERS

Malaria is a problem on the Andamans, so take precautions. It is also essential to drink bottled water at all times, or use a water filter.

Karnali
Malakheti   Dillikot
8167m
Dhaulagiri ▲
⑬
Nepalganj   Pokhara
⑰
Butwal   **Kathmandu**
Namai
⑮
8848m
Mt Everest ▲
⑭
Bhaktapur
⑯
Sun Kosi
Dhankuta
Birganj
Biratnagar

0	100	200	300	400	500 km
0	100		200		300 m

NEPAL

I f only one country in the world deserved to be tagged "King of the Mountains," then Nepal would surely be it. With near on 80 percent of the country dominated by the Himalaya, it's no surprise that Nepal is the world's premier high-altitude trekking destination. And deservedly so. The trekking opportunities are incalculable and the quality is for the most part simply outstanding. Yet, to be blinded by the beauty of the mountains would mean missing out on the country's numerous other attractions. The Terai region in the south of the country, for example, forms part of the Ganga Plain and is one of the country's best places for spotting wildlife, and the Tharu people who live there are distinctly different from the highland Nepalese tribes. But in any region you will be struck by the relaxed and purposeful disposition of the Nepalese, and their willingness to welcome you. They place a lot of emphasis on their religion, whether Hindu or Bhuddist, and their associated array of wonderful temples and colourful clothing are a distinctive feature of the country.

Lamjung Himal seen from Siklis in the Annapurna range

NEPAL

13 A Rare Annapurna Trekking Sanctuary

by Steve Watkins

Mention Nepal and the subject of trekking is rarely far behind. The magnificent Himalaya mountain range hosts a multitude of trails and a tribal culture that has barely changed for thousands of years. I leapt at the chance to take a six-day hike on a relatively unexplored route in the Annapurna Conservation Area.

For lovers of mountains, Nepal is a veritable paradise on Earth. Over three-quarters of the country's land area is taken up by the awesome mountains and foothills of the Himalaya range, so it would be possible to hike and climb every day for life and still not cover all the routes on offer. Since the first attempts to conquer the world's highest peak, Mount Everest, the escapades and adventures of mountaineers and trekkers in Nepal have spawned a whole library of books and articles, which have helped turn the country into the most popular trekking destination in Asia, if not the

world. Widespread rumours of over-crowded trails and peaks seem to have done little to deter other thrill-seekers, perhaps because for most visitors those rumours rarely match up to reality. However, I was still a little sceptical about the claim made by the UK-based operator Specialist Trekking Co-operative that on the trail they recommended, in the especially popular Annapurna region, it was likely that we would not meet any other trekkers at all. The six-day circular trek from Pokhara to Siklis is located within the region protected by the Annapurna Conservation Area Project and was off-limits to commercial tour operators until the late 1990s.

There are basically two ways to go trekking in Nepal. One involves staying at tea houses—locally owned, simple houses that provide cooked meals and beds—and the other is to go camping, which means taking porters and all the gear needed to be self-sufficient. Both have their merits, but the camping option allows travel in more remote areas where there are no tea houses. Our trek was one of the latter and I, trekking alone, was joined by no fewer than four porters, a chef, and a guide from Specialist Trekking Co-operative, owned and run by famous Himalayan mountaineer Doug Scott and his wife, Sharu. As we stood at a Kathmandu bus stop on a chilly December morning waiting for our bus to Pokhara, I felt the huge pile of gear that we had with us would have done justice to

3 You need to be used to regular physical exercise and preferably have some previous experience of hiking. Some of the days involve over 6 hours of walking, with regular ascents and descents of steep hills.

★ Although this was a camping trip, it was not the rough-style camping that I normally practise on my own. The operator supplied good tents (which are put up and taken down by the porters) and comfortable bed rolls, and the chef cooked up three huge feasts of good-quality food each day. There is also the mandatory fresh cup of tea delivered to your tent at wake-up time.

 This particular Annapurna hike is a camping trail only, so you need to be self-sufficient. You need to carry camping gear, cooking gear, and food (these are supplied by most trekking tour operators) in addition to your own personal clothing. It can get very cold at night and can rain hard or be gloriously sunny at any time of year, so you should go prepared for any eventuality. It is essential to have good trekking boots that you know are comfortable.

ACAP: PROTECTING THE ABODE OF SNOWS

The Annapurna region of Nepal receives over 50,000 trekkers each year, making it the most popular trekking destination in the country. Add to these all the porters and guides who accompany groups, and it is easy to understand that this area of the Himalaya, which translates as "Abode of Snows," is prone to environmental and social problems related to the levels of tourism. In 1986, the King Mahendra Trust for Nature Conservation (KMTNC), a non-governmental organization comprising of several groups from around the world, set up the Annapurna Conservation Area Project (ACAP) to help protect the environment, whilst managing the development of eco-friendly tourism that benefits local communities too. All trekkers to the ACAP area are charged an entry fee of 1,000 rupees, which is then spent on various projects, including reforestation, supplying fuel efficient stoves to tourist lodges, building micro hydro power plants, and running clean-up programmes.

an Everest expedition. Pokhara was an 8-hour bus journey away, but the wondrous scenery along the Prithvi Highway, including the whitewater rapids of the Trisuli River and the constant backdrop of the Himalaya's snow-covered summits, made the time pass relatively quickly. At Pokhara bus station, we avoided the crowds of taxi hawkers by paying the bus driver an extra sum to drop us off at the trek start point, Milanchok village, about a 40-minute drive north.

Despite the early morning departure from Kathmandu, it was quite late in the afternoon by the time we loaded up our packs, tiptoed across a dilapidated, bamboo bridge and began hiking up the east bank of the fast-flowing Seti Nadi River. It was amazing to see just how much equipment the porters were able to lift in their baskets, which are carried by a tumpline, or headband, that fits on the forehead. Not only did they easily manage such heavy loads, but most of them were wearing just flip-flops too! I felt slightly over-dressed with my modern backpack and high-tech walking boots.

Soon the track began to zig-zag up the valley side until we reached a wide, open ledge dotted with mudbrick houses coated with clay. Up ahead, we caught our first glimpse of the dramatic pyramid summit of Macchapuchhare, which literally translates as Fishtail Mountain (its summit, from certain viewpoints,

resembles a fish's tail). This 6,997m (22,956ft) peak, which was to dominate the views for the first few days of our trek, is strictly off limits to mountaineers owing to its fragile, thin rock summit. With the sun beginning to set, the peak turned first pink and then rust red as we entered the small village of Ghachok, our overnight stop. Without the warmth of the sun's rays in the valley, the temperature plummeted, and I donned all my clothing in an attempt to stay warm as the porters erected the tents in the garden of one of the village houses. While the chef, Janak, cooked up a three-course dinner, including curried vegetables and chicken, I watched the last of the light show on Macchapuchhare and spoke to Mahesh, my guide, about the Indian cricket team's chances of beating Australia in a forthcoming test series. Strangely, Nepalis seem to be almost as crazy about cricket as the Indians, despite not having a strong national team themselves.

A NOMADIC ENCOUNTER

Once I had snuggled up tight in my sleeping bag, I forgot the cold night air and enjoyed a peaceful sleep, save for a few bouts of barking from the village dogs. One of the unwritten rules of trekking is that no matter how much walking needs to be done in a day, it is mandatory to get up at 6am. The shock of leaving my sleeping bag before the sun came up was

somewhat mitigated by the prompt delivery to the tent door of a cup of tea, along with a bowl of hot water to wash in. The real reward, however, was to see the dawn light sliding down the mountains. Although my stomach had barely dealt with processing the previous night's dinner, Janak produced hot porridge, omelettes, and pancakes for breakfast. I was going to have to do some hard trekking to work off all the calories!

Just before departing, Dhan Bahdur, the elderly man who owned the land we had camped on, came out and agreed to escort us along the myriad tracks that lead out of the village. Scrambling up a bank, we crossed and climbed terraced fields, where a large troop of monkeys, including several newborn babies, were playing and feeding. Near the edge of the fields, a semi-nomadic mountain shepherd, named Shiva Lal Gurung, was tending his goats and sheep. Wearing traditional tribal dress, a felt hat, and a short, white waist wrap, together with the

modern addition of black Wellington boots, Shiva explained how he spent the monsoon season grazing his herd high up in the mountains, in a small valley below Macchapuchhare. In winter, to avoid the freezing temperatures, he retreated down to the edge of the village, where he lives in a ramshackle temporary shelter. His tanned and hardened face paid testimony to the tough existence that he leads, but there was no doubting his happiness with his lot in life. With big smiles, we parted company with Shiva and Dhan Bahdur, and briefly ascended before dropping steeply back down to the Seti Nadi River.

A rather new-looking cable suspension bridge, partly built and funded by the renowned British Ghurka military regiment, who recruit solely from this region of Nepal, made crossing the river easy. Then the trail headed up a series of ledges towards the village of Chaur. As we reached the second ledge, the sound of drumming drifted over from the other side of the valley and we could just make

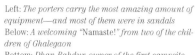

Left: *The porters carry the most amazing amount of equipment—and most of them were in sandals*
Below: *A welcoming "Namaste!" from two of the children of Ghalegaon*
Bottom: *Dhan Bahdur, owner of the first campsite we stayed in*

out a funeral procession winding its way down the hillside. Fascinated, Mahesh and I joined a couple of local people and sat for almost 2 hours to watch the entire ritual. The drummers were at the head of the procession, while the deceased, an 84-year old woman from Ghachok, was carried behind them on a wooden stretcher. Other mourners transported large bundles of firewood to be used on the riverside funeral pyre. The ritual was elaborate and carefully performed. A stone platform was built and filled with wood before the body, wrapped in a bright green cloth, was placed on top and covered with more wood. Meanwhile, the woman's daughter was inconsolable and anguished on a nearby rock. The priest and other senior village men then walked anticlockwise around the pyre to light it. Within a minute, the fire had taken hold and the mourners gradually dispersed to leave the woman's body to burn and subsequently be washed away down river.

Our path continued upwards on a wide, stone stairway and took us past several teenage girls bent heavily forward under the weight of their firewood loads. Chaur village is tiny, and characterized by narrow, cobbled streets bordered by stone walls and conical bales of hay stacked on head-high platforms, probably to prevent mice and rats eating it. The Gurung tribal people rely on agriculture to earn an income, but this amount often

SICK OF HEIGHTS

The majority of treks in Nepal involve days at heights of 3,000m (9,800ft) or more, the height at which the effects of altitude on the human body will probably begin to emerge. Contrary to the popular statement that there is "less oxygen" the higher up a mountain you go, the increased breathing and heart rate is in fact due to a fall in oxygen pressure within the lungs. The lungs simply cannot inflate so much. Between 3,000m and 4,000m (9,800ft and 13,100ft), shortness of breath, headaches, and sleeplessness will probably be all that most trekkers will experience, but go higher and it is important to be aware of a condition known as Acute Mountain Sickness. Vomiting, vertigo, and a decrease in the capability of the brain to function properly, such as slurring speech, is a sign that sufferers need to descend as quickly as possible. It may not be necessary to descend completely as going down even a few hundred metres/yards can make a significant difference to how a trekker feels. Perhaps the most effective ways to reduce the chances of suffering from altitude sickness are to drink plenty of water while ascending, and to ascend slowly to allow the body time to acclimatize.

pales against the money sent back by Gurung soldiers chosen to join the British Gurkhas. Originating from Tibet, these hard-working, unassuming people are now found throughout the Annapurna hill region. Comparatively few trekkers have ventured this way, so our presence was enough to cause a stir of intrigue among the local children, who peered through the gate and over the walls of the school as we hiked past. Whenever I made eye contact with them, they flashed cheeky, shy grins before turning to their friends in giggles of laughter.

STAIRWAY TO INDIGESTION

While Mahesh and I had been watching the funeral, our porters had surged on ahead, so we now had to make a concerted effort to catch up with them. The trail split into two, one path going high over a hill and the other criss-crossing the Sardi Khola River. Guessing that the heavily laden porters would have opted for the low-level route, we briefly removed our boots, waded across the river, and followed an indistinct path through heavy bush. Re-crossing the river on a very rickety bamboo bridge, we began to wonder whether the porters were indeed in front of us or were somehow waiting for us back at Chaur village.

Eventually, a bellowing call from up the narrowing valley heralded our regrouping and we all sat by a small stream to enjoy lunch in the glorious sunshine. While food stops are always a very welcome part of the day, the incessant, steep hill climb we encountered immediately after restarting left me wishing I hadn't opted for the extra helpings of chips. The trail followed yet another stone staircase and in between catching breaths I marvelled at the amount of work involved in building such an extensive network of pathways.

Twenty minutes later we entered the village of Ghalegaon and stopped briefly to watch a family at work and play in front of their thatch-roofed, mudbrick house. While a young girl sifted chaff from the wheat by pouring it into the breeze from a large plate, her father sat stripping bamboo leaves to make a basket or woven mat. Behind them, a group of young men sat hunched in a circle playing a card game called "Marriage"—though I doubt that the winner gained a bride. Almost all Gurung marriages are arranged by the parents, and there are strict rules to ensure that youngsters marry partners from outside their own village. As we left, two children cried out "*Namaste*!", the widespread Nepali greeting, closely followed by requests for sweets.

Sweetless, Mahesh and I continued climbing, quickly gaining height on the steep track, until we finally reached a flattened ridge with spectacular views across to Macchapuchare and down to distant valleys. Soon after, the porters arrived and gratefully dumped their luggage. One porter, Bacchu, stretched out on the floor and remarked, "It is hard to get work in Nepal and then you get it and it is still hard!" While dinner was prepared, I walked up to a small Buddhist shrine above the camp and admired the surroundings. Although things seem so peaceful and idyllic in the mountains, Mahesh had impressed on me how important it was to keep all our valuable gear close to us while we slept in the tents. It is not unknown for thieves to slip into camp at night and cut open tents to steal backpacks, boots, or anything else they can get their hands on.

A LAND OF ELVES AND PIXIES

By morning, heavy cloud had closed in, cloaking the forested slopes above us. The cool temperature was a blessing as the day was to bring no respite from our ascent into the mountains. However, there was to be a change in scenery, as the trail climbed up for almost 2½ hours through an enchanting rhododendron forest. The dank air, contorted tree trunks, and moss-draped branches had me wondering where the elves and pixies were hiding. My legs were now well acclimatized to the uphill work and I really enjoyed following the path that has been worn down over the centuries by the astounding daily journeys of the tribal people. It is not uncommon for villagers, some of whom passed us in the forest, to hike, barefoot, 60km (40 miles) or more in a day with their loaded baskets, to get to regional markets. Occasionally, the tree cover thinned and allowed snapshot views of the surrounding snow peaks.

After a brief snack break at the top of the climb, we traversed past Tara Hill Lookout, another trail campsite, and down through the more established ecocamp at Nayaule. Nearing Siklis village, which is at an altitude of 1,980m (6,496ft), the forest petered out and we contoured around open slopes that offered stunning vistas along the Madi Khola Valley. Almost 6 hours after leaving Ghaegaon, we descended to our camp spot just to the west of Siklis. Once we were settled in, a welcoming party arrived, consisting of a few hundred sheep and goats that took great delight in inspecting the tents, three herders, and a group of four women from nearby Parju village selling souvenirs and drinks. Whilst the sheep and goats were fine specimens, I restricted myself to buying a few bead bracelets, a tiny silver casket, and a bottle of beer.

Next morning, the cloud had cleared and we were treated to inspiring, breakfast-time views of the snow- and

BIRTH OF A MOUNTAIN RANGE

About 70 million years ago, during the Upper Cretaceous period, two landmasses, the Eurasian plate and the Indian subcontinent plate, collided in the Tethys Sea. As a result, the rock folded, forming valleys and ridges that subsequently transformed themselves, via further lifting and folding, into the highest mountain range on Earth today, the Himalaya. Although the last major changes to the range occurred around 600 million years ago, the mountains are still on the move. The Indian subcontinent plate is shifting northwards at the snail rate of 2cm (1in) per year, which is forcing the Himalayan peaks skywards at about 5mm (⅛in) each year. So, if you don't climb Mount Everest soon, it will just keep getting harder and harder—though of course, each new successful climber can claim to be the first to climb the world's highest summit!

ice-bound peaks of Lamjung Himal, 6,986m (22,920ft) and Annarpurna II, which soars to 7,937m (26,040ft). Now, if hiking uphill sounds like hard work, then it may come as some surprise to find out that hiking downhill is even more taxing, especially on the knee joints. As the sun's rays crept down the valley walls, we began the steep, 820m (2,690ft) climb down a stone stairway to the Madi Khola River. Nearing the small village of Siklis Phedi (*phedi* means bottom of hill in Gurung), we were forced to stand aside as a pack of load-carrying mules scaled the steps under the guidance of two young boys wielding sticks. At the bottom of the valley, the path crossed a large suspension bridge over the turbulent Boto Khola River, a tributary of the Madi Khola, and twisted into Dudh Pokari village. After a brief rest to eat fresh mandarins bought from a village shop, our trekking party hauled itself back into action and continued down the west bank of the Madi Khola River, accompanied once again by blue skies and intense sunshine. At lunchtime, I took the opportunity to soothe my overworked feet by soaking them in the freezing, glacial waters of the river. This helped immensely to prepare me for the stiff 2-hour climb to finish the day at Ghyamrang village.

HONEY RAIDERS

Our camp spot was on a terrace just below the village school and it didn't take long for word of our arrival to spread among the children, who came to watch over our every movement, save for my visit to the toilet tent! The village school is one of the projects that Specialist Trekking Co-operative is involved with. The completion of a new school building with new classrooms had allowed the 60

or so children to be split into smaller age groups. The following morning, we arose early to join Gumbahadur Gurung, the school headmaster, and Dasrath Sapkota, one of the school's two teachers, for a tour of the new building and a chance to meet some of the children. It was a great surprise to be welcomed like royalty, with two children coming out to place garlands of beautiful, golden marigold flowers around our necks. Despite having very limited funds for writing materials and text books, the teachers do a very commendable job in educating the children in various subjects, including English.

After a school photo session, we said fond farewells and began the trek back down to the Madi Khola River and on to Jyamdo village. There we stopped at a family house to sample a *lhassi*, a fatty, yogurt-like drink made from buffalo milk.

Left: *The fast-flowing Seti Nadi River*
Inset left: *Siklis camp, with the Lamjung range in the background*
Inset right: *Nomadic mountain shepherds*
Right: *Mahesh enjoys a rest in the sun before our final leg up to Sahure Bhanjyang*

I personally found it hard to stomach. The owner of the house offered Mahesh the opportunity to take future trekking groups into the hills to see the honey hunters at work. These men scale trees and cliff faces to collect honey from natural hives and use only smouldering leaf torches to subdue the bees. Unfortunately, it was the wrong time of year for us to go as the honey had already been harvested, in September and October. The rest of the pre-lunch hike followed a narrow path that undulated along the river bank.

During lunch, we witnessed the local "electric fishermen" at work. Although this activity was banned some years ago, these men continue to use two long bamboo prods that carry live wires linked to two 12-volt car batteries carried on the back of the head fisherman. The prods, one with a less than adequate plastic bag on the handle to protect the handler from shocks, were plunged into the water to stun nearby fish with the current, causing an audible buzzing. Helpers with fishing nets then scooped up the fish as they floated down river. Most of the men seemed to have foot problems (some had deep lacerations to their heels) from spending so much time in the freezing water, and it was disturbing to see them taking any fish they caught, with no regard for maintaining future stocks.

Back on the trail, we moved away from the high mountains and followed terraced fields to our last overnight camp, at

TRAVELLERS' TIPS

❑ Whilst Nepal's "classic" treks, such as Everest Base Camp and the Annapurna Sanctuary, are very much worthy of the tag, there are many other, lesser known routes that are equally magnificent. So don't ignore treks that you haven't heard of.

❑ Do not go rushing off at the start of a trek. Allow your body time to adjust to the daily rigours of hiking and stretch your muscles in the morning before setting out. Cold weather and cold bodies add up to pulled muscles.

❑ Take a good book to read, as the nights are long, though you will probably want to sleep longer than normal anyway.

❑ On the photography front, some hill people want to have their photos taken and others don't, so ask first and respect their wishes.

Bhagowatitar village—by far the biggest settlement we had seen on the trek, though it boasted only a couple of hundred inhabitants. A super slap-up meal, complete with an end-of-trek cake somewhat miraculously produced by Janak, was washed down with a couple of beers. There was still one more short day of hiking left that took us up to Sahure Bhanjyang village and then down a winding trail to the shore of beautiful Lake Begnas. We then finally boarded a bus back to Pokhara.

It had seemed a fanciful claim from the operator that this region of the supremely popular Annapurna trekking area was rarely visited, but we had indeed not encountered another trekker during the 6-day trip. Instead, I had a relatively brief but deeply stimulating personal encounter with Nepal as it has been for many centuries and as it was in my pre-trip dreams.

PLACE NAMES

Spellings of villages, towns, and rivers vary widely and the only real guide is the sound of the name, rather than how it is spelt, e.g., *chok*, meaning "village," is often spelt *chowk*. Bear this in mind if you are looking for the names on a map. I have adopted the spellings used on the Nepa Maps *Treks around Pokhara—Siklis-Shyaklung* map.

GOING IT ALONE

INTERNAL TRAVEL

Pokhara is Nepal's second most popular tourism destination after Kathmandu, so transport options are good. Several "tourist" bus services, which are direct and reasonably comfortable, depart Kathmandu from the Thamel end of Kantipath Road, with most leaving in the early morning (6am to 9am) for the 7- to 8-hour journey. The buses stop off at restaurants en route for breakfast and lunch. Perhaps the best bus service in terms of comfort and bus quality is run by Greenline, who operate from their own terminal just east of Thamel on Tridevi Marg. They have departures at 7am and 8am, but it is advisable to book ahead. Several airlines, including Royal Nepal Airlines Corporation and Necon Air, operate daily flights to Pokhara from Kathmandu, which takes less than 1 hour. They may cost a lot more than the bus service but you get the added bonus of enjoying breathtaking views of the entire Himalaya Range (sit on the right-hand side from Kathmandu and left-hand side to Kathmandu).

WHEN TO GO

There is a very strong trekking season in Nepal, from October to May, with October and November being the preferred months for most visitors. I trekked this low-level route in early December, a quiet time for trekking, and the weather was still superb, though a little chillier at night. High trekking passes are usually closed from December to March, but the weather in Nepal has had little pattern to it over recent years, so there are no hard and fast rules. Beware that itineraries can change at short notice and even relatively low-level treks can be affected by snow.

PLANNING

Specialist Trekking Co-operative run trips out of the United Kingdom only (though they offer land price only packages that must be booked via the UK office). However, there are so many operators in both Kathmandu and Pokhara that prices have tumbled. Remember that the less you pay, the more likely it is that the gear that the operator supplies will be inadequate, and less likely it is that their porters and guides get a fair wage.

HIRING EQUIPMENT

Nepal, and Kathmandu in particular, is renowned for its rip-off outdoor equipment. Many big brand names adorn sleeping bags, backpacks, and fleece jackets. However, it is almost entirely fake, and the low prices reflect this. Genuine brand name equipment is sold in a few specialist shops, but costs much what you would pay in the U.K. or U.S. The fake gear is not all poor quality and may be sufficient for most trekkers' needs, but there are reports of some potentially dangerous manufacturing tricks. "Down" jackets have been found to contain carpet underlay, which would offer no insulation when it is sodden, and sleeping bags are deliberately overrated for their warmth factor. A highly recommended trekking shop for hiring and buying equipment in Kathmandu is Shona's Rentals (Tel/Fax: 01 265 120), on Jyatha Road in Thamel (just opposite Kilroy's Restaurant).

HEALTH MATTERS

Apart from altitude sickness (see p. 136), the health problems travellers are likely to encounter in Nepal relate to food and drink hygiene. Whilst not everyone is afflicted with a stomach upset during their stay, it is wise to expect it. I heard reports of sickness originating from both cheap and expensive restaurants, so that is really no way to judge it. Generally, if a restaurant is busy with locals and/or travellers then it should be a safe bet. On the trail, boil mountain water for at least 10–15 minutes, or treat it with iodine tablets or a purification filter. In the villages, beware of milk-based products, as the milk is unlikely to have been pasteurized. Stick to bottled water, tea, or bottled drinks.

WHAT TO TAKE

- ❑ Good, comfortable hiking boots and socks.
- ❑ Trekking poles (walking poles that collapse down for packing).
- ❑ Waterproof jacket.
- ❑ Several thin, warm layers of clothing, such as fleece jumpers.
- ❑ Thermal underwear.
- ❑ Shorts.
- ❑ Long trekking pants.
- ❑ 3–4 season sleeping bag (depending on how high your trek goes)
- ❑ Warm gloves and waterproof shell gloves.
- ❑ Warm hat/balaclava.
- ❑ Good sunglasses (preferably with large lenses or special mountain glasses).
- ❑ Medical kit.
- ❑ 1 litre (1¾-pint) leakproof water bottle.
- ❑ Torch.
- ❑ Sun hat.
- ❑ Sunblock.

14 Himalayan High Riders

by Steve Watkins

Nepal may be noted for its Himalayan trekking trips, but the same mountains also harbour trails that make for awesome mountain biking. I organized a five-day guided tour that took in the Kathmandu valley rim, the Himalaya viewpoint town of Nagarkot, and a spectacular, remote road to the Tibetan border.

Kathmandu and the surrounding valley is a place of contrasts that seems to inspire in travellers either love or hate. Those who hate the city itself usually place the undoubtedly bad, but finally improving, traffic pollution problem at the top of their list of reasons. Yet, escaping from the smog to find a healthy, thrilling adventure does not require anything more than a reasonable amount of energy and a mountain bike. Peter Stewart, the Australian owner of Kathmandu-based operator Himalayan Mountain Bikes (HMB), has lived in and biked around Nepal for 6 years and he bubbled over with enthusiasm as we discussed all the possible routes I could take

on the tour. Even though I had not even turned a pedal over yet, I was already wishing I had more time to explore. Eventually, I settled on a 5-day trip that would take me through a hilltop wildlife reserve to Nagarkot, a town renowned for its views of the Himalaya mountains, and then on to a luxury camp, called Borderlands, near the Tibetan border in time for Christmas Day.

The following afternoon, Suresh, my guide and a competitive mountain bike racer, met me at the company's Thamel office and organized a taxi out to their bike storage depot on the Kathmandu ring road. After sorting out helmets and bike settings, we leapt aboard and

 Hills and biking equals sweat and effort, so you need to be fit to undertake this ride. Previous biking experience is essential, unless you are very fit from other endurance sports. Short parts of the route that I rode involved technical riding, but there are route options available to avoid some of these. All the hill climbing has its rewards, however, as you get to experience some exquisite downhills too.

 This tour takes in remote parts of the Kathmandu Valley, so accommodation options are limited. The simple lodges offer very basic but reasonably comfortable beds and local meals. The exceptions to this are in Nagarkot and at the Borderlands camp resort, where accommodation and food are far better.

 Bikes, helmets, and repair tools are supplied by the operator. It is worth taking your own biking clothing, including gloves and shorts, good biking footwear, and a small daypack or bum bag for carrying food and extra clothing on the trail.

Above: Riding the ridge from Jhule Post
Left: Buddhist temple at Nagarkot; if your eyesight is good you can see Everest from here
Below: Our audience watched with interest as we checked our bikes at Karma Lodge

pedalled through the heavy traffic to the turn off for the road to Kakani, a small village some 27km (17 miles) northwest of the city. Within just 10 minutes our riding environment changed from smoke-belching trucks and buses to shady trees on a quiet, winding road that skirted the Nagarjun Forest Reserve, home to herds of wild deer. Suresh had warned me that the road to Kakani was a continuous climb, but the gradient was fairly gentle and constant, so I managed to develop a comfortable pedalling rhythm. Soon, the forest ended and the magnificent, deep valleys of the Himalayan foothills opened up around us.

Although the road was relatively quiet, it was still necessary to keep a wary eye out for vehicles as we negotiated the endless corners. Drivers in Nepal are

incredibly skilled at squeezing through the narrowest of gaps, but I didn't want to test their ability by getting in the way, especially as the consequences of getting it wrong would probably have entailed a long tumble down the mountainside. After the hustle of the city, it was refreshing to see tribal people quietly going about their business. The Newari people who inhabit these hillside villages are successful market traders and the large size

of their traditionally styled, mudbrick houses bore testimony to their wealth.

FLOUR GHOSTS

Just beyond the village of Mudkhu, some 250m (820ft) higher than Kathmandu, we pulled over for a drink and to admire the view down to the Kolpu Khola river valley. Back on the climb, the road was occasionally covered with thick carpets of millet. The villagers lay it out on the road to dry it and to have the threshing carried out by the wheels of passing vehicles, including ours! To aid the cause, I deliberately wove my way over each millet section even though it made pedalling heavy going. Further up the hill we again took a break to visit a small corn-grinding operation housed in a ramshackle shed. Powered by noisy diesel engines, the grinders churned out flour so fine that it hung in the air and even settled on the machine operators, turning them into ghostly figures. Farmers from the local area bring their raw corn here to be processed before selling it in Kathmandu's markets.

Our route continued skyward and my legs began to feel the effects of the sustained effort, while superfit Suresh looked as if he had hardly increased his pulse rate. We were now over 1,750m (5,740ft) high, but still had another 300m (980ft) of climbing to go before reaching Kakani. If the stress of exercise had caused us to forget the dangers of oncoming traffic, the sight of a mangled taxi lying halfway down a step ravine was enough to put us back on full alert. According to locals, the taxi had plunged off the road three days earlier, killing the driver. As we neared Lower Kakani, my legs were starting to struggle and I felt dismayed when Suresh announced that our overnight stop was another 4km (2½ miles) up a steeper hill. Clicking down into my "last resort" gear, I barely managed to keep the pedals moving and half expected to see snails overtake me as I crawled past an army barracks. It came as a great relief to see Suresh sitting on the steps of the Kakani Lodge, holding out a bottle of orange juice for me.

With the sun gone, the temperature plummeted and I wolfed down my dinner just so that I could get to my warm bed as quickly as possible. By morning, my legs had recovered and a breakfast of omelette and pancakes restocked the energy reserves for what promised to be an exciting ride through the Shivapuri Watershed and Wildlife Reserve. Persistent cloud cover and hazy air conditions took the edge off the views but provided a welcome break from the heat, as we hit our first off-road section. After shouldering the bikes for 10 minutes up a rough, terraced slope, we continued riding on a single-track trail through thick bush to the army post entrance to Shivapuri Reserve. Several gun-toting soldiers emerged from an office filled with "dit-dit-daa" sound of Morse code messages being relayed over a radio.

SHIVAPURI SLICE

The Shivapuri Watershed and Wildlife Reserve measures 9km (51/2 miles) from north to south and 24km (15 miles) from east to west. At its heart is the 2,732m (8,963ft) high Shivapuri Peak, and the whole area is known for its steep terrain; over half the park has a slope greater than 30 percent. Sitting between subtropical and temperate climates and at verying altitudes, the reserve has a fascinating ecological system that includes four distinct forest types. These range from pine and oak to upper mixed hardwood, including rhododendron, at higher altitudes. It receives an annual precipitation of 2,727mm (107in), which travels via series of reservoirs and pipelines to supply 35–45 percent of the Kathmandu's Valley's water requirements.

From Kathmandu to the Tibetan border

axle-deep rivulet washouts that criss-crossed the trail. At times, the forest cover opened up and we were treated to hazy vistas over a vast expanse of ridges and hills. We had become used to the gently traversing track, so it came as a bit of a shock suddenly to plummet down the hillside on a writhing jeep track until we eventually splashed through the Jamle Khola (*khola* means river in Nepali). However, what comes down must go up in the world of mountain biking, and we dropped through the gears to begin a 40-minute climb up a rock-strewn channel to another army post.

By mid-afternoon we had reached the Buddhist temple at Nagi Gompa, which looked somewhat sorry for itself with its array of very faded prayer flags tangled around nearby bushes. Near there, we stopped to talk to a gang of playful children who wanted to know where we were from and how old we were. Then it was time to push on. The downhill to Sundarijal was a wild and thrilling descent, full of drama and tension. We danced the bikes over rocks and ruts, held on tight through sand and gravel patches, and splashed into narrow streams. Braking hard to stay on course around switchback bends, we only rarely dared look up for long enough to absorb the views.

KARMA GAMES

Ten minutes after reaching the bottom and crossing the Bagmati Khola, a major river that later flows through Kathmandu, we pulled up at our overnight stop, the Karma Lodge, a whitewashed two-storey house offering basic accommodation. With clearing skies, we were in for a very cold night and I added extra blankets to my bed to try to keep warm. Although

Casually, they inspected our modern bikes and were amazed at how lightweight they were. To enter the reserve, it cost me, the "foreigner," 250 rupees and Suresh, the Nepali, just 10 rupees, but I knew the fee funded the protection of the area and had no qualms with the discrepancy. I just felt lucky that I didn't have a movie camera with me, as the fee for that was 3,000 rupees!

The Shivapuri watershed area is one of the principal sources for drinking water in the Kathmandu Valley, supplying over 30 million litres (6.5 million gallons) every day. The watershed became a reserve in 1982 in order to protect the hills and rivers from the accelerating environmental degradation that accompanied the burgeoning population growth in the valley. Forests were being decimated partly to satisfy the demand for fuel and building timber and partly to open up more space for cultivation, all of which led to increased levels of serious soil erosion. Two years later, in 1984, the area was extended and became a wildlife reserve too. In all, there are 21 Royal Nepal Army posts guarding the wall that demarcates the reserve's 120sq.-km (46sq.-mile) area.

Initially, our route snaked along a narrow, rocky path surrounded by trees, which occasionally arched over to form natural tunnels for us to swoop through. It was fast and engrossing action and we needed to concentrate hard to avoid getting caught out by the numerous

Karma Lodge felt like a special, almost spiritual kind of place, it was actually named after the owner's 14-year-old son. In the morning, I sat and watched Karma and his brothers play *pangara*, a simple game where each boy has a small hoop and a long stick, and races along trying to keep the hoop rolling. While they played on the track, a troop of monkeys marauded through the grounds in search of food. Although this was the only sign of exotic animal life that we saw during the trip, Shivapuri is also home to several endangered species, including leopards and leopard cats.

scraping the back tyre, I spent most of the descent with the back wheel locked up and sliding as I tried to restrict my speed and guide the bike around and over the obstacles. By the time we rattled to a halt at Jhule army post, adrenalin was whooshing around my body. I felt like running back up to have another go, but Suresh assured me that there was plenty more to come on the way towards Nagarkot. He was not wrong. After eating and drinking at the army post store, we went down, down, down, on an exposed ridge for a further 50 minutes, a great reward for all the climbing of the past

There is nothing quite like an early morning hill climb to wake up weary limbs, and the one from Karma Lodge was a 2½-hour epic that took us well over 2,000m (6,561ft) high. The track's gradient was generally not too severe and I found myself thoroughly enjoying the ascent. Eventually, we began to traverse the hillside until, at a switchback bend, Suresh and I left the main track and took on a scintillating, technically challenging, steep descent down a deep, sandy single track littered with big steps. Standing on the pedals with my backside almost

couple of days. This was about as good as mountain biking gets, and we soon passed through the villages of Chauki Bhanjyang and Jarshang Powa.

Nagarkot was beckoning, but we needed to earn our arrival. From the village of Kattike Dada, we faced a final ½-hour climb on a contorted, dusty jeep track to our overnight hotel, the very comfortable Peaceful Cottage. Nagarkot is an unusual Nepalese village in that it owes its existence entirely to tourism. It is set on a pretty, forested hilltop but the numerous hotels and lodges are not particularly charming. However, it's only the view that people come for. From most hotels, including ours, the magnificent view of the Himalaya range stretches all the way from 8,598m (28,208ft)-high Kanchenjunga, the world's third highest peak, to the 8,167m (26,794ft)-high Dhaulagiri. If you have good eyesight, you may be able to see Mount Everest too, though the bump on the horizon is apparently a little disappointing. I use the word "apparently" because Mother Nature was in a strange mood that December and the entire Himalaya was cloaked in heavy cloud. I did catch a peek of a summit

out of Nagarkot, we passed a new Buddhist temple, a brilliant white dome topped off with painted Buddha eyes, built in the grounds of the Himalaya Resort Hotel. After all the descents of the previous day, normal service was soon resumed as we climbed for 40 minutes to an observation tower located on a hilltop, some 2,600m (8,530ft) up. From there we joined a forestry track and descended through pine trees until we emerged at Gimireghaon, a tiny settlement. The village children's eyes virtually popped out of their heads when they spotted us and one came running over to tell Suresh that

through a fleeting window in the cloud cover, but had to resort to buying a panoramic mountain-view poster to see what I was missing.

FAME AND FOOLISHNESS

Slightly disappointed, Suresh and I set off the following morning on our final and longest day of biking. The Tibetan border was 75km (47 miles) away and it was Christmas Eve. If we wanted to celebrate Christmas in style we had no other option than to reach the luxury Borderlands adventure camp near there. On the way

Above left: *Stopping en route for a refreshing drink of water from the Jamle Khola*
Above: *What goes down must go up—but the view was ample compensation*

he had seen him on TV during a recent mountain bike race.

Basking in Suresh's reflected glory, I tried to impress the villagers by riding down a steep banking. The front wheel snagged in a ditch and I flew over the handlebars. Brushing off the dust, I took an embarrassed bow, remounted, and rode off to the sound of communal laughter. Beyond the larger village of

NEPAL

Nala we followed a footpath through terraced fields and had to give way to three giggling tribal women carrying big basketloads of wood. It seemed everyone had heard of my downfall. All too soon, we rolled into the noisy, dirty, bustling town of Banepa on the main Kathmandu highway. Following our encounter with the rural beauty of Nepal, I struggled to cope with the culture shock and wondered about the country's future given that so many rural Nepalis are moving to towns like these.

The scenery on the road to Dhulikel improved a bit and by the time we stopped for lunch my spirits were soaring again. Perhaps the imminent 27km (17-mile) descent into the lush Panchkhal Valley, on the Arniko Highway, had something to do with that. There was no need to pedal and the ride passed in a blur as I cut the corners like a racing driver. It was fun watching local people having to take a second look to make sure that I wasn't on a motorbike, as I sped past them. From the bottom of the hill, the further we pedalled the more enchanting the scenery became. The valleys became deeper and narrower until we reached Dolaghat, at the confluence of two mighty rivers, the Sun Koshi and the Indrawati. Standing on the village's bridge, I could not ignore our road snaking up along the valley side. We settled back into the saddles for another long climb. Over a small pass, the road dropped to the edge of the awesome Bhote Koshi River, one of Nepal's noted rafting rivers. Our good progress along the undulating road was only briefly interrupted by a puncture in my rear tyre, but it was soon repaired and we continued to Baelphi, where we stopped for a snack. The end was near, and on reaching the dingy market village of Barabhise, just 10km (6 miles) from Borderlands, I began to congratulate myself on a fine ride. However, the tail of our journey held an unwelcome sting.

The surfaced road ended (the popular belief is that Nepal does not want to facilitate links with Chinese-controlled Tibet for security reasons) and we were subjected to a hellish last hour, in dwindling light. Incessant buses and trucks kicked up thick clouds of choking dust and I had to dig deep into my mental reserves to maintain some forward movement on the very rough, stony track. This section of road to the border is usually closed for much of the rainy season because of frequent landslides. A yellow sign up ahead had "Borderlands" written on it but it was a "2km ahead" sign. I put my head back down, covered my nose and mouth with one hand, and slowly continued through the dust storm to the camp. Exhausted, we were both overjoyed to reach the peace of the remarkable Borderlands. Set in beautifully landscaped gardens on the bank of the thundering Bhote Koshi, this luxury adventure camp is a real treasure. At the atmospheric, open-sided, thatch-roofed bar, lit only with kerosene lamps, Suresh and I met up with the other dozen or so travellers who had wisely opted for this little dash of Nepalese paradise as their own Christmas presents. With a cold beer in hand and the festive party just warming up, we celebrated a memorable Himalayan ride.

HIGHLY SKILLED NEWARS

Regarded as the original inhabitants of the Kathmandu Valley, the Newar tribe is still the most dominant group in the region, numbering over half a million. They have Mongoloid features, speak the distinct Newari language, and are renowned worldwide for their art and craft skills. Drawing on influences from both Buddhism and Hinduism, the Newari artists create woodcarvings, metalwork sculptures, and elaborate religious paintings, some of which can be seen decorating the majestic temples of Kathmandu, Patan, and Bhaktapur. The Newars are also famed for their love of dancing, including the masked dance called *Lakhe*.

GOING IT ALONE

WHEN TO GO

Mountain biking is possible year round in Nepal but the best time is from October to April, when the skies are most likely to be clear and conditions dry. The monsoon season is from mid-June to September, but mountain biking on wet trails can be a whole heap of fun if you are that way inclined. Anyway, it doesn't usually rain all day.

PLANNING

It is possible to venture off alone on your mountain bike in Nepal, but the costs of organized tours are very reasonable. With these you get the benefit of being able to travel lightweight (the operator moves your gear to the overnight stops) while being guided to all the best riding routes. There are a few mountain bike operators in Kathmandu, and Himalayan Mountain Bikes are among the best for quality of guides and hire bikes. Trips can be tailor-made, and there are various accommodation options on most routes. Some HMB trips can also be booked in the U.K. via Specialist Trekking Co-operative. Whilst it is advisable to book ahead, late bookings can sometimes be taken, especially for shorter rides around the Kathmandu Valley, which may need only one or two days' notice. Be aware that operators who offer cheap prices will have to cut their costs somewhere, which can mean poor equipment or inexperienced guides. There are several international operators running biking trips to Nepal, including UK-based companies Karakoram Experience and Exodus.

TRAVELLERS' TIPS

On long riding days always keep a stock of snacks, such as Power Bars, chocolate, or biscuits, in your daypack in case your energy flags between village stops. If you are riding in a group, try not to be dragged along at a pace that is too high for your levels of fitness. It is a holiday after all. It is far better to have a fairly constant output of energy rather than short bursts of high action. Ask the guide to oil your bike chain every morning to ease your pedalling.

HEALTH MATTERS

Potential health problems are generally related to dehydration, long exposure to intense sunshine, and poor food-and-drink hygiene. Take on board plenty of fluids while you are riding and keep your energy levels up by eating regularly. Pasta and rice are good staple parts of a riding diet. Always use sunblock and wear a sunhat. Be careful about eating food in the villages because hygiene levels may not be up to much. Dishes such as vegetable fried rice are a good bet. Buy bottled water whenever you can; otherwise treat all water with iodine tablets or a filter. There are small stores on most routes selling water, soft drinks, and snacks.

WHAT TO TAKE

- ❏ Mountain bike (see below).
- ❏ Riding shoes (hire bikes do not have cleat pedals).
- ❏ Biking shorts, gloves, and helmet (operators can supply them too).
- ❏ Small daypack or bum bag.
- ❏ Bike water bottle.
- ❏ Warm layers of clothing.
- ❏ Waterproof/ windproof/ breathable jacket.
- ❏ Sunblock.
- ❏ Sunhat.
- ❏ Sunglasses.
- ❏ Torch.

FLYING BIKES

Many riders may prefer to take their own bikes over to Nepal. All international airlines carry bikes as part of your luggage allowance, but they have various regulations about how to prepare the bike for transit and different attitudes towards charging for the service. The surest way to get your bike accepted is to pack it in a bike box, the large cardboard boxes that manufacturers use to deliver the bikes to retail stores. Good bike stores will give you one for free. To fit the bike in the box, remove the pedals and wheels and loosen off the handlebars to twist them flush with the bike frame. Pad any sensitive parts, like derailleur and gear shifters, with foam, and fit basic wheel axles into the front forks and back wheel position to stop them getting crushed by other luggage. Tape the box up thoroughly and don't put pedals or other small parts separately in the box (they will fall out if it gets torn). Most airlines do not charge for carrying bikes as along as the total weight of your luggage is within the allowance.

15 Terai Trunk Route

by Steve Watkins

In a country renowned for its mountains, the low, flat lands of Nepal's Terai region offer a stark contrast. What this lush agricultural area lacks in big peaks, it makes up for with big wildlife in the captivating Royal Chitwan National Park. I spent three days exploring the park and a nearby Tharu tribal village, on elephants, in boats, and by foot.

When you first see the pancake-flat lands of the Terai region, which occupy a mere sliver across the southern edge of Nepal, you might well assume that their only role is to further emphasize the magnitude and majesty of the Himalaya mountains to the north. Look again, however, and it starts to become clear that this land, with its long tribal history, is in itself a fascinating part of Nepal's identity. Most visitors still stick to the mountain areas but, thanks in part to the wildlife-rich Royal Chitwan National Park, the Terai is increasingly becoming a "must see" destination for Nepal-bound adventurers who want a little diversity. To explore the national park and some of the surrounding Tharu tribal villages, I booked a three-day package, which included elephant treks and boat trips, at the Gaida Wildlife Camp, one of the exclusive lodges located within the park's boundary.

With most tours in Nepal, just getting to the start is an experience in itself, and the journey from Pokhara to Narayanghat, the entry town for the national park, was no exception. After marvelling at the view from the bus window of the western Himalaya snow peaks, we enjoyed an awesome ride on a road that clung to the vertical rockface of the deep Kali Gandaki gorge. As we entered the Terai region, the decrease in hills was matched by an increase in temperature and humidity. After spending the previous two weeks in the mountains, I found it strange to see so many people, including women in brilliantly coloured saris, riding around on bicycles—most of which were old Chinese, one-speed contraptions perfectly suited to the terrain. With

Above: *Elephants are good swimmers and not as ponderous on land as they may at first appear*
Left: *A Tharu village house inside the Gaida Wildlife Camp, a tranquil and protected jungle zone*

the sun's rays beating down on an endless view of golden yellow mustard fields, it was hard to believe that the Himalaya mountains were so close; so close, in fact, that it was still possible to see them on the horizon.

Fortunately for travellers, the tourist buses drop passengers off at the relevant points for all the major national park lodges. I jumped straight off the bus and into the back of a Gaida Wildlife Camp

This is a very easygoing trip, unless you fancy getting personal with a tiger or rhino. Armed only with a sense of adventure, you can enjoy relaxing boat and elephant rides or gentle forest walks—so it is suitable for families too.

★★ The Gaida Wildlife Camp lodge is within the park boundary and offers wonderful, eco-friendly accommodation in exclusive bunga-lows decorated in rustic style. There is no electricity (generators are too noisy) but the kerosene lamps and candles only add to the cosy atmosphere. Outside the park, there is plenty of accommodation to suit travellers on a low budget.

No special equipment is needed for this trip.

jeep for the short ride, including a river fording, to the lodge. Set on the bank of the Dungre Khola (*khola* means river in Nepali), a small tributary of the large and serene Rapti Khola, Gaida is one of only six lodges allowed within the park boundary. A major advantage, apart from the tranquillity of being in the protected jungle zone, is that they can keep and use their own elephants for taking people on rides whenever they want to go and for long enough to see more remote parts of the park. Lodges outside the park, of which there are many, can only link in with the limited supply of government-owned elephants, so at peak times you may find that you have to wait for a day or so after you arrive; also, the rides are time restricted. Settling into my delightful wooden bungalow, surrounded by tropical trees and large-leaf plants, I was already wishing my stay was longer than two nights. Sitting out in the oval garden, I sipped a fruit punch while Basanta Rayamajhi, the amiable Gaida manager, outlined the three-day programme. He told me that the camp was the second oldest in the park, having been established in 1976.

NO HOUSEHOLD PET

First up, I joined fellow travellers Theresa and Eric, from the United States, at the elephant stable to get to know how these wondrous creatures live and work. Vishnu, the camp's resident naturalist, explained that although wild Asiatic elephants used to live in the park, the ones used here today have all been trained from birth. Asiatic elephants are smaller than their African counterparts, growing to around 3m (9ft) high and weighing up to 5 tonnes/tons. If you fancy having one as a pet, then break open your chequebook because these beasts eat like there is no tomorrow. A normal daily diet includes 300kg (660lb) of grass and leaves, supplemented by 20kg (45lb) of a mixture of rice and molasses known as *kuchi*, and all washed down with 200 litres (45 gallons) of water. This voracious appetite is due to their energy-sapping size and inefficient digestive system, which means they gain little sustenance from what they eat.

Each elephant at Gaida has a team of two people who care for it and drive it. The phanit is the most experienced of the two and drives the elephant by sitting on the back of its neck and using subtle leg commands or tugs on its ears to guide it through the jungle. Voice commands used to be used but the sound of the phanit's voice was enough to alert wildlife in the vicinity, making it difficult to spot anything. This phanit–elephant relationship is a long and trusting one, built up from the very early days in the elephant's life. Mahouts are the people who look after the elephants' daily needs, including washing and feeding, though the term mahout is frequently misused to signify the phanit's role. Elephants are good swimmers in calm water and not as ponderous in their land movement as they may first appear. When panicked, they have been known to reach speeds of 40kph (25mph) and routinely travel at 4kph (2.6mph), about the same walking pace as yours and mine.

After demonstrating some of the leg commands on one of the camp's oldest elephants, Vishnu offered us the chance to try the traditional mounting technique of walking up the elephant's trunk. Theresa was bravest and went first. The phanit gave the command and the elephant curled the end of her trunk to make a step. Theresa proceeded to walk up the trunk and needed to grab the elephant's ears to get onto its head. Suddenly realizing how high off the ground she was, Theresa momentarily stalled, lost her balance, and ended up upside down and straddling the raised trunk in an impromptu comedy act that would have befitted any circus clown. I would have laughed more, but it was soon my turn. The elephant's skin felt as tough as a gnarly old tree trunk and was sparsely covered with short, spiky black hairs. Looking into her wise black eyes, I

DON'T LET SLEEPING ELEPHANTS LIE

Although elephants find it easy enough to lie down and are frequently seen rolling around in mudpools, they can sleep only while standing up. Their bodies weigh up to 6 tonnes/tons, so any extended period of time spent lying on their sides would lead to disastrous damage of internal organs. With so much mud to play in, water to squirt around, and tourist-carrying to do, it is lucky that the elephants actually need only about 2 or 3 hours' sleep every day. Ultimately, many elephants die because their teeth erode away, leading to a fatal inability to eat. However, they do grow six sets of molars during their lifetime and live on average for around 70 years.

apologized profoundly and clambered up to her head and onto her back. This was my first non-zoo encounter with elephants and I instantly became an admirer.

Primed with our newly learned know-how, we strolled through to the elephant loading point, a wooden platform built level with the elephants' backs to assist passengers in getting on and off. The phanits coaxed their charges into position and we clambered into the special, wooden-framed saddles. As the elephant moved off with a lolloping, rhythmic gait, it took me a while to work out how to sit comfortably on the saddle. After careful experimentation, I found that dangling my legs off the front corner provided the best protection from the incessant to-and-fro motions. We had only reached the Dunghre Khola, just a short distance from the camp, when a greater Asian one-horned rhinoceros (subsequently referred to as simply rhino for brevity), appeared out of the tall, dense grass and thundered off into the river. It was quite a shock to see one so early, and even more sobering to realize that it had been hanging around in what basically is the camp's front garden! Vishnu's earlier advice about never wandering out of the camp without a guide suddenly seemed more convincing.

The rhino quickly disappeared into the thick forest on the other bank, so Krishna, my phanit, eased our elephant into the river. It is not surprising that elephants, with such bulk and such thick skin, have trouble keeping cool. They sweat only from the top of their toenails and have multitudes of blood vessels close to the surface of their big ears, which help to regulate their temperature, but their favourite cooling tool is water. If the saying "as happy as pigs in mud" rings true, then the same can be said of elephants and water. Even a stern tug of both ears by Krishna failed to stop our transport grinding to a halt in the middle of the shallow river for a drink and quick splash around. Although the elephants show great willingness to work for the phanits, there is no doubting who has ultimate control in deciding just when the work will take place.

SAMBAR STAND OFF

The Royal Chitwan National Park has three distinct types of environment: grasslands, riverine forest, and sal forest. On the other side of Dunghre Khola, the elephant trudged on paths through the beautiful and dense riverine forest, which includes medium-height khair trees interspersed with the larger simal trees and a plethora of undergrowth bushes. All the shrubbery makes for excellent hiding places for the wildlife and initially it seemed that our first rhino maybe our last animal too. Yet Krishna knew these lands and the animals' behaviour so well that when things appeared to be too quiet he would turn the elephant onto another trail and search elsewhere. His efforts were rewarded when a small group of sambar deer crossed our path, initially

Above: *A greater Asian one-horned rhinoceros, to give him his full name, spotted near our camp*

without noticing our presence. The chunky-looking, dark brown sambar is the largest deer species in the park; adult males weigh around 320kg (700lb). As soon as they spotted us, the deer froze and pricked up their ears. We stopped too, and for a few moments there was an intriguing and tense stand-off before the deer sloped off into thicker bush. Other animals do not perceive elephants as a threat, so although we were sitting on top, the deer and rhino only really see the elephant and we are allowed to get very close.

Beyond the riverine forest, we entered a flood plain covered in long, golden, swaying grass. If the forest provides good shelter for animals, then the thick, tangled grasslands are an even better hideout. The grasslands are the principal reason why visitors only rarely see the most vaunted creature in the park, the tiger—or Royal Bengal tiger as it was previously known. Krishna had seen just two in the entire year. According to latest estimates, there are around 80 tigers in the park and throughout the 2 hours we were out on the elephant trek, the desire to see one was

overwhelming. Every blade of grass that moved and every leaf that rustled made my pulse rate rise, my eyes focus hard, and my mind imagine orange-, white-, and black-faces peering from the grasses. The possibility of seeing one was almost as exciting as actually seeing one. The tigers melt into the background easily, but the rhinos find it harder to hide and we were treated to an almost non-stop parade, some with miniature baby rhinos in tow. Even when we were up close to the rhinos, they barely lifted their heads for more than a few seconds to check out the scene before getting back to feeding on the grasses.

A HEAVY COLONIAL TOLL

These prehistoric, armour-plated battering rams, which can live for up to 70 years, fear nothing, except humans. Or humans with guns, to be more exact. The supposed mythical and medical powers linked with virtually every last inch of the rhino's body, with the horn being the most prized part, has led to it being widely hunted. It was disturbing to learn the extent of some rhino massacres carried out by colonial high-fliers in the name of entertainment. During one unparalleled

Right: *Tharu woman tending her crops*
Far right: *Village girl weaving a grass mat*

GRASS CUTTERS PAY WITH LIVES

Whilst the Royal Chitwan National Park has been an undoubted success in preserving ecological diversity and the habitats of wild animals, the park has had adverse effects on the local people who are trying to survive daily life in the vicinity of the park. The rhinos eat their crops, the tigers kill their livestock, and the resources of the park are out of bounds. To alleviate the suffering, which was giving rise to tension between locals and park management, the national park is opened up for two weeks every year, in January, to allow local people to collect the abundant tall grasses that they use to build their houses and for various other purposes.

By paying a small fee, the families can gather as much grass as they want during the two-week period, without the use of vehicles or oxcarts. Over 70,000 people pour in to take advantage. The only problem is that the rhinos, sloth bears, and tigers don't take a two-week holiday during the grass-cutting extravaganza, and every year a dozen or so people are killed. However, the rewards are obviously deemed to be worth the risk, as the grasses can be used as thatch or sold to local businesses for a healthy profit.

hunt in 1939, the Viscount of India's party killed 38 rhinos, in addition to 120 tigers, 15 bears, and 27 leopards. To put that in some perspective, there were only 20 tigers left in the entire park in the 1970s and just 80 nowadays; and only about 400 rhinos remain today. Should you inadvertently find yourself staring eye to eye with a rhino, don't try running, because they are swift and agile, despite their 2-ton bulk, and can execute sharp turns. It is better to stay calm and stand still, as the odds are the charge will be a false one, unless the rhino is cornered or if it is a cow defending her calf.

Whilst the rhinos are marvellous for attracting visitors, they are deemed a complete menace by farmers in areas surrounding the national park, as they regularly destroy crops, especially wheat. All around the park perimeter and beyond there are wooden watchtowers in which farming families take turns to camp out each night in order to scare off any rhinos that venture onto their land.

With the reddening sun melting onto the grassland horizon, Krishna turned our elephant homeward and we ambled back through the forest. Dusk is always a good time for wildlife spotting and we stumbled across two flighty herds of chital, or spotted deer. Graceful and svelte, with rich brown coats speckled with white dots, the chitals leaped and bounded through the undergrowth, letting out piercing cries to warn the rest of the herd of our approach. Up in the treetops, a silhouetted troop of common langur monkeys were making their final forages of the day. Krishna took us back into the Dungre Khola down a steep bank, and it was remarkable how well the elephant coped with such testing terrain. Back at camp, we dismounted and watched the elephants enjoy a frolic in a mudbath, another method these beautiful creatures use to keep cool. The mud dries out and is lighter coloured than their own skin, which helps to reflect the sun's rays.

Following a delicious buffet dinner of traditional Nepali food—rice, curries, and vegetables—Vishnu treated us to an enlightening illustrated talk about the park and its wildlife. Although the high humidity levels in the Terai had badly damaged several slides, we were introduced to common leopards, wild boar, and sloth bears, the most aggressive and potentially dangerous creature in the park for humans.

Next morning, I arose before dawn and joined another guide, Duki, for a brief sunrise stroll along the riverbank. The river was blanketed in fog, which subdued almost all sounds, so when the deep red sun managed to penetrate the murk it made a serene and mystical scene. Spider webs built in tree branches and bushes glistened with dew and we encountered several elephants being taken out for early morning exercise by the phanits. The big activity for the day was to be a 3-hour boat trip down the Rapti Khola (*rapti* means beautiful), followed by a short walk through the grasslands to Gaida's tented camp, a lower-priced and more remote accommodation option for travellers wanting to sample life in the wilds. To maintain tranquillity and enhance the chances of spotting animals and birds, Gaida only use humanpowered dugout canoes on the river. At first it felt rather unstable, but once I had settled down into my low seat and Assa, my boating guide, had begun poling us downriver, it all became very relaxing. Rapti Khola is home to two species of crocodile, the gharial crocodile and the marsh mugger. Our luck was in as we

spotted a gharial on a sandbank after only ten or so minutes. These slender-nosed, endangered creatures are very nervous and pose no threat to humans, while the marsh mugger has a short, stubby snout and is more aggressive, taking large animals, such as deer, and very occasionally unwary humans. Neither species wanted to hang around when we got close to them, launching into the water with a powerful swish of their tails.

INTO THE TIGER NEST

Crocodiles are undoubtedly the highlight of the Rapti Khola trip, but the river is also home to scores of exotic birds—526 species have been noted here. Assa was quick to point out an osprey soaring above the water in search of prey. Around the river's edge, black-and-white sand martins flitted through the air in search of tiny insects before returning to their nests, which are burrowed out of the sandy banks. One of the most endearing bird species found on the river is the rusty orange-coloured ruddy shelduck, locally known as love ducks. These strong fliers migrate across the Himalaya mountains from Siberia to the Terai every winter. They earned their love ducks tag because they mate for life. By the time we pulled into the bank to disembark, we had also spotted, amongst others, little egrets, intermediate egrets, small pied kingfishers, and black ibis.

The laid-back journey had lulled us

FURTHER READING

Heart of the Jungle by K.K. Gurung (André Deutsch Ltd, 1983). A classic, if slightly outdated, book that gives a thorough background to the park, the animals and birdlife, and the local people. It is available in Kathmandu's bookshops, including Pilgrim Books in Thamel. Black-and-white photographs and lovely line drawings of the animals and birds are included.
Royal Chitwan National Park—Wildlife

Heritage of Nepal by Hemanta R. Mishra and Margaret Jefferies (The Mountaineers, 1991). A more up-to-date and slightly more comprehensive guide to the park than *Heart of the Jungle*, giving an overview of the region, the Tharu people, and environmental problems, in addition to detailed information on the animals and birdlife found in the park. Colour and black-and-white photographs are used throughout.

into complacency, but Assa's announcement that we may, if we were lucky (!), see a tiger on our 20-minute walk through the grasslands snapped us out of it. To prove his point, Assa strolled along the small beach, scouring the sand until he found a tiger pawprint, a large one, and reasonably fresh too. The 20-minute hike suddenly took on the dimensions of a marathon for survival. Torn between the desire to see a tiger and the onset of terror that would surely ensue, our pace along the dirt track ebbed and flowed. Assa had seen one on this stretch of track the previous year but, thankfully and regretfully, we did not witness a repeat performance. After a brief visit to the Gaida tented jungle camp, we boarded a jeep for the 1-hour return journey to the lodge.

In the late afternoon, I joined Vishnu for a visit to nearby Bachauli, a traditional Tharu tribal village. Some anthropologists claim that the Tharu are the original people of the Terai region but owing to a complete lack of written history about the tribe, the claim has always been hotly debated. Alternative theories include them being descended directly from Buddha—but their language is distinctly different from that spoken by Buddha. Others believe that they originate from Himachal Pradesh in northern India. This theory claims that when Islamists attacked the Hindus of Himachal Pradesh, the Hindu rulers sent all their princesses, along with servants, to a hideout in the (then) dense forest of the Terai. Most of the Hindu men died in battle, so the princesses instead married the servants, which could explain why Tharu women still serve their husbands food by balancing the plate on their feet, the lowest and least holy part of their body, as a sign of superior status. There were two options for reaching Bachauli, by foot through the fields or by oxcart along a track. Having sat on an elephant and in a boat for the best part of two days, I decided my legs needed a workout and opted to walk.

TRAVELLERS' TIPS

Whilst the crashing sound of elephants passing through the forest doesn't seem to upset the other wildlife, the sound of a human voice is enough to send them scurrying for cover. If you want to optimize the chances of seeing anything, be as quiet as possible when on the elephant ride and resist the temptation to shout instructions at the phanit. He will be well aware of wildlife in the area and knowledgeable about the best spots for taking photographs. Take the warnings about wandering around the park alone very seriously. Tourists and guides have been killed in the past.

TRIBAL INDIFFERENCE

Our trail wound through fields of yellow mustard, where Tharu women, tall and slender in appearance, worked in small groups to tend the crops. Although the Tharu people have inhabited the area for centuries, many families do not own the land they work on. In 1950 the government introduced land registration but the under-educated Tharu were not aware of the implications and failed to register their interests, thus losing the land. The landless now work on other people's property under one of two systems, *theka* or *bighaa*, which entitles them to shares in the crop.

Bachauli village, like most Tharu villages, is a collection of mud-and-grass huts built around a central communal area. The hut builders utilize mud from a site about 6km (4 miles) away (the local mud is not sticky enough) and the grass is collected from within the national park during the annual collection period. It was relatively quiet when we arrived as it was a market day in the nearby town of Narayanghat, but it was pleasant to see the people still there simply getting on with their lives and not overly interested

Above: Human-powered dugout canoes maintain tranquillity and increase the chance of spotting animals and birds

in my arrival. As I wandered down the dusty tracks between the houses, I noticed that the mud huts had no windows, just tiny vent holes. Vishnu explained that the Tharu believe that the evil eye can see through windows and affect their lives, though he added that the lack of windows also helped to keep the interior cool during the scorching summer months.

At one house, the owner allowed us inside to see the kitchen. With no windows and only a shaft of light through the door and the dim glow of the fire to light the interior, it was incredibly dark. The owner's wife squatted at the fireside on the impeccably swept mud floor stirring a pot of boiling rice. There was no furniture, just a few woven grass baskets holding chillis and tiny silver fish. Fishing is an important part of Tharu life. They use woven circular nets or fine nets strung on triangular wooden frames. Leaving the kitchen, I spotted two triangular nets hanging from the roof eves. We strolled through the rest of the village,

watching girls weaving grass mats, children playing chase games, and teenagers huddled in a small room watching Indian soap operas on television. Our departure was heralded with as little pomp as our arrival and I left relieved that our presence in the village had such minimal effect on the lovely Tharu people.

As my flight back to Kathmandu did not leave until 11:30am, the following morning I took the opportunity of a brief, dawn elephant ride back into the park. Fog once again cloaked the river and forest but made for a distinctly different feel from the earlier sunset ride. Having spoken to other travellers who have visited the Royal Chitwan National Park, I realize that experiences differ quite widely, depending mainly on where you choose to stay. My three days at Gaida Wildlife Camp had been so relaxing and enjoyable that it felt like a week. However, the real benefit of staying inside the park is that the activities, including the elephant rides, are on offer pretty much whenever the fancy takes you. Such freedom to explore and observe wildlife, coupled with the tranquillity, is priceless, so go on treat yourself.

GOING IT ALONE

INTERNAL TRAVEL

There are several ways to get to Royal Chitwan National Park. Daily tourist buses, including those operated by Greenline, run from both Kathmandu and Pokhara. Alternatively, you can visit the park on your way into Nepal from India. Local buses link the border crossing at Sunauli with Narayanghat, from where buses and rickshaws run to Sauraha. If you want to save time, consider flying from Kathmandu to the airport at Bharatpur, just 45 minutes' taxi ride from Sauraha. Be aware though that this flight is often delayed or cancelled due to the foggy morning conditions in the Terai, occasionally for several days at a time.

WHEN TO GO

December is a great time to see the Terai region, as the fields are awash with yellow mustard flowers. However, the occasional early morning foggy conditions can delay any wildlife-spotting trips, though I found it a particularly enchanting time to explore. From November to February the weather is cool, with average temperatures ranging from mid- to high 20°C (75°–85°F), but be prepared for chilly nights. March to May is pretty good too, though the temperatures are already heading towards 40°C (105°F). Once the monsoon season arrives in June, high temperatures, high humidity, and high afternoon rainfall levels last until October, though the park is at its most lush during this period. The best time to spot tigers is in February, after the grass cutting festival, as there are fewer places for these shy cats to hide.

PLANNING

You can book direct with the various lodges within or outside the park, including the Gaida Wildlife Camp. Bookings for Gaida can also be made in the United Kingdom through Specialist Trekking Co-operative. A multitude of agencies in Kathmandu offers trips to Chitwan, some are not overly clear about exactly what you get for your money. One recommended agency is Manjushree Travel & Tours in Thamel, who offer a range of accommodation options. With so many low-priced lodges and hotels outside the park in Sauraha, it would rarely be a problem to just turn up and find something. There are agents in Sauraha who can organize elephant treks and boat trips.

HEALTH MATTERS

Contact your doctor about the latest recommendations for malaria prevention in the Terai. You should take a course of anti-malarial tablets. At dusk, cover up all exposed areas of your body and apply insect repellent and then sleep under a mosquito net. Avoid drinking water at the lodges unless you are sure of its purity. Choose soft drinks or tea and coffee instead, to be safe. The heat and humidity can have a draining effect on your body so be sure to drink plenty of liquids at regular intervals, even if you are simply relaxing on a boat trip for a few hours. Wear a sunhat and use high-factor sunblock.

WHAT TO TAKE

- ❏ Light clothing, including shorts and lightweight, neutral-coloured trousers (the rhinos don't like bright colours) and long-sleeved shirt.
- ❏ Warm jumper for the evenings (thicker from December to February).
- ❏ Closed, comfortable walking shoes or boots.
- ❏ Sun hat.
- ❏ Sunblock.
- ❏ Insect repellent.
- ❏ Mosquito net.
- ❏ Torch.
- ❏ Water bottle.

Below: *Luxury in the wild—the sleeping quarters at Gaida Wildlife Camp*

NEPAL

16 Running the Bhote Koshi

by Jill Gocher

Rafting down one of Nepal's raging white-water rivers is just what is needed to give an edge on a trip to this enchanting country. For a short, two-day trip that promised plenty of thrills I decided to try the Bhote Koshi.

Sitting in an ungainly rubber raft, dodging rocks while crashing down a raging whitewater river is not everyone's idea of a good time, but for me, the experience was both exhilarating and revitalizing—a perfect antidote to city stress and urban overkill. One of Nepal's many raging white-water rivers, the Bhote Koshi starts its life high up in the Tibetan Plateau, before rushing and winding its way down into eastern Nepal. With Grade 4 and 5 descents in the upper section, and 2 to 3 in the lower section, it is a wild running river. Yet it is also a steep descent, classified as a technical, rather than high volume river, requiring a "reactive crew" while allowing scope for skilful manoeuvring on the part of the rafters.

But first we had to get there. Interminable is the word that best describes the ride. We arrived at the Equator Expeditions office in Thamel in Kathmandu at 7am, and from then on the morning progressed slowly as we awaited late arrivals and last-minute organization. The motley crew gradually assembled. There were to be 18 rafters in all: two New Zealand girls, a German-Chinese man, an Australian, a few British, three Slovenians, a few Dutchmen and a Dutch couple, and an assortment of American new agers. We were accompanied by the Nepali guides, headed by Pravin, and several British kayakers who wanted to tackle the river's technical twists for a few days in their own high-powered, high-tech craft.

READY TO GO

At last we were ready to leave. Dodging the morning "Tiger Balm" vendors and shoeshine boys, our group headed down Thamel's busy streets to the bus. The small vehicle was quickly loaded to the hilt with backpacks, mattresses, sleeping bags, water bottles, and the other paraphernalia that is needed for an overnight rafting expedition. Rafters, guides (including the team leader, Pravin), helpers, and hangers-on climbed on to the bus and we were finally off, heading east along the Kathmandu–Tibet road for a the 3-hour ride. Rafts, paddles, vests, and helmets we collected along the way.

We were headed first to the Sukute Beach Adventure Camp. Run by Equator Expeditions, this comfortable camp is fitted with a large dining/entertainment pavilion and a washing/toilet block with hot water. Accommodation comes in the form of semi-permanent roofed tents, with hammocks strung across the front

Anyone with an average degree of fitness, good reflexes, and an ability to follow simple commands can enjoy the rafting experience. An adventurous attitude is an asset, but the guides always group like-minded people together and the timid will find they are not overtaxed. A desire to get wet and the ability to swim are useful attributes. Because the trip is so well organized, hassles are rare.

On a rafting trip, falling into the cold water is almost a certainty. Good companies do all they can to make the trip comfortable and ours was as comfortable as possible.

The tour company provides all the specialist equipment needed, including tents, mattresses, rafts, life vests, helmets, paddles, and first-aid equipment. Bring a thermal vest or wetsuit if you are rafting in the winter months. Open action sandals are best for the feet.

entrance, enjoying prime river views. The camp is a good place to relax between river jaunts, and some people stay for days, doing a kayaking course or just enjoying the peaceful, rural atmosphere. The staff gave us a short welcome, assigned us to our tents, stored our baggage, and, after allowing us half an hour to explore and settle in, announced lunch. The abundant, mostly vegetarian food was enlivened with plenty of salads, cheese, and canned tuna—a simple yet satisfying meal.

Then we piled back into the bus. Rafts, paddles, and vests at the ready, we headed another 22km (14 miles) up to the rafting point, just below the Lomasangu Dam.

FIRST GLIMPSE OF THE RIVER

From our elevated position in the bus, the river seemed small, mild, even boring. Where were the splendid Grade V conditions I had prepared myself for? "Don't worry," said Mark, one of the Australian helpers, "you will find there are a few surprises. It's not half as tame as it looks." As we reached our put-in point, the river still looked tame—pretty, but tame—as it gurgled its way through forested hills and green farmland. "Looks like we'll be in for some serious Grade I rafting," someone commented. The two New Zealand girls, Sue and Josie, were indignant to the extreme. "Aw, we were promised Grade V and this is not even a decent Grade I," exclaimed Sue, who comes from Queenstown—New Zealand's premier rafting centre. "This is kid's stuff."

As these two girls seemed to know what they were doing, I decided to stick with them, fancying myself as one of the experienced rafters. Most of the group were gung-ho guys in their 20s, enthusiastic first-timers, but not that keen to share their expected macho thrills with mere girls, even experienced ones.

TEAM LEFT, TEAM RIGHT

The process continued. Our three rafts were pumped up with powerful foot

RIVER GRADES

- ❑ **Grade I** Has flat water, no rapids, barely a splash: no fun at all.
- ❑ **Grade II** Has a small bubbling, current with small roller-coaster rapids: all fun and no danger, but no adrenalin-producing thrills either.
- ❑ **Grade III** Needs a trained guide to steer rafters through: can be quite exciting and technical, requiring some degree of skill.
- ❑ **Grade IV** The rapids start to be seriously big, uncontrollable, unforgiving, and exhilarating: thrills galore and adrenalin will start pumping.
- ❑ **Grade V** The limit—only for the adventurous, with highly trained crews: serious thrills and a huge sense of achievement on completion of the descent.
- ❑ **Grade VI** Considered unmanageable, unnavigable, and unrunnable: most expeditions porterage around these, and only serious daredevils or thrill seekers even consider to attempt a descent.

pumps (great exercise for the thighs). Teams were chosen. Pravin wanted to put all the women into one raft and give us a "soft" ride, but this suggestion was met with fierce opposition from me and the New Zealanders. We wanted a "hard" ride and the chance to show our toughness. In the end we shared the raft with three guys. Six of the men teamed up to become "the Tigers," "macho dudes" who were going to take on the river.

Before any rafting team takes to the water, there is a mandatory lesson on dry land. We donned our plastic helmets, life vests, and aluminium paddles, then practised the various manoeuvres that would be needed in times of high activity on the river. We were told the basic instructions: "paddle forward," "paddle backwards," "team left" (everyone leaps to the left

side of the raft), "team right" (everyone leaps to the right), and so on. Although the commands are simple, they need to be obeyed, and promptly, in times of high waters.

Most Nepal rafting companies practise safe rafting and each group is accompanied by at least one or two kayakers who make the run ahead of the rafters. This has the twofold purpose of checking the waters and showing the rafting guides the best line to take through the rapids, as well as being on hand in case anyone experiences difficulties when they fall from their raft. Six kayaks accompanied our group. We were ensconced in heavy-duty Avon self-bailing rafts, with three rafters on each side. With a guide at the back to give directions and steer the raft out of trouble (or into trouble, as the case may be), even beginners can have a great experience.

Into the Swim

Finally we climbed into our respective rafts to begin the descent. It started off easily enough, with calm waters allowing us to perfect our manoeuvres and learn to work together as a team. The three rafts followed each other in quick succession, drifting to and fro across the river.

Then the rapids started, bringing with them a whole new world of exhilarating,

Above: *Kayakers stay ahead of the rafts to find the best route down*
Top inset: *Everyone has to wear a plastic helmet for safety*
Bottom inset: *Our accommodation was comfortable and offered superb river views*

adrenalin-pumping thrills. We handled the first few sets of rapids without incident, laughing uproariously at the Tigers, who all fell unceremoniously into the river. Then the rapids got steeper, the

NEPAL'S WILD RIVERS

Nepal has some of the world's best rafting rivers and several are listed amongst the world's top ten. Enterprising foreign white-water experts, especially New Zealanders, are continually surveying the mountains for new adventures.

Running a river can take anything from hours to five or six days, or even, for serious rafters, ten days or more. Rafters spend several hours a day actually descending the river, then set up camp on a beach for the night, with time to relax and enjoy the natural surroundings.

❑ **Trisuli** Probably the first river to be used for serious commercial activity, this is still quite popular, although more with tour groups than adventure seekers. I was discouraged from this descent by guides from one tour company who told me that it was old hat, a bit bland, and generally not worth the bother.

❑ **Karnali** Nepal's longest river, starts from the base of Mount Kailash, Tibet's holiest mountain, and runs south, forming the major drainage system for western Nepal. This is one of the world's best big volume rivers, providing a classic expedition of around 11 days. The river passes through deep canyons before opening out to jungle, then on to the plains of the Terai and the Gangetic plains.

❑ **Sun Koshi** "The River of Gold" has been rated by those in the know as one of the world's top ten rafting rivers. A big-adventure, big-volume river, it rises near Shisha Pangmama, high in the Tibetan Plateau, then runs eastward, draining some of the world's highest mountains. The rafting trip descends the river for some 270km (170 miles) on an 11-day journey.

❑ **Kali Gandaki** The river starts its descent from the Tibetan Plateau into the Kingdom of Mustang. Dropping spectacularly, this holy river has carved the world's deepest gorge between the peaks of Mount Annapurna and Dhaulagiri. Grade III and IV rapids are common. It was opened to commercial rafting in 1991.

❑ **Marsyangdi** Opened to rafting in 1996, the Marsyangdi is another "raging river." It offers some of Nepal's most exciting Grade IV and V rapids during the six-day descent. The first section is so good that it is rafted twice, two days running. Because the rafting point starts in a remote area, the actual rafting takes only three days.

waves got bigger, and concentration was required.

Swirling, bucking, plunging through the white water, we were making a great ride, as we worked our way through the centre of the maelstrom. I opened my mouth to yell, letting off excess energy and fighting any fear. Then suddenly, with no warning at all, my mouth filled with water. I was actually in the water, momentarily disorientated, and gasping for air. The downward action of the waves dragged me under, time after time, as I fought to stay clear of the surging foam. As someone described it, it's like being in a washing machine. The buoyancy of the life vest kept me afloat as I gulped lung-fuls of air, trying not to panic. Gasping and coughing, I managed to pull myself together and struggled towards the boat grabbing thankfully at the ropes that circle the outside. Strong hands took hold of my vest and hauled me in, leaving me, like a big fish, in an alive, but shocked heap at the bottom of the still bucking raft.

THE WILD RIDE

I had all of two seconds to get my breath back, and no time for sympathy or commiseration, before I had to take position again and start paddling through the next set of rapids. Humbled, I grabbed my paddle and made the motions. I pride myself on my good sense of balance and ability to stay in a raft, so I found the whole falling-in experience quite humiliating, and I was bemused at being unable to figure out what happened. Usually, you are aware that a fall is coming, and can prepare yourself a little mentally, but this came out of the blue. The raft simply bucked me out. A fall certainly generates a new respect for the river and the incredible power that is contained in these rushing waters.

Unlike many of the most memorable rapids on Nepal's rivers, the rapids on this lower section of the Bhote Koshi are not named, so it is difficult to recall the sequence of thrills. Several of the descents offered pure excitement without terror, while others caused the raft to buck and toss like a wild horse, so that staying inside took a conscious effort, requiring hard gripping with the feet, thighs, and knees as well as leaning well into the centre of the raft. But even these precautions didn't guarantee a dry ride! To minimize chances of going overboard when going through the bigger rapids, you should hold on to the raft and try to keep your weight towards the centre of the boat.

After about 2½ hours of action, the sun started dropping behind the hills and there was a chill in the shadows. Then the camp hove into view—a welcome sight indeed. Thoughts turned immediately to hot showers, warming drinks, a cigarette, and warm dry clothes.

The night was spent eating and relaxing over beers or rum punch, getting to know our fellow rafters. Food was plentiful, with plenty of carbohydrates to recharge the energy levels. Later, some sat around playing guitar and dancing, while others sidled quietly off to the quiet, warm sanctity of their tents.

THE SECOND DAY

The second day was very much a repeat of the first, except that we started our ride off in the morning. After a hearty breakfast of eggs, toast, fruit, and loads of tea or coffee, we made a relaxed start around 9am, piling back into the bus to drive back up to the put-in point.

The new rafters had gained a lot of confidence during the first day, and the Tigers had developed into a strong team—except for one, who decided a little less excitement would suit him better and changed places with one of our group.

For me, the natural excitement of the river is enough, but there were some who wanted more. They wanted to tip their rafts and experience life a little closer to the edge. I noticed a bit of guarded chat in the front of the raft and sidelong glances at Pravin, presiding over his oar, at the back. Sue and Josie were obviously up to something. Sure enough, bored with the lack of Grade V thrills, Sue and Josie were hatching a plot to overturn us in one of the bigger rapids—a nice surprise for the rest of us.

I put my foot down—hard on the bouncy floor of the raft—and voiced my objections. I have a great respect for the river and, having travelled in boats where men risk their lives getting through dangerous rapids, I have difficulty in enjoying manufactured adventure. Just handling the raft and rapids well is thrill enough.

In the end, we didn't tip the boat, but somehow on a particularly steep patch both Mariana, the Slovakian woman, and I were tipped out. This time at least we knew it was coming, and we were prepared.

GOING BACK

Back at Sukute Beach, there was another surprise in store. After lunch we were to raft for further hour or two downstream. The rapids were small, but it was a beautiful afternoon, so we ended our trip with an idyllic, if unexciting ride. We passed by more villages, watching the children bathe and women washing in the river. Greetings were exchanged with boys who showed off their special tricks, somersaulting noisily into the waters. And so it went on, until we reached the put-out point. Our bus was waiting and, with great efficiency, rafts and rafters were despatched back to base.

Top: *You can be tossed out before you know it when the raft hits a rough spot*
Above: *Loading the kayaks onto the truck at Sukute Beach—with everyone helping we were soon ready to go*

During our return journey to Kathmandu we saw the mighty Himalaya range lit by the setting sun. All eyes turned to the right, trying to figure out which of the mountains was Everest. Possibly we saw it. I really don't know. We stopped the bus and everyone scrambled out to take photographs and enjoy the spectacular sight. Then, as darkness surrounded us, we continued the journey, cosy and contented, back to the confines of Kathmandu.

SAFETY IS NO ACCIDENT

According to the Equator Expeditions rafting brochure, "safety is no accident." To use their own words, "We have a minimum of two safety kayakers on all our trips, plus one Western guide in peak season, with first aid and EMT qualifications. Combine this with the high-calibre experience and proficiency of our Nepali guides and you have the best team on the rivers and mountains in Nepal." The kayakers find the best line through each rapid and are on the spot should anyone need a helping hand.

GOING IT ALONE

INTERNAL TRAVEL

For rafting trips, transportation to and from the base (either Kathmandu or Pokhara) is included in the package. From Pokhara to either base it is a 6-hour bus journey—quite a pleasant journey on the tourist buses ($5), which depart each morning.

The other alternative is a 30-minute flight ($60)—highly recommended at least one way for the panoramic views over Nepal's luscious terrain.

WHEN TO GO

The post-monsoon months of mid-September till late November are the prime months for rafting. The waters are high and the weather is not too cold. The winter months of December, January, and February are rather too cold, although wetsuit wearers can still enjoy some good rafting. The summer months of late March to early June are also prime time, as the spring snow melts fuel the rivers to about one grade less than their highest. The monsoon season from mid-June to early September is not busy for rafting. The rivers are full and only overnight trips on the Trisuli and Seti Rivers are available.

PLANNING

Obviously any rafting expedition is done in a group, but it is very easy to book your trip in either Kathmandu or Pokhara (for the Kali Gandaki River). There is no need at all to book from your home country. Plenty of single travellers sign up for these trips, and it is always easy to meet companions.

Prices for rafting trips vary considerable. Overnight trips start around $60, then week-long expeditions rise dramatically to several hundred dollars. It pays to ask around at the various rafting companies to check options as well as prices.

HEALTH MATTERS

While trying foreign food is always an adventure, it can also be hazardous. Nepal is justifiably notorious for its lethally unhygienic cooking conditions and for decades travellers have been warned against eating salads and locally produced ice creams. As a constant traveller in Southeast Asia, I rarely have stomach problems but during my five weeks in Nepal, I had three separate and quite serious disturbances. Beware of what you eat and try to check the cleanliness standards in kitchens. Never take ice and check the seals of bottled water to ensure there has been no tampering. Waterborne parasites are one of the most common causes of stomach upsets and they are no fun.

In Kathmandu stick to the excellent new restaurants that have opened around the Thamel district.

Trekking companies usually ensure that their food is hygienically prepared, so there is no need to worry while you are on an actual trek.

On a positive note, the medical suppliers around Thamel are well versed

with foreigner's stomach ailments and a quick description of the symptoms will result in the dispensation of the correct medicine without any real need to see a doctor.

WHAT TO TAKE

Although the rafting company provides specialist equipment, individuals are responsible for their personal belongings, which should include:

- ❏ Sleeping bag (for hire in Kathmandu (in Thamel) or Pokkara.
- ❏ One set of warm dry clothes for the beach and evenings.
- ❏ One set of rafting clothes—T-shirt and shorts (from November to March a thermal top is recommended).
- ❏ Towel.
- ❏ Suntan lotion.
- ❏ Bathing suit.
- ❏ Personal toiletries,
- ❏ Water bottle.
- ❏ Water purifying pills (although the company provides boiled water).
- ❏ Cap/hat.
- ❏ Torch/batteries.
- ❏ Sun glasses (with string retainer so you don't lose them in the river).
- ❏ A first-aid kit.
- ❏ Mosquito repellent.
- ❏ Camera.

Below: *Meditation before the descent calms the nerves*

NEPAL

17 On Horseback to the Kingdom of Lo

by Jill Gocher

Remote, medieval, and other wordly, Lo Manthang is the capital of the feudal Buddhist kingdom of Lo, or Mustang, in northern Nepal, where the culture and customs follow Tibetan traditions. No roads lead to the region. I set out on horseback along the trail that follows the Kali Gandaki River, an important and ancient salt trade route, connecting Tibet to Nepal and, beyond, to the Indo-Gangetic plains.

As the tiny plane descends into the barren valley, its wingtips almost touch the sides of the mountain. All around us is the great Himalaya massif, and then the majestic snow-covered peaks of Nilghiri, Telicho, and Daulghiri usher us into the Jomson Valley. The dramatic spectacle has left an awed silence in the passenger cabin. Then, with the relief of a safe landing, comes an exhilarated commotion of laughter and fast talk.

Thin air, bitingly cold temperatures, and steep mountain passes make the journey a bit of a struggle, yet many people who make the journey, and enjoy it, are in their 40s and 50s.

★ Sleeping in tents, battling against cold winds, washing in a small basin, enduring icy nights and trekker's food make you realize the true worth of a hot shower. As you pass through villages, expect constant requests for sweets, face cream, pens, and shampoo from these people who have little in the way of modern Western comforts.

Excellent fleece jackets, down parkas, trekking boots, sleeping bags, and general trekking gear can be hired or bought in the Thamel area of Kathmandu far more cheaply than in other countries. You need trekking boots (although I used clogs), fleece sleeping bag liner (available in Kathmandu), rope to lengthen stirrups if you are taking a horse, ski poles (a lot of people seem to use them as walking accessories—although they are unnecessary on a horse), heavy moisturiser in great abundance (the air is cold and very drying to the skin), sunglasses (in the thin air above 3,650m/12,000ft, the sunlight is very bright and UV-proof sunglasses or goggles are an essential).

The flight on the aptly named *Cosmic Air* plane has transported us away from the mundane and we disembark in Jomson to another world—an ancient and remote Buddhist world of *chörtens* and *gompas*, where the tinkling bells of pack-horses, mules, and goatherds take the place of traffic noise and motorbikes; where yak butter tea replaces Nepali *chai*. Somewhere over those mountains, we lost 100 years. This 20-minute plane ride from Pokhara crosses an indefinable boundary that lies somewhere between the fecundity of the lowland plains and foothills and the crisp awesomeness of the high mountains.

While even Pokhara is relatively remote, the main bazaar of Jomson (or Jomoson) is a tiny village, with all traces of the Western world erased. Flat-roofed, Tibetan-style, stone houses line the main street, interspersed with a few simple but pleasant tourist hotels. The smell of wood smoke scents the thin, cold air.

Small and sturdy mountain ponies stand tethered to the few trees and the occasional horsepost that dot the dusty road. Their Tibetan-style carpet saddles add a touch of the exotic to the scene as their owners—wild-looking, mountain men—tout for business. Herds of goats, with bells tinkling in the thin air, pass through the main road accompanied by their human escorts, who whistle and shout instructions. Their backs are daubed with bright colours, one group a fluorescent green, another hot pink, each easily identifiable to their owner. A group of horses loaded down with timber ambles past, on its way to a building site up the trail.

DZONG SAM

Jomson (its name is derived from the old *Dzong Sam*, or New Fort), is located in Lower Mustang, another stop on the millennia-old Kali Gandhaki salt trade route. The river's trail leads to one of the most used of the 12 Nepali passes linking the Tibetan plateau with the Indian plains. Because of the relatively low altitude, the pass remains open for most of the year. Over the centuries, this has allowed swift and relatively large-scale trade of salt, brought down from the marshy salt lakes west of Lhasa and traded for other essential goods along the way. Jomson is the regional administrative centre and also the departure point for all treks and departures to Upper Mustang, higher up the Kali Gandhaki Valley.

We spend the first day here. Having doubled our altitude in the half-hour flight from Pokhara (Jomson is already 2,713m or 8,800ft), we need to spend time acclimatizing. We sit and talk, gazing out of the big picture window onto the street below. The warm and sunny dining room at the Trekker's Lodge is a great place to build up our strength for the trials that lie ahead—a thought to ponder as we eat our way through the menu of potatoes, pasta, and the odd attempt at Mexican or Italian cuisine.

Even after this first day of effortless acclimatizing I find the effects of the change in altitude quite unsettling. Sleepiness is the strongest symptom, combined with feelings of disorientation, lightheadedness, and headaches. The second night is the worst and I awake in the cold darkness hyperventilating and gasping for breath. The symptoms disappear after a few days, but it is essential to allow the body time to adjust before ascending higher. Many factors affect the body's reaction to altitude, including age,

where you normally live, and fitness levels. Smokers generally have a tougher time, although some seem to breeze through without any problem.

The other two in our group, John and Marcie, intend to walk to Mustang, but I want to make the journey in the traditional way—on the back of a horse. Being over 40 and, although reasonably fit, in less than perfect physical shape, I prefer to enjoy the experience rather than try to prove that I am an athlete.

THE GROUP

The size of the groups on this Mustang journey ranges from two to an unwieldy 14 or 15. Our group of three is pleasantly small, which is a distinct advantage. While relationships can be more intense in a smaller group, there are fewer egos to please, which allows for increased flexibility and a better chance of a cultural experience. Two yuppie Buddhists from Washington DC and one writer could be an interesting combination. We are escorted by an underfed bunch of eight porters, Jok the cook (who isn't), and Shiva (pleasant enough, but his Hindu outlook means he has no knowledge of the Buddhist region through which we are travelling).

Getting a horse proves to be a little more complicated than I expected. As it is not part of the tour, I must pay extra for the privilege. I walk around Jomson speaking to different horse owners, but they are not keen to accompany me all the way to Lo Manthang and back for less than a few hundred dollars—an unrealistic price. I decide, on the advice of Shiva, to hire horses day by day from villages along the way.

THE LAST TEA HOUSE— KAGBENI

Our first day of the journey is an easy 3-hour walk along the river bed to Kagbeni, a medieval village that stands at the junction of the Kali Gandaki and Jhong Khola, a smaller tributary. Once a *dzong* (palace fort) ruled the area from the hills above this small trading town, but it succumbed to the powerful rule of Ame Pal from Lo Manthang back in the 15th century.

The narrow cobblestone alleyways and primitive mudbrick houses of the older part of town hint that little has changed over the centuries. Animals are housed in the dark lower storeys, roughly hewn wooden steps lead to the sunnier, human living quarters above. Doorways are decorated with heads of sheep and goats or buffalo skulls—symbols of the B'on Po religion that predates, but still incorporates, Buddhism.

The square, red Kag Chode Thupten Samphel Ling Gompa, a 15th-century Buddhist monastery, stands alongside the Jhong Khola River. The *gompa* was once home to over 150 monks, who came from the surrounding 12 villages. It was active up until the 18th century, but, with money problems and a decreasing interest in traditional culture, the numbers have dropped to about 35 and visitors are requested to pay a "donation" of 100 rupees to help with restoration costs. Across the gorge of the Jhong Khola River, long-disused meditation caves are set high in the eroded cliffs.

Kagbeni is a stop on the Annapurna circuit, a cultural crossroads where traditional inhabitants are outnumbered by

trekkers, guides, porters, and adventurers of all descriptions. The tea houses make great meeting places and tables are filled with Goretex-and Polartec-clad trekkers telling colourful tales of their exploits as they slurp down endless bowls of trekker's food—tomato soup, chips, steaming bowlfuls of spaghetti, and pancakes. Several groups are heading for Mustang and it looks as if it's going to be a busy trail.

At the edge of town a big sign in English marks the beginning of the restricted area. Trekkers come to gaze at the view up the Kali Gandaki Valley to the endless, barren mountains that characterize Upper Mustang. The police post stands near by and we stop in to have our permits checked before proceeding further.

INTO THE FORBIDDEN KINGDOM

There is nothing like starting a journey on a high note. The trail out of Kagbeni leads straight uphill through loose gravel.

There are two paths to Chele, our destination that day. In the drier months, most locals follow the flat river bed, a far easier walk than the path that the tour groups take, along the hills. Shiva, a mountain man himself, doesn't appear to notice the difference between a flat surface and an almost perpendicular incline. He just keeps plugging on, oblivious to the tortured gasps of his group.

After lunch the wind comes up strongly. Each day, regular as clockwork, it starts up at midday, whistling through the deep gorges as it surges down to the heated plains far below. Although the air is clean, the wind carries copious amounts of dust, and we wrap our faces in scarves and bandanas as a precaution.

On the first night all the groups stay at Chele, a small village high above the Kali Gandaki. The hillside hamlet blossoms into a tented camp for the night, as every flat surface flowers with blue tents, baskets, and backpacks. Groups of porters busy themselves setting up tents and the tables and chairs they have carried on their backs all day. Dark shelters echo with the noisy hiss of kerosene pressure stoves as the cooks get to work preparing their group's dinner.

Far left: *Young monks studying at Mustang*
Left: *Ancient* chörten *(Buddhist shrines) dot the mountainside, marking boundaries and holy places*
Below: *Prayer flags dance in the thin, cold wind*

NEPAL

THE MINIMUM IMPACT CODE

Go gently in an area where the culture is as strong as the environment is fragile.

❑ **Travel ecologically** In Upper Mustang horses and ponies are traditionally used both for transportation and as pack animals. The local people are not really used to accommodating porters. To maintain tradition and to minimize the environmental burden created by porters, it is recommended that ponies be used instead.

❑ **Protect wildlife** Owing to the limited carrying capacity of the desert environment, wildlife densities in Upper Mustang are very low. Species include the snow leopard and wild ass. It is illegal to interfere with wildlife or their habitat in any manner, or to purchase any item made of rare or endangered animal parts. Please respect the fragile ecology of the area by refraining from walking on vegetation or collecting plants and flowers.

LIFE ON THE TRAIL

I wake in the freezing cold morning to a cheery call of "water ready." A bowl of warm water is the day's bathing option. I emerge reluctantly from the warmth of my almost adequate sleeping bag and the doubtful comfort of my blue tent to a beautiful clear sky. Minutes later a cup of tea (*chai*) appears, heralding another carbohydrate-rich breakfast. This sort of trekking brings a new appreciation of any luxury. Life follows a regimented order, with no time or energy for diversions. Wake up, get up, wash (the face and possibly feet), breakfast, pack, toilet, then start the day's journey. Whether you are walking or riding, you need to concentrate your energies for the physical tasks ahead.

In addition to acclimatizing to the altitude, our bodies need to adjust to the new demands of strenuous walking in high places. An hour or two of exercise a week does not prepare you mentally for constant motion and extra physical effort. After initial shock, each day sees an increase in physical endurance and mental power as the relationship between body and mind strengthens.

Interesting things happen to you when you're walking in the thin, cold, air. As one American woman said "ten days of trekking is better than five years on the (analyst's) couch." With none of the diversions and distractions that make up our everyday lives, the mind clears. The great spaces of the mountains allow time to reflect, even as one's perceptions heighten. Cynics will put it down to the low air pressure, but it is possibly a result, too, of the vast silence and space that you encounter along the way.

TASHI DELEK

You meet a surprising number of people on the trail. Sheep herders bring their animals down to Jomson en route to the markets of Pokhara. Groups of pilgrims pass by, and local Lo people make short journeys between towns. Government officials ride proudly by on their horses, importantly bound on secret missions. Then there are the groups of porters, liaison officers for the trekking groups, mule packs, and the tourists themselves, heading towards Mustang, or happily returning, their minds filled with visions of hot showers and chocolate. Somewhere along the path, the greeting of the trail changes form the Nepali/Hindu *namaste* to *tashi delek*, the universal greeting used in Tibetan-speaking lands.

Having the luxury of a 13-day permit, we travel more slowly than the majority of the groups, stopping each day after 4 or 5 hours' trek. This allows us the opportunity to explore some of the hamlets and *gompas* along the way.

One of the most enjoyable days of the trip starts with the walk from Chele to Samar—a 3-or 4-hour journey. I leave ahead of the others, following the porters along the rocky path, high above a magnificent deep gorge to a pass at 3,480m (11,400ft). The sunlit morning air is completely still, and the only sound in the otherwise vast silence is the tinkling bells of the grazing horses and sheep on farmland across the steep river valley.

Descending along an easy trail into the tiny township, I come across a group of village women. Dressed in their traditional *chupa* (Tibetan dress) and striped woollen aprons, they stand in a field, winnowing the buckwheat, millet, and wheat that form their basic diet. Behind them, the snow-capped peaks of the Himalaya look down benignly. As they winnow, they make a thin whistling sound, calling the wind to help separate the grains. I immediately go and sit by them, revelling in this archaic but idyllic pastoral scene, enjoying a well-deserved rest and feelings of great well-being in the warm midday sun.

ALWAYS THE MOUNTAINS

The huge scale of the landscape dwarfs any attempts at human endeavour. While it seems that we have journeyed many miles, each time we reach a pass or stop for a rest and look around, the towering snow-capped peaks of Nilgiri and Dhaulagiri are there, mocking our puny efforts with their grandeur.

Two of the passes we ascend are almost 4,000m (13,120ft) high. The last high pass, the Nyi La at 3,950m (12,960ft),

marks the southern boundary of what constitutes the ancient Lo Kingdom.

At this pass travellers have built up a huge cairn of stones, chanting the words "*so soh*,"(good luck), "*lha–ghyalo*" (may the gods win). We meet with a breathtaking panorama: deeply eroded gorges and bare peaks, bearing a more than a passing similarity to the Grand Canyon, reach as far as the eye can see, with no sign of life to alleviate the tedium—just the chill, whistling wind and endless space. For a moment, just a moment, I stand and ask myself "what on earth am I doing here?" But like most moments, it passes, to be replaced with a new acceptance of this alien environment.

Once again I feel comfortable, and, sitting astride my sturdy horse with the ridiculously short stirrups that bring my knees almost up to my chin, jockey style, we make our way down to Ghame, one of the larger towns in Mustang.

THE LONGEST MANI WALL

Passing through the village of Ghame, we come to what is probably the longest *mani* wall in Nepal. Over 100m (330ft) long, this prayer wall is painted in earthy greys, terracottas, and creams. The pigment is taken directly from the clay-rich cliffs near by.

This *mani* wall has been in existence for centuries, dating back to the days

FOOD AND DRINK

One of the important ways to avoid stomach problems is to wash your hands before each meal. Another important point to remember is—never drink tap water. Always ensure it is boiled or treated before use. Eat only freshly cooked food. Never consume food that has been exposed for some time.

Trekking companies provide all food during treks, except for the nights spent in Kagbeni and Jomson. Although guests have some choice in their food, cooks favour high carbohydrate foods (pancakes, potatoes, chappati, and fried foods). I had to demand fresh vegetables and no amount of asking brought fresh meat, although it was sometimes available in the villages.

A few extra food supplies can relieve the culinary boredom. Salamis/sausage, yak cheese, and dried beef jerky (an excellent brand is available in some Thamel supermarkets) all work well while nuts, dried fruits, and muesli bars make good, reviving snacks. During the autumn months, delicious fresh apples can be purchased along the way.

when Guru Rimpoche first brought
Buddhism and the tantra to Tibet. The
wall is built up of flat rocks engraved with
the universal Tibetan mantra *om mani
padme hung* or the invocation *om
benza-guru-pema-sete-hung*.

Ghame's *mani* wall is the first of the
numerous Buddhist monuments, *chort-
ens*, and prayer walls that we pass along
the way–although few are as spectacular
as this one. They dot the wayside, marking boundaries and holy passes,
containing within them holy relics of
lamas and ancient religious texts.

INTO LO MANTHANG

The last day's trail from Tsarang into Lo
Manthang seems one of endless expecta-
tion. So many times we reach a high point
and look eagerly down, but see only more
mountains and rough trails, with no sign
of the ancient kingdom.

Then, finally, we hit the last pass. The
trail broadens to a wide, flat plain and a
trail the size of a normal road—a great
ride for a good horseman. My reluctant
steed refuses to make anything more than
a slow trot—possibly the world's most
uncomfortable gait and certainly, for a
not-too-experienced rider with short stirrups, not a gait to be encouraged. With
great relief on my part (and, no doubt, on
the part of the horse) he lapses back into a
relaxed walk and we make our way excitedly into the ancient walled city of Lo.

My first impression of Lo Manthang is
one of dismay. Have I journeyed for days
only to arrive at an overburdened tourist
trap? Conspicuously dressed in bright
reds and blues, a group of European
tourists wanders through the ancient
capital, clicking cameras in unison at
everything in sight. It is a fine and quite
embarrassing example of a cultural colli-
sion, but fortunately it lasts only minutes
before the group moves on.

As they move off, the true nature of
the town begins to assert itself. Men and

Above: *Kali Gandaki valley bathed in late afternoon sunshine*
Top inset: *My guides were always friendly*
Middle inset: *Freshly painted prayer wheels*
Bottom inset: *Saddling up*

took over the village of Lo Manthang. He became the first king, building a strong fort (*dzong*) overlooking the town. He founded a dynasty that can be directly traced through 25 successions to the present king, and established fortress towns and monasteries in a kingdom that, at its peak, stretched along the Kali Gandhaki as far south as Muktinath.

As the Gorkas united the numerous principalities and feudal kingdoms of medieval Nepal during the 17th century, Mustang became part of that country, although its armies never entered the kingdom. The king (or raja) maintained his title and a degree of autonomy until 1951, when Mustang was incorporated more closely into Nepal.

Mustang gained some notoriety in the 1960s when the Tibetan Kampa guerrillas used it as a base in the warfare against the invading Chinese in Tibet. The region was closed until 1991. Even today, the Nepalese presence in Mustang is little more than cosmetic.

Many pleasant hours can be spent exploring the narrow streets of the ancient town. Three ancient *gompas*, Champa Lha Ghang, Thubchen Lha Ghang, and Chhoedhe Gompa date back to the 15th century. While both Champa and Thugchen are at present undergoing a much-needed renovation, Chhoedhe is very much in use. It is also the home to a monastic school for young monks.

women sit in the late afternoon sun in the main square. Some spin their prayer wheels, absorbed in their task of sending prayers heavenwards. Others spin rough yak wool into single threads, to be used later for weaving bags, and other necessities. The majority sit quietly relaxing, engaging in desultory chat.

For centuries, Lo Manthang marked the border of Ngari, or Western Tibet, a region that swept from from Lo and Dolpo in the east as far as Ladakh in the west. It dominated the salt trade route along the Kali Gandaki, overseeing and taxing goods ferried between Tibet and India. This remote area was long part of Tibet, with the main cultural and religious inspiration coming from Lhasa.

In 1380 the Tibetan warlord Ame Pal

LOCAL CUSTOMS

- ❑ Do not remove any religious artifact from the area.
- ❑ Respect local customs in your dress and behaviour. Women should wear skirts not shorts or revealing shirts; men should always wear shirts.
- ❑ Avoid outward displays of affection.
- ❑ Nudity is strictly prohibited.
- ❑ Ask permission before taking photographs and respect people's rights to privacy. Try not to be intrusive.
- ❑ Do not give anything to beggars unless they are genuine religious mendicants.
- ❑ Encourage young Nepalis to be proud of their culture.
- ❑ Remember that your trip has a great impact on the natural environment and on the people who live off its resources.
- ❑ Don't put your hands or lips on communal food plates or drink containers; don't offer used food off your plate—it is considered *jutho* or contaminated, and is unacceptable.

BACK TO JOMSON

The trip back to Kagbeni was faster than our trip in and, as we neared the end, much sadder. It is a special privilege to be able to enter a place so remote and untouched by the modern world. Even though a large percentage of the Mustang population now leave the towns during the winter months, journeying south to Pokhara, to Kathmandu or further afield to northern India, they retain their traditional culure and beliefs. Visiting as I did, you would not be aware that the population empties during the time of snows.

After letting the others go on ahead, I sit down to gaze one last time at the now familiar landscape. As I sit, two figures clothed in black make their way up the steep hill, walking fast. It is two villagers from Lo Manthang, Dolma Tsering and her mother, whose fitness at the age of 65 would leave most Westerners gasping.

They stop to sit for a minute and I give them an apple then take pictures, promising to send them to Lo Manthang for their spring return. They are on their way south, to spend their winter months in Kathmandu. After sitting for a while they stand up, quickly stride away, their dark robes flapping in the breeze as they disappear over the hill and out of sight, my last vision of this magical land.

Strangely, Jomson seems much changed after our 14-day absence. Accustomed now to the tiny hamlets of Upper Mustang, we find that what had appeared as a small hamlet on first encounter has grown to the size of a minor metropolis. Apart from the airport, there are shops, restaurants, hotels, horses, telecommunications, and a quiet bustling air of commerce. Tibetan people from the nearby refugee camp trade goods and souvenirs, and tourists are there in numbers. We have arrived back in "civilization."

SAFETY TIPS

Watch where you are walking With the rocky trails, it is necessary to spend a lot of time looking at your feet to avoid slipping, stumbling or falling down. This is just one more good reason to take a horse.

Acute Mountain Sickness When the body has insufficient time to acclimatize to a higher altitude, symptoms such as dizziness, headaches, sleepiness, loss of appetite, fatigue, disorientation, shortness of breath, loss of balance, and hyperventilation may occur in the early stages. It can happen to anyone at heights over 2,500m (8,200ft). A dry cough may also develop (the Nepali cough.)

The only treatment is to give the body time to acclimatize. If symptoms appear, don't ascend until they disappear. If they persist or worsen, it may be necessary to descend until the symptoms disappear. The drug Diomox is helpful in lessening the symptoms, as long as they are not too severe.

GOING IT ALONE

INTERNAL TRAVEL

As this is a restricted zone, every departure must be in a group. The smallest acceptable size is two.

A Mustang journey is expensive, whichever way you look at it, and this is on top of the flight to Kathmandu.

Permits can be arranged for 10 days, for $700. This allows enough time for a fast walk in and out and a visit to the ancient capital.

For a 13–15 day permit, there is an additional charge of $70 per day.

Expect to pay around $1,000 for the compulsory government liaison officer who must accompany each departing group.

Then a trekking company will charge from $50 upwards per day for the entire trip, probably starting from Kathmandu.

Airfares to Pokhara and Jomson and back to Kathmandu will cost another $232.

WHEN TO GO

The Trekking season operates from late March to early November, although by November you can see the snows moving closer and the winds are chill.

FINDING A TREKKING COMPANY

With access to the Internet, it is quite easy to find out what different companies are offering. The prices seem to vary as much as the quality of the services. You can arrange your itinerary, dates, and all those basics over the Internet before leaving.

For Mustang, while it is possible to pick up a group on arriving in Kathmandu, it is worth doing at least a little preliminary investigating before leaving. The best option is to put together your own group.

HEALTH MATTERS

Most of the following will prove useful, even if you don't take a fully stocked medical kit.

Take water purifying tablets (although your porters will give you freshly boiled water it can be greasy, tasting like weak dishwater). It is far better to take water from unpolluted streams where possible and treat it. Buy the two-part pills that neutralize the taste of the iodine. Take scissors, tweezers, bandages/dressings/plasters, blister pads, aspirin, sewing needle/thread, antiseptic/antibiotic cream.

The following medicines can easily be bought in Kathmandu at one of the pharmacies in Thamel.

❏ **Diamox** reduces the symptoms of AMS. Acetazolamide can prevent mild cases of AMS by increasing the respiratory rate. It also reduces the accompanying nausea and headaches.
❏ **Paracetamol/Disprin**—for altitude headaches.
❏ **Sudafed**—for sinus.
❏ **Antibiotics** sinus, ear, bronchial, urinary tract, etc can all be treated with Norofloxacin 400mg (good for dysentery and urinary tract infections) or Azithromycin 250mg—a one-dose-a-day drug

(for 5 days) also suitable for penicillin allergic patients.
❏ **Metoclopramide** 10mg—for relief of vomiting and nausea (these proved to be very useful for one of our group)
❏ **rehydration salts** (almost a necessity)
❏ **Tinidazole** 500mg—an antibiotic effective for several stomach complaints including *giardia* and *amoebic* attacks.
❏ **Immodium**—good if you need to travel and you have a bad stomach.
❏ **Mycostatin** (vaginal pessaries)—infections can flare up after completing a course of antibiotics.

WHAT TO TAKE

Clothes
❏ Trekking boots.
❏ Warm jacket (layering is best—a sleeveless fleece vest and a down jacket are good).
❏ Gloves (Polartec or thick fleece).
❏ Hat/balaclava.
❏ Windproof outer trousers.
❏ Woollen/fleece socks.
❏ Thermal underwear.
❏ Good UV sunglasses.
❏ Day pack.
❏ Sweater.
❏ T-shirts.
❏ Two pairs of trousers.

Others
❏ Torch (for reading in your tent and nighttime toilet excursions.)
❏ Water bottle and purifying tablets.
❏ Extra batteries.
❏ Sunblock.
❏ Lipchap stick.
❏ Heavy moisturiser (the air is cold and very dry).
❏ A good book.
❏ Camera, plenty of film, polarising filter, UV filter (for the mountains).
❏ First-aid kit.
❏ Extra food.

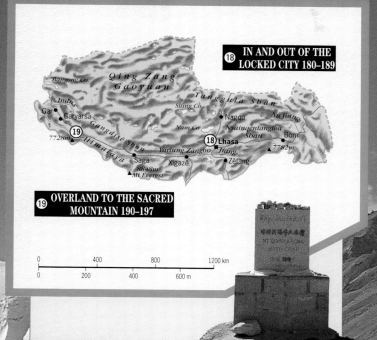

TIBET

Flanked by the Himalaya and Kunlun mountains, the Tibetan plateau is one of the highest places on Earth, where Mount Everest shows its glorious face, and passes soar to more than 5,000m (16,400ft). It takes a special kind of traveller to set foot in this fascinating, windswept desert, curved by green valleys and sand dunes, and where nomads roam with herds of yak, sheep, and goat. Throughout Tibet, there exists an undercurrent of myths and legends sought by worshippers who make pilgrimages to its sacred lakes and mountains. Buddhism is the philosophy, and paintings, stupas, and scriptures are treasured in hill-top, golden-roofed monasteries run by the few monks that still practise here.

Lhasa is the modern commercial, trade and sightseeing hub, yet little of its origins as the forbidden city of the Buddhist Kingdom remains. Again, it takes a determined traveller to slip beneath the skin of what's new to glimpse a way of life that is rapidly disappearing.

The road to Mount Everest, on the border between Tibet and Nepal

18 In and Out of the Locked City

by Lee Karen Stow

Lhasa, historically the forbidden city, a locked kingdom within the land of snow, is open to tourists at a price. I squeezed through the heavy presence of the Chinese military and became lost in the throng of pilgrims, on a rigorous, compelling, and often nerve-wracking adventure in the Tibetan capital.

Known in the Tibetan language as the ground of the gods, Lhasa sits on the north bank of the Kyi Chu River, in the province of Ü. It was seventh-century King Songtsen Gampo who introduced Buddhism to Tibet. He created a palace on the site of the present Potala Palace, the famous cream and red fortress that once housed successive Dalai Lamas, neither elected presidents nor hereditary monarchs, but manifestations of Avolakitesvara.

The Dalai Lama line can be traced back to a nephew of 14th-century monk Tsongkhapa, who was recognized as an incarnation of Avalokitesvara, the Bodhisattva of Compassion. A bodhisattva is a person who delays reaching the state of nirvana in order to help other beings: the present Dalai Lama, Tenzin Gyatso, is said to be the 74th manifestation of Avalokitesvara.

All this is in a confusing nutshell; and, as you progress through Tibetan temples and bite at the country's history a piece at a time, it becomes even more bewildering. And that's without the added myths and legends.

What is clear is that in 1950 the Chinese Army invaded Tibet in what they say was a "peaceful liberation." Communism was enforced, suppressing the Buddhist religion, and the Dalai Lama and his government were forced to flee to exile in India. In 1965 the Tibetan Autonomous Region (TAR) was founded, dragging Tibet further into the claws of the Motherland.

With the lure of get-rich-quick schemes in the early 1980s and an increase in tourism, Chinese Han immigrants arrived in great numbers, swelling Tibet's population. A new, Chinese town encroached on Lhasa's Tibetan architecture and much of the old "Shangri-La" disappeared, to be replaced by concrete squares, office blocks of steel and reflective glass, and security cameras perched on religious sites. What used to be sacred is now on show, at a cost, to tourists. Olive-green uniformed military direct traffic, keep eyes on everyone, or sprawl lazily outside noodle restaurants, having shoes polished and puffing on cigarettes.

 Physically demanding, high-altitude trekking at up to 5,200m (17,000ft) is not for the faint-hearted. Performing *koras* around Lhasa's monasteries is not difficult, but altitude may affect energy and health. High-altitude cycling over mountain passes and bad roads, coupled with dust, intense sunlight, and no recovery services, requires a good degree of stamina.

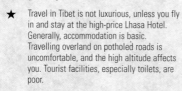 Travel in Tibet is not luxurious, unless you fly in and stay at the high-price Lhasa Hotel. Generally, accommodation is basic. Travelling overland on potholed roads is uncomfortable, and the high altitude affects you. Tourist facilities, especially toilets, are poor.

 Take good-quality hiking and camping gear. If you are going to cycle, choose a mountain bike, which grips the roads better than a trail bike.

Into the land of snow

The 1-hour flight to Lhasa got off to an incredible start. The China South West Airline plane rose quickly over the smog belt of Kathmandu in Nepal, leaving behind green folds of pine valleys draped with waterfalls and heading towards a tremendous bird's-eye view of the snowy Himalaya range. Its anchor, Mount Everest, materialized to the left, seemingly level with the wing tip, its well-conquered summit cutting a white, imperfect, inverted V shape out of a thick blue sky. I was lucky. I had a clear view from my envied position, seat A next to the window (if you are flying back from Lhasa, ask the check-in clerk for seat F).

Touchdown came quickly at the military-manned, shiny Gongkar Airport terminal, Everest disappeared behind the tail, and I joined a long queue for immigration. Passengers drank mineral water and popped painkillers to cope with the headaches caused by the sudden ascent to 3,680m (12,074ft). I stood obediently in line, reading a list of 12 rules to which visitors must adhere while in the People's Republic of China.

A tough way in

Generally, to visit Lhasa you must travel in a group on a tour approved by the Chinese government. It is possible to wander Tibet independently, but you need a lot of time, a neat plan of entry, the knack of sorting out your own red tape, and luck. And even then you cannot be guaranteed entry. As my time was limited I had gone for the straightforward option and signed up with a travel agency in Kathmandu for what they told me would be a "fly-in, drive-out" tour, accompanying four others in a Land Cruiser. At the end of the tour, we would return overland by vehicle to the Nepalese border.

Imagine my horror when I emerged through immigration at Lhasa to find myself stuck with 27 tourists dangling cameras round their necks. In unison they all bowed to an unconvincing welcome from a gum-chewing Tibetan tour guide, who hurriedly threw *katahs*, white scarves used for special occasions, around our necks. "Welcome to Tibet," she mumbled, before herding us onto a coach and picking up a microphone to jabber about the wonderful surfaced road from the airport and how, because rice cannot be grown this high, the Tibetan farmers grow barley instead. I was panic-stricken. I always travel independently, not like a sheep. Almost choking from the *katah*, I refused to hop off for a "photo opportunity, everybody!" of a painted Buddha on the side of a rock obscured by electricity cables. I had to escape.

Everyone told me it would be impossible. I was on a group visa and no one can split from a group. Next morning, I declined a sightseeing tour and knocked on the door of the Chinese doctor at the hotel. "I'm not well," I announced. The doctor clasped my wrist, agreed my pulse was racing and diagnosed exhaustion and altitude sickness. He advised me to rest and fly back to Lhasa instead of travelling overland, and wrote an official letter. I was taken off the group visa, but not before handing over an extra $228 for a flight ticket, $80 fine for an individual visa, and an assurance to the Tibetan director of the government-run tour agency that I would not talk to monks or discuss politics, and that I would inform them of my whereabouts at all times.

Within reason, I was free to wander. So, after rest and recuperation, I switched hotels, turning my back on a swimming pool, and a room with towelling slippers and cable television at the Lhasa Hotel in the Chinese karaoke part of town. Instead I took a dormitory bed with dirty sheets at the Snowlands Hotel. It may seem a daft thing to do, but Snowlands sits in the Tibetan part of Lhasa known as the Barkhor, strides from the Jokhang, Tibet's spiritual heart. It is also heavily frequented by other Western travellers in search of company and companions for trekking and cycling. Not surprisingly, the most talked-about

destination is Everest and the most visited site is the Potala Palace, for centuries the seat of the Dalai Lamas.

To the Potala Palace

The Potala Palace was named after Mount Potala in India. The fifth Dalai Lama began the present structure in 1645. He died before it was finished, but his death was kept a secret for more than a decade, until completion in 1694.

Despite new, sun-reflecting office skyscrapers and banks, the Potala and its 13 storeys cannot be dwarfed. At night, no lights shine from its windows, behind which are around 1,000 rooms and more than 30 chapels. Noticeably, the Potala is no longer a functioning monastery, rather a tourist attraction with the atmosphere of an abandoned mausoleum. Its treasures—stupas (shrines), *thangkas* (silk wall hangings), and gold tombs of past Dalai Lamas—are mostly behind glass partitions. Those monks who still wander the labyrinth, in and out of the queues of shuffling pilgrims, are caretakers, wiping away dust, clipping charred candlewicks, and refilling butter lamps.

Some monks are spies, confided our guide nervously, before pleading with us not to ask political questions as her answers would be monitored. Oh, and if

Top: *Potala seen through the prayer flags from Chokpuri Medicine Hill*
Above: *Copper-coloured prayer wheels line the walls of the Potala Palace*

we wanted to take photos inside, it would cost 90 yuan ($10) each. Even without such warning, one feels a sense of uneasiness while filing through the Potala corridors with their plastic knee-high litter bins in the shape of black-and-white Chinese pandas. We were allowed to take photos only on the roof, where you are invited to don a hideously fake Tibetan costume and be photographed against the golden eaves.

Performing the Kora

One morning, slabs of raw yak meat were being piled on market stalls in the shadow of the Potala, while Tibetan women tested the freshness of yak butter by carving off a knob from yellow oblongs.

Through the busyness, pilgrims carried rosary beads, counting prayers by rubbing a bead through thumb and finger, as they began the *kora*, a clockwise circumambulation around the palace. I followed, along a corridor flanked by stallholders selling plastic flip-flops and acrylic cardigans. Copper-coloured prayer wheels were fastened in a continuous row to wooden brackets under a sloping tin roof that kept off the rain. Cylinders contain prayers written on parchment and when spun on their butter-greased axis, the prayers are repeated countless times.

At first I turned every wheel, then every other one, spinning over the heads of beggars who sat in the dirt underneath, holding out grubby yuan notes and wanting more. Two monks, resplendent in saffron robes, chanted in unison, and a stonecarver displayed rows of flint-sized *mani* stones bearing the Tibetan mantra *om mani padme hum* (Hail the Jewel in the Lotus). A gap appeared in the wall to the left, revealing a grassy patch on which a woman squatted openly to urinate.

SUMMER'S RETREAT

The biggest shock for me, second to the mummifying of the Potala, was the Norbulingka (meaning Jewel Park), known as the Summer Palace of the Dalai

Above: *Norbulingka, where the 14th Dalai Lama hid to escape from the Chinese army in 1959*

Lamas. The seventh Dalai Lama built the first Summer Palace in 1755 and began the annual tradition of vacating the Potala by way of a grand procession of monks, musicians, and splendidly dressed aristocracy and dignitaries.

In his autobiography, *Freedom in Exile* (published by Little, Brown & Co., U.K.), the 14th Dalai Lama remembers: "The day I quit my gloomy room in the Potala was undoubtedly one of my favourite during the whole year. It began with a ceremony that lasted for 2 hours (which seemed like an eternity to me). Then came the great procession, which I did not much care for. I would rather have walked and enjoyed the countryside, whose fresh outpourings of natural beauty were just beginning to show themselves in delicate shoots of green."

It was from the Norbulingka that His Holiness the 14th Dalai Lama escaped the Chinese army, disguised as a soldier, in 1959. His private rooms, dominated by his ceremonial seats, audience throne, and wireless set are well-kept. Pilgrims pile yuan notes at the foot of his robe, wrapped in a cone as though a magician has waved a wand to make him vanish.

183

TIBET

FOOD AND DRINK

Tsampa is the staple food of Tibet and is barley flour mixed with butter. It is not only eaten, but also given as offerings in temples. *Chang* is an alcoholic drink made from fermented barley. The most popular drink among the locals is yak butter tea, churned in a long wooden tube with added salt. It's greasy and an acquired taste. Yaks also are responsible for hard yak cheese, dried yak meat (which keeps for months), and sharp yak yogurt. At restaurants, Chinese noodle and stir fry meals are common, though the Tibetan specialities of vegetable or yak meat *momos* (steamed or fried dumplings) with a dish of soy sauce, or *thugpa* (noodle soup with meat or vegetables) are delicious.

For an entrance fee of 25 yuan ($3), you enter the Norbulingka through an arch that punctures a faded perimeter wall to what the Chinese have turned into a public park. In reality, it's a landscape of dilapidated gardens and palaces, many of which are locked, and a horrifying zoo of bears and wildcats confined to tiny cages. A fountain trickles into a basin scattered with torn entrance tickets. In one temple the throne of the 13th Dalai Lama is flanked by sawn-off plastic cola bottles stuffed with marigolds, and upright Chinese vases filled with fake flowers underneath Christmas tree baubles.

INTO LHASA'S HEART

A fraction of the old Tibet still breathes at the gold-roofed Jokhang temple. This is the holiest shrine in Tibet because it harbours an image of Sakyamuni, the historical Buddha. Monks wearing deep-red robes struck up a chorus of music on drums and horns on the arrival of tourists. Others polished butter lamps or hand-moulded crimson butter statues.

There is not much left of the structure's seventh-century origins, save a few carved pillars and arches. There is however, an array of religious sculptures, paintings of guardian kings, deities, and historical figures who left their mark on Tibet: the Guru Rinpoche (an 8th-century Indian Buddhist master, who helped establish Buddhism in Tibet) and Tsongkhapa (14th founder of the Gelukpa sect of Tibetan Buddhism, of which the present Dalai Lama is one). Throughout the day, pilgrims trace the Jokhang's labyrinth, mumbling or prostrating on the paved slabs, worn smooth from centuries of devotion. From the Jokhang's ornate roof, you glance down over shaven heads of monks as they slide spread-eagle on the floor in worship.

AROUND THE BARKHOR

Circling the Jokhang is the famous Barkhor Circuit, another *kora* and an octagonal parade of activity from dawn until dusk. I didn't have a choice about not walking this *kora*, as I was promptly carried along with the throng. I was accidentally hit in the face by a spinning prayer wheel and I had my nose squashed up against a Tibetan woman's extensive headdress. It dripped with turquoise stones, nuggets of pure blue set on strands of pink cloth that were wrapped within her black plaits. The Barkhor is the main commercial hub for the Tibetans. It has changed markedly over the years: where once Tibetans sold yak butter, horse saddles, and sunflower seeds, Chinese traders have set up stalls to hawk fake turquoise and coral, souvenir daggers, jewellery, fluffy slippers, and wolfskin hats.

TAKING THE BUS TO DREPUNG

Next day I caught a rickety bus to Drepung Monastery. Founded in 1416 as one of the largest of the monasteries belonging to the Gelukpa sect and at one time supporting more than 7,000 monks, Drepung lies 8km (5 miles) west of Lhasa. I lost count of the scores of monks spilling from a temple, beckoning me to follow them, but there are nowhere near as many now as there were originally.

First I performed the *kora*, climbing up pale sandy boulders, my feet in time to the rhythm of birdsong. A monk, robed in maroon, led the way up the path. We rested by a stream where a woman was washing sweaters. I offered the monk dried papaya. He then sped on his way, his sandals flapping, while I continued, passing strings of prayer flags and piles of pebbles left by pilgrims as offerings.

Drepung *kora* is no tough hike; it is rather pleasurable. Afterwards, I wound my way round the medieval alleyways of the monastery until I came across a trio of monks figuring out how best to slice through a gnarled tree root. They had already created an impressive wall of chopped logs in preparation for Tibet's cold winter. Around the corner, a flock of monks flitted along the path. "Come, come...this way," they beckoned. I followed through passageways, under archways, skipping down stone steps and up a wooden stairway to a temple porch where a colony of discarded shoes was arranged in pairs. Melodious chanting drifted from a doorway hung with thick fabric, and held me spellbound until I felt like an intruder and turned to leave.

OUT TO GANDEN

Many travellers hire a Land Cruiser or take a public bus (it leaves at dawn) from Lhasa for Ganden Monastery, regarded as the finest monastic complex outside town. Its focal point is the silver and golden tomb of Tsongkhapa. The tomb which contains only a few of his remains as his body and its original tomb were destroyed during the Chinese Cultural Revolution of 1966 to 1976, launched by Mao Zedong (Tse Tung). Mao's Red Guards worked the Tibetans into a frenzy to bring about the destruction of dozens of religious sites.

Trekkers use Ganden as the starting point for a 4-day Ganden–Samye trek, a difficult route of around 80km (50 miles) that crosses two 5,000m (16,400ft) passes and connects Ganden with

another important monastery, 1,200-year-old Samye. The road to Ganden spans a river and runs through Tibetan farmsteads, away from a Potala that floats on the horizon like a ship at sea. In villages, yak heads hang over doorways of houses with off-white walls that slope inwardly to a thatch of brushwood. Farmers with pitchforks heap straw into piles, tractors putter along, and donkeys balance bulging saddlebags.

The Land Cruiser I had hired for a day trip dodged black pigs, cows, children, and wagons loaded with logs until it turned right, up a rubble path that swerved in hairpins to where Ganden sits cradled in the hillside at 4,500m (14,764ft). To me, the monastery's buildings of varying shapes, in ochre, pink, white, and fawn, resembled faculties of a great university.

WRATHFUL DEITIES AND BLUE BODIES

Inside Ganden Monastery, a hothouse of Tibetan government until it moved to the Potala, a monk gave me an impromptu tour of the Main Assembly Hall, an atmospheric interior of 108 columns soaring to lacquered beams festooned with silk. He pointed to a sculpture of Tsongkhapa, and on the back walls he ran a finger over the vibrant colours of Vajrapani, the Bodhisattva of Energy, found on many a monastic wall. Vajrapani wears a tiger skin around his blue-black body, holds the flaming red of a thunderbolt, and sports an eye in his forehead. Another wall depicts Mahakala, a protector deity who clutches a tiara of laughing skulls and a skull cap with fangs as pointed as his own. Shri Devi, protector of Lhasa, is also blue, wears a tigerskin cloak, and rides a beast of a horse. I remembered the awesomness of these mythical creatures a few days later as I gazed up at another beauty—the highest in the world.

EVEREST BASE CAMP

From Lhasa, you can go on a drive to Everest Base Camp, pausing at Tingri,

TIBET

where you can drive on or do a three–four day trek to the mountain. As we rolled along in our Land Cruisers behind a line of donkeys, heading for Tingri, we watched lightning slash through navy clouds in the distance, with the Himalayas running along the horizon to the right. It rained heavily, so our group of five abandoned camp and knocked on the door of a Tibetan guesthouse. The lady of the house, whose black plaits were inter-twined with purple threads, hung a paraffin lamp in the window, turning darkness into cosiness.

The restaurant-tearoom was also her family's kitchen, lounge, and bedroom. Its walls seemed to hug the three long seats that framed the room, thick with woven rugs. Rows of Thermos flasks stood on a shelf, next to a chest painted with white lotus flowers.

The road winds away from Tingri to a single track, cutting through the rubble and pale terracotta boulders that is the Qomolangma National Nature Reserve. Yaks with shaggy black coats pull tufts of grass from the glacial jumble.

Finally, Everest's Tibetan face rises into view at a staggering 8,850m (29,035ft). I saw her block the valley like a gorilla, her brow frowning and shoulders hunched as if protecting her root to the ground. Snow plumes puffed around her ears in a vision so grand and intimidating I nicknamed her King Kong's mother.

Unlike the mountain's Nepalese face, Everest in Tibet stands in striking isola-tion, as though broken free of her Himalayan neighbours. We milled around the Base Camp (5,200m/17,060ft), know-ing that somewhere up on those treacherous slopes a team of Spanish mountaineers had reached Base Camp Three, halfway to the summit.

In 1953 Edmund Hillary and Sherpa Tenzing, part of a British expedition led by John Hunt, were the first climbers to conquer Everest. Since then scores of climbers have succeeded or perished. Many of them set out from where we stood, a patch strewn with rocks and a

lonely place to spend the night. A Queen of Spades playing card, cracked photo film canisters, ring pulls from lemonade cans, discarded cigarette butts, and rusty soup tin lids lay among the pebbles.

Behind us stood Rongbuk (or Rongphu) Monastery, perhaps the highest on Earth. Established in 1902, the monastery was completely destroyed during the Cultural Revolution. Once there were 300 monks and nuns here; now there are 10 monks and 21 nuns. Their spiritual leader fled to Nepal. Over the past decade, parts of the monastery have been restored and painted brightly with images of buddhas and protective deities. Two nuns wearing deep russet robes, beaded bracelets, and woolly hats giggled at us; one kneaded in her hands a ball of *tsampa*, the staple food of Tibetans, made with barley flour. A bowl of juniper smouldered in the courtyard, sending spirals of incense into the air.

BIKING OUT OF LHASA

Everest Base Camp is a stop-off point on what is probably the roughest, toughest,

Far left: The ornate, gold-roofed Jokhang temple, Tibet's holiest shrine, was built in the seventh century, although little of the original structure remains
Above: Monks at Jokhang temple greet visitors with music
Left: The endless knot, depicted on Jokhang's roof, is a common symbol in Tibet and symbolizes time, harmony, and love entwined

and most exhilarating trip out of Lhasa: by bicycle, on the 920km (575-mile) route to the Nepal border and on to Kathmandu along much of the Friendship Highway. I am not an experienced cyclist, but one look at the condition of the roads convinced me that it would take someone with the stamina of an ox. Not me.

During the monsoon season there is risk from landslides, and a good bout of rain immediately turns a mud road into chocolate pudding. All roads are perforated with potholes and sometimes are washed away completely. Bike repair shops are non-existent, and a lack of decent accommodation facilities means cyclists have to carry everything with them: camping equipment, enough food, and water.

TIBET

TIBET UNDER CHINA

In 1950, the Chinese Communist Army (under the leadership of Mao Zedong) invaded Tibet, claiming the country as part of the "Great Motherland." For the next nine years, the Dalai Lama and his people tried to coexist peacefully with the Chinese authorities, but the continuing and worsening repression culminated in the Lhasa Uprising of 1959. Since that time 1.2 million Tibetans (a quarter of the population) have lost their lives, and thousands fled or are still fleeing across the Himalaya to freedom, where they live as refugees in India and Nepal.

The present and 14th Dalai Lama, Tenzin Gyatso, was 16 when the Chinese invaded Tibet. He fled to exile in India and established the Tibetan Government in Exile in Dharamsala, India, from where he travels the world pursuing a "Peace in Action" campaign for the Tibetan people. In 1989, in recognition of his efforts to achieve peace and freedom for his people, His Holiness was awarded the Nobel Peace Prize.

On the positive side, you cycle through a dramatic, lunar landscape of peaks whipped like cream and bald slopes speckled by dazzling lakes and shot through by rushing rivers, and the momentous sight of Everest.

Whether you go by Land Cruiser or bike, the Lhasa–Kathmandu overland journey passes over the Khamba La (4,794m/15,728ft) and Karo La (4,960m/16,273ft) passes. From the first you can spot the beautiful Yamdrok Tso Lake (Turquoise Lake). The route then drops to Gyantse on the north bank of the Nyang Chu River, and on to Shigatse at 3,860m (12,664ft), notable for its Tashilunpo Monastery, traditional seat of the Panchen Lama, who was the second spiritual leader of Tibet. After Shigatse, there's another high pass to cross, the Lhakpa La at (5,160m/16,929ft) before the road winds to Shegar town and then to Tingri at 4,340m (14,239ft). If the sky is clear, this is a tremendous place to pause and admire Everest, Makalu I (8,470m/27,789ft) and Cho Oyu (8,150m/26,739ft) to name just three.

Further along is Nyalam, then a descent down the valley of the Bhote Koshi to Zhangmu and the Friendship Bridge, the border with Nepal, and what now seems a paltry 2,300m (7,500ft).

I decided to take the easy route back—by plane. As Everest loomed into view again, a black and white Audrey Hepburn movie followed the mobile phone commercial just as the hostess served the cheesy sandwich. The movie would not be finished by the time the plane descended into Kathmandu's belt of smog. Unfortunately, I could say the same for the sandwich.

OTHER ACTIVITIES

❑ Visit Nam-Tso Lake, across a corner of Tibet's cold, windswept northern plains. Allocate 3 days for getting there and time to trek. A longer circuit around the lake is for very experienced, well-equipped trekkers only, and can take more than two weeks.

❑ Hire a cycle (from backpacker hotels and guesthouses) in Lhasa and take a day's ride out to Drepung Monastery or Sera Monastery, another well-known Gelukpa monastery, founded in 1419.

❑ Go to Kailash-Manasarovar, the sacred mountain and lake, overland by Land Cruiser or, if you have ample time, cycle.

❑ Horse riding: Snowland Travel (above the Pentoc Guesthouse, the Barkhor, Lhasa) organize two-day horse treks, staying overnight in nomad tents.

GOING IT ALONE

INTERNAL TRAVEL

Travelling in Tibet depends on the current political conditions. The information given here could well be out-of-date by the time you travel. A valuable source of information is the website of the Tibet Information Network (TIN; see page 000), which offers current advice to travellers.

One-hour flights from Kathmandu Tribhuvan International Airport to Gongkar Airport, Lhasa, are with China Southwest Airlines, and operate two or three (in high season) times a week. Flights go alongside Mount Everest. Flights also arrive in Lhasa from Chengdu in China. Individual travellers cannot buy air tickets without a TTB permit (Tibet Tourism Bureau). A travel agency can easily fit this up, but you will probably have to arrange a package tour. Other main routes are by bus from Golmud or the Nepalese border to Lhasa or Shigatse. Driving, rather than flying in, is a better way to acclimatize to the high altitude. Hitchhiking is illegal, and drivers can be fined if caught.

WHEN TO GO

Tibet is cold in winter, cool in summer. Sunlight is extremely intense, through it's chilly in the shade. In one day in summer, temperatures can range from 29°C (85°F) to 4°C (40°F) at night. In winter, nights can drop to –9°C (16°F), snowfall blocks high passes and high-altitude trekking is not advised. Generally, April/ May to October is a pleasant time to go, though monsoon rains in July and August can wash away

unsurfaced roads outside of Lhasa, particularly near the Nepalese border.

PLANNING

Getting in to Tibet is an adventure in itself, since the Chinese government prefers tourists to join a group with a guide. They have tight rules concerning the required Tibetan Permit. The easiest way to visit Tibet is with a group, following a prearranged itinerary. Usually you cannot break up a group visa and, if you do manage it, it's to your financial cost. It's possible to travel independently, but you need time, patience, and an understanding of the rules—and nothing is guaranteed.

Remember, you could place individual Tibetans at great risk if you hitchhike, stay with them, or talk to them about sensitive and political issues. If conditions in Tibet are tense, more travelling restrictions will be in force. Check the website for a list of annual sensitive anniversaries and security alert periods. At any time, travellers are advised not to become involved in any demonstrations or calls for Tibetan independence.

HIRING AN AGENCY

Many conditions (guides, accommodation, transport) in Tibet are controlled by the Chinese government and tourist agency—not the company with whom you arrange the trip. The government considers their hotels to be luxurious, but facilities for tourists are dire; there is a lack of hot and cold water on the road, and tourist hotels are large concrete blocks in fenced compounds, with unheated

rooms, dirty carpets, and broken chairs.

ORGANIZING A GROUP

Individual travellers can advertise for other travellers to join them on an overland trip to the Nepalese border and Kathmandu via Everest Base Camp, with 3–4 days' trekking if desired. Once you have enough members, visit a travel agency in Lhasa and negotiate a price to be split between all of you. Be prepared for the occasional truck/jeep breakdown on the road and make sure you have enough time for the journey. And don't forget to check the required permits/visas.

HEALTH MATTERS

Unless you have been acclimatized beforehand, you might find flying in to Lhasa painful. Ample liquid intake and rest are advisable. Because of insufficient medical facilities in Tibet, it is essential to have full medical insurance, which includes air evacuation.

WHAT TO TAKE

❑ Warm, quality trekking clothing.
❑ Warm sleeping bag.
❑ Hiking boots.
❑ Iodine tablets.
❑ Flashlight and home-bought batteries.
❑ Ample toilet rolls.
❑ High-energy snacks.
❑ Water bottle.
❑ Daypack.
❑ UV sunglasses.
❑ Medical kit.
❑ Scarf/mask to protect lungs from dust.
❑ Camera with UV and polarising filters.

Kathmandu is a good place to hire camping gear and outdoor clothing. Bikes can be bought in Lhasa, but many cyclists prefer to fly in with their own.

TIBET

19 Overland to the Sacred Mountain

by Lee Karen Stow

*In remote western Tibet—a lofty plateau of snowy peaks and arid scrub deserts—
stands the sacred Mount Kailash. I travelled overland on a rugged four-week
expedition to see Hindus and Buddhists perform the hardest pilgrimage in Asia,
paying homage to the gods that live here, on the roof of the world.*

Topped with snow, with its four sides matching the points of the compass and one face slashed by a swastika—the ancient Buddhist symbol of luck—Mount Kailash rises like the white, rounded nose of a rocket ready for take-off from its own mountain range. Its cone stands 6,714m (22,028ft) in isolation so distinctively, any traveller is prompted to stand in silent worship.

It is mainly pilgrims of the Buddhist and Hindu faiths who circumambulate Kailash's base in their hundreds, a religious *kora* that wipes away the sins of a lifetime. Tibetans regard Kailash as Kang Rinpoche, "jewel of snow," while Hindus believe the peak to be the centre of the universe and home of Shiva, the destroyer and transformer of life. What is fact is that four of Asia's rivers, the Ganges, Indus, Sutlej, and Tsango-Brahmaputra, have their sources within 100km (62 miles) of the mountain.

LEAVING KATHMANDU

Three hours into our drive from Kathmandu, the bus we had hired to take us to the Nepalese border in Tibet admitted it couldn't climb the muddy hill and slid to a defiant halt. Other buses became stuck in a similar quandary, and passengers were obliged to pile out and either push or walk. We waited for back-up (a better bus with wheels thick enough to make mincemeat of the slush) and took the opportunity to get to know each other.

We were six British women and one man: Amy the veterinary surgeon; Sarah the doctor (fortunately); June, aged 60 (retired and an intrepid explorer); Zara, a Tibetologist with a profound knowledge of Tibetan art and culture; Judy, a therapist; Carl, a lawyer; and me. We had met briefly the previous evening at the Hotel Utse, a Tibetan-run hotel in the tourist throng of Thamel in Kathmandu, and again early next morning as we set off, with a trio of rickshaws carrying our luggage, to meet the Nepalese crew who would take care of us for a month. Worryingly, we were missing Passan, the cook.

The replacement bus smelt of urine and had acquired strangers, I thought, as it struggled up a pine-matted valley striped by waterfalls and hung with thin cloud. White rapids of the Brahmaputra rushed beside in a

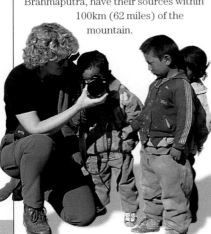

Left: *The children at Tingri were fascinated by our cameras*

Right: Prayers are printed on flags so the wind can escort them to the heavens

torrid frenzy. Half-naked children devoured what was left of our packed lunches, and butterflies the size of our hands disappeared over ravines in a relaxed scene that was in stark contrast to the one we were about to set foot in.

Bold red letters across a hardline concrete gateway spelled out something like "Welcome to China." It was the Friendship Bridge, and time to alight and lug our luggage through the Chinese, military-manned checkpoint where our passports were kept until the following morning, to complete immigration. This meant we were forced to spend our first night in Tibet in a filthy hotel in Zhangmu, with a grime-encrusted squat toilet with a vomit-inducing stench. Zhangmu is heavily populated by Chinese, who trade cheap waistcoats, towels, quilts, and the local currency (yuan) and sing badly in the karaoke bars until late, when the incessant barking of stray dogs drowns them out. At dawn you are blasted awake by Chinese homilies broadcast from speakers stuck on roofs. "Respect the Motherland!" the radio screeches.

Leaving our bus at the border and feeling relieved that our cook Passan,

 This is a challenging trip at high altitude with burning sun rays and below-freezing temperatures at night. Snow is not uncommon, even in summer. The 53km (33-mile) Kailash *kora* is a tough hike because of the altitude and its difficult climb over the main pass of 5,630m/18,47ft.

 It is an uncomfortable journey overland on bad roads that are often washed away in parts. Western Tibet does not cater for tourists. Accommodation is in tents and occasionally Tibetan-run guesthouses with no running water and terrible toilets, or Chinese-run, concrete hotels.

 You need complete camping equipment, although tents and ground mats are usually provided by the agency with whom you travel. Take a sleeping bag and good quality outdoor wear (preferably a down jacket) and thermals.

had appeared, we and our luggage piled into battered Toyota Land Cruisers, each driven by a Tibetan driver. Our Tibetan guide, Tsering, was in charge. Behind us followed a truck carrying tents, fuel, and food. This was the start of our trip proper, an expedition to stretch our stamina, both physically and emotionally, in the last breath of a once-forbidden kingdom rapidly being swallowed by China.

TAKING THE SOUTHERN ROUTE

Millions of years ago, Tibet rested at the bottom of a vast sea. When the two super-continents of the world collided, the land

TIBET

rucked like crumpled paper, creating the highest mountains on Earth, anchored by Mount Everest. Through this barren landscape cuts the southern route, one way to Kailash, passing through the towns and villages of Saga, Zhongba, Paryang, and Darchen, and topping mountain passes that stagger to more than 5,000m (16,400ft), fluttering with prayer flags of reds, blues, greens, whites, and yellows. This is when our driver, Basang, lifted his hat in tribute, shouting "Lha, So, Lha So!" (May the gods be victorious!), and the headaches of altitude hit.

Travelling to Kailash is no luxury. Mostly we camped underneath an ink sky scattered with stars that seemed close enough to steal and stamped by a full moon whose silver disc traces the outline of Tibet's "rabbit in the moon."

At the few guesthouses along the route we drank jasmine tea from soup-bowl cups. Only June and Zara could stomach the salty yak butter tea. I remember sitting next to a woman who picked at the flesh of a sheep's skull, its rows of teeth still clinging to its jaw. She plucked out the eye to crunch, slowly.

One day, we woke to discover a sand storm had collapsed our toilet tent and demolished the kitchen tent, inviting stray dogs to a feast of cheese and drinking chocolate. Another morning, our tents sagged under the weight of 7.5cm (3in) of snow and one Land Cruiser failed to budge after 3 hours of attention from our on-the-spot mechanics.

Days stretched long, as we drove for hours at reduced speed on cracked roads so bad it took 2 hours to crawl 65km (40 miles). Bumps twisted our spines, numbed our backsides, and had us crawling into our sleeping bags at night, relieved at the chance to be horizontal.

DIAGNOSIS WITH THE LOCALS

The hardship was rewarded when children waved, smiled, and shouted "*tashi dele!*", hello. Villagers and nomads with squashed faces and high cheekbones crowded round our opened windows

when we broke down or stopped to answer the call of nature.

Tibetan women wear long *chupas*, belted with buckles that are engraved with religious scenes and from which hang spoons, keys, and nose scrapers. Their jewellery varies according to their wealth. One woman had turquoise studs fastened in an earlobe that had obviously been home-pierced. A chunk of coral dangled on a red cord from the hole. Turquoise, Tibetans believe, is good for the liver, coral ensures a healthy heart, while a striped zee (a type of agate) is highly prized.

Sarah, the doctor in our group, revealed her profession and treated a gash on a man's scalp. Soon, a makeshift surgery formed on the grass as more Tibetans arrived clutching bellies and pleading for cures for all sorts of ailments. One woman wanted to know if Sarah could heal the holes in her shoes. I queued up with the others as I was suffering breathlessness because of the altitude and a headache so tremendous it felt like my skull was crushed in a sandwich of concrete. Fortunately, I wasn't ill enough to have to descend to a lower altitude, unlike Judy and Carl, who had to abandon the expedition altogether. They returned to Kathmandu and left us five, all women.

PRAYING ON THE FERRY

Shortly before we reached Saga, we rattled across plains dotted with nomad tents, a patchwork of yak skins against the mountains. Nomads move from pasture to pasture, trading Indian cottons, China tea, and salt from the lakes. As nature dictates, they transport their families, yak herds, and ferocious, black, husky-type dogs known as mastiffs.

Saga, a modern town growing from the wilderness just when you believe there's no population anywhere around, is reached via a comical apology for a ferry—planks of cracked wood on iron beams. This dodgy catamaran is pulled along on cables strewn across the rushing Brahmaputra.

The long trek to Mount Kailash runs parallel to the Nepalese border

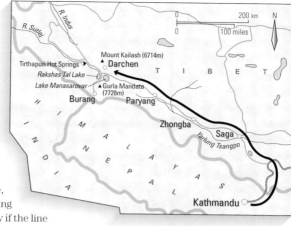

Once you are across, you drive to a depressing sprawl of Chinese, white-tiled, lavatory-type buildings with blue glass—Saga town. There's a military barracks, a satellite dish, brothels, shops selling smelly cabbage, and a post office offering international calls only if the line works. Not wanting to stay at the seedy guesthouse, we camped away, in the company of stray dogs pawing the ground for more scraps from our vet, Amy.

STRANDED

Next day we progressed to Zhongba, where we became stranded for two nights: the crankshaft on our supplies truck had given way. Zhongba has the split personality of a derelict ghost town supposedly abandoned because of the sand winds, and a new town. Around it is a wasteland of broken glass, sheep skulls, a pony's leg, a crusty yak skin, jaws, teeth, and something's vertebrae. We wouldn't camp here, so we piled into dormitories at the guesthouse and ate in the sitting room of a Tibetan woman whose head-dress, a mass of turquoise nuggets, rested on ebony plaits. These she unravels every 10 days to shampoo.

An iron stove fuelled by sheep droppings and marked with a pipe chimney rising through the bamboo in the roof, kept us warm and fried Passan's onions and potatoes. Afterwards, we had home-soured yak yogurt sprinkled with sugar. From the top of a dresser the woman pulled down a thigh bone of dried yak, which Basang wedged steady in his armpit while he carved off strips with his penknife. When he had had his fill, the owner replaced it on top of the dresser, for the next diner.

Our night was sleepless, because of dogs yapping at the moon, but next day the truck was fixed and we soldiered on, around potholes the size of gardens.

Eventually, almost two weeks since leaving London, and after long drives through terrain so dusty it's like being in a vacuum cleaner, we arrived at the Chang, overlooking Lake Manasarovar. We stood dumbfounded at the spectacle that we had travelled miles to see and, as is customary, Basang began driving the three circuits around the fluttering prayer flags. On the second lap our Land Cruiser ran out of fuel. Typical.

BAD WEATHER AT KAILASH

At 4,574m (15,000ft), Lake Manasarovar, a bolt of beckoning blue between the bookends of Gurla Mandata and Mount Kailash, is circled by a red crust of moss and caramel sands sloping up russet hills that rise to snow summits. Manasarovar (*Mapham Yum-tso* in Tibetan, meaning "victorious lake") is connected to the smaller Rakshas Tal Lake by a channel, and bears five of originally eight monasteries erected at points around it.

We asked the caretaker to unlock Chiu Monastery (sparrow monastery), occupied by three monks and built on a copper-coloured outcrop where Milarepa, an 11th-century poet, imagined paradise. The *lhakan* (house of god) is the hub of the monastery, a square room with walls smothered in fabric into which are stitched *thangkas* (silk hangings depicting religious scenes).

A group of pilgrims had just completed the *kora* around the lake and were receiving blessed water beside an altar lined with flickering butter lamps. Along one wall runs a library of ancient texts, the 108 spoken words of Buddha, each wrapped in cloth and held between slices of painted wood. The texts are labelled with small squares of fabric and are removed by monks who chant from them.

Nearby is the actual cave of Milarepa, dominated by a statue of Guru Rinpoche (the Tibetan nickname of the Tantric Buddhist master Padmasambhava, meaning lotus-born), surrounded by treasures supposedly left by him. Around the site are *mani* walls (stoves carved with Tibetan mantras), prayer wheels of gilded copper, and a large *chörten* (a small temple filled with religious offerings). At the foot of the monastery are hot sulphur springs, whose water is piped into tiled baths for visitors. There are guesthouses here, but we preferred to camp by the water's edge, and prepare ourselves for Kailash and the *kora*, one of the most challenging pilgrimages in the world.

Refreshed, we drove to the town of Darchen, the starting point of the *kora*. It's capital D for dump: a drab gathering of traders' tents and hawkers who crowd round your Land Cruiser to scrape necklaces of fake turquoise down the glass. But here is where we had to pass our passports through yet more red tape, hire yaks to carry our supplies around the *kora*, and by law spend a night at overpriced and filthy lodgings. To make matters worse, it hailed hard ice nodules that rapped the roof like a woodpecker. We prayed for morning and escape.

Morning came and we never went. Bad weather had set in at Kailash and the yak man warned it would worsen. So we abandoned our *kora* temporarily and headed out to Tirthapuri, the third most holy pilgrimage site in Western Tibet and the tremendous Kingdom of Guge. Here Zara was in her element, explaining the intricacies of the medieval murals for which the place is famous.

But when we returned to Darchen the sun shone dazzlingly brightly, softening the edges of the dump. Next morning the yaks' backs were packed with supplies and we finally set off, striding along a rubble track towards a Kailash sharp against a sky as blue as a cornflower.

Left: *Tuje Chempo (Lake of Great Compassion)*
Right: *Tarboche flagpole, with Mt Kailash in the background*

THE KORA'S BEGINNING

To perform the *kora* is to accumulate merit. As this is a holy site, it should be visited with respect. If you don't understand Buddhism or Hinduism, think of the mountain as the abode of your own god or simply as something infinitely mightier than you.

Kailash is ringed with auspicious signs, from Buddha's footprints and sites where great spiritual teachers have meditated to rocks shaped as buddhas and waterfalls cascading like horse's tails. The way ahead is undulating, over sparse grass and dry soil to prayer flags and a silent spot strewn with clothing as offerings. A Tibetan pilgrim raised his hands and stretched out before the flags and towards the southern face of Kailash, at the foot of the Lha Chu Valley. We circled the flags to head for the Tarboche Flagpole. This is replaced annually on the anniversary of the Buddha's enlightenment in May/June. If the flagpole remains straight when it is erected, all is well. If it bends towards Kailash, it's famine, disease, and possibly death. If it bends away from the mountain, it means great alarm.

We stood beneath the two-legged Chörten Kangnyi, an archway from which goats' heads twirl in the breeze. Kailash loomed to the right, its summit pristine and unconquered. Pilgrims dashed along,

threading rosary beads through their fingers, while prayer wheels whizzed round catching sunlight. Walking towards us were four Bön followers (Bön is the Tibetan religion predating Buddhism), who perform the *kora* anti-clockwise.

By nightfall we were camping in front of Kailash's north face, shivering in the freezing breeze that blew from her. By morning, the nearby stream had frozen and the ground around our tents lay hard and crunchy. It was our big day, crossing the feared Drölma-la Pass, a continuous ascent of 200m (656ft) up to the climax at 5,630m (18,472ft). We set off before sunrise, with toes and fingertips numb from cold. A litter of clothing and clumps of human hair marked the Shiwa-chal cemetery, where you leave something to ensure a smooth transition between this life and the next.

It took us more than an hour to crawl along the rocky corridor, pausing frequently to rest. Our yaks overtook us, picking their way effortlessly over boulders. But we knew it was worth all the pain when we finally reached Drölma-la, a slate-grey, rocky pass festooned with red, blues, greens, and yellows—a multitude of prayer flags, *mani* stones, yak skulls, and horns looking spectacular against a snow-streaked backdrop. We tied our own prayer flags and watched the wind blow our messages to the heavens. Passan arrived as nonchalantly as the yaks, swinging our box of breakfast eggs, to dish out dried fruit and hot lemon.

We relished the fact that the hard bit was over, although we knew we had to descend on the other side. The way down was knee-cracking, but the Tuje Chempo (Lake of Great Compassion) shimmered a glorious welcome. As we skipped—albeit stiffly—into camp, feeling well pleased with ourselves, we almost stumbled on a Tibetan nun, face down on the path. Her hands, stretched out beyond her head were clad in leather slippers and she protected her body with a leather apron. A mask kept the dust from her lungs, though her forehead was cream with

sand. This tiny Tibetan was prostrating all the way to the *kora's* end.

THE KORA'S END

Our final day's walk was free of tricky ascents. We began with a peep into Zutul-puk Monastery, where Milarepa is said to have meditated and built a cave.

We followed through high-sided valleys, the domain of eagles, before the final trail through a canyon of blazing red and orange rock stratas, striped with green. Cairns, built ever taller by passing pilgrims, led the way to a gaping mouth through which the Barkha Plain ran to the emerald waters of Rakshas Tal Lake.

A final prostration point signalled the end of the *kora*, after which we paused for thought, then brought out the packed lunch of chappatis and boiled eggs.

With the yaks unloaded and our equipment returned to our unpredictable truck, we turned our noses up at grubby Darchen and sped for Lake Manasarovar, to submerge our aches in the hot sulphur springs and spend a night beside the holy water. The delightful Passan baked us a chocolate cake in the shape of Kailash, smothered in icing for the snow. As we hugged our hot water bottles, watching the candle flicker in the draught, none of us thought about the long drive to Kathmandu. Basang, however, was relishing the prospect of retrieving his leg of dried yak.

WARNINGS

At some border crossings officials have demanded additional travel permit fees from foreigners.

Avoid becoming involved in any demonstrations or calls for Tibetan independence, and beware of video-taping or photographing such incidents.

Local authorities will react strongly if you are found carrying letters or packages from Tibetan nationals to be posted in other countries.

GOING IT ALONE

INTERNAL TRAVEL

Most people reach Kailash by arranging an overland drive. There are no flights, trains, or public transport. Allow 17–21 days, plus at least four days for the *kora*, depending on road conditions and how often your vehicles break down. Generally, there are three main routes to Kailash: the northern route, which can be accessed from Lhasa or Kathmandu; the southern route, often not passable in the monsoon owing to river overflow; and the Kashgar route, a bleak landscape and tough, but apparently incredibly beautiful. An alternative to the overland driving is to fly to Simikot (about 50 minutes from Kathmandu), trek for about eight days to Kailash, perform the *kora*, and then trek back. Allow about 24 days, including time at Lake Manasarovar.

WHEN TO GO

May to June and from the end of August to October are the seasons for visiting Kailash, although the first couple of months are busy with pilgrims. In midsummer there can be problems with monsoons washing away roads and bridges. Snow is not uncommon whenever you visit, and you should always be prepared for bad weather.

PLANNING

Prior permission is required from the Chinese authorities for travel to Tibet (see Planning, p. 189). Most travellers journey from Kathmandu or Lhasa on a prearranged itinerary. You can travel on a prepaid, organized tour booked in your own country or through one of the travel agents in Kathmandu. This is more expensive, but the hassles, red tape, and arrangements are all taken care of. The best trip is a fixed departure overland tour in four-by-fours, because the journey helps you adjust to the altitude. It's a tedious, arduous journey of three to four weeks (depending on whether you wish to include a visit to Everest Base Camp), but a good group would stop at sites along the way and spend time at Lake Manasarovar.

FINDING A GUIDE/GROUP

Because of the restrictions on travelling independently in Tibet, you would be wise to book your expedition to Kailash through a travel agency, which can sort out all the red tape and provide you with drivers, vehicles, expedition team, cooks, food, fuel, tents and the necessary permits for travel. Shop around for the best prices and conditions. If booking in Kathmandu, remember to read the small print of the contract between you and the agency before you sign, and ask lots of questions. Travellers in Lhasa can post advertisements on hotel walls to get others together to share the costs and then approach an agency to organize the journey.

EQUIPMENT HIRE

You can buy trekking gear in the Thamel area of Kathmandu, although the quality of goods may be slightly substandard, but inexpensive. Sleeping bags and other equipment (even a down jacket) can be hired.

On the Kailash *kora*, you can hire a yak for 60 yuan (about $8) per day to carry your tent, food, and equipment, for a minimum of 3 days. Remember, if the weather is bad and you don't trek, there's no refund.

HEALTH MATTERS

Recommended immunizations are: polio, tetanus, typhoid fever, yellow fever (if coming from a tropical African/South American country), hepatitis A, rabies, hepatitis B, TB, diphtheria. The extreme altitude may cause altitude sickness, so take ample liquids, rest, and take any symptoms—including headache, nausea, insomnia, and loss of appetite—very seriously. If you do develop symptoms of acute mountain sickness, descend to a lower altitude immediately. If ignored, mountain sickness can lead to potentially fatal problems. You can buy drugs to help the condition, but it's best to check with your own doctor before you travel.

WHAT TO TAKE

- ❑ Warm sleeping bag.
- ❑ Rain and windproof jacket.
- ❑ Thermal underwear.
- ❑ Down jacket.
- ❑ Walking boots.
- ❑ Fleece.
- ❑ Gloves.
- ❑ Woolly hat or balaclava.
- ❑ Sun hat.
- ❑ Very high-factor suncream.
- ❑ Lip balm.
- ❑ Sunglasses.
- ❑ Water bottle.
- ❑ Camera.
- ❑ UV and polarizing filters.
- ❑ Snacks—dried fruit, cereal bars, chocolate, packet soups.
- ❑ Personal medical kit.

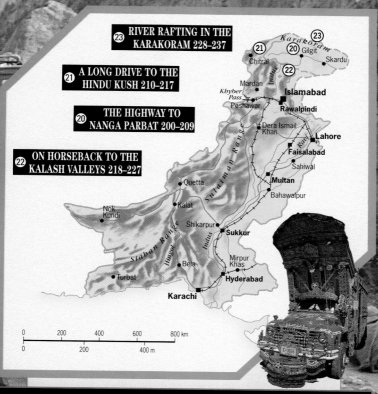

Map labels: Karakoram, Chitral, Gilgit, Skardu, Mardan, Indus, Khyber Pass, Peshawar, Islamabad, Rawalpindi, Dera Ismail Khan, Lahore, Faisalabad, Ravi, Sulaiman Range, Sahiwal, Multan, Quetta, Bahawalpur, Kalat, Nok Kundi, Shikarpur, Sukkur, Siahan Range, Hingol, Bela, Indus, Mirpur Khas, Hyderabad, Turbat, Karachi

| 0 | 200 | 400 | 600 | 800 km |
| 0 | | 200 | | 400 m |

PAKISTAN

Northern Pakistan, where the following adventures are set, is a world apart, a mountain fastness that has become accessible to foreign travellers since the opening of the Karakoram Highway in the 1970s. The region is dominated by the world's greatest mountains, the Western Himalaya, Karakoram, and Hindu Kush. These stupendous mountains and their interlocking valleys and tumbling rivers make north Pakistan one of the greatest adventure destinations for trekking, river rafting, jeep safaris, and cultural tours as well as high altitude mountaineering. Here you will find 8,000m peaks rising like glittering castles above vast glaciers and sun-scorched desert valleys. Here too are a thousand valley oases where irrigation has transformed barren ground into terraced fields and fruitful orchards. In the beautiful districts of Diamar, Gilgit, Hunza, Baltistan, and Chitral you will meet warm-hearted, generous people whose traditions are among the oldest in the world.

Mountain guide Abdul Wakeel (second left), with Tato jeep drivers on the road to Nanga Parbat

20 The Highway to Nanga Parbat

by Des Hannigan

Throughout its 1,300km (812 miles), the spectacular Karakoram Highway passes close to some of the world's highest mountains, including the 8,125m (26,656ft) Nanga Parbat. To reach the Nanga Parbat area, I followed the KKH 350km (218 miles) to Raikot Bridge, where things become even more spectacular.

More and more people are "doing" the Karakoram Highway these days. Special tour coaches head north from Islamabad to the northern capital of Gilgit and then continue through the district of fabled Hunza to the Khunjerab Pass on the Pakistan-China border. From here the road continues to Kashgar, one of the biggest bazaars in the world. There is a counterflow of travellers from the Chinese side of the border, but there is something special about heading north along the KKH on its tortuous way through the interlock of the world's greatest mountain ranges, the Himalaya, Karakoram, and Hindu Kush. You breathe in at Islamabad and you exhale in China. It's all breathtaking.

You can travel along the KKH by crowded bus, by carnival-coloured truck, by van, by jeep, or even by bicycle. What you travel in depends on what you can afford, of course. Bussing it along the KKH is the cheapest option and offers authentic local colour and sensation. There are disadvantages with bus travel, however. Pakistan's buses are wildly decorative inside and out, but are often dingy. They can take 18 hours to get from Rawalpindi to Gilgit, and 22 hours to reach the Baltistan town of Skardu. On buses, you travel through the night for much of the way with little chance of seeing anything. You may find yourself turned out on a cold mountainside helping to clear landslide debris from the road; you cannot choose your travelling companions; opportunities for photography are minimal; and if stomach bugs have got you, then all that local colour and sensation pales along with your face. There are fast-track "luxury" Coasters and Hiace minibuses that make the journey along the KKH more bearable, but on public transport generally, you need to grit your teeth, grit everything else, and dream of fantastic destinations to come.

1 A trek to Fairy Meadows is an ideal first Himalayan experience. You may suffer mild breathing difficulties during a short stay above 3,000m (9,800 feet), but walking in the Fairy Meadows area is undemanding and very pleasant. A bigger challenge is to trek from Fairy Meadows to Nanga Parbat base camp, which is located at just under 4,000m (13,000ft). The route is not difficult, but you should first acclimatize for a few days at Fairy Meadows or move up to Beyal campsite as a middle stage.

★ Accommodation along the Karakoram Highway ranges from very basic charpoys (simple beds under a canopy), through basic hotels, to hotels with en suite facilities and good restaurants. Accommodation at Fairy Meadows is in tents, furnished with sleeping mats. There are two toilet shacks with single units used by both sexes. Toilets are of the squat type. Washing facilities are basic. All three campsites at Fairy Meadows have dining huts where meals can be ordered.

⚒ Normal trekking clothes and boots are sufficient. A four-season sleeping bag is advised for spring and autumn camping at Fairy Meadows.

THE KARAKORAM HIGHWAY

- Conceived in the wake of a border agreement between Pakistan and China in 1964. Took 20 years to complete.
- Opened 1978, but foreigners have been allowed to travel along the road only since 1986, so the trip still seems exclusive.
- 80 million kilos (80,000 tons) of cement used to build the road and its 114 bridges.
- 8 million kilos (8,000 tons) of dynamite were used to shift 30 million cubic metres (43 million cubic yards) of mountainsides.
- Official figures claim there were about 500 deaths among the Pakistani and Chinese workers, with a similar number being seriously injured. True casualty figures are rumoured to be much higher.

SHORT NOTICE

This time I travelled the KKH by car, courtesy of the long-established tour company Travel Walji's, with whom I had arranged at short notice a trek to the Nanga Parbat base camp area for myself and my 18-year-old son, Tim. Walji's run the Avis concession and one of their hire cars was going north on the KKH to Gilgit and Hunza to rendezvous with a client for a return trip to Islamabad. We were heading for Raikot Bridge, to the south of Gilgit, where we were to meet a mountain guide for our trip to Fairy Meadows, the idyllic campsite below Nanga Parbat's north face.

We left Islamabad at 6am on an October morning in a Toyota Crown saloon to do the KKH in style. Our driver was an immaculately dressed Kashmiri called Mir Razaq. He was a superb driver. In Pakistan you overtake with determination or you barely move at all. The KKH, especially, is a fairly narrow "two-lane" highway, but we were soon to realize that Mir Razaq's judgement and confidence at numerous constrictions and blind corners was impeccable. Our other travelling companion was Walji tour officer Sadruddin Hunzai, who was heading north to visit his family in Atabad in Hunza. Sadruddin was a quiet, dignified man and a fount of information to us on our journey along the KKH.

We headed west through the calm of early morning Islamabad to join the Grand Trunk Road to Peshawar. The section of the GT between Islamabad-Rawalpindi and Peshawar is a frantic stream of traffic by day. Built-up to either side for most of the route, the road breeds its own atmosphere of dust-laden exhaust fumes. Traffic was sparse at first, but by the time we climbed through the Margalla Pass, a raw gash blasted through Islamabad's encircling hills, the flow of vehicles had increased greatly; a mauve haze of carbon monoxide began to darken the sky. The car raced northwest with its horn blaring in disharmony with those of every truck, bus, pickup, and Suzuki that fought for space on the Peshawar road.

ANCIENT CITY

About 30km (19 miles) from Islamabad, we turned off the GT and soon passed the famous archaeological site of Taxila, ancient city of Gandhara, the old name for the Peshawar Plain. The site and its ruins represent human settlement from about 1000 B.C. through to the 6th century A.D. However eager you are to reach the mountains, you should try to fit in a day's visit to Taxila. Beyond Taxila the road enters the North West Frontier Province through a countryside of low, straw-coloured hills. We drove through countless small villages that were thronged with youngsters heading for school amid the vivid clutter of morning markets and an apparent chaos of farmer's trucks, donkey carts, and meandering cattle jamming the road.

The big market towns of Haripur and Havelian came next, and were even more crammed and noisy. In another 20km

PAKISTAN

(12 miles) we reached the garrison town of Abbottabad, administrative centre of the Hazara district.

Beyond Abbottabad, the KKH starts to climb into the Black Mountains through wooded hills, which are terraced with fields of corn and rice paddies. We passed the settlements of Battal and Sharkool and reached Battagram, a bustling bazaar village where everything, from bread to guns, seemed to be on sale. About 20km (12 miles) north from here we reached the Indus at the Chinese-built Thakot Bridge, where the mighty river flows pearl-grey and dense as mercury between the crumbling walls of gaunt mountains. Beyond Thakot Bridge you have the feeling that this is where the KKH really begins as the road enters the forbidding but awesome district of Kohistan.

THE UNGOVERNABLE

Kohistan was the ancient land of Yaghistan, the "Ungovernable," and today there are valleys and enclaves to either side of the KKH where the Pakistan government still has little control. The ungovernable applies to natural as well as political forces. Building the KKH meant an almost bare-handed struggle with the most difficult terrain in the world. It took 20 years.

Left: *The Karakoram Highway Memorial, on the KKH beyond Gilgit*
Below: *The high peaks of North Pakistan are permanently covered by snow*
Right: *There's no limit to the amount of decoration local drivers can pile onto their vehicles*

In Kohistan the Indus gorge squeezes between sheer mountainsides. Here the road runs along a narrow rock shelf that had to be blasted from the cliffs. The charges were placed by men lowered on ropes from higher up the mountain and the work here claimed more lives than on any other section along the KKH. This is where you first experience the Northern Areas' "hanging" highway effect. The road runs between rock and river and beneath beetling overhangs that have been shattered by blasting. There is nothing but thin air between the edge of the road and the bed of the Indus, hundreds of metres below. Travelling north, you have to overtake on the outside edge, forcing your way past the lumbering, high-sided trucks that hog the middle of the narrow road.

For passengers, "eyes left" is the wisest option; at least you can divert your attention from all that empty space on the right by taking a close-quarters' look at the fantastic kitsch art work and carving that covers most Pakistani trucks and buses. Garish colours, vivid motifs, bulging chrome, plastic knickknacks, and a juke-box selection of klaxon blasts, are the universal themes.

WEST BANK

At the village of Dasu, the KKH descends to the riverbank and becomes less nerve-wracking. Now the road crosses to the west bank of the Indus, then wriggles its way northwards for about 25km (15 miles) to where it turns sharply east and passes through the shanty bazaar of Shatial. The valley widens and becomes more desolate; the Indus cuts its way through a wide river plain of dark grey sand. About 15km (9 miles) beyond Shatial the KKH enters the Northern Areas and the district of Diamar, then continues across the desert-like river plain to Chilas, where we were to spend the night. It had taken Mir Razaq barely 9 hours to drive from Islamabad, including stops; this was fast travelling for the KKH. He looked as if he had just been out for a stroll.

We reached Chilas in the dark and checked in at the roadside Panorama Hotel, a pleasant mid-range place with a

good restaurant. Supper was the inevitable, but tasty, mutton khorma, rice, and vegetables that you grow accustomed to in the North. We were joined by the guide who was to accompany us to Fairy Meadows, Abdul Wakeel, one of Walji's excellent mountain guides, who comes from the nearby village of Bunar Das. Abdul was a slightly built, wiry man in his late twenties. He was to be an invaluable and extremely likeable companion for the next few days. The following morning dawned bright and clear, and with Abdul aboard we drove the 25km (15 miles) from Chilas to Raikot Bridge, where we parted company with Sadruddin and Mir Razaq and where we began our brief but fascinating association with Nanga Parbat.

NANGA PARBAT

The north face of Nanga Parbat, the "Naked Mountain," is the biggest gable end in the world, the western wall of the Great Himalaya. From the summit of the mountain, this north-facing wall descends through several thousand metres of stupendous landscape towards the ashen gorge of the Indus River. Nanga Parbat is Kashmiri by name, but is known locally as Diamar, as is the surrounding district—a derivation of *Diva Meru*, the Heavenly Mount. It is more land mass than mountain; there is no truly distinguishing summit but rather a merging of several summits with their interlocking ridges and high cols. Nanga Parbat is altogether more awesome than even the most elegant, the most distinctive of 8,000m (26,250ft) peaks. Above 5,000m (16,400ft) there is permanent snow; the unremitting whiteness is broken only where blue-black facets of vertical rock are blasted clean by the wind.

Getting anywhere near Nanga Parbat's upper reaches is possible only for mountaineers of the highest calibre, but for ordinary mortals simply prowling round the approaches to the mountain is reward enough. It also takes time just getting that close, as Tim and I were soon to learn. At

Raikot Bridge we transferred to a skeletal-looking jeep that was stripped of its side-windows. Abdul climbed into the front alongside the driver and minutes later the jeep was barrelling up a stony track between rust-coloured boulders as big as houses. This was the track to Tato village and Fairy Meadows. It sliced up the bare hillside in a great loop then rose steeply into the mouth of a narrow gorge that was hemmed in by towering cliffs. Nobody warned us to brace ourselves.

The track to Tato has been gouged out of the cliff faces that flank the southern wall of the gorge. It rises (in tandem with your adrenalin count) for several twisting miles with overhanging blades of rock above and with vast echoing drops below. I will not dwell for too long on the sensationalism of this track. It made the KKH seem like a five-lane motorway. Enough to say that after a jeep drive to Tato you will never be quite the same again.

SUPERB DRIVERS

Local jeep drivers control transport between Raikot and Tato, not least because they helped build the track and they now maintain it. They are superb drivers. The story is that many youngsters in the Northern Areas start handling jeeps at about age 12. There is a local saying that translates roughly as "all the bad drivers have dropped out..." Caught as you are between Heaven and Hell, you must trust in this, unless you want to trudge from Raikot Bridge for 4 parching hours to the road's end above Tato and then for another 2 hours through the thin air to Fairy Meadows. I settled for convenience and white-knuckled sensation.

"This is not like English roads?" said a grinning Abdul from the wildly swaying front seat. My grin was fixed.

The higher you climb, the less nerve-wracking the cliff-side corniche becomes. After about an hour the track leads to the village of Tato amid narrow fields of maize and with square-cut houses clustered along the banks of the gushing stream of the Raikot Gah. The jeep track continues above Tato for a few hundred metres as far as the Nanga Parbat Fairy Point Hotel, an attractive cluster of timber shacks where we eased dry throats with delicious *chai* (or tea), in the shade of trees, and where Abdul arranged for two local porters to carry our gear up to Fairy Meadows.

To Fairy Meadows

It takes about 2 hours to walk the 5km (3 miles) to Fairy Meadows. The track leads steadily uphill along sub-alpine slopes clothed with pine, spruce, cedar, and juniper. Below your feet the Raikot Gah tumbles down its rocky bed. Ahead, Nanga Parbat dominates the horizon. At Tato, we had reached 3,000m (9,800ft), all within a bare hour of leaving Raikot Bridge. Now, on foot and uphill, any guilt I had about not shouldering my own rucksack faded quickly as the reduced oxygen pressure of the higher altitude made me gasp for breath.

Reduced oxygen pressure above 2,500m (8,200ft) will affect your breathing in the mountains of Pakistan and you need to understand the causes and recognize the symptoms (see page 136). Even for the fittest people, the feeling is uncomfortable. I found that my breathlessness eased as soon as I stopped moving; but it returned within a few laboured steps. Most people suffer in this way when they first reach altitudes above 2,500m (8,200ft), especially if they have come directly from sea level. During the few days we spent above 3,000m (9,800ft) Tim and I were affected, but not so much so that our overall experience was spoiled. The astonishing beauty of the surroundings makes up for it all and most people acclimatize within a few days as their bodies adapt to changes in the air pressure.

Camp International

Fairy Meadows' main campsite, Raikot Sarai, stands on a pine-fringed, grassy shoulder overlooking the Raikot Glacier and with stunning views of Nanga Parbat.

TRAVELLERS' TIPS

Dress conservatively in rural Pakistan. Shorts or revealing tops are not advised for either men or women. Exposure, by foreigners, of bare skin other than hands, feet, and face is an affront to many Muslims. Most of the people of the Diamer district are Sunni Muslims and have strict observances including purdah, the veiling of women. You should not photograph women. Even framing a landscape with women working in the foreground may cause offence. Western women should consider wearing a *dupatta*, a loose headscarf, when in bazaars. This may avoid hostile glances and occasional negative comments. This is not capitulation. Rural Pakistan is no place to make points of principle.

The air is sweet with the scent of pine resin. The atmosphere at Raikot Sarai is very friendly. This was Camp International. There were Pakistani, German, British, Spanish, Dutch, and French trekkers at the site. Most had come with organized groups but we also met independent travellers with impressive backgrounds. Gerhard and Hedwig Dopler were an Austrian couple who were on an extended backpacking trip that had already taken them through China to Pakistan. Even here the "small world" syndrome operated. We ran into the British mountaineer Victor Saunders, whose inspiring book, *Elusive Summits*, I had been reading only a few weeks before.

At Raikot Sarai you can hire prepitched tents and mattresses and there are a few chalet beds available (these definitely need to be booked ahead). The camp is very well managed by the genial Aziz Rehman Raees and there is always a cheerful crowd of cooks and porters around the timbered dining hall and kitchen. Meal times are easygoing, communal events. You can eat outside in what amounts to one of the world's greatest alfresco restaurants. The food is the standard fare of North Pakistan and is well prepared. The cooks vary the menu as best they can, given the difficulties imposed by Fairy Meadow's remoteness and by the unpredictability of visitor numbers. For breakfast, bowls of piping hot porridge are followed by tasty omelettes. Be prepared; the omelettes are often spiked with chillies—perfect if you like it hot. Mountains of fresh chapatis and *chai* go without saying. Evening meals are usually mutton or chicken dishes with sidebowls of vegetables and platters of rice.

Below: The track to Fairy Meadows is the ideal place for a first walk at high altitude
Right: Local roads, like the Karakoram Highway, often follow a precarious route between sheer cliff and sheer drop
Right inset: The bustling northern town of Gilgit

BEYAL

The next morning, Tim, Abdul, and I walked the few kilometres to Beyal, the summer herding settlement higher up the valley from Fairy Meadows. The trail led through shady pine woods, out onto the high escarpment above the Raikot Glacier and then continued across grassy meadows alongside the Beyal River. We pestered Abdul with questions about the area, all of which he answered with patience. His father, Ahmed Mir, is *nambardar*, a head man, at Bunar Das village. During the early years of the 20th century Abdul's grandfather had guided British officials on their way through the Himalaya to and from Srinigar in Kashmir to Gilgit. As a guide, Abdul was thus maintaining a great family tradition that was steeped in the history of the Northern Areas. He worked also in other areas of Pakistan, and was very aware of his country's culture and history.

BRUSHWOOD BUILDINGS

Beyal is a huddle of timber and brushwood buildings set in broad meadows at the valley head. There is a summer campsite here, where we ate lunch from heaped platters of mutton khorma, with a tasty vegetable mix and with rice, dhal (lentils) and chapatis, all washed down with piping hot *chai*. Then Tim and I set off up the valley towards the high bank of moraine beyond which lay the icy whiteness of Nanga Parbat. On the way we met Gerhard and Hedwig Dopler, who were reconnoitring their planned trek to Base Camp, a good 4 hours higher. Both were feeling the effects of oxygen depletion and were taking sensible precautions by acclimatizing day by day.

Nanga Parbat Base Camp seemed only a stone's throw from Beyal, but, for me at least the effect of altitude was still a handicap. We needed more days acclimatizing if we wanted to explore any higher. For now Tim and I veered from the main path and panted our way up steep slopes through the pine forest to reach the dramatic escarpment's edge above the Raikot

Glacier. Far below lay the black frozen waves of the glacier. On its far side a narrow band of white ice skirted the raw slopes that rose to Buldar Peak and Chongra Peak. To the south, the broad apron of the Raikot icefield spread below Nanga Parbat's mighty face. When you are confronted by the greatest Himalayan mountains you begin to understand how local people believed that the glittering high peaks were fairy castles. They seem to float above their rooted lower slopes. Legends of Diamer tell of the djinn and pari, fairies who lived on top of Nanga Parbat in a *shell-battekot*, a castle of "glass stone."

PAKISTAN

PAKISTAN

ALPINE MEADOWS

On our second day we wandered through the remarkable alpine meadows that surrounded Fairy Meadows. In the cultivated terraces that lined the valley slopes all the way down to Tato, the maize and corn had been gathered in. It was the end of the season and soon everyone, including the herders of Beyal and Fairy Meadows, would move down to the Indus Valley leaving the high pastures to the muffling snows of the Himalayan winter. For now, life at Fairy Meadows went on happily. In the evening after supper, trekkers, cooks, and porters gathered round a big log fire at the edge of the campsite. Soon the night air was filled with the sound of drumming and the throaty singing of Diamar songs. Empty oil cans became drums; the songs had the same cadence and pace as Irish folk ballads. In the flickering, smoky light the men leapt into impromptu dance; they whirled round the fire in rhythmic, staccato movements reminiscent of Spanish flamenco dancing.

On our last morning we left Fairy Meadows soon after dawn. Abdul had advised an early start because a number of groups planned to leave that day and we did not want to have to join a queue for a jeep at Tato. Our gear was soon packed and was carted off by porters, leaving us a fast, but easy walk down from the campsite. Soon we were driving down the jeep track, towards Raikot Bridge and the Indus Valley, this time with less apprehension than on the way up. Back on the KKH, we drove from Raikot Bridge by jeep the 78km (49 miles) to Gilgit, where, reluctantly, we parted company with our good friend Abdul.

GILGIT

Gilgit is a vivid and wonderful town that will bring you up short with its frenetic bustle. This is the historical focus of the Northern Areas. Its position in the river plain at the junction of the Hunza and Gilgit Rivers and 20km (12 miles) from the Indus Valley makes it the natural junction of all the valleys that slice through the districts of Ghizr, Gilgit, Diamar, and Skardu.

You are sucked in to Gilgit's seemingly chaotic bustle from the word go. If this is your first visit to a rural Asian town, then brace yourself. Nothing in Gilgit even approximates to the shopping malls, cafés, restaurants, and foodshops in Europe or America. Western standards have no relevance. Open-fronted butchers' stalls are curtained with blood-streaked, fly-crawling carcasses above a shamble of goats' heads and offal. These stalls stand cheek by jowl with soot-encrusted chapati bakeries, *chai* houses, fruit vendors, clothes shops, and hardware stores.

The constant stream of jeeps, Suzukis, buses, lorries, and vans fills the air with dust and exhaust fumes. A tangled web of electric cables sags above your head. On foot, be careful; you tread a thin line between the risk of a glancing blow from a klaxon-blaring jeep and the ankle-snapping minefield of fragmented pavements and open drains to either side of the street. Vehicles apart, bazaars such as Gilgit's are the closest you'll ever get to the realities of medieval markets long lost in Europe. Love it for what it is. This is the authentic rather than the "themed."

NANGA PARBAT

An ascent of Nanga Parbat was first attempted in 1895 by the British mountaineer A.F. Mummery and two Gurkha porters. All three disappeared without trace. Subsequent expeditions led to more deaths, including those of several German climbers and sherpas during the 1930s and two British army officers in 1950. The death toll earned Nanga Parbat the macabre nickname of "Killer Mountain." The peak was eventually conquered by the remarkable Austrian climber Hermann Buhl, who made a solo ascent in 1953 only a few weeks after the first ascent of Mount Everest by Edmund Hillary and Tenzing Norgay.

GOING IT ALONE

INTERNAL TRAVEL

There are buses daily between Islamabad/ Rawalpindi and Gilgit ($5–$6). The journey can take up to 18 hours and can be uncomfortable. Smaller companies run more amenable 20-seater Toyota Coasters on the route, and these may cut the journey by about 3 hours ($6–$8). Prices to intermediate stops are proportionate. Hiring a private car between Islamabad and Gilgit will cost you $160 one way.

Pakistan International Airlines runs one to three flights a day between Islamabad Airport and Gilgit using Fokker F27s, ($50 one-way; this is the "foreigners" fare and is substantially more than what Pakistani nationals pay). The trip takes a magical hour and is an experience in its own right. However, weather conditions can wreak havoc with schedules. Cancellations over several days can create a backlog of frustrated travellers. Reservation well in advance is essential, and even then you cannot count on everything going to plan. If your flight is cancelled, make sure you reconfirm your booking for the next day or you may lose your place. Try securing a seat on the right-hand side for best mountain views on the Islamabad–Gilgit flight.

You can reach Raikot Bridge from Gilgit on southbound NATCO buses to Raikot Bridge ($1.5). Private jeep hire, Gilgit to Raikot Bridge, is about $40. Raikot Bridge to Tato is $16 and is not negotiable.

WHEN TO GO

June to mid-October is the best period for a visit to the Fairy Meadows area. The campsites at Fairy Meadows are open during this period. September–October is usually dry and is a cooler time of year, although it can be very cold at night above 2,000m (6,500ft).

PLANNING

Tour agencies in Pakistan organize week-long trips to the Nanga Parbat area, including transport to and from Islamabad/Rawalpindi, or from Gilgit, and will arrange accommodation at KKH hotels and at Fairy Meadows and Beyal campsites. They can also supply a guide, who will engage porters to carry your gear, where necessary. You can make your own arrangements, first travelling by public transport or private vehicle hire to Raikot Bridge. It is wise to hire a jeep from Raikot Bridge to Tato rather than make the exhausting 4-hour hike in the often savage heat. At Tato you can always find local men and boys for hire as porters to Fairy Meadows ($2.50). The campsite managers can usually arrange guides and porters for longer treks. Reservations for camping at Fairy Meadows should be made a week or two in advance.

HEALTH MATTERS

❏ Full travel insurance, including cover for medical and evacuation costs, as well as extra cover for adventure sports, is essential.
❏ Inoculations to guard against hepatitis A, typhoid, meningitis, tetanus, and polio are strongly recommended. Seek doctor's advice on these matters well in advance of travelling. Protection against malaria should also be taken. Protection against rabies and Japanese B encephalitis may be considered, although risk of contraction is small. Seek prior medical advice.
❏ Treat even bottled water with iodine tablets. Try to drink at least two to three litres of water per day. Do not drink river water, even if your guides may do so with impunity. Do not use ice cubes.
❏ Avoid eating salads or cold food. Fresh fruit is plentiful in many parts of northern Pakistan. Some authorities advise peeling fruit before you eat it. The problem is that even as you peel, you may transfer bacteria from the peel to your hand and back to the peeled fruit. The dilemma is entirely yours.
❏ Use waterproof sunscreen with high protection factor. The sun's rays in the mountains can be very intense.
❏ Carry a small first-aid kit to include pain killers, antiseptic, plasters, and bandages. Ask your doctor's advice about dysentery tablets and antibiotics.

WHAT TO TAKE

❏ Sunblock.
❏ Sun hat.
❏ Good, comfortable walking boots and trekking clothes.
❏ Four-season sleeping bag for camping at Fairy Meadows.
❏ Loose, concealing clothing, especially for women.

21 A Long Drive to the Hindu Kush

by Des Hannigan

Travel in North Pakistan is generally along unsurfaced and often very rough jeep tracks. One of the greatest jeep safaris of all is the 577km (360-mile) journey from Skardu to Chitral via the remote Deosai Plateau and the Shandur Pass.

lways go against the grain, they say. It makes for a more interesting life. I had this dangerous maxim in mind after making several trips up and down the north–south axis of the Karakoram Highway. Going east to west across North Pakistan's great mountain-ranges seemed a more fascinating option, however; it would be like crossing a gigantic T or, in reality, crossing the "Roof of the World."

high Deosai Plateau by rough tracks to the village of Astor and then to Gilgit, a journey of 225km (140 miles). From Gilgit it is another 352km (220 miles) west to Chitral along a track that leads across the magnificent Shandur Pass.

Right: *The windswept, grassy plain of Shandur Pass is marked by an army checkpoint*

The town of Chitral lies at the western end of this east–west axis; the town of Skardu lies at its eastern end; midway between the two lies Gilgit, "capital" of the mountains and the linchpin of the KKH. Skardu is linked to the KKH and to Gilgit by a paved road that runs through the stupendous upper gorge of the Indus River and is a glorious journey in itself. More enticing, however, is a high-level route that loops south from Skardu and crosses the remote 4,000m (13,123ft)-

Above: *Winter was definitely closing in as we started across the Deosai Plateau*

This makes the overall Skardu to Chitral trip 577km (360 miles) long, most of it through remote mountain country and on very rough tracks. You start in the Karakoram, clip the Western Himalaya, skirt the Hindu Raj, and end at the Hindu Kush; a mountain odyssey par excellence.

KARAKORAM HEARTLAND

Skardu is the capital of Baltistan, the heartland of the Karakoram. Just 80km (50 miles) to the south lies Kashmir, a well-savaged bone of contention between Pakistan and India. Yet the overwhelming splendour and scale of Baltistan, home to the Karakoram's greatest cluster of peaks, somehow insulate the region from the outside world. To the southeast, beyond the mountains, lies Ladakh and the beautiful Vale of Kashmir. To the northeast, beyond the breathtaking peaks of K2, Masherbrum, Broad Peak, and the Mustagh Tower, lies the high plateau of China. In Skardu you feel satisfyingly landlocked at the heart of a mountain wilderness.

 Provided the jeeps you travel in are reliable and your drivers likewise, you should cope easily with this long but delightful trip.

 The tracks through the mountains can be very rough in places, so do not expect cushioned luxury. However, it is remarkable how easily you will adjust to the rocking and rolling of the jeep. There is enough diversion in the beautiful scenery and fascinating villages through which you pass. If you are camping on the Deosai in July or August, take plenty of insect repellent.

 Wear normal outdoor clothing, including sturdy boots. If you are travelling in late autumn, make sure you have warm, weatherproof outer clothing and carry all-season sleeping bags. The Deosai can have snowfalls as early as October, and above 2,500m (8,200ft) it can be chilly at night at any time of the year if you are camping.

Skardu has a rough and ready charm. It seems less claustrophobic than Gilgit and Chitral, the two other main towns of North Pakistan, perhaps because it is perched above the wide river plain of the Indus and seems more open. A sphinx-like craggy hill, the Rock of Skardu, rises above the town to add some perspective within the encircling rim of higher mountains, the outliers of the mighty Karakoram to the north and of the remote Deosai to the south. Halfway up the rock stands the ruins of Karphocho Fort; the slog up to the fort is worth the effort for the views alone. Skardu's main street merges College Road, the busy Naya Bazaar, and Hameed Garh Road in one long, dusty corridor. Leading south from Naya Bazaar is the older Purana Bazaar, the most atmospheric in Skardu.

THRONE ROOM

I was staying with my son Tim at Skardu's PTDC K2 Motel, a great favourite of mountaineering and trekking groups. I had arranged the first section of the trip across the Deosai Plateau to Gilgit with the Skardu-based Baltistan Tours, whose very able manager, Yousuf Wazir, had organized things with admirable efficiency in spite of the lateness of the season.

Yousuf's only concern was that the high Deosai was usually snowbound from November to May. It was now late October, the first snowfalls had been reported from the plateau, and the seasonal tent "hotels" on the Deosai had packed up for the winter. The Skardu to Gilgit trip is best done over two or three days, but with snow already reported we aimed to make a crossing to the village of Astor in a day. This meant an 8-hour trip to Chilam, the first settlement on the Astor side of the Deosai. Going all the way to Astor could take up to 12 hours. A delay or a breakdown would not be much fun. We would do it, said Yousuf, *inshallah*, God willing. Tim and I had good sleeping bags and cold weather gear for less spiritual reassurance.

AGED JEEP

The next morning we met our driver, Ghulam Medhi, a young, tough-looking Balti with the look of a man who could tackle anything. Our jeep was an aged, but solid American model built like a tank. It was painted black and had the bulging, muscular look of an Andalucían fighting bull, a fanciful impression that I found reassuring. Yousuf Wazir had collected some basic supplies for our trip. He

had news of more snow flurries on the high plateau, information that was greeted with solemn but sage nods all round. We left for the Deosai just before midday, under lowering clouds.

The road to the Deosai climbs steadily south from Skardu between the fractured, unsteady walls of the Sadpara Gorge and above the tumbling, breakneck waters of the Sadpara River. Within the hour we reached Sadpara Lake, a beautiful place but today a leaden sheet under grey skies.

Beyond the lake, the track wound its way steeply through the narrow stream gorge of Sadpara Nullah. At 2,500m (8,200ft) we seemed to run fast-forward into late autumn. The riverside willows and birches were medallioned with golden leaves, sunbursts in the otherwise dreary landscape of this increasingly gloomy day. Soon, however, the last trees were left behind and we reached the rocky pass of Ali Malik Mar at 4,000m (13,123ft), the savage gateway to the Deosai proper and an even faster forward introduction to winter. As we moved onto the plateau, horizontal streamers of snow whipped across the bleak landscape. Ghulam bent low over the wheel peering through the murk.

ROLLING HILLS

The rolling hills of the Deosai were smeared with snow and blackened with peat. We huddled inside the jeep. Ghulam had slotted in the side windows in the lower *nullah* (gorge), but the bitter wind still spiralled round our heads. Another half hour's driving along a muddy track and, miraculously, the murk of low-lying cloud and scudding snow was pierced by shafts of brighter light. Suddenly, the mist and snow evaporated and were replaced by dazzling sunshine that revealed the vast, exhilarating expanse of the Deosai.

Now we could appreciate the awesome size of the plateau. The high altitude is emphasized by the distant corona of blindingly white mountains that encircle the Deosai. Ahead of us, the track ran across low hills for some kilometres then crossed the gurgling streams of the Shatung and Barawai Nala rivers.

We rattled on along the track as it cut a straight line across the plain alongside the glittering Barwai, then crossed the river by a weather-beaten swing bridge at Bara Pani. About 600m (650yd) downstream from the bridge, on the south bank of the river, lies the summer base of the Himalayan Wildlife Project, closed for the winter but in summer worth a visit. Within its remit is the protection of the rare Himalayn bear. There is a seasonal tent hotel by the bridge, a useful halfway stage in a summertime crossing of the Deosai.

As we began a steady climb away from the river the bleak weather closed in once more, reminding us that summer was long gone. Soon we reached the Sheo Sar Lake, a blurred, grey sheet barely seen through the mist and snow. We were in a full blizzard by now, the jeep moving slowly in a lumbering, jerking motion along the brutal, rocky track through the Chhachor Pass. We rifled our lunch pack and chewed on cheese and biscuits as we rode along.

WINTER DEOSAI

A short way beyond Chhachor, the track became much softer and muddier as it descended rom the 4,000m (13,123ft) line. The flurries of snow became fitful until they merged into soft drizzle and finally ceased. You could almost hear a metaphorical gate clang shut behind us on the winter Deosai. There would be few crossings of the plateau from now on. Soon we reached Chilam, a scatter of buildings and army compounds.

We could have found basic accommodation here but, although darkness was

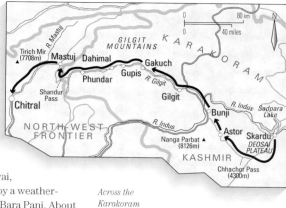

Across the Karakoram

falling, I was keen to push on to Astor, a good 3 hours away. Ghulam drove masterfully through the dark. As time passed and as confusing junctions loomed, I began to wonder if we would ever reach Astor. Suddenly Ghulam bellowed, "Astor!" and jabbed his finger in the air. We peered out from under the jeep's canopy and there, high above us, as high as the Milky Way it seemed, were the dim lights of a village strung out along the edge of an escarpment. Minutes later we drove into the brightly lit and welcoming courtyard of the Kamran Hotel. I would have given Ghulam a medal if I'd had one.

ASTOR

The next morning we woke to brilliant sunshine and cloudless skies. Before breakfast I strolled through Astor, a bustling little village of steep, dusty lanes, clamped between great hills and with greater mountains above.

From Astor we drove down the exquisite upper reaches of the Astor river valley. Neat fields of rice and maize rose in elegant terraces from the opposite bank. The rough track wound its way between interlocking mountains, with always the gurgling, leaping river forging the way ahead. In the lower reaches of the valley, the dark mountains rose higher and closed in, the river lost its gaiety and sank deeper into the rocky trench of the valley between vast, crumbling walls.

Left: *The wonderfully sited Phundar guesthouse*

rock and roll mercilessly. Yusuf never seemed to move a muscle as he drove, yet you felt at ease all the time. The trip to Chitral would take us three days and we planned to stay at Government Inspection bungalows on the way.

The morning after our arrival from the Deosai, we left Gilgit for the Shandur and Chitral in one of Walji's well-maintained jeeps. The weather seemed set fair for several days of brilliant sunshine and there was not the same mood of urgency as there had been prior to our Deosai crossing. We were heading deep into the mountains, but mainly through sheltered river valleys at a much lower altitude. Life seemed simple and uncomplicated. Unknown to us at the time, the political world of Pakistan was about to change dramatically as the ruling government became embroiled in events that were to end with a military coup. In the remote Karakoram and Hindu Kush it's easy to miss such things.

Our road led northwest from Gilgit along the green corridor of the Gilgit River. The river was a jade-coloured ribbon, its banks shrouded with slender poplars that were already showing their autumnal colours of red and gold. We passed through villages that seemed well supplied with schools and clinics, two of the great socializing institutions that the remarkable Aga Khan Foundation has brought to the remoter areas of the North.

A few kilometres on from Shenote and just past Gulapur are the ruins of Sher Qila, "the fort on the rock;" the fort's 19th-century watchtower survives on a high spur on the north bank of the river. We drove as far as Ghakuch, where we stopped at a roadside eating house, a dark, unadorned place where we were

Soon road and river parted company until we were running down a typical Himalayan corniche, towards the mighty trench of the Indus Valley, shrouded by canopies of rock above and with vast drops into the echoing gorge far below. It becomes commonplace in North Pakistan, this edge-of-the-world wandering.

At the mouth of the Astor Valley, at Ramghat Pul, we branched off the main track south and crossed the river by a swaying suspension bridge onto the line of the old Gilgit-to-Srinigar road. Our route took us directly north along the sun-baked southern slopes of the Indus to the garrison town of Bunji. Here we joined the KKH and fairly bowled along the last 40km (25 miles) of surfaced highway to Gilgit, where the first section of our east–west odyssey ended and we said fond farewells to Ghulam.

WEST TO CHITRAL

In Gilgit we renewed acquaintances with old friends from Walji's, whose Northern Areas' general manager, the genial Naunihal Shah, had arranged our trip to Chitral. Our driver for this stage was Yusuf Mohammed, a Walji's driver I had been with before and who was a veteran of numerous trips across the Shandur Pass. Yusuf Mohammed seemed always to have effortless concentration and control on the rough and troublesome tracks of the mountains. Over such terrain you

served piping hot plateloads of equally unadorned mutton korma, rice and dhal for lunch. On we went through the sunlit valley; at one point we stopped for a few minutes to watch a lively village football match with its crowd of enthusiastic spectators. A few hours later we reached Gupis, where the Gilgit River begins life as the confluence of the Ghizr and Yasin rivers. This was our first overnight stop and we stayed at a delightful Inspection bungalow that had the faded charm of older times in its dusty, dimly lit rooms and on its shady veranda.

To Phundar

The next morning dawned as crystal clear as the day before. It was a short trip to our next overnight stop at Phundar, but we were to travel more slowly than yesterday because the road beyond Gupis was much rougher. The track unwound through the valley of the Ghizr River, and in 10km (6 miles) we reached the beautiful Khalti Lake. Just beyond the lake the track passed beneath dark cliffs, then through a narrow pass where the river ran broad and shallow, glittering in bright ripples across its stony bed. Soon we emerged into the upper valley of the Ghizr and into ever more brilliant light.

The higher we climbed into the mountains, the more golden the colours became. By the time we reached Phundar, the leaves of poplars, acacias, willows, and birches had become even more luminous. The blue of the sky deepened, the river glittered even more brilliantly, and above it all the ragged peaks and ridges of the Hindu Raj and Hindu Kush gleamed silver-white.

Phundar is reached by a steep, tortuous track up a great wall of glacial moraine above the confluence plain of the Ghizr River with the rivers of Bahushtaro Gol and Chhashi Gol. The Inspection bungalow at Phundar, where we were to stay, stood on the crown of the morainic ridge. Below, to the east, lay the placid waters of Phundar Lake; to the west of the ridge lay a broad flood plain through which the Ghizr flowed in great lazy curves, and where skeletal lines of poplars interrupted the flat, sandy fields.

Towards Shandur

After a restful night at Phundar we drove west through a string of villages linked by the green and gold of poplars and by a mosaic of ochre fields and rocky walls. The harvest was long over, but everywhere people were threshing corn and were spreading corncobs and fruit to dry on the flat roofs of the houses; children peered out at us from behind walls, groups of men, squatting outside village shops and *chai* (tea) houses, raised their hands in lazy salute.

Now the houses thinned out and the land became more barren and raw as we rattled through the scattered settlements of Teru and Barsat and entered the broad, shallow valley of the Khokhush River. Soon the track swung abruptly to the west and we began to climb towards the Shandur Pass on a wheel-crunching, wheel-spinning, rocky track alongside a tumbling stream. In time the track levelled off and entered the wide valley of the Shandur. The pass stands at an altitude of 3,730 m (12,237ft) and is more of a long, grassy plain than a pass. It is flanked by low mountains whose crests are frosted with ice and snow. At Shandur Top, the middle of the pass, there is a Pakistani Army barracks and a checkpost that marks the border between the Northern Areas and the North West Frontier Province.

POLO GROUND

We stopped at the checkpost and had *chai* with the officials outside their tents. The Shandur is famous as the site of the highest polo ground in the world. The famous Gilgit-Chitral Polo festival is held in July in the natural arena of the Shandur. At the heart of the pass are two shimmering lakes that reflect the surrounding peaks. At its western end, the darkly impressive peak of Ushill Dhar, 5,350m (17,552ft), fills the horizon, signalling the abrupt descent from the Shandur into the deep Laspur Valley.

We descended hundreds of metres into the valley and back to a world of gold-leafed poplars and green meadows. At Baruk village we stopped at a roadside eating house and sat in the mellow sunlight enjoying the remains of the previous night's chicken supplemented by potatoes in spicy sauce and cake-like *khasta shapik*, a type of local bread that is exceptionally tasty. Then we drove for kilometre after kilometre due north, through the desolate lower reaches of the Laspur Valley along narrow shelves in the shaley slopes and above wind-eroded gullies that plunged in twists and turns to where the Laspur River foamed along its rocky bed far below. Just below the village of Mastuj, the road turned sharply west once more and we rattled down the valley of the Mastuj River through the still golden light until we reached the lush fields of rice, wheat, and barley and the orchards of the lower valley. Far ahead the snowy bulk of Tirich Mir, at 7,706m (25,282ft) the highest peak in the Hindu Kush, filled the horizon. Across the valley, to the east, the dark icy heights of Pal Zom seemed to block out a sky already dense with evening cloud; ahead of us lay interlocking bluffs. The valley grew narrow and squeezed itself through rocky gorges, then spilled out onto a widening plain, only to narrow once more.

At Buni village, without warning, we coasted onto a metalled road and with the merest relaxing of his arms, Yusuf Mohammed seemed to welcome that soothing surface after those endless miles of rock and roll. Two hours later we came down onto the ever-widening plain of Chitral. The lights of the town were like blurred candles in the purple dusk, the air had grown chilly and by the time we crossed the Chew Bridge over the Chitral River and entered the dimly lit and crowded bazaar, it was fully dark. The blue and gold colours and intoxicating light of the past three days had faded from the air.

POSTSCRIPT

The next morning I phoned my wife, Pauline, in England, from a corner shop in Chitral bazaar. She told me, with some anxiety, that there had been a military coup in Pakistan a couple of days before, and were we all right? Amazement and disbelief were my first reactions. The shop was crammed with Chitralis who were glued to the smallest portable television set in the world. I craned to look, expecting military propaganda on screen. They were watching cricket.
"Everything's perfectly normal," I said. This was the Hindu Kush.

GOING IT ALONE

INTERNAL TRAVEL

There are daily bus links between Islamabad/Rawalpindi and Skardu ($5–7). The journey can take up to 22 hours. There are daily buses between Gilgit and Skardu ($2) and the trip takes about 6 hours. Private transport between Gilgit and Skardu costs $50.

Pakistan International Airlines runs one flight a day between Islamabad Airport and Skardu using Boeing 737s ($50). This is the "foreigners" fare and is substantially more than Pakistani nationals' fare. The trip takes the same magical hour as does the Gilgit flight and is an experience in its own right. Cancellations over several days can create a backlog of frustrated travellers. Reserving seats well in advance is essential and even then things do not always go to plan. If your flight is cancelled, make sure you re-confirm your booking for the next day or you may lose your place.

There are daily mini-bus links between Chitral and Peshawar ($5). The journey takes 12 hours or more. You then need to travel by bus, train or plane to Islamabad. Private transport from Chitral to Peshawar or Islamabad costs about $180.

There are two PIA flights a day from Chitral to Peshawar on F27s ($50). The flight takes 95 minutes. There are frequent cancellations owing to weather conditions. Reservations strongly advised.

WHEN TO GO

You can cross the Deosai Plateau between June and October. From mid-October onwards there is a risk of snowfall. The plateau is impassable between November and May. During June and July the Deosai can be plagued with mosquitoes and you should use insect repellent, and mosquito nets if you are camping. Expect extremes of heat and cold at altitude throughout the year, especially on the Deosai where there can also be fierce winds even in summer.

The Shandur Pass can be crossed between May and October. If you want an uninterrupted and peaceful crossing avoid the period covering the July polo festival at the Shandur Pass. You can make a visit to the festival a part of your trip, if you're gregarious, and if you can fight your way there with the hundreds of other jeeps and trucks.

PLANNING

There are more than enough jeeps and drivers for hire in Skardu and Gilgit for crossings of the Deosai Plateau and the Shandur Pass, but bear in mind the need for being confident about the reliability of both vehicle and driver. You can arrange jeep hire through reliable agencies or through hotels. Jeep hire from Skardu to Gilgit is about $180 and from Gilgit to Chitral about $200.

There is a good choice of hotels in Skardu, Astor, Gilgit, and Chitral. Summer tent hotels operate on the Deosai and at the Shandur Pass. If you want to stay in a Government Inspection bungalow, or "rest house" along the Gilgit–Chitral route, you need to book through the office of the Chief Engineer in Khazana Road, Gilgit, tel: 0572 3375. If you arrange the trip through a tour agency, it will book for you.

OTHER TRAVEL OPTIONS

Crossing the Deosai Plateau from Skardu to Chilam on foot can make an enjoyable trek, and you can always get transport onwards to Astor and Gilgit. Very experienced mountain bikers have made the Deosai crossing. It is worth looking for a tour agency who could arrange a crossing by pony. Any of these options is best undertaken in late summer to early autumn, when the Deosai mosquitoes are less rampant. If you do not want to make a full crossing of the Deosai, you can arrange private jeep hire for half-day round trips onto the plateau from Skardu.

The Gilgit–Chitral trip across the Shandur Pass can be done by combining public transport, cargo jeep transport, and walking. There is no public transport beyond Gupis other than cargo jeeps. Few cargo jeeps cross the Shandur Pass. In the higher reaches of Ghizr, walking is specially pleasant and there is a trekking route from Barsat to Mastuj through the Chamarkhan Pass, as an alternative to crossing the Shandur Pass.

HEALTH MATTERS

See recommendations on p. 209.

WHAT TO TAKE

❑ Insect repellent and mosquito net (for camping) if you are crossing the Deosai June–July
❑ Clothes for extremes of heat and cold at any time of year.
❑ All-seasons sleeping bag.

PAKISTAN

22 On Horseback to the Kalash Valleys

by Des Hannigan

The Kalasha are a non-Muslim people who live in the Hindu Kush, near the Afghan border. Their complex culture is thousands of years old, and visiting the Kalasha homeland is a privilege as much as an experience. I made the trip on horseback, a fast-disappearing mode of transport in the area.

You can lead a horse to water, but when it really wants to drink, leading it away is another matter. I found this out the hard way in the blistering heat of a Hindu Kush afternoon high above the Chitral River and several dry, dusty miles south of the town of Chitral itself.

I was astride an Afghan pony on my way to visit the Bumburet Valley, home to the remarkable Kalasha people, or Kalash, as they are generally known. The Kalash are subsistence farmers who are noted for their rich and complex culture

Right: *There's always room for one more on a local truck*
Far right: *Stupendous views out over the Chitral valley to the Hindu Raj mountains*

and for the decorative dress of their womenfolk. There are only about 3,000 Kalash, and they are the only non-Muslim people in the entire Afghanistan-Pakistan landmass. The Kalash valleys of Bumburet, Rumbur, and Birir are 35km (22 miles) south of Chitral. There are several agencies who organize an increasing flow of visitors to the Kalash. Most people travel by jeep or by minibus, but I wanted an alternative, less dusty way of reaching the valleys. Besides, the Kalash deserved a measured approach, and travel by horseback seemed one way of recapturing some of the atmosphere of a less frenetic age.

 3 You do not need to be a very experienced rider to handle the docile Afghan ponies used on treks of this nature. However, you do need to be fairly firm with your mounts and know how to control them and turn them by using the reins. Within the confines of the Kalash valleys, walking is not demanding, but if you undertake a trek on foot between the valleys, you may suffer some effects of altitude.

★★ Specify that you want Western-style saddles and you should not be too saddle-sore. It can be very hot and dusty at times riding through the Hindu Kush. Hotels in the Kalash valleys offer amenities that range from all mod cons to basic facilities.

 Wear normal outdoor clothing, including sturdy boots. Wear thick trousers or jodhpurs for riding. A sun hat is essential.

PAKISTAN

Frenetic was not the word you would use to describe the wiry little Afghan ponies that took my son Tim and me, and our Afghan guide, Hamid Allah, to the Kalash. These were work horses. They were nameless, and a horse with no name seemed a forlorn creature. I dubbed my mount "Hangover," having realized within minutes he had a ferocious thirst. You know the feeling. Hangover's thirst meant frequent mid-morning stops at wayside streams along the winding road to the village of Ayun. His pace quickened as the sun passed the yardarm, but whenever he found a roadside stream, he dropped his head, drew in water mightily through bared teeth and would not stop until I hauled him away by rein, mane, and ears. Tim was riding a livelier grey, and with much more style than I could manage.

MOUNTAIN INN

We had arranged our horse trek through the tour agency Hindukush Trails, which has a liaison office at the Mountain Inn in Chitral. The Mountain Inn is famous for its delightful garden and its secluded position at the southern end of the town's busy bazaar. Here, amidst autumnal blossoms and leafy shade, I met Hindukush Trails' representative Babu Mohammad, a noted mountain guide and a man of great warmth. The traditional base camp on the approach to Tirich Mir, the highest peak of the Hindu Kush, is known as Babu's Camp—a reflection of Babu's stature in the mountaineering and trekking community. It was late in the season for arranging treks, but Babu never faltered. He conducted business in that wonderful way of things that you learn quickly to expect in Northern Pakistan. No fuss, no problems; everything is undertaken in a relaxed, sociable manner; any potential difficulty is addressed fully, then solved with calm detachment. You drink tea, you discuss, you ponder, you consider the possibilities. Soon, everything can be arranged, *inshallah*, God willing.

I made it clear to Babu that I was not an experienced horse rider. I have lived most of my life around horses but have not ridden many, nor felt entirely at ease with them. Tim was more able, but neither of us was an ccomplished rider. Babu smiled; there was no way he would turn us loose on anything other than docile mounts. But when I saw the Afghan ponies that cantered into the courtyard of the Mountain Inn two days later, I still felt a minor flutter of anxiety. They were handled at speed and with some panache by their tough-looking riders and, in the close confines of the buildings, they looked to be several hands higher than they actually were.

WESTERN SADDLES

Two of the riders were the owners of the horses. The third was a young Afghan who was to be our guide. This was Hamid Allah; he wore an old camouflage jacket over his *shalwar kameez* (baggy trousers and long shirt) and a skullcap of golden thread perched on his head. Babu had specified "Western" saddles for Tim and me. Hamid's pony was the smallest of the three and was heavily loaded with fodder, yet I never saw this sturdy little creature falter once during our journey. As always, half the neighbourhood turned out to watch our departure from the hotel courtyard, and soon we were ambling gently through Chitral's southern quarter to the amused, and bemused, glances of passers-by.

To ride on these old tracks was a pleasure, however. Hamid had little English to our nonexistent Pushtu, but he was extremely good-natured and patient, considering our slow pace. Time ambled by. Distance was covered eventually. Sometimes we cantered along the empty tracks, although the infamous "rising trot" is a motion I have never quite managed painlessly. We rode between the grey-green waters of the Chitral River and the barren foothills of the high Hindu Kush range that runs into Afghanistan, a mere 25km (15 miles) to the west. Nothing seemed to flourish in this arid land, but once we spotted a huge, lime-coloured lizard, with a tail over a metre long, race uphill in a strange wobbling motion. It looked big enough to saddle up.

TIRICH MIR

Our first day's riding eventually took us high above the Chitral River onto a rocky bluff from where, far to the north, we could see the snow-covered Tirich Mir, the highest peak in the Hindu Kush. From the other side of the bluff we looked down on the confluence of the Ayun and Chitral rivers within an intricate and colourful landscape of irrigated fields and orchards. On the eastern side of the Chitral Valley, the grey and ochre hills of the Hindu Raj, struck through with thick veins of marble, soared into the blue sky. The contrast with the vivid colours of the valley was striking.

We stayed overnight at Ayun, where we visited Shahzada Khush Ahmed ul Mulk at his beautiful home at Balawosht, high above the Ayun Valley. Khush Ahmed is a member of the Chitrali royal family. He is in his 80s, a remarkable man who in his time has travelled great distances on foot and on horseback throughout the North West Frontier Province and Afghanistan. He was a key

ORIGINS OF THE KALASH

There are numerous "Creation Myths" that claim to explain the origins of the Kalash. There is an enduring but unprovable belief among the Kalash themselves, some of whom are fair-skinned, fair-haired, and blue-eyed, that they are descended from deserting Aryan soldiers, or from a General Shalaksha, of Alexander the Great's army, which passed through the Hindu Kush in the 4th century B.C. It seems more likely that the Kalash represent a resilient ancient culture that may have Middle Eastern, and even Mediterranean characteristics.

figure in the humanitarian care and resettlement of the thousands of Afghan refugees, who fled into the NWFP in the wake of the Soviet occupation of Afghanistan in the 1980s. Still exiled, they are forgotten by the outside world.

Later, Tim and I eased our riding muscles with a brisk walk through the lush meadows of Ayun. We climbed high up the green slopes, then walked along the bank of a main irrigation channel. In the Hindu Kush, as in all the great mountains of Asia, bountiful water is the blessing bestowed by glaciers on desolate valleys. The clever disposal of this water is what transforms raw alluvium into green oases. Here, at Ayun, this water is even used to drive an electricity generator. The channel we followed had been cut along the steep slopes of the northern side of the Ayun Valley and drew off water from higher up the river. We followed the channel to a spectacular viewpoint. Below, at the valley mouth, the wide river plain was a dense pattern of fields and orchards that were lush with growth. The Ayun River curved round its northern edge. A thunderous waterfall, the final torrent of all the gathered threads of the hillside irrigation channels, poured into the river.

they tend to dress in *shalwar kameez* and are indistinguishable in dress from their Muslim neighbours. Kalash women, however, still wear their vivid and colourful clothes, jewellery, and headgear. Their main dress is a black tunic-like robe; they are the Siah Posh, the "wearers of the black robes." The robes are highlighted by beautiful coloured embroidery at the neck, shoulders, cuffs, and hem.

It is the accessories of Kalash dress that are truly striking. The tunics are belted with broad cummerbunds in red or purple, again threaded with embroidery. Most vivid of all are the headdresses worn by Kalash women over their plaited hair. For everyday use there is the *shushutre*, a cap-like headband with a long tail, decorated with cowrie shells, buttons, and beads in bands of brilliant colour. The more elaborate *kopas* is a ceremonial headdress, worn also in winter. It consists of a woven cap with a very broad tail sweeping back from the crown of the head, again with intricate decoration of shells, beads, coins, and buttons. Kalash women also wear numerous bangles and rings and layers of necklaces made out of orange, red, and white beads. You may see older women, and children, with their faces stained with a black paste made from crushed goat's horn. This is applied to protect the skin from wind and cold.

KALASH VILLAGE

From the check post it took us an hour to reach Anish, a Kalash village, where we turned off the main track to reach the delightful little Jinna Kalash Hotel. The hotel was a simple two-storey building, the upper storey being a line of rooms unfurnished except for beds and fronted by a narrow balcony. Hamid tethered and fed the horses in an adjoining meadow. We sat in the shade of the balcony and drank fresh *chai* (tea), then ate a simple

TO THE KALASH

The next morning Hamid, Tim, and I left Ayun in sunlight that was almost too hot to bear. Our road took us through the wide central bazaar of the village and on up the dusty track that led along the southern side of the Ayun Valley. Here we moved in and out of glaring sunlight and cool shade, where the track ran beneath great overhangs of beetling rock. Below us the river poured over its rocky bed. The horses ambled on in their gentle, dogged fashion until we reached the junction of the Bumburet and Rumbar valleys and a crossing of the Ayun River to where a government checkpost commanded the way ahead. Here Tim and I had to sign in and pay a permit fee, before turning northeast into the Bumburet Valley.

Soon the hills opened out and the valley grew green as the road wound between sunlit meadows and tall trees. We began to notice the distinctively dressed Kalash girls amongst groups of Muslim youngsters who played in the meadows and peered down at us from the wooded slopes of the valley. Kalash men once wore traditional costume, but today

CHITRAL SHOPPING

Chitral's Shahi Bazaar and New Bazaar are purdah bazaars and local women are not seen. Foreign women, preferably with a male companion, can frequent the bazaar. They may draw curious glances, although attitudes are easing all the time. It is still sensible for both males and females to dress conservatively. Numerous shops sell Chitrali hats, (*pakols*), *chunghas* (gowns), waistcoats, bags, and light rugs, all in a soft woollen cloth called *patti*, often with intricate embroidery. There are numerous shops selling Afghan and Chitrali rugs, jewellery, antiques, and precious stones. For sizzling hot tikkas, or pakora (deep-fried vegetables), or roasted corncob, try the wonderfully scruffy Goldpur Road, leading off the central PIA Chowk.

lunch of potato stew and chapatis. Before long we were approached by a young man who introduced himself as a Kalash guide. This was Taj Muhammad, a native of the valleys and of Kalash stock, although his father had converted to Islam in the late 1940s. Taj had been brought up a Muslim, but retained strong links with Kalash relatives. He had a cool, almost urban, sophistication and was an accomplished linguist; the ideal person from whom to learn about the Kalash.

After lunch we said goodbye to Hamid Allah as he took off back to Chitral, mounted on the packhorse and leading old Hangover and the grey behind him. With a cheery wave, Hamid disappeared in a cloud of dust and at a terrific pace.

OTHER TREKKING OPTIONS

It may be possible to arrange a horse-trekking itinerary in the Chitral area that does not necessarily take in the Kalash Valleys. Longer horse riding trips are possible. You can also trek by foot between the Kalash valleys. You can make an enjoyable two-day, 14km (9-mile) trek from Bumburet to Rumbur over the Donson Pass and the Kundyak An Pass. You should hire a local guide because of some difficult route finding. A day trek can be made from Birir to Bumburet; again a guide is essential. You should be aware of the possible effects of altitude (see page 136).

I reckoned he would cover the distance to Chitral in a few hours compared with our relaxed amble of the past 2 days. Tim and I walked with Taj to the village of Krakal, where we visited a Kalash household and talked with relatives of Taj's. In Bumburet, the Kalash villages all occupy the steep north slope of the valley and catch the best of the sun. The Kalash build sturdy timber houses, usually of pine and cedar with layers of pebbles and stone between the planks of wood. The dwellings are often in tiers, the roof of the lower house being used as a veranda by the one above. Cooking is done on a small central hearth, above which is a small hole in the roof to vent smoke.

KALASH TRADITIONS

We visited other homes, where we talked to Kalash families and shared bowls of walnuts, dried grapes, and apricots. On a sunny veranda we met Taj's uncle who spoke of the Kalash traditions and practices. Taj was able to translate answers to our many questions about the remarkable survival of the ancient Kalash culture. The Kalash religion is complex and has numerous deities who are worshipped at open altars of stone, or in wooden temples called Han, where ceremonies are also held. Beliefs are firmly based on animism and a powerful duality: the pure, *onjeshta*, and the impure, *pragata*. The pure is associated with high pastures, goats, and shrines. Women are considered to be *pragata* because of menstruation and childbearing. They are not allowed near the *onjeshta* regions of the high pastures or near goat and cattle barns. During menstruation and when they give birth, women stay isolated in a special house outside village limits. This is the Bashali House. These matters are only part of an intensely complex culture, but you need to be at least aware of them when visiting the Kalash valleys.

Kalash farmers use traditional methods and implements, although mechanical harvesters have now appeared in the valleys. You will still see bullocks drawing wooden ploughs. Kalash fields are not terraced as in other parts of the Hindu Kush but the Kalash utilize irrigation channels. Crops include maize, wheat, millet, barley, and beans. Wine is produced from plentiful grapes and some tobacco is grown. The Kalash orchards are full of walnuts, mulberries, pears, apples, apricots, and pomegranates. Goats are an important possession, and some sheep and cattle are kept. The herds are moved to high pastures in summer.

SURVIVAL

There are only 3,000 Kalash in the three valleys. Kalash culture has survived because of centuries of isolation and because groups of Kalash throughout history resisted domination by outside influences such as Islam. Whether or not Kalash culture, in its authentic form, will survive 21st-century influences is another matter.

That evening, after a simple supper of meat and dhal, Tim and I sat on the balcony of the Jinna Kalash Hotel and spoke with a fellow traveller, a Danish girl who had been in Bumburet for several weeks and who was deeply interested in the Kalash and their culture. We talked about the pros and cons of tourism's potentially destabilizing effect on the Kalash. The consensus was that so long as tourism is discreetly managed and is thoughtful and respectful, then visits to the Kalash, by Westerners especially, could be a major force in preserving Kalash identity in the face of other more immediate influences, such as Islam. The amplified calls to prayer from several valley mosques already dominate life in Bumburet. Wholesale logging, mainly by outside contractors, of cedar and pine in the upper Kalash valleys is damaging the ecology of the Kalash environment. There are complex matters at stake here; we were certain of that.

SCHOOLS

The following morning the ever-patient Taj took me hither and thither through the valley. The Kalash have good educational facilities and various Western organizations have established health and

---

PHOTOGRAPHY

One of the great features of Kalash culture is the colourful and intricate jewellery and clothes worn by Kalash women. Photographing Kalash costume is irresistible to tourists and the Kalash are happy to oblige. You should always ask permission and give some thought to striking up a rapport, however difficult this may be given language differences. Try not to merely "point and shoot." Please do not photograph Kalash women if they are washing by the river. In recent times the situation over photography has become complicated because of the thorny matter of payment for taking photographs. Some commentators feel that this is a regrettable development; others feel that the Kalash should benefit directly. If you are concerned about the situation you should ask the advice of your tour guide. Please remember that there is a substantial Muslim population in the Kalash valleys and that you should not photograph Muslim women.

social welfare centres. We visited several schools and I spoke to a group of bright and charming girl students with a roll call of evocative names. Durdana Bibi, Gul Naz, Gul Bigim, Masran, Shaheen Gul, and Arab Gul were all modern in their outlook, but were sharply aware and proud of their traditions and their singular culture. I was intrigued to learn that several of the girls had visited Greek islands that I knew well, as guests of a Greek health foundation that is active in the valleys.

Later, Taj and I climbed the northern slopes of Bumburet, then followed an irrigation channel to the village of Brun. Here the timber houses of the Kalash occupy a narrow sequence of terraces on the stony, upper slopes below steep mountain walls. Just above the village is a sacrificial site where goats are ritually slaughtered and then roasted on a ceremonial fire. On an isolated spur above the village stood the Bashali House, set apart by its elevated

position against a background of sunlit mountain and intense blue sky.

Eventually, Taj and I made our way down awkward slopes on steep shortcut paths until we emerged behind the Jinna Kalash Inn. It was time for Tim and me to return to Chitral, and after a quick lunch we left by jeep. Taj came with us as far as Ayun, where he hopped aboard a cargo jeep that would take him directly to town. At Ayun we paid a brief visit to Khush Ahmed ul Mulk before driving on to Chitral. Here in that world of purdah bazaars, of the strictly male *shalwar kameez*, plain waistcoat and Chitrali cap, there was little chance of even catching a glimpse of anything so remarkable as those colourful Kalash headdresses.

Right: The elaborate headdresses of the Kalash women immediately distinguish them from their Muslim neighbours
Below: Cheerful Chitrali schoolboys

GOING IT ALONE

INTERNAL TRAVEL

There are daily mini-bus links between Peshawar and Chitral ($5). The journey takes 12 hours or more. Private transport from Peshawar or Islamabad to Chitral costs about $180.

Pakistan International Airlines runs two flights a day from Peshawar Airport to Chitral using Fokker F27s ($50. This is the "foreigners" fare and is substantially more than Pakistani nationals' fare.) The flight takes 95 minutes and is dependent on good weather conditions. Cancellation of flights over consecutive days creates a backlog of frustrated travellers. Reserving seats well in advance is essential, and even then things do not always go to plan. If your flight is cancelled make sure you reconfirm your booking for the next day or you may lose your place.

WHEN TO GO

Access to Chitral by road from the south is by the Lowari Pass. This is closed by snow from November until May. From May to October the Kalash valleys are free of snow and travelling is pleasant. If you choose to trek between the valleys, note that the higher passes may have snow in April and late October.

PLANNING

Horses are best hired through an established tour agency such as Hindukush Trails. Hiring independently is difficult for strangers to the area. Jeep trips to the Kalash valleys can be arranged through hotels or through tour agencies Public transport jeeps go daily from Chitral to the Bumburet Valley (50 cents). There is one jeep per day to Rumbur Valley (50 cents). These jeeps can be overcrowded. Agencies will arrange for a Kalash guide. If you arrive independently in the Kalash valleys, it is best to hire a Kalash guide if you want to visit Kalash homes and move around the Kalash communities. Usually a Kalash guide will track you down almost as soon as you arrive in the valleys. Fees for guiding are open to negotiation, but expect to pay about $5–$6 for a day, and tip proportionately if you wish to.

If you are travelling on horseback to the Kalash, camping is a good option during the summer months. There are few accommodation options between Chitral and the Kalash valleys, but if you are hiring horses through a tour agency, they will arrange accommodation. There is a good choice of hotels in the Bumburet Valley from the luxurious to the basic. Hotels in the Rumbur and Birir valleys are fairly basic, but adequate.

SIGHTS IN CHITRAL

The early 20th-century Shahi Masjid mosque, at the bottom of Shahi Masjid Road (leading down from PIA Chowk) is a spectacular building, with magnificent umbrella domes. Nearby, on the riverbank, is Chitral Fort, much of which is in ruins. In 1895 British Indian troops were besieged here by forces of the Chitrali royal family for a month, before being relieved by British reinforcements marching from Gilgit across the snow-bound Shandur Pass.

HEALTH MATTERS

❑ Full travel insurance, including cover for medical and evacuation costs, as well as extra cover for adventure sports, is essential.

❑ Inoculations to guard against Hepatitis A, typhoid, meningitis, tetanus, and polio are strongly recommended. Seek your doctor's advice well in advance. Protection against malaria should also be taken. Protection against rabies and Japanese B encephalitis may be considered, although risk of contraction is small.

❑ Treat even bottled water with iodine tablets. Try to drink at least two to three litres of water per day. Do not drink river water, even although your guides may do so with impunity. Do not use ice cubes.

❑ Avoid eating salads and cold food. Fresh fruit is plentiful in many parts of North Pakistan. Some authorities advise peeling fruit before eating it. The problem is that even as you peel, you may transfer bacteria from the peel to your hand and back to the peeled fruit. The dilemma is entirely yours.

❑ Use waterproof sunscreen with high protection factor. The sun's rays in the mountains can be very intense.

❑ Carry a small first-aid kit, to include pain killers, antiseptic, plasters, and bandages. Ask your doctor's advice about dysentery tablets and antibiotics.

WHAT TO TAKE

❑ Sun hat.
❑ Long, thick trousers.
❑ Strong boots.

PAKISTAN

23 River Rafting in the Karakoram

by Des Hannigan

The glacier-fed rivers of North Pakistan slice through the broad valleys and narrow gorges of the mighty Karakoram mountains. This rafting trip down the Hunza and Gilgit rivers passes through some of the finest mountain scenery in the world.

You hang on tight when a river raft starts its bobbing glide into white water and minor mayhem. Photography fails as exposure and focus go haywire in a world of crashing spray, wobbling views, and rocking horizons. Your priority is to stay in the raft.

It was mid-October and we were hurtling down the icy waters of the Hunza River on the first day of a three-day rafting trip in the far north of Pakistan. The Chinese border lay 90km (56 miles) upstream at the Khunjerab Pass, the junction of the Karakoram and Pamir ranges. Overnight a first breath of winter had come from that vast northern heartland. Snow powdered the slopes above 3,000m (9,900ft) and turned the upper peaks into

 Rafting on the Hunza and Gilgit rivers is well within the capabilities of those with average fitness and energy, but you need to be fairly agile. Being a competent swimmer is an advantage in the unlikely case of capsize. No special training or skill is required by crew because the safe handling of the raft is the responsibility of the river guides. A spell as bow paddler is enjoyable, provided you have fairly strong arms and good co-ordination.

 You may feel uncomfortable at first beneath layers of wetsuit, waterproofs, buoyancy aid, and helmet, but they are essential for your safety. Be prepared for the occasional equivalent of a bucket of cold water in the face. Overnight accommodation is in hotels.

 All specialist equipment, including wetsuits, wetsuit boots, waterproofs, buoyancy aids, and safety helmets is supplied by the tour organizer. In autumn, thermal underwear can help to keep you warm if there is an early cold spell. Bring dry clothing in a sealable plastic bag.

pure white fantasy castles that were periodically obscured by gloomy clouds. The grey-green waters of the Hunza seemed bleak and hostile at first; but we were wrapped up to the gills in wetsuits, waterproofs, lifejackets, safety helmets, and heart-warming enthusiasm—loving every minute of it, in fact. As the raft accelerated into yet another stretch of frantic rapids, I stowed the cameras in watertight containers and settled for helter-skelter adventuring through the foam.

My 18-year-old son Tim and I had arranged our rafting trip through tour operator Travel Walji's local office at Gilgit, 180km (112 miles) to the south. The company has very skilled river guides who have been trained by American experts and who underpin their expertise with infectious enthusiasm and the friendliest of natures. Walji's rafting programmes are flexible, so with our limited time we had settled for a 4-day trip. This included 1 day's travel by jeep along the Karakoram Highway to our starting point at the village of Sust, on the Hunza River, 60km (37 miles) from the Pakistan–China border. Our river guide was Attaullah Khan, who came from Hunza. Atta was in his 20s; he was an instantly likeable man and had a rich sense of humour.

DESOLATE LANDSCAPE

We travelled north by jeep from Gilgit, following the Karakoram Highway alongside the Hunza River and through a shattered desolate landscape of the kind that gave rise to the ancient name *kara koram*, the "dark crumbling rocks." Until the KKH was built in the 1970s, the only route to Hunza and to China was along a perilous cliffside track on the west side of the river. Surviving sections of this track can be seen, still clinging to sheer rock faces. Such was the area's isolation that the first jeep reached Hunza only in 1957. The district was ruled by its royal family until 1974, when it became a sub-division of the Northern Areas.

The whole area between Gilgit and Hunza is watched over by the mighty peak of Rakaposhi, 7,788m (25,551ft). From the KKH near the village of Chalt, 60km (37 miles) north of Gilgit, the elegant summit of the great mountain dominates the southern outlook, though it is often wreathed in cloud.

From Chalt, the KKH continues through the district of Nagar and then, at the village of Pisan, the highway crosses the river into Hunza. Soon we reached the chief town of Hunza, Karimabad, where we stopped for lunch and visited the splendid Baltit Fort, historical home of the Mirs, the traditional rulers of Hunza. The original village of Baltit, which surrounds the fort, has been absorbed into the expanded settlement of Karimabad. This modern name celebrates Prince Karim, the present Aga Khan, spiritual leader of the Nizar Ismaili sect of Islam, to which a majority of Hunza people belong.

KARIMABAD

Take time to wander round Karimabad. The town is a snakes-and-ladders' mosaic of terraced fields and leafy orchards, framed by cobbled lanes and stone walls beneath towering mountains. Icy, opaque water from the Ultar Nala, the steep valley that descends from the high ground below the Ultar peak, supplies a network of irrigation channels that transforms whole patches of raw earth into green oases. Karimabad is now crammed with gift and souvenir shops and is emphatically a tourist town; but its integrity is intact, its location magnificent, and the friendliness of its people unforced. There were children everywhere, bright-eyed

with curiosity and eager to greet us in English with precise, clear voices. In the numerous craft and jewellery shops lining the narrow streets you will find traditional Hunza clothing and artefacts for sale, though often at inflated prices.

From Karimabad we drove the 90km (56 miles) to Sust through increasingly dramatic mountain scenery. At Sust you enter frontier territory. The old village of Sust lies out of sight above the KKH. On the road itself is the modern settlement, a creation of cross-border trade and customs control. The road at either end of modern Sust is lined with carnival-coloured lorries; the main settlement is crammed for several hundred metres with immigration and customs checkpoints, shops, food stalls, garages, and roughshod hotels and eating houses. Browse the shops here by all means, but expect anarchic pricing and be prepared to haggle for goods of all sorts from cooking pots to bolts of silk.

We stopped overnight in the friendly and comfortable P.T.D.C. Hotel at the northern end of Sust. Later that evening Atta's fellow river guide, Ahsanullah Baig, arrived with our raft and equipment on a jeep driven by one of Walji's remarkably efficient drivers, Mir Ahmad. For supper that evening we had the standard chicken khorma, boiled rice, and dhal. From your room in rural hotels in the Northern Areas you get used to hearing "supper" being pursued squawkingly round the backyard an hour or two before serving. The pursuit always ends with an abrupt, neck-wrung silence.

THE ENEMY

Over supper Atta talked enthusiastically about river rafting. The sport has its own special language and mythology, as with all adventure sports. "Always face the enemy" is the key lesson, we were told—the enemy being river rapids. A raft skipper needs to "read" the way ahead for crucial signs of danger that are often hidden by the complicated hydraulics of fast-moving water. Partially submerged boulders create "pour-overs" that can cause disaster. Certain pour-overs form the vividly named "frowning hole" that creates a "stopper" in which a raft can become trapped, immobile at first but with the risk of being turned turtle. The friendlier sounding "smiling hole" creates a widening downstream flow that takes the raft safely clear. A "drop" is a river-wide "hole" that can capsize a raft and drive it under, holding it submerged in a contrary thrust of water. Eddy lines, the wrinkles and scars on the river's surface, are an important indication of what kind of hazard lies ahead.

All this rafting talk was exciting stuff, but Atta assured us that we would be unlikely to meet major hazards and that, if any did loom ahead, we would raft out and portage round the danger, even though he and Ahsan could handle most challenges on the river. Tim and I were holiday rafters after all. That night it snowed on the high ground and poured with rain below the 3,000m (9,900ft) line. A rising river might add to the fun, I thought, as I woke intermittently to bouts of thunderous rain.

DULL DAY

Next morning the rain and snow had stopped but the day was damp, cold, and sunless. The dull light reduced the mono-chrome colours of the mountains to even gloomier tones. Atta, Ahsan, and Mir Ahmad were busy in the hotel forecourt inflating the raft and rigging its safety gear, oar frames, and stow boxes, helped by the good-natured staff of the PTDC Motel. The overnight rain had not increased the river's volume very much, Atta said, but the water would be cold, the air icy. We changed into our wetsuits, struggled into hefty waterproofs, and buckled on buoyancy aids and helmets.

Sust was as lively as it had been the previous day. Frontier towns never sleep. From the centre of the settlement we drove the jeep, with raft on roof, down a rough track to the rocky riverbank. We were followed by a crowd of curious onlookers who watched intently as we slid the raft into the edge of the stream. We were using a 4.5m (15ft) hypolan inflatable, a "self-bailer" that ejects any washed-in water through small drainage ports, called grommet holes, in its inflatable floor. This type of raft is symmetrical: it has a matching bow and stern, and is

Right: *Kharamabad bridge, a nerve-tingling cable suspension construction over the Hunza River*
Inset: *Always "face the enemy," the white water ahead*
Below: *The spiky Tupopdan peaks*

steered by a central oarsman assisted by two paddlers kneeling in the bows. Atta took Tim and me through the safety drill, with lucid explanations of what to expect and how to cope with the unexpected. We would experience average Grade III rapids with occasional III+ and IV out of a range of Grade I to V; in between there would be plenty of easygoing Grade I glides and Grade II ripples.

River runs of Grade III, with the odd Grade IV thrown in, are more than enough to give rookie rafters plenty of excitement, and the experience is well within most peoples' capabilities, especially when in the safe hands of experienced river guides. Tim, being a good deal fitter than I am and having experience as a sea canoeist, was appointed bow paddler with Ahsan. Paddlers need to co-ordinate well and to have strong arms, but bow paddling is a chance for novice rafters to join the action.

ON THE WATER

Tim and I had reconnoitred the first kilometre (½ mile) of riverbank to the south of Sust the previous afternoon and were ready for a quick succession of Grade IIIs to start with. We were not disappointed.

HUNZA

Beautiful Hunza has for long been depicted as a legendary "Shangri La," an earthly paradise whose people enjoy longevity and enviable good health. The realities of life, in what is still a harsh, unforgiving environment, are far less rosy, of course, but you will find a more easygoing attitude in Hunza than elsewhere in the Northern Areas. Most Hunzakuts belong to the Ismaeli sect whose spiritual leader is the Aga Khan. Women in Hunza go unveiled in public. Respect for people's privacy is expected at all times, however, and you should not photograph women without careful and courteous inquiry.

Within seconds of casting off, to the muted cheers of the onlookers, Atta skilfully oared us into midstream as the raft slid into the first boulder-strewn white water. There was a moment's uncertainty when the side of the raft skidded down the smooth, swollen flank of a huge boulder, and then we were away, rocking through the boiling water. Ahsan and Tim paddled as Atta called out instructions in what became a recognizable litany of "back paddle" or "forward paddle." I lorded it in the stern, one foot jammed into a foot thong that would keep me inboard if I was jerked backwards. One hand gripped the safety rope, the other the raft frame. We swept forwards towards the narrowing river gorge and the towering walls of the 6,000m (19,690ft) mountain of Jurjur Khona, which seemed to block our way ahead in the formidable way that all great mountains do.

For the next few hours we rafted through an exhilarating sequence of boisterous rapids and smooth waters between the huge echoing walls and steep alluvial fans of the river gorge. Rafting, like canoeing, is one of the least intrusive, least environmentally damaging activities. The river runs, and you run with it. There is no fuel-related pollution, no noise (other than your whoops of excitement), no damage to vegetation or to the fabric of the landscape, and very little disturbance of wildlife. Between bouts of white water, you glide down river with a sense of calm detachment.

RIVERBANK AUDIENCE

On our effortless way south we passed the villages of Gircha, Jukulgar, and Mor Khun, whose field workers crowded to the banks to wave us on. Along the pebbly shores, where duck shooters had built boulder hides, crowds of youngsters ran to shout greetings and to marvel at this high-tech craft. Atta described how youngsters make themselves buoyancy frames of sealed plastic bottles and then launch themselves down river. Inflated goat skins were once used for perilous river transport throughout these mountains and even today such rafts are still in use and upcountry people travel long distances downriver spread-eagled across a single inflated inner tube or on multi-tubed rafts.

ACTIVE GEOLOGY

On this first day we made the best of the rapids between Sust and the village of Khaibar, 20km (12 miles) downstream. At one of the best runs we were defeated by the active geology of the Karakoram. The section had suffered recent rock falls and there were ugly razor-sharp fins of rock peppering the river. Atta decided to "line" the raft along the riverbank by pulling it along from the shore with fixed ropes. Even as the raft was being carefully manipulated along the east bank, a clattering slide of rock and sand tumbled down the western wall of the gorge and crashed into the river with an odd hissing sound, as if it was hot.

Several kilometres on, the day ended on a huge pebble beach, near the village of Khaiber and conveniently close to the Karakoram Highway, from where Mir Ahmad could bring the jeep to the water's edge. Here we loaded the raft onto the roof of the jeep and then headed south along the KKH for an overnight stop at the village of Passu.

BLUE SKIES

The next morning we woke to dazzling sunlight and cloudless blue skies. From Passu we drove back north and rafted in close to our previous day's stopping-off point. Immediately we hit rapids with the familiar excitement of a downhill run through tumultuous water. Today, the heat was fierce and we soon discarded our waterproofs as we moved out of the narrow river gorge into the wider world below the Tupopdan spires. Here, glacial damming of the Shimshal River, followed by catastrophic breaches and floods, has created a vast river plain of shingle and sand. The plain was made more desolate by its submergence in 1974 beneath a

temporary lake that swamped the Hunza Valley for 20km (12 miles).

To the west of this breathtaking arena lies the great snout of the Batura Glacier, black and gritty where it looms over the Karakoram Highway. In the distance, the peaks of the Batura Wall pierce the skyline like glittering teeth. To the north the great wall of Tupopdan soars from the river's bank, a vast Gothic-like frieze, ribbed and fluted and multicoloured, from grey through furnace red to the gleaming white of snowfields below black summit pinnacles. At the eastern end of this great wall, the Shimshal River pours from its deep valley to swell the Hunza where it spreads into numerous placid streams across the river flats. The fields and dwellings of Passu crowd together on the west bank.

BRIDGE GAME

On the east bank of the river, massive alluvial fans spill down from snow-dappled crests. High on the steep slopes, local people had spelled out celebratory messages in white stone as greetings to the Aga Khan on his visit to Hunza in the early 1980s. In the middle of the river plain we pulled out onto a shingle beach beneath a rocky island. A short scramble led to the top of the island where old walls indicated fields once used for grazing before the expanded river system isolated them. From here there were inspiring views of the Passu Glacier and

the glittering white fang of Shispar Sar, 7,611m (24,970ft), and the bulkier Ultar, 7,388m (24,239ft). In a stone pit on top of the island we found some old rubber tyres. Atta explained that during annual festivals, tyres are carried high up the mountain wall above the alluvial fans and are then set alight and sent rolling down the slopes in a fiery cascade.

We rafted for another kilometre (½ mile) or so, then pulled out on the east bank of the river beside Atta's "special treat." This was the Kharamabad Bridge, an astonishing cable suspension bridge surfaced with widely spaced planks and branches. The bridge runs high above the split channels of the Hunza River for well over a hundred metres (or yards) and has all the challenging characteristics of bad dreams and one-wrong-step-and-you're-doomed jungle dramas. Atta, Ahsan, and Tim strolled across the trembling planks with ease. I took photographs, then followed like an old cat. In high winds the experience is even more moving, but Atta explained that local women cross daily with heavy loads balanced on their heads. Local youngsters, as young as seven, run across at full speed, of course.

Above: *The water boiled around us as we rounded a large boulder*
Right: *Baltit Fort, Karimabad*
Left: *Shishpar peak*

LIZARDS AND DINOSAURS

Later we ate lunch of canned tuna fish, cheese, and biscuits on the river bank; there's no gourmet fare when you're out on the river in this rafting game. We watched tiny lizards like miniature dinosaurs scuttling among the rocks. We were at the heart of the kind of raw, primeval landscape that might well have once spawned dinosaurs. After lunch we drifted on lazily through quiet waters and occasional bursts of friendly rapids until we reached the village of Gulmit, site of the one-time summer palace of the ruling princes of Hunza. Beyond Gulmit, another convenient landing point gave the jeep access to the riverside. With the raft loaded onto the jeep's roof, we drove into the village and up to the Marco Polo Inn, where we were to stay the night.

The Inn is owned by the charming Raja Hussain Khan, greatgrandson of the last ruling Mir of Hunza. It is a delightful place, more classic hill station than conventional hotel in style. The rooms are fronted by a veranda that looks on to a garden awash with colourful geraniums and snapdragons against a background view of the great mountain wall of distant Tupopdan to the north and the high Gulmit Glacier to the west. Adjoining the hotel is the family home, an outstanding example of traditional Hunza building, complete with intricately carved doors. Raja Hussain Khan showed us round the tiny museum that also adjoins the hotel, and with great kindness took us on a tour round Gulmit, an attractive terraced settlement below steep cliffs. We visited the weaving centre in the village where Hunza craftswomen produce exquisite carpets.

MOUNTAIN CAMPAIGN

Later we visited one of the Northern Areas' most distinguished residents, Shah Khan, another member of the Hunza royal family. Shah Khan was a leader of the 1947 mountain campaign in which poorly armed soldiers of the Gilgit Scouts regiment, under commanders such as Shah Khan, drove the forces of the Maharaja of Kashmir back through the mountains of the Western Himalaya. The action secured the Northern Areas as semi-autonomous kingdoms until their full absorption into Pakistan in 1974. I had brought greetings to Shah Khan from a mutual friend, the accomplished British mountaineer Mike Banks, who had made the first ascent of Rakaposhi in the 1950s, as a member of a British expedition of which Shah Khan was liaison officer.

Back at the hotel we enjoyed a superb meal prepared by a Walji's expedition cook, the extremely good-natured Nizam-ud-Din, who had joined us at Passu. Chicken soup was followed by *karahi*, braised mutton, with tasty side dishes of dhal and *palak*, spinach in a spicy sauce, and *alu*, tiny potatoes in a more subtle sauce. Atta and Ahsan had gone south to Karimabad for the evening and the next morning they had news of a problem. The only access to the rafting-in point for the rapids south of Gulmit had been blocked by a new farm wall and our best run of the day was effectively lost to us. We had a quick conference and decided to head south by road to Gilgit, where we could run the lively rapids of the Gilgit River instead.

THE GILGIT RIVER

The lower Gilgit River has a succession of Grade III and Grade IV rapids, with one of the best runs located at the heart of Gilgit town, where the Chinarbagh Bridge crosses the river. The glorious sunshine of the previous day had gone and like our first day at Sust, grey, gloomy weather settled over the mountains. We rafted in about 24km (15 miles) upriver from Gilgit and hit Grade IV rapids immediately. This was followed by long, benign stretches of Grade I with occasional Grade II and III. The closer we got to the town the larger the riverbank audience became. At one point the river is compressed through a boulder neck, a Grade IV known as the Water Pipe. It is only a few feet below the edge of the riverside road and here an excited crowd waited to watch us as we crashed through.

Ahead lay the Konodas Bridge, which crosses the river from Gilgit's Kashmir Bazaar. Atta had warned us to expect a crowd of spectators and he was right. The bridge was dense with onlookers as we

raced beneath. A hundred metres (yards) before the next fast run, youngsters on the shore shouted and hooted good-naturedly as we slid past in midstream. "They're saying goodbye," Atta told us with a grin. "They never expect us to make it through this next one." Cool comfort. Atta and Ahsan often ran the Gilgit for practice during the spring months, when the water is high, and they had turned turtle (without mishap) at this particular rapid more than once; hence the ghoulish anticipation of the local youngsters. At this time of year, however, the run was a reasonable Grade IV and we shot through with ease.

Darkness was falling now. Ahead loomed the Chinarbagh Bridge and below it a full-blooded Grade IV, short-lived but fierce. It was a suitable signing off. We rolled through the tumbling crests, fighting the corkscrew twist of the river to pop out beyond the bridge, our momentum carrying us in a final dying glide onto a convenient sandy beach where Mir Ahmad and Nizam-ud-Din waited with the jeep. Within the hour Tim and I were at our hotel, showered, changed, and ready for dinner—minor veterans of Hunza rafting, with unforgettable memories of the world's most spectacular mountains.

THE GULMIT FOLK MUSEUM

The museum at Gulmit is crammed with impressive memorabilia of Hunza history and tradition. It is small, but has a richly authentic atmosphere. Among examples of Hunza costume and domestic objects there are some marvellous eccentricities, including the tiny, toy-like rifle given to a ruler of Hunza by the English soldier Lord Kitchener in the early 20th century. You can purchase handmade artefacts in colourful Hunza designs here. The entrance fee is 40 cents (an additional donation is appreciated).

GOING IT ALONE

INTERNAL TRAVEL

There are regular bus links to Gilgit from Rawalpindi/Islamabad, operated by NATCO (Northern Areas Transport Company) and Masherbrum Tours, both of whom run daily services and a few night services ($5–$6). The journey by bus to Gilgit can take up to 18 hours. Smaller companies run 20-seater Toyota Coasters on the route and these may cut the journey by about 3 hours ($6–$8). Private hire car is the most comfortable option ($160 one way).

The quickest way of getting to the Northern Areas is by air. Pakistan International Airlines runs one to three flights a day between Islamabad Airport and Gilgit using Fokker F27s ($50 one-way approx.) This is the "foreigners" fare and is substantially more than Pakistani nationals' fare. The trip takes an hour and is an experience in its own right. Weather conditions can wreak havoc with schedules. Cancellation over several days creates a backlog of frustrated travellers. Reserving seats well in advance is essential and even then things do not always go to plan. If your flight is cancelled be sure to reconfirm your booking for the next day or you may lose your place. Try securing a seat on the right-hand side for best mountain views on the Islamabad–Gilgit flight.

WHEN TO GO

The best periods for rafting in Northern Pakistan are April to May and September to mid-November. During these periods river flow in the main raftable rivers is low enough to give exciting runs. September to mid-November is the best bet for good runs coupled with clear skies and balanced temperatures, although it can be cold from mid-October onwards. From June to the beginning of September the flow can be dangerously high, although certain sections of river can be run during July. In winter the weather is often too cold and the river gorges can be snowbound.

TIPPING

Tipping or *baksheesh* (a gift or donation) is a way of life in Pakistan. Anyone who supplies the slightest service to you may expect a tip. In hotels and restaurants an average 20–30 cents should suffice for services. When hiring vehicles, or when on trek, the tipping of guides, drivers, and cooks is usually expected. There is a hierarchy, of course, with guides being tipped more than drivers or cooks who, in turn, are tipped more than porters. If you are on an organized trek, ask the trek leader or the tour agency manager for advice on tipping.

FINDING A GUIDE/ EQUIPMENT HIRE

There are few tour companies in Pakistan with the capacity and experience to organize white-water rafting, but Walji's Adventure Pakistan offer excellent rafting trips under the guidance of extremely well trained river guides and with first-class rafts and equipment. Walji's rafting programme covers everything from half-day rafting on the Gilgit River to two-or three-day trips. They also offer multi-day rafting adventures on various rivers, often incorporating trekking as well. Depending on availability, the company will tailor a rafting trip to suit your needs. A sample price for five-day white water rafting is $495; single supplement $60. This includes road transport, accommodation (usually in tents but, where convenient, hotel accommodation can be arranged at extra cost), food, and equipment; half-day rafting costs about $80, including supply of equipment. Rafting trips can be arranged through Walji's Islamabad office or through their Gilgit and Karimabad offices.

TRAVELLERS' TIPS

❑ Always comply with your river guide's instructions.
❑ If you feel there is something you would rather not attempt, do not be afraid to say so. Professional guides always respect client's wishes.
❑ If you have to change out of your wetsuit in the open, make sure that local people cannot see you.
❑ Taking action photographs from aboard a river raft can be dangerous, especially if you stand unsecured when the raft is running through rapids. Make sure that the raft has watertight containers in which you can store your cameras when not in use.

HEALTH MATTERS

See recommendations on p. 209.

WHAT TO TAKE

❑ Change of clothing in a sealable plastic bag.
❑ Thermal underwear (not in high summer).

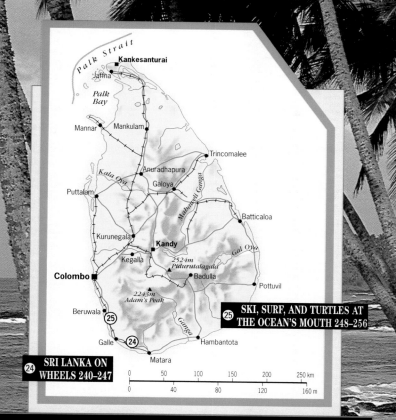

On the map:

Kankesanturai

Palk Strait

Jaffna

Palk Bay

Mannar Mankulam

Trincomalee

Kala Oya Anuradhapura

Galoya

Puttalam

Batticaloa

Kurunegala

Mahaweli Ganga

Kandy

Gal Oya

Kegalla *2524m Pidurutalagala*

Colombo Badulla

Pottuvil

2243m Adam's Peak

Beruwala (25)

Galle (24)

Gangai Hambantota

Matara

(25) **SKI, SURF, AND TURTLES AT THE OCEAN'S MOUTH 248–256**

(24) **SRI LANKA ON WHEELS 240–247**

Scale: 0 50 100 150 200 250 km
0 40 80 120 160 m

SRI LANKA

Ringed by 1,585km (985 miles) of coastline, Sri Lanka appears as a droplet of water falling from the southern tip of India. It rises from palm-fringed beaches washed by the Indian Ocean, through dry tropical forests to its highest point, Mount Pidurutalagala 2,524m (8,281ft). Basking in an average temperature of 27°C or 80°F (much cooler in the hills) the island is watered by two monsoons.

An abundance of spices attracted the Portuguese and Dutch to the island in the 15th century until the British arrived, establishing tea, rubber, and coconut plantations, developing the railways and founding the legal and commercial system. Sri Lanka became independent in 1948, yet English is widely spoken and tea is still the biggest export. Other visitors have included Lord Buddha, emissaries of King Solomon in search of jewels for the Queen of Sheba and explorer Marco Polo. Today's traveller comes to dive the coral reefs, windsurf down rivers, hike up mountains, track elephants and leopards, meditate with monks, or walk barefoot to a Buddha.

The beaches of Sri Lanka's west coast are the epitome of a tropical paradise

24 Sri Lanka on Wheels

by Lee Karen Stow

On an island crisscrossed by surfaced roads, gravel lanes, and dirt tracks, the blaring horn rules the way, shooing everything in its path. On two wheels I share these dusty thoroughfares with cyclists, stray cows, bullock carts, and BMWs, before heading for the wilds of the jungle and a traffic jam of a different kind.

Sri Lanka appears tiny on the world map; just 353km (220 miles) from north to south and 183km (114 miles) from west to east at its fattest part. No highway or fast motorway serves its main cities and towns, but that doesn't stop drivers careering along choked main roads as though they're competing in the Grand Prix. The only language of the road is "beep," and the rule for overtaking is that there isn't one. Drivers simply go for it, passing a bus or bicycle on either side at wobbling speed.

A newspaper report dated July 1999 stated that people living at busy intersections have a high lead content in their blood, and that the pollution is worsening owing to rising numbers of vehicles on the road, many of which run on diesel. You ride behind a cloud of black smoke

1 You have to be highly alert to cope with the traffic on the busy roads. But walks are pleasant and climbs are manageable if done when the weather is cool.

★ Riding buses, trains, and tuc-tucs is uncomfortable; and rest stops are at squat toilets and diners with dodgy food. Accommodation ranges from basic guesthouses with mosquito nets patched with tape to reasonable and clean hotels. Expect cockroaches.

✕ If you're planning on some serious motorbiking, take your own helmet. A puncture repair kit is useful for bicycles. Waterproofs are essential in the monsoon season. It will probably be too hot for leathers, but you should consider wearing protective gear. Take a camera, plenty of film, polarizer, and UV filter, and binoculars to spot wildlife on safari. A tent and sleeping bag are needed for camping and a mosquito net is a good idea.

belching from buses lopsided with passengers. You lather on the sunblock and by the end of a long, hot day, a film of grime covers your face.

Looking back, however, I had some great times on the road. Truly hilarious is the rickshaw/three-wheeler/two-two/tuc-tuc—call it what you will. One morning, in search of a bank, I hopped into the back seat of a tuc-tuc. This cheaper alternative to the taxi has no doors and the driver sits hunched in the cramped cockpit surrounded by tassels of silk-thread, their sheen faded with the sunlight. There's a shrine to Buddha on the dashboard. One driver had a custom-built horn that whistled at passing females.

For total freedom on the road, the brave can hire a moped or motorbike. It's hair-raising, but only on two wheels can you pause to watch women hang washing on the tombs of a cemetery in a shanty town; or take photographs of Buddha rising from the corners of road junctions; or watch two children squashed into a red plastic washing up bowl taking a shower under an outside tap; or halt while a funeral cortège, half a dozen men carrying a coffin, crosses a roundabout.

When I told a local that I wanted to hire a motorbike and go sightseeing, he gawped at me and said I was insane. It didn't help that the owner of the guesthouse where I was staying had lost a leg in a motorbike accident. But I'd heard about the quiet back roads that slither along the coast and wind up towards the cooler hill country. It was merely a case of finding the way.

Two's COMPANY

I began slowly, as a pillion passenger, along the busy Colombo to Galle coastal road that slithers through the popular southwest resorts, squeezing my legs in tight as we rode, for fear a bus overtaking on the other side might slice off my kneecaps. I soon decided this was a foolish idea, took a bus south to Tangalla, and picked up my wheels there.

At Tangalla I convinced Jake Lee, a student from England, to come motorbiking with me. Jake was taking a weekend off from his 3-month placement as a teacher of English at a college and children's home on the outskirts of Colombo run by a Buddhist monk.

A boy who lived near the beach at Tangalla offered us his brother's Honda 125 for the day, at 500 rupees. The bike looked well cared for, but we realized we wouldn't be insured and discovered that the engine had been drained of oil, so we declined the offer and hired a similar model from Vigtha Enterprises in Tangalla (500 rupees for half a day).

There was only one crash helmet available; so we borrowed the owner's— to his dismay. Now, recalling rolling over squashed coconut husks, banana skins, and cowdung and being chased by stray dogs, I think we must have been mad to even contemplate tackling Sri Lanka's roads. Yet within minutes we bravely overtook a tuc-tuc and headed down the coast with the sandy wind on our cheeks.

The road south, once it passes Matra, is not so bad. It is a beautiful stretch, hugging the shoreline where deep fringes of

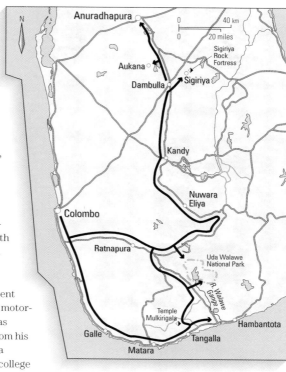

Exploring southern Sri Lanka

coconut palms bow to rocky inlets and moon-shaped bays. After Tangalla the road is quieter and verges (for refuge) become wider.

The route leads to Hambantota, into a contrasting, dry terrain. We stopped for chilled cola at a restaurant by the edge of a sheet of water that hides crocodiles by day and acts as a launchpad for waterfowl. Though it was monsoon season, it rained only once, lashing down hard until the sun came out and dried everything so intensely that steam rose from our sleeves.

Nearing Hambantota, we reached a spread of shallow saltpans, shimmering pink and grey—a surreal setting, like a scene from a science fiction movie. Women, clad in baggy skirts, blouses, and headscarves to keep out the relentless sun, hack relentlessly at water fields with heavy iron dredges. Once loosened, the

SRI LANKA

salt is raked into growing crystal mounds on which the women stand. We could not imagine such monotony. The women stop occasionally to drink water under the attention of male supervisors, who make sure visitors don't take photographs.

We retraced our route and headed inland to the Temple Mulkirigala (actually five temples), reached by climbing

dozens of steps past monkeys playing on wall tops. The caves, dating back 2,500 years, are dressed with Buddhas of varying sizes and poses under ceilings painted with Buddha scenes. Jake and I took turns keeping an eye on the bike while the other one climbed to the temples, stopping to accept monkey nuts from Buddhist monks.

It was here that we noticed our right ankles and shins were sprayed with engine oil. The bike had sprung a leak. And the milometer had packed up too, so we didn't know how far we'd come. Jake suggested we return to the hire shop, and I offered to ride us back. This was fantastic, cruising at a steady 48kph (30mph), passing paddy fields and men on bicycles balancing live fish on the handbars—until a tic from a cow flew into my eye, hitting the eyeball like an arrow.

I lost sight, screamed in agony, swerved, and brought us to a halt in a shallow ditch. Villagers rushed out to see the commotion, and instead of helping, stared and giggled. By the time we arrived back at the hire shop, my eye was red, sore, and watering and our trousers

Left: *Chatting to a monk at Mulkirigala temple*
Above: *Motorbike is a popular form of transport along Sri Lanka's busy west coast*
Right: *Aukana Buddha—built by the master*
Below right: *Buddhist monks*

felt as greasy as a mechanic's rag. But the ride had certainly been memorable.

AWAY FROM THE OCEAN

To tour inland from the south is to filter on country lanes slithering by pea-green rice paddies, water buffaloes, and rubber plantations. Scarecrows stand on the exposed rafters of part-finished houses to ward off evil spirits. Colonial houses with ornate verandas, abandoned by the British when Sri Lanka achieved independence, are mostly well preserved. Road signs are non-existent: you ask, or you guess. Roads themselves are generally in good condition, but after monsoon rains they can become potholed. To remedy this, the villagers are given a pile of chippings, which they use to patch the gaps.

Borrowing a bicycle from a villager, I rode around, swerving to avoid a herd of buffalo emerging from the bushes. I stopped at a tank, a huge artificial lake

built centuries ago and scattered with lilies, for a swim with the locals, who washed their cottons with vigour. I bought a plastic shopping bag from a hardware store and a few clay cooking pots as souvenirs, and balanced the lot on the handlebars, riding along under white flags hung from electricity pole to pole, signalling a funeral and leading to the house of the deceased.

Roads up into the hill country and the former British settlement of Nuwara Eliya become narrower and steeper (the buses have sick bags on the seats).

243

SRI LANKA

As coconut palms fade into acres of tea plantations, hairpin bends lead to a landscape scattered with waterfalls and pine forests, reminiscent of Scotland. It rains a lot here, temperatures drop to 7°C (45°F), and you need woolly jumpers.

An extremely busy, yet interesting, road is the A1, Colombo to Kandy. You whizz by cane furniture stores and stalls of cashew nuts manned by pretty "cashew nut girls" clad in pink or green saris. To head north to Anuradhapura is to tunnel through a dark canopy forest of mahogany, teak, and ebony trees on the way to the heartland of Old Ceylon, in the Kurungewala district, an interior of villages that have changed little in decades.

A VILLAGE IN THE JUNGLE

I had heard of the Ulpotha Sanctuary, back in England, and checked in for a week. This 12-acre indigenous village at the base of the Galgiriyawa Mountains has a history stretching back thousands of years. Legend says that pilgrims travelling in search of Lord Kataragama, an incarnation of the god-child Murugan, believed the village to be the sacred site associated with the god because of the seven hills in the surrounding jungle.

Ulpotha had been abandoned for decades when, in 1994, farmer and prophet Mudiyanse Tennakoon began, with the help of friends, restoring the village and reviving its traditional methods of organic farming. It opens for a few weeks each year to guests who practise yoga and meditation to get back in touch with nature.

My room was a mud and cowdung hut, or *asana* (meaning "divine seat"), separated from a paddy field by a pumpkin patch. Meals were a banquet of yams, melons, mango, jackfruit, okra, breadfruit curry, rich red rice, and buffalo curd, served in clay pots on huge square straw mats on the floor. By design, there is no electricity. Time is measured by the day's rhythm and night is lit by oil lamps.

Tennakoon sometimes lives here. He is 67, willowy thin, with silver hair and a silver beard. He sleeps where he feels comfortable, usually on a mat with his cotton wrap for a blanket. He took me to meet Sandeep, his six-year-old grandson who practises yoga and becomes tangled up in the bends of his knees, and later we meet the village shaman.

The shaman sits on the floor of his grubby, limewashed room and reads sliced limes as though they are tea leaves. He read mine and told me I travel too much. As a remedy he took a pinch of sandalwood, wrapped it in a banana leaf, popped it into a paper envelope, and wrote something on the outside. It translated as: "Take once every day for four days, with water."

Next day, Tennakoon invited me to join him in chanting. First, I had to shower out in the open, shielded by a circular fence fashioned from palm leaves. I turned a wooden handle halfway up a palm trunk and out rushed a cold waterfall. Freshly washed, I wrapped myself in muslin cloth and climbed inside a wicker coffin, the steam bath. Water boiled in pots underneath, spouting herbal steam between the holes in the weave. Ten minutes after, Karunaratne, the treatment man, lifted the lid and motioned for me to sit on a rock for him to pour minerals over my head. The grains collected in the creases of the muslin.

Dry and smelling of herbs, I joined Tennakoon in an open temple, facing that same paddy field. He sat cross-legged, in front of a makeshift altar of burning oil and incense, and opened his book at the *Dhammapada*, a religious text belonging to the Buddhist scripture. The language is written in Pali, curved like musical notes and running like ants across the thick, white parchment.

The wind rustled the palm leaves but failed to blot out Tennakoon's chanting. He had been asked to perform this ritual for the good of Ulpotha, a bit like asking for rain in times of drought, or peace in times of war. "When I am chanting I call upon the whole planet; every piece of nature, even a rock, is a living thing," he said.

OUTINGS TO THE BUDDHAS

One inland adventure that I could not miss was climbing Sigiriya. Built around a massive rock as a royal citadel in the 5th century and famed for its frescoes, Sigiriya is best climbed early morning when the air is cool. The correct way is to stroll through the pleasure gardens, which represent the good things in life, then enter a labyrinth of stairways before ascending 200m (650ft) to the top and to enlightenment.

In 30°C (85°F) afternoon heat, our small group from Ulpotha struggled up the steps, clasping the wrought-iron railings. With our sarongs billowing like tents in a storm, we finally reached the flat summit and its 360-degree view of green interrupted by giant mirror-like water tanks.

At Reswehara we saw a 12m (39ft) unfinished Buddha, sculpted by a student from the grey granite cliff. The story is that 1,500 years ago a competition was held between a master and his student to carve twin statues of Buddha at two separate places. Whoever finished first would ring the bell. When the teacher completed his masterpiece and rang the bell, the student laid down his tools and went to look. Overwhelmed at the standard of his master's workmanship, the student abandoned his own carving. You can see the master's magnificent effort at Aukana, 32km (20 miles) west of Sigiriya. It is a warm, golden effigy with a hornet's nest growing under the elbow of the raised right hand, in the fashion of a drooping sleeve.

By dusk, we arrived at Dambulla, 19km (12 miles) from Sigiriya, just as the "mother of all caves" was closing. Monkeys rummaged through leftovers by the roadside as we discarded our shoes and walked barefoot to the temple and its trio of elaborately painted caves, crammed with Buddhas and as old as the 1st century B.C.

FROM BUDDHAS TO ELEPHANTS

Just as memorable as my motorbiking experiences was my encounter with the elephants at Uda Walawe National Park. Reached from Colombo via the gem-mining town of Ratnapura, Uda Walawe spreads alongside the Walawe Gange River. You can motorcycle or drive up to the park entrance, then board a 4WD for a guided safari.

Estimates suggest the park holds around 300 Asian elephants, spotted deer, wild boar, water buffalo, and a variety of birds, from egrets, peacocks, and herons to cormorants.

Visitors, once they fathom the complicated entrance fees (you pay extra if you choose a 4WD with a roof, for example) can stay overnight in a bungalow or pitch a tent at the designated campsite, taking care not to encounter leopards or

---

BUDDHISM

Buddhism, the personification of all noble virtues and qualities of passion and wisdom, is the main philosophy of the island, followed by Hinduism, Islam, Christianity, and Catholicism. Sri Lanka received Buddhism in the 3rd century B.C., after which colossal stupas were crafted in stone, clay, brick, and stucco. Bronze, ivory, sandalwood, and sometimes gold were used for the smaller ones. The first statue is believed to be the Thuparama, the oldest Buddhist shrine in Anuradhapura. There are three positions of Buddha: fearless with right hand raised; in meditation; and reclining. One reclining position showing his feet together (sleeping) and the other with one foot slightly pulled back (nirvana).

You will see Buddhist monks wearing red or orange robes and Buddhist nuns dressed in yellow robes dyed using saffron. They have no money, and are looked after by the villagers, who donate food to the temples.

Above: Tuc-tucs are standard local transport—cheap, hardy, and easy to use, but even they are vulnerable to punctures on these roads

As we watched the wildlife, I noticed that neither guide nor driver was armed, and our vehicle was not equipped with a radio to call base should we hit a problem. It didn't worry me until we rumbled along the track and came across a couple of elephants stripping bark to our left. We stopped to take photographs and noticed more elephants behind, including two young calves. Cracking noises of branches to our right told me we had come between a herd—a big one. No worries, assured the guide.

But the elephants didn't want us there. They preferred to dine in peace and we were too close for their liking. So they decided on a plan of action. A mother, her teats heavy with milk, positioned her great brown hulk behind the jeep, inches from the door. Her coin-shaped eyes glared yellow and her flesh-mottled ear tips flapped annoyingly. I could count the bulging veins on the wrinkled skin of her belly.

venomous snakes, particularly the cobra and Russell's viper.

The safari itself normally lasts up to 3 hours and is best done in the early morning or late afternoon, when animals approach the watering holes. Elephants here are rarely poached for their ivory because few Asian elephants carry tusks; at the time of writing, the park had three with tusks. If you spot one you are considered lucky. An elephant tusk and a leopard seen on a safari means you are very blessed.

After a few minutes we spotted an elephant bull between the stilt-like trunks of trees, half hidden by a belt of high grass. Further along, on the spongy green banks of the reservoir, a father and calf grazed. Pelicans swooped overhead, fish eagles hunted, and white-necked storks stood as statues.

Two others took the front and the rest closed in on either side. Attempts by the guide to shoo them with his baseball cap made the situation look pathetic. And when the female to the rear began pawing the ground and reaching her wet trunk in to sniff us, I really wanted to go home.

We remained motionless for half an hour at least. I was counting elephants, not minutes. Up to 50 mooched round us and background rustles in the bush suggested they had back-up. I tried to make conversation to help pass the time, but the question of "how much training did you do to become a guide?" resulted in the worrying answer of "three weeks, madam."

Eventually, the elephants lost interest and cautiously sloped away, leaving me with palpitations. I confess it was the closest I have ever been to an angry elephant, and I shall never forget it.

GOING IT ALONE

INTERNAL TRAVEL

Mopeds and motorcycles can be hired in Colombo and at various resorts down the coast, including Hikkaduwa and Tangalla, and also inland at the historic city of Kandy. The wise don't rent a bike from hectic Colombo, but instead take a bus to the quieter places and start their tour along less traffic-choked roads. Bicycles can be borrowed from a number of places, even local villagers, but these are not the greatest machines in the world. Expect hard seats, weak brakes, and frequent punctures.

A tuc-tuc has no meter, so you negotiate a price beforehand, taking care to stress that you ride them all the time and so know what it costs (even if you don't). Sometimes you can bargain the driver down to what seems like a pittance to you but a substantial fare for him.

WHEN TO GO

From November to April, outside the monsoon season, is a busy time for the southwest, when the ocean is more suited to swimming. March to April are the hottest months of the year. In the monsoon, some areas can be flooded. In the lowlands, the temperature averages 27°C (80°F), and can drop in the central hills to as low as 10°C (50°F) at night. The southwest monsoon brings rain to the western, southern, and central regions from May to July.

PLANNING

A popular thoroughfare is the A2, Colombo through Galle to Matara (160km/100 miles), which runs right down the southwest coast, but this can be extremely dangerous to tackle. Drivers in Sri Lanka seem to possess a "couldn't care" attitude, so long as they get to where they're going. The southern corner and inland towards the east is far safer, as are some roads inland.

Whilst most of Sri Lanka remains unaffected, fighting between the security forces and the Tamil Tigers continues in the north and east, and Foreign Office officials advise you not to visit these areas. Some national parks are also off limits too, so it is best to check before you plan your route. Inland areas can be reached by car or bike.

VEHICLE HIRE

Before hiring a moped or motorcycle, check that it is in good condition and full working order. Check brakes, tyres, and oil leaks, and make sure that the price includes a helmet (if you don't have your own) and insurance.

HEALTH MATTERS

People in Sri Lanka will tell you the country has no malaria, yet the Hospital for Tropical Diseases in London states that Sri Lanka is a high-risk malaria zone (lower in districts of Colombo, Kalutara, and Nuwara Eliya). A yellow fever certificate may be required if you are coming from a tropical South African/South American country. No other vaccinations are legally required, but the following are recommended: Tetanus, diphtheria, typhoid, hepatitis A, hepatitis B, and rabies.

Sri Lanka has a high risk of infected food and water. Drink only bottled water, and check that the seal has not been broken. Avoid ice in drinks and any fruit juices made with water, and stick to boiled tea plain or served with boiled milk. Peel all fruit and be cautious of ice cream that may have melted and been refrozen.

WHAT TO TAKE

- ❏ Currency: you cannot buy Sri Lankan rupees outside the country and so you have to change your money or travellers' cheques on arrival at the airport, or in hotels and banks.
- ❏ Sunblock for the face and a high-factor suncream for elsewhere.
- ❏ Riding goggles to protect your eyes.
- ❏ For the monsoon season, waterproofs and your own umbrella (Sri Lankan umbrellas break). At other times, cool, lightweight clothing and warmer items for the hill country.
- ❏ You might prefer to take your own crash helmet, and a puncture repair kit for bicycles.
- ❏ Camera.

Below: *Karunaratne pours a cocktail of minerals over a guest at Ulpotha Sanctuary*

25 Ski, Surf, and Turtles at the Ocean's Mouth

by Lee Karen Stow

Sri Lanka is surrounded by water; an ocean of coral reefs, sunken wrecks lost from colonial fleets, and crashing surf—a ring of cobalt supporting wooden canoes that haul in tuna and shark. Into the ocean flow freshwater rivers, some laced with crocodiles and monitor lizards, others fit for a ski, or two.

Wide, brown, and flat, the Bentota Ganga River feeds into the Indian Ocean at the point where two foliage-clad hills part as a gaping gateway, on the southwest coast of Sri Lanka. Like the calm before the storm, the river runs smooth through a tropical jungle corridor of juniper, mango, and papaya trees. Bamboo shoots up as sticks, and coconut palms clutch their fruit, like bunched grapes.

As it nears the ocean, the thick green vegetation thins out into patches of honey sands. A lone wooden canoe rests on the shore, its paint flaking from 29°C (85°F) heat. Soon the river is sucked through that gaping chasm, until the roaring surf grabs it, churns it up, and sweeps it away for a thunderous crash on the nearby tourist beaches.

Inside the mouth, the river is salty. I know this because I swallowed litres of the stuff, getting wrapped in soggy palm fronds while trying to pull myself upright—back straight, arms out, elbows locked—during my first waterski lesson.

Waterskiing was my second choice. I had intended to dive but it was July monsoon and the scuba-diving season was non-existent along the west coast because of rough, wind-ravaged seas, strong undercurrents, and reduced visibility. Conditions like this can sweep even the fittest swimmer to his death.

REEFS AND SHARKS

However, when the season is ripe for diving (November to April), you can take boat dives out to wrecks of Dutch and Portuguese sailing ships lost during monsoons in the 16th and 17th centuries, often laden with cargoes of cinnamon and other spices taken from the island.

You can submerge to offshore coral, sandstone, and crystalline reefs that are magnets for fish, reptiles, invertebrates, and plants. Hikkaduwa is about 100km (62 miles) south of Colombo, on the main coastal road, and is known for its underwater coral gardens and marine sanctuary, spied through a snorkel mask, on a dive, or from a glass-bottom boat. The reef, with its corals is separated from the shoreline by a shallow lagoon, 2–3m (6–10ft) in depth. Turtles are known to

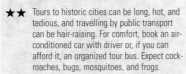

Scuba divers should be qualified and hold the required and recognized certification. Beginners can try waterskiing and windsurfing, though it takes a few starts to gain your balance. During the monsoon, the seas are too rough for scuba diving and often dangerous for swimmers.

Tours to historic cities can be long, hot, and tedious, and travelling by public transport can be hair-raising. For comfort, book an air-conditioned car with driver or, if you can afford it, an organized tour bus. Expect cockroaches, bugs, mosquitoes, and frogs.

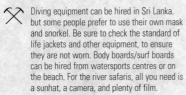

Diving equipment can be hired in Sri Lanka, but some people prefer to use their own mask and snorkel. Be sure to check the standard of life jackets and other equipment, to ensure they are not worn. Body boards/surf boards can be hired from watersports centres or on the beach. For the river safaris, all you need is a sunhat, a camera, and plenty of film.

paddle in and out, among more than 150 species of fish, from damselfish and wrasses to surgeonfish and moray eel.

There is diving, too, from the fishing town of Negombo, further north, but I was told conditions here are not as good as elsewhere. To the south are the dive sites of Dodanduwa, the rocky reefs off Gintola and Ralagala, Unawatuna, where you can hire a traditional wooden canoe and snorkel to see parrotfish, and the Buena Vista Coral Reef, where there's a chance of spotting the blacktip reef shark.

An alternative is to fly 640km (400 miles) west to the Maldives, where 1,200 low-lying islands are protected by a coral reefs cut by several deep natural channels. The best time to dive the Maldives is November to May .

BACK TO SKIS

Sadly, for me diving was off the menu, so I took to the river. Watersports centres line both banks of the Bentota Ganga (reached by turning right off the coastal road from Colombo to Galle). Jetskis and scooters flit across the surface like skimming pebbles. Scooters are wider than jetskis, have an outboard motor, and are easier to control because they don't reach such high speeds. Sometimes there's parasailing. But it all depends on the depth of the river at the time of the year—and it needs to be deep.

I spent my six "starts" at waterskiing struggling behind the speedboat. As soon as the boat revved its engine and pulled away from the wooden jetty, I ended up on my back, skis flying off towards the palm trees or pointing skywards. Successful skiers zoomed by, waving at me. I gave up, and hopped on a water scooter, whirled from bank to bank, and then decided to ditch the life jacket in favour of a potato and cabbage curry.

That evening, quite by chance, I discovered that the riverbank is home to Chandrasiri Silva, 1992 Sri Lankan champion for waterskiing mono and barefoot. So next day I called on him at his

watersports centre and handed over the rupees. Called Siri for short, he greeted me with a blast of Bob Marley, a leftover habit from his champion skiing days in Jamaica. He'd been watching me the day beforehand and hadn't laughed.

He told me to sit on the riverbank grass, bend my knees, and clutch a ski handle at the end of a rope that he had fastened to a palm trunk. He showed me the correct way to stand up at waterskiing until the tree bowed with the strain. "It's not how strong you are, it's how you hold yourself—knees bent, head confidently forward, chest out, arms straight and shoulders up," explained Siri. "It's balance." I waded out into the river and donned the skis while Siri started up the motor boat.

In seconds, we were off. After three attempts I stood up, racing along over the frothy wake of the speedboat at 60kph (37mph). I rode waves, turned curves, and headed upstream towards an iron railway bridge, its trains overspilling with people. I flew towards those jaws of the ocean mouth, my skis gliding as though sliding over crisp snow.

Back at the jetty, Siri hadn't finished. He pulled off his pendant of miniature gold skis (a champion's prize), perched on his mono board, and raced behind the speedboat, weaving from left to right, leaning so low the spray arched over his head like a waterfall. He spun his stocky body back to front as though waltzing, and waved.

SLOWING IT DOWN ON SAFARI

One way to catch breath is to take a riverboat safari upstream for 3 hours, sunning yourself in a wooden motorboat painted orange, blue, and green and with a canvas suntop. It's a safari without big game, of course—more seafood restaurants, dive centres, beer gardens, and ice cream parlours, in fact. Half-hidden in the foliage are plush riverside chalets belonging to wealthy Sri Lankans who had come for June's Full Moon weekend of *Poson poya*, celebrating the coming of Buddhism to Sri Lanka. Mothers held up their babies as we passed. Children splashed in the shallows.

Crows picked at scraps on a rubbish heap. A trio of elephants took a bath, one lifting a papery ear so the man could rub a soapy sponge behind it. Naturally, on this touristy adventure, there's a shop, but at least it's an authentic wooden hut on stilts over the water.

The salesman, built like Tarzan and dressed in a cream loincloth, motioned for us to pull over and feel the wispiness of his saris. As transparent and light as organza, the saris hung from a tree pole, in rich colours of emerald, sapphire, purple, crimson, and yellow; some were printed with golden elephants. They felt better quality than those hawked on the beach and cost the same (400 rupees). I bought one and in return, Tarzan placed a necklace of jasmine flowers around my neck, sliced off the top of a king coconut, and plunged a straw into it.

I drank the sweet coconut milk back on board, cruising passed a trio of monitor lizards sprawled on a branch in the shade, their front legs draping over either side as though fed up with swimming. Crocodiles live further upstream and are apparently best seen on a morning boat trip, when it's cool enough for them to venture from the shade.

A local lad, sitting astride his wooden catamaran fashioned from a pair of dug-

Right: *Bentota River carves a corridor through a jungle of mango undergrowth*
Below: *Chandrasiri Silva, former waterski champion, in action*

SRI LANKA

out canoes and held together by wooden planks, sailed up to us. He held aloft a baby crocodile, which he kept as a bribe, its back leg fastened to a string he used as a lead. "Photo, madam, photo?" he begged. I wasn't buying. Nor did I want to see the "Sri Lankan monkey, madam" kept at a beer garden.

On the return cruise we sidetracked through an undergrowth of mango trees, a web of roots rising from brown water dappled by sunlight. We bobbed down to avoid branches that hung like skeleton fingers. "Jungle," announced the boat driver, puffing his chest proudly. A five-colour kingfisher perched in wait.

As we slowly motored back to our starting point, the sun began to set over the point at which the smooth river drains into the surf of the ocean, tinging it rose then burning it orange—a tremendous sight. Siri was waiting, iced cola in a glass, Bob Marley on the CD player, and his photo album open at Jamaica.

RIDING THE SURF

For all of this, I stayed at Beruwela, which marks the start of a 130km (81-mile) stretch of fudge-coloured sands. A tourist hotspot with the usual beach sellers, beggars, elephant with a bell round its neck giving rides, and a few lewd suggestions from the beach boys, Beruwela is lively.

In monsoon, when the sea is rough, its spray is like steam evaporating from boiling waves. The offshore breeze is hot, swaying the palm trees along the beach, and daring to dislodge the coconuts. Someone tries to sell you batiks, which are not batiks but cheap, printed fabric. A man sits behind his market stall set out with neat rows of shells from the deep, oyster pink and as creamy as ivory. Another sells baseball caps and straw hats hung on stalks dug into the sand.

I hired a body board, waist-high and as light as cardboard, and battled my way with it through tugging current until I stood chest deep in ocean. Waves pulled my thighs sideways and tried to shove me back to shore. The trick is to harness this power by waiting for a big wave, watching it break into thousands of white horses galloping furiously, then hold the body board with both hands titled from your pelvis and wait. When the frothy lip of the wave lifts you, throw your body onto the body board, hold on tight, and, if you've timed it correctly, the wave will carry you with it to the shore. As the foam fizzes in both ears, you become part of the wave.

To THE TEMPLES

I would say Beruwela was not a backpackers' or singles' hangout (you need

---

TURTLES

Sri Lanka is visited by five of the world's seven species of marine turtle: the leatherback, the loggerhead, the hawksbill, the green, and olive-backed ridley. All are listed by the International Union for the Conservation of Nature as either threatened or endangered; many are accidentally caught and killed in fishing gear. Even though turtle eggs are protected by legislation, poachers steal them to eat or, more likely, to sell for profit. Tortoiseshells are also collected, and tourists are persuaded not to buy tortoiseshell souvenirs.

---

somewhere like Hikkaduwa, further south, for that) so much as a sunset-tinged paradise for couples and honeymooners. All along this coast, however, are guesthouses, B&Bs, and beach bungalows. Dozens of excursions transport you in air-conditioned minibuses to Sri Lanka's hinterland and historic sites—the kind of places where you know you'll be badgered into buying postcards.

Begin with the city of Kandy and its golden-topped Dalada Maligawa (or Temple of Tooth), said to house the sacred tooth relic of the Buddha. Each July/August, for ten days, a replica of the tooth casket is carried in a procession known as the Esala Perahera,

---

ON THE MENU

Fish, of course, is on every coastal menu: seer fish (white and tasty), tuna, deep-fried sprats, crab, lobster, prawns. Rice is the staple food, white and served with curries loaded with chillies and spices (many restaurants will tone down the dish on request). A *sambol*, like a curry made from ground coconut, onions, and chilli can be painfully hot. Meals are usually eaten in the Sri Lankan way: the food being scooped up with fingers of the right hand and pushed into the

mouth with the thumb.

Breakfast is a hopper, a bowl-shaped pancake with a cooked egg in the centre, or string hoppers, mixed from rice flour and coconut milk and twirled into white birds' nests. Chilled papaya juice is refreshing, but the best drink of the day has to be a pot of the famous Pure Ceylon tea, served with boiled milk or lemon. Sri Lanka is a giant fruit salad, made up of pineapple, watermelon, mangosteen, mango, custard apple, papayas, rambutan, melon, guavas, and of course, coconut.

THE COCONUT

The white coconut tree is very valuable; nothing is wasted. Its milk is used in curries and the flesh grated for use in meals and sweets. Shells are fashioned into souvenirs, or used as cups for catching latex drawn from the rubber tree, or burnt and ground to make carbon powder.

After the outer husk has been soaked in water for two weeks, the fibre is soft enough to hack off with a wooden pole. When dry, the fibres are twisted into rope, woven into rugs, or used as mattress stuffing or for brooms. Trees last 60–70 years and, when fruits finish, can be used for wood. The hard palm trunk is ideal for beams, while the leaves can cover roofs and walls.

Sri Lankans slice off the top of a young, king (yellow) coconut, insert a straw, and sell it as a refreshing, sweet drink called *thambili*. Coconuts left on the tree to mature are picked and scraped of flesh, which is squeezed to make a milk. The milk is heated and the extracted oil is strained and used by women as hair conditioner. Unfortunately, the king coconut trunk is too soft for use.

accompanied by music, costumed elephants, and dancers.

Colombo, Sri Lanka's commercial capital is undoubtedly worth a visit, although tour operators at home will tell you not to linger long, fearing terrorist bombings or shootings. Colombo is not a pretty sight; it's a chaotic culture shock, with rubbish-chocked gutters, urine-soaked station platforms, and pollution so apparent it leaves the taste of exhaust-fumes in the mouth.

For the traveller in need of eclectic bustle, however, Colombo is a cooking pot of horn beeps, banana crates, curry smells, designer suits, stray cows, and barefoot wanderers. Roads are heavily congested with cars, buses, bullock carts, tuc-tucs (three-wheeled, cheap alternatives to taxis), cyclists, and moped riders with tempers. Majestic City is an air-conditioned shopping mall with fast-food biriani in the basements and escalators to shops that sell cut-price designerwear. I saw more Western faces here than on Beruwela beach, many of them stocking up on known-brand jeans for less than $20.

Twelve kilometres (7 miles) away is Mount Lavinia, a tidier suburb of reasonably priced guesthouses and a beach. I stayed along Beach Road—one end is passed by frantic drivers on the Colombo to Galle coastal road, and the other is sliced by a rusty railway track before it peters out to sands, with seafood restaurants, jogging city workers, long-haired travellers, and martial arts enthusiasts. To sit here at dusk, savouring the aroma of fried prawn, watching a boy perform a karate kick to the sea, and being jolted by the rumble of a crowded train behind, while the skyscrapers of Colombo in the distance flicker like Manhattan is to see a Sri Lanka not found in a glossy travel brochure.

A few yards down from this beach there's a headland of rocks coated in green moss and seaweed and known as the Bay of Mount Lavinia. Above, folks sip Pure Ceylon tea on the terrace of the Mount Lavinia Hotel. Built in 1806 by a colonial governor as a mansion for himself and his lady love, Lavinia, it's dubbed as one of Sri Lanka's finest hotels (the most expensive room is the Governor's suite, at $300 per night). Tourists come to see the place and to laugh at the porter who has to wear long, white socks.

ON TURTLE WATCH

I stuck to the coast and booked a driver called Sandeep, who knew all about coconuts and Buddhism. He wanted to share everything with me, stopping every few minutes and urging me to take a photo, whatever the scene. He took me southwards on the coastal road, pausing

Above: *Galle fishermen waiting for a tug on the line*
Left: *King coconuts for sale at a roadside stall*
Right: *Watch hut at the Turtle Conservation Project at Rekawa Beach hatchery, near Tangalla*

by the stilt fishermen of Galle who perch on stakes driven into the seabed.

Using skills handed down from their fathers, the fishermen cast out their lines and sit and wait for a tug from a fish, or—like one enterprising fellow—50 rupees from someone wanting to take a photo.

I asked Sandeep about turtles, and he pulled up outside the Bentota Turtle Hatchery, run by Mr. Kithsiri Kannangara. Eggs laid by the turtles are collected and reburied inside protective fencing to prevent poachers stealing them to sell to people for consumption. After incubation, turtles are kept in tanks, swimming relentlessly like clockwork toys, before they are released to the ocean. I held two-day-old greens, hawksbills, and loggerheads, each no bigger than an apple.

Over the last 20 years almost all of the marine turtle nests on the south and southwest coast of Sri Lanka have been ransacked by poachers. Researchers have calculated that the turtle population will decline to extinction within the next few decades, unless it recovers with the help of sustained conservation measures.

Mr. Kannangara is a one-man band and receives no government funding for his project, existing on donations and tourist purchases. You can become a turtle conservation volunteer for a couple of months or longer, living with him and his family, collecting and monitoring eggs, putting turtles to sea, raising awareness of the turtles' plight, and cleaning tanks. Work is available all year round. According to some marine experts however, keeping new-born turtles in tanks may not be such a good way of helping their survival.

shift is the busiest time, when turtles crawl up the beach to lay their eggs. These turtles are studied, and any unusual characteristics, such as barnacles and cracks in shells, are logged before they are tagged through the rear flipper. Once the eggs are laid, the turtle takes about 2 hours to cover the hole with sand, using her flippers. These eggs are measured and counted.

AMBUSHED

By nightfall we stood silently near the nightwatch hut, on a 2km (1¼-mile) stretch of pale sand—a remote bounty paradise—that is the hatchery. The ocean roared like a pride of hungry lions, the waves periodically blotting out the swaying lights carried by catamaran fishermen in the offshore distance. Nest protectors quietly patrolled the sand, flashing torches when they stumbled upon a green or rare leatherback. A few inquisitive tourists arrived by tuc-tuc to watch.

"Quick, you're just in time, we've got a nest of hatchlings coming out," whispered Christine, a volunteer from Australia, waggling her torch frantically. We squinted through the darkness. Hundreds of tiny greens spilled from their hole in the sand, scattered around our feet faster than ants, and flapped desperately towards the waves. Statistics show that one in a thousand hatchlings survive the onslaught of the ocean and its predators. The sight of so many, frantically pursuing their destiny, and the thought that most of this charging army will not survive even the night, is humbling.

They conclude that in the first days hatchlings are in swimming stage and by the fourth day they are in feeding stage, by which time they have lost the aim to swim. So, when hatchlings are released they tend to hang around the shoreline rummaging for food and in full view of flying predators.

The Turtle Conservation Project (TCP), further down the coast at Tangalla, believes turtles should hatch naturally and be allowed to make their own way to the ocean, unassisted by human hands. It carries out a marine turtle tagging and conservation programme, and employs former turtle egg poachers in the belief that their knowledge and time spent protecting rather than stealing will benefit the turtle population.

TCP's head office is in Tangalla, but the hands-on beach work is carried out 15 minutes away by tuc-tuc at Rekawa, one of Sri Lanka's most important nesting grounds for greens, leatherbacks and, on rare occasions, the hawksbill. The night

GOING IT ALONE

INTERNAL TRAVEL

There are no internal flights within Sri Lanka. Sri Lanka looks a small island on a map, yet is difficult to get around because there are no fast highways, just main roads heavy with traffic. Trains are usually over-crowded in all classes, with passengers hanging from the doors. Trains run from Colombo Fort station to many places of interest, but are slower than the buses.

The best option, if you don't fancy tackling the roads in a hire car, is to take a bus; there is so much competition between the private bus companies, you can jump on one virtually anywhere. Fares are cheap and it's a first-hand way of seeing Sri Lanka. The express services are faster and air conditioned.

Radio cabs charge around 34 rupees per kilometre; check the taxi is metered before you ride. Bargaining on tuc-tuc fares is normal.

WHEN TO GO

Most holidaymakers visit Sri Lanka's west coast between November and April, out-side the monsoon season. I visited in June/July and saw only one day of rain, though the rough ocean was not suitable for diving. March and April are the hottest months. In the monsoon, some areas can be flooded. Sri Lanka is 880km (550 miles) north of the equator. In the lowlands, the tem-perature averages at 27°C (80°F), and can drop in the central hills to as low as 10°C (50°F) at night. The southwest monsoon brings rain to the western, south-ern, and central regions from May to July.

PLANNING

A good start to your trip would be to stay at a guest-house in Mount Lavinia, an hour's taxi drive from the airport. Many independent, like-minded travellers start out from here on hikes and other adventures. Then travel down the coast road all the way to Tangalla, stopping at resorts to swim, dive, or snorkel. Take excursions inland to the historic cities and return to Colombo or make a final beach stop in Negombo.

FINDING A GUIDE

Hire a trained and regis-tered Tourist Guide who carries a licence issued by the Ceylon Tourist Board. These can be booked through the tourist centres.

EQUIPMENT AND VEHICLE HIRE

Before diving, check that the establishment is fully professional and registered with a recognized diving institution. You can hire diving equipment, but do check it carefully. Also check that the centre is insured before setting off. Jetskiing is usually not cov-ered by insurance.

I didn't dare hire a car in Sri Lanka because driving conditions are hazardous, but there is a reasonable choice of them in Colombo. If you hire a car, make sure it's air conditioned.

LOCAL CUSTOMS

Sensitivity is called for when choosing what to wear. Shorts and beachwear are taboo at places of wor-ship and should be confined to the beach. When enter-ing a temple, remove shoes and headwear. Women should have legs covered and wear sleeves down to their elbows.

HEALTH MATTERS

Sri Lankans will tell you the country has no malaria, yet the Hospital for Tropical Diseases in London states that Sri Lanka is a high risk malaria zone (lower in dis-tricts of Colombo, Kalutara, and Nuwara Eliya). A yel-low fever certificate may be required if you are coming from a tropical southern African/South American country. No other vaccina-tions are legally required, but the following are rec-ommended: tetanus, diptheria, typhoid, hepatitis A, hepatitis B, rabies.

Sri Lanka has a high risk of infected food and water. Drink only bottled water and check that the seal has not been broken. Avoid ice in drinks and any fruit juices made with water, and stick to boiled tea, plain or served with boiled milk. Peel all fruit and be cautious of ice cream that may have melted and been refrozen.

WHAT TO TAKE

❏ Currency: you cannot buy Sri Lankan rupees outside the country and so you have to change your money or trav-ellers' cheques on arrival at the airport, or in hotels and banks.
❏ Sunblock and high-factor suncream.
❏ For the monsoon sea-son, waterproofs and your own umbrella.
❏ At other times, cool, lightweight clothing (but avoid white, which dirties within minutes).
❏ Buy sarongs for next to nothing to wear as beachwraps, and to cover up at temples.
❏ Snorkelling/diving mask and snorkel.

INTRODUCTION

Contained in the first section of these "Blue Pages" are lists of selected contacts relevant to the 25 adventures related on pages **18–256**. Because the adventures are personal accounts, the information provided here will reflect each author's own experience, and therefore details will vary accordingly. Remember also that some contacts are in remote places, so be sure to call or write in advance before setting out. None of the places in the Contacts or the A–Z have been vetted in any way by the publishers and, although some of the companies were used by our writers, this is no guarantee they will still be run by the same people or to the same standard of proficiency.

The Contacts section gives details of companies used by our authors and complements the Activities A–Z in the second part. Below is some general information to help you plan your own adventures.

INTERNATIONAL DIALLING CODES

Telephone and fax numbers given in this section of the book begin with the area code. When dialling from outside the country, prefix this number with the international network access code of the country you are in, followed by the country code. When dialling from within the country, prefix this number with a 0 e.g. (033) 511 8767.

International Network Access Codes

For calls from the U.K. 00
For calls from the U.S. 011

Country Codes

India 91
Nepal 977
Tibet (China) 86
Pakistan 92
Sri Lanka 94

EMBASSIES AND CONSULATES
British Embassies

For more details of U.K. Government offices visit their website at www.fco.gov.uk

India
Chanakyapuri
New Delhi 1100021
☎ (11) 687 2161 **fax:** (11) 687 288/20065

email:
bhcndvis@ndf.vsnl.net.in
website: www.ukinindia.org
Office hours: 10–2 and 3–6

Nepal
P.O. Box 106
Lainchaur
Kathmandu
☎ (1) 410583/411281/414588
fax: (1) 411789/416723
email:
britemb@wlink.com.np
Office hours: Mon–Thu 8:45–1 and 2–5:30; Fri 8:45–1:45

Tibet
There is no British representation in Tibet; refer to:

British Embassy
11 Guang Hua Lu
Jian Guo Men Wai
Beijing 100600
China
☎ (10) 6532 1961
fax: (10) 6532 1937/1930
email: consularmail@peking.mail.fco.gov.uk
Office hours: 8:30–12 and 1:30–5

Pakistan
Diplomatic Enclave
Ramna 5
P.O. Box 1122
Islamabad
Pakistan
☎ (51) 822131/5

fax: (51) 823439
email: bhcmedia@isb.com-sats.net.pk
Office hours: Mon–Thu 10–6; Fri 10–2

Sri Lanka
P.O. Box 1433
190 Galle Road
Kollupitiya
Colombo 3
☎ (1) 437336/451924–6
fax: (1) 430308/335803
email: bhc@eureka.lk
Office hours: Mon–Thu 8–4:30; Fri 8–1; Visa Section: Mon–Thu 8–10

AMERICAN EMBASSIES

For more details of U.S. Government offices visit their website at www.americanembassy.com or www.webofculture.com

India
Shanti Path
Chanakyapuri 110021
New Delhi
☎ (11) 688 9033/611 3033
fax: (11) 332 9499

Nepal
Pani Pokhari
Kathmandu
☎ (1) 411179
fax: (1) 419963 (Chancery)

AMERICAN EMBASSIES (CONT'D)

Pakistan
Diplomatic Enclave
Ramna 5
Islamabad
Pakistan
Mailing Address:
P.O. Box 1048
Unit 62200
APO AE 09812-2200
☎ (51) 826161-79
fax: (51) 214222
Office days: Sun–Thu

Sri Lanka
210 Galle Rd
Colombo 3
Mailing Address:
P.O. Box 106
☎ (1) 448007
fax: (1) 437345/446013

ACCOMMODATION PRICES

Hotels listed in the Contacts
and A–Z sections have been
split into four price categories.
Some parts of the world are
generally cheaper than others
but a rough guide is as follows:

$ = under $40
$$ = $40-$85
$$$ = over $85

---

1 CAMEL SAFARI IN JAISALMER ► 20–27

OPERATORS—GENERAL
Travelplan
Jaipur
☎ (141) 222332/223050 **fax:** (294) 410213
email: tplanjai@datainfosys.net
tplanjod@datainfosys.net
Run by Mr. Virendra Singh from his head office
in Jaipur, Travelplan has offices in the other
major cities of Rajasthan—Udaipur, Jodhpur,
Jaisalmer, and Bikaner. Their transport fleet
includes cars (small & large), minivans, and
large coaches; well-mannered, English-
speaking drivers are available. Experienced
staff will organize adventure tours such as
camel, horse, jeep, and motorcycle safaris and
trekking in the hills of Rajasthan, and make
hotel/flight/train reservations.

OPERATORS—SAFARIS
Note: The author's safari was made, inadvertently, with the tour desk operated by Hotel
Golden City in Gadi Sagar Road (☎ (2992)
51664). This is not recommended.

Caravan Safari
Ghandi Chowk
☎ (2992) 51330
Organizes jeep and camel safaris, and camp-
fires/dinner dance trips to the sand dunes.

Paradise Hotel
See Accommodation, below, for details.
Offers one of the better quality budget safaris,
for as many days as required.

Safari Tours
Gandhi Chowk
Jaisalmer
☎ (2992) 51058 **fax:** (2992) 51158
email: rewlaresort@hotmail.com.
This upmarket safari company offers good
tents, good food, air mattresses, barbequed
dinners, Rajasthani dancers, VIP handling,
skilled camel handlers, jeep safaris, etc. They
also have a desert camp for luxury lovers.

Sahara Travels
Ghopa Chowk
1st Fort Gate
Jaisalmer
☎ (2992) 52609
The charming and professional Mr. Bissa, otherwise known as 'Mr. Desert', is one of the

longest-running camel operators in town. He operates jeep tours, jeep safaris, camel safaris, and makes transport reservations, all for reasonable prices. Highly recommended, he often escorts his groups personally.

GETTING THERE

Anyone with time should consider taking the trains which run from from Delhi through to Jaipur, then on to Jodhpur and Jaisalmer. Sleepers are available, but because of the need to book and change trains several times, some prefer to take a hire car or the faster and cheaper and (far less romantic) bus.

INFORMATION

Some of the better safari companies are very happy to give information about the trips they offer. For example, the Sahara Travels office (above), right outside the fort gate in Jaisalmer.

ACCOMMODATION

On the safari all accommodation is provided, whether in tents or under the stars.

Hotel Simla $

Jaisalmer Fort
☎ (2992) 53061
Located within the fort, this tiny hotel has original "Arabian nights" styled rooms, and is close to many restaurants and sights. Free pick-up service from the railway station.

Hotel Suraj $

☎ (2992) 53023
Behind the Jain temple inside the fort, this small and intimate 500-year-old, carved sandstone *haveli* has retained much of its original charm. Rooftop views are an additional bonus.

Jawahar Niwas Palace $–$$

No 1 Bada Bagh Road
P.O. Box No 1
Jaisalmer 345 001
☎ (2992) 52208/52288
fax: (2992) 52611/52288
Boasting beautiful architecture, this former royal guest house has been renovated to international tourist standard. Friendly and gracious staff do everything to ensure their guests' comfort. Specialty Rajasthani cuisine from Royal Jaisalmer kitchens, available on request and on special occasions. Definitely worth a visit. Has hosted many luminaries over the years.

Paradise Hotel $

☎ (2992) 52674/52417
Located inside the fort, this well-run budget hotel has a grassy and shady courtyard, rooftop restaurant, and good views over the town and desert.

FOOD AND DRINK
8th July

Inside the fort, overlooking the passing parade, this restaurant is run by an Australian-Indian. The menu is imaginative (they even have Vegemite, that great Australian favourite!); fresh juices, and tasty vegetarian fare.

Jawahar Niwas Palace

Bada Bagh Road
☎ (2992) 52208/52288
For a special night, make a group booking and sample authentic Rajasthani food in tented luxury in the grounds of this hotel.

The Trio

Ghandi Chowk
Mandir Palace
Jaisalmer
☎ (2992) 52733
A popular and well-run restaurant serving all kinds of Indian specialities—definitely worth a visit.

> ## 2 HUNTING TIGERS IN THE FORTRESS GARDEN
> ► 28–35

OPERATORS

The offices below are near each other, close to the railway station on the other side of the bridge—a 5-minute walk away.

Rajasthan Tourism Development Corporation (R.T.D.C.) Office

Vinayak Tourist Complex
333 Ranthambhor National Park Road
This well-run government office arranges things such as pick-ups and drop-offs efficiently. It also provides accommodation, and has a restaurant with efficient staff and quite acceptable food.

Project Tiger Office

The Park has been under the Project Tiger scheme since 1972 and it is possible to book your Park excursion at the office.

GETTING THERE

Ranthambhore is an easy train ride from Jaipur on the main Bombay line. It is also accessible from Agra and Kota.

ACCOMMODATION
Hotel Tiger Moon $$

☎ (22) 640 6399 (Mubai Reserv.)
This relatively luxurious hotel, close to the park, has deluxe cottages and a swimming pool.

Jhoomar Baori Castle $$

Jhoomar Baori
☎ (7426) 20495
Located on the top of a hill surveying the entire surrounding area, this hotel was once a former royal hunting lodge. Although renovation would be in order, the hotel exudes plenty of quirky charm and the rooms are extremely comfortable, especially the two suites. Book ahead during the busy months.

R.T.D.C. Vinayak Tourist Complex $

See Operators, above, for details.

Sawai Madhopur Lodge $$–$$$

Ranthambhore National Park Road
☎ (7426) 20541/20247/20719
fax: (7426) 20718
Run by the Taj group, the hotel is a former hunting lodge built in the 1930s by Maharajah Sawai Man SinghII of Jaipur for his hunting trips to Ranthambhore. The lodge has hosted many celebrities and VIPs over its lifetime.

FOOD AND DRINK

There are no independent restaurants near Ranthambhore and guests tend to eat at their hotels, which offer reasonable Indian food. The Taj Sawai Madhapur Lodge offers the best and most expensive food.

3 TRACING THE MUGHALS
▶ 36–43

OPERATORS
Uttar Pradesh Tourism Office

64 Taj Road
Agra
☎ (562) 360517
Runs a small and convenient booking office on the platform at Agra's railway station. Book tours to the Taj and Fatepur Sikri when you get there—the tours are designed to coincide with the train's arrival, so no time is lost.

INFORMATION
U.P. Tourism Office

See above for details.
Helpful and well-organized, the office has both brochures and abundant information to hand out.

ACCOMMODATION
DELHI
Imperial Hotel $$$

Janpath
New Delhi
☎ (11) 334 1234/5678 fax: (11) 334 2255
Beautifully renovated and decorated, the Imperial exudes a quiet grandeur. Old lithographs decorate the walls, floors are polished, flowers abound and staff, dressed in white, glide quietly by. The Spice Garden Restaurant is well worth a visit for its decor alone. A well-located oasis of peace in busy Delhi.

Nirula's Hotel $$

L Block
Connaught Circus
☎ (11) 332 419 fax: (11) 335 3957
email: delhihotel@nirula.com
website: www.nirula.com
Located in one of the old colonial blocks, the hotel is a bit pricy but offers comfort in a convenient location.

Y.M.C.A. Tourist Hotel $

Jai Singh Road
☎ (11) 336 1915 fax: (11) 374 6032/6035
email: ymcath@ndf.vsnl.net.in
Clean, secure, and uninspiring in a quiet but central location close to Connaught Circus. Better rooms have T.V. and air conditioning. The restaurant serves reasonable food, especially the Indian selection, and there is a swimming pool and tennis court. Credit cards accepted.

AGRA

In Agra, I stayed in Taj Ganj to get the atmosphere of the artisan's village. This centuries' old enclave has plenty of cheap accommodation and can be noisy, although the better rooms are quite acceptable. Enjoy dining on tiny rooftops overlooking the Taj, but be aware that certain of the cheaper guesthouses deliberately poison their guests as a profit-making scheme they have made up with hospital staff—the reputable guest houses generally have posted up a notice of reassurance.

Hotel Kamal $

☎ (562) 330126

email: siit@del2.vsnl.net.in

A well-run, clean establishment. The rooftop restaurant looks directly to the Taj, without any need to crane your neck.

Laurie's Hotel $

MG Road

☎ (562) 364536

A former colonial hotel that once hosted Queen Elizabeth. Although Laurie's could do with a tighter management, it manages to retain a little of its earlier charm with big rooms, solid walls, and an air of peaceful neglect.

Mughal Sheraton $$$

Taj Ganj

Agra 282 001

☎ (562) 331701 **fax:** (562) 331730

One of Agra's best hotels, set in a large garden park—an oasis of quiet and calm.in the midst of all the bustle.

Taj Khema $

Nice-looking hotel close to the Taj, run by the State Government Tourism Dept, U.P. Tourism.

FOOD AND DRINK

Bhojnalay Restaurant

Pawan Hotel

Sadar Bazar

Agra

☎ (562) 363716/262442

They serve the best *thali*, south Indian food, and vegetarian dishes in town, for a very reasonable price. Conditions are scrupulously clean—you can even put your arms on the table without flinching.

Taj Keema Restaurant

Taj Mahal Eastern Gate

☎ (562) 330140

Does an excellent Indian buffet lunch for a very reasonable price. Within easy walking distance of the Taj.

4 At Play in the Valley of the Gods ► 44–51

GETTING THERE

FLIGHTS

Indian Airlines

Delhi Booking Office

☎ (11) 463 1337 **fax:** (11) 462 4322

website: www.indianairlines.com

Operates a comprehensive, efficient flight schedule throughout the country and operates several air pass systems if you want to fly around the country or within certain regions. Flights to Kullu from New Delhi on Mondays, Wednesdays and Fridays, take 1 hour 20 minutes, including a brief stop at Shimla. Weather conditions, especially in winter, may cause delay or cancellation, but book flights as far in advance as possible as they are popular and the planes used on this route only carry 20 or so.

Jagson Airlines

12th floor, Vandana Bldg

11 Tolstoy Marg

New Delhi

☎ (11) 371 1069

Also operate the New Delhi–Kullu route on a daily basis.

OPERATOR

Himalayan Journeys

P.O. Box 15

The Mall

Manali 175 131

Himachal Pradesh

☎ (1902) 52365/53355 **fax:** (1902) 53065

email: himjourn@de13.vsnl.net.in

website: www.himalayanjourneysindia.com

This professional company is located at the very top end of the Manali main street, past the small roundabout. They offer an extensive range of adventures from rafting and trekking to jeep safaris and heli skiing. The beginners' ski packages last 1 week and include 6 nights at Solang, a qualified instructor and all meals. Ski touring trips are tailor-made to suit your level of ability and desires. There are some magnificent routes available, including several that take in summits. Their staff are qualified mountain guides and speak good English, but perhaps more importantly are fun companions. All tours include specialist ski equipment and camping gear where necessary. A heli-skiing package will take in some of the world's best long powder runs.

ACCOMMODATION

Hotel Fifty-Five $$

H-55 Connaught Circus

New Delhi 110 001

☎ (11) 332 1244/332 1278 **fax:** (11) 332 0769

email: hotelfiftyfive@hotmail.com

This lovely small hotel in the centre of New Delhi has won the National Tourism Award for

Best One Star Hotel three times and justifiably so. With its friendly atmosphere and well-furnished, comfortable rooms that boast en-suite bathrooms, hot water, and satellite T.V., it is a haven in the melée of India's capital. It may seem a little overpriced now, but for peace of mind in this range, it is hard to fault. They also exchange currency, but do not accept credit cards. Beware, though, that they do not pay commissions to taxi drivers, so if you reveal it as your destination, you may be subjected to the infamous Delhi taxi driver scam of taking you to another hotel that does pay commissions!

John Bannon's Guest House $$

The Manali Orchard
Manali 175-131
Himachal Pradesh
☎ (1902) 52335/52388
This small and personal place, still run by John himself, predates Manali's hotel-building frenzy and remains a popular place to stay. Set in a lovely orchard about 5 minutes' walk north of the main street, it has large, comfortable rooms with en-suite facilities and great views down the valley. John is a source of inspiration and knowledge about things to do locally.

5 OFF THE RAILS IN DARJEELING ► 52–61

OPERATORS AND CAR HIRE
Juniper Tours and Travel

email: nischal13@hotmail.com.
Can organize air tickets to Nepal, car hire, and guides. No trekking but the staff are helpful and well-organized.

SD Enterprises

103 Wembley Park Drive
London HA9 8HG
U.K.
☎ (020) 8903 3411 fax: (020) 8903 0392
email: dandpani@dircon.co.uk
website: www.users.dircon.co.uk/dandpani
Check the internet for India Railways' trains and timetables, and book directly from London. This company will look after you way ahead of when you need to go. Also have information on the Darjeeling Toy Train.

Wanderlust Travels Ltd

M-51/52 Palika Bhawan
(opp. Hyatt Regency)
New Delhi 110066
☎ (11) 467 9059/410 2180/611 889
fax: (11) 688 5188
email: wandtrvl@bol.net.in
website: www.wanderlustindia.com

ACCOMMODATION
DARJEELING
Cedar Inn $$

Jalapar Road
Darjeeling 734101
☎ (354) 54446/53916/56764
email: cedar@dte.vsni.net.in
Perched high on a hill near the signal station, overlooking the whole of Darjeeling, this new hotel is possibly the best in town. It is a bit of a walk to the town, although scenic, and taxis are available for the return journey. Comfortable rooms with a view, many with a fireplace. International phone calls, colour cable T.V. The friendly staff are able and willing to make all travel arrangements and to give advice.

Hotel Shangrila $$

The Mall
5 Nehru Road
Darjeeling 734101
☎ (354) 54149
This quirky old hotel has only 3 huge rooms, looking down over the Mall. Each has a fire-place and a bathroom with hot water. Friendly and helpful staff try their best to help guests enjoy their stay. Good restaurant downstairs.

Windamere Hotel $$–$$$

Observatory Hill
Darjeeling
☎ (354) 54041/2 fax: (354) 54043/54211
email: windamere@vsnl.com
Darjeeling's most famous and snootiest hotel. Nostalgic and comfortable, it provides an authentic 50-year time warp experience. A wonderful bar that has hosted royalty, moun-taineers, Tibetan traders, and celebrities over the years. All meals included in the tariff. Rooms are smallish and cosy.

PELLING
Norbu Ghang Resort $$

Pelling
☎ (3595) 58245/58271/58272
fax: (3595) 56271
email: netuk@sikkim.org
This attractive new hotel located in a garden setting has views over the mountains to Kachenjanga Mountain, Sikkim's holy mountain.

West Sikkim
Garuda Hotel $

Small hotel, popular with backpackers, offering basic budget rooms and traveller's food.
☎ (3595) 50614

Hotel Phamrong $

Upper Pelling
West Sikkim
☎ (3595) 58218/50660 **fax:** (3595) 58281
This is probably the most established hotel in Pelling, used by both groups and independent travellers. Attached bathrooms, and very welcome hot air heaters on request.

Food and Drink

In Pelling restaurants are scarce, to say the least, so eating in the guesthouses is the thing to do. Traveller's food and passable Western-style food is the order of the day.

---

6 Rhinos and River Dolphins in Assam ► 62–73

Operators
Wild Grass

Barua Bhavan
107 M.C. Road
Uzan Bazar
Guwahati 781001
☎ (361) 546827 **fax:** (361) 630465
e-mail: wildgrss@gw1.dot.net.in
Founded over 10 years ago, Manju Barua's tour operation is highly recommended for its efficiency and attention to detail—can arrange everything from straightforward transport and accommodation packages to Kaziranga National Park to offbeat options like the sandbar camping expedition. Packages are tailor-made and offer terrific value for money. Knowledgeable, English-speaking guides.

Getting There
Flights

Most people fly to Guwahati or Jorhat on scheduled domestic flights from Calcutta or Delhi. Wild Grass can arrange pick-up and road transfer to Kaziranga from either local airport.

Indian Airlines

☎ (33) 236 0730 (Calcutta) or (11) 566 5301 (Delhi)
Daily flights to Guwahati from Calcutta and Delhi. Services from Calcutta to Jorhat twice a week.

Jet Air

☎ (33) 511 8767 (Calcutta) or (11) 685 3700 (Delhi)
Reckoned to be the most efficient domestic airline, Jet Air flies daily to Guwahati from Calcutta and Delhi, and Calcutta-Jorhat twice a week.

Buses

Buses for Kohora/Kaziranga leave from the Paltan Bazaar by Guwahati's railway station. Regular buses are operated by the Assam State Transport Corporation, but private bus companies are more reliable and comfortable.

Green Valley Travels

Sipukhuri
Guwahati
☎ (361) 544636
Private bus company providing regular services to Kaziranga in air-conditioned buses.

Information

There are information counters at the airport and the railway station.

Assam Tourism

Station Road
Guwahati
☎/**fax:** (361) 547102
Has limited resources.

Accommodation
Eco-Camp $

Potasali Village
Tarajan
P.O. Gamani
Sonitpur
Assam 784103
☎ (3714) 44246 **fax:** (3714) 44175
e-mail: assamangling@yahoo.com
An eco-friendly fishing camp (open Oct–Mar) run by the Assam (Bhorelli) Angling & Conservation Association just outside the Nameri National Park. Accommodation is in 6 spacious and comfortable twin-bedded tents (4 with en-suite showers and toilets) arranged around a grassy plot. Linen, blankets, and mosquito nets are provided and the camp canteen provides delicious local (tribal) and Indian food. There is also a spartan 9-bed dormitory and 3 rooms with 3 beds sharing the wash block, or campers can pitch their own tents. The camp gets busy with anglers and their families on weekends.

INDIA

Hotel Belle Vue $

M.G. Road (Post Box 75)
Guwahati 781001
Assam

☎ (361) 540847 **fax:** (361) 540848

Great site perched above the Brahmaputra and convenient for the city centre, but the Belle Vue has seen better days. Large, plain rooms with air conditioning and en-suite bathrooms. The cavernous and empty dining room offers Chinese, Indian, and Western menus. (Note: Apparently, the similarly priced **Brahmaputra Ashok**, just down the road, is a better option, ☎ (361) 541064 **fax:** (361) 540870.)

Wild Grass Resort $

Kaziranga
Golaghat
Assam 785109

☎ (3776) 62011

Charming colonial style lodge completed in 1991 and set in tree-shaded gardens with a swimming pool. There are 18 airy twin-bedded rooms with en-suite showers, creaky wooden floors, and rattan furniture; tents are also available. In the main building the Bamboo Grove restaurant serves good Indian food, Western cereal, eggs, and toast at breakfast and a lunchtime buffet, and the veranda is good place to enjoy a cold beer. There is a warm welcome from manager, Ronesh Roy, and guests soon relax in the friendly atmosphere.

FOOD AND DRINK
Paradise Restaurant

G.N. Bordoloi Road
Guwahati

☎ (361) 666904

As befits its status as the top Assamese restaurant in town, the Paradise boasts air conditioning, glass-drop chandeliers, and oodles of formica. But ignore the décor and order a *thali*, a set meal which offers a taste of 8–10 different dishes. There are meat or vegetarian options and the waiters will explain what's what. The menu also runs to assorted curries and Chinese dishes.

7 LIFE AND DEATH ON THE GANGA
➤ 74–83

OPERATOR
Manjushree Travel & Tours

P.O. Box 2563
Thamel
Kathmandu

☎ (1) 430952/428284/436885
fax: (1) 227644
email: manjushree2563@hotmail.com

Very efficient and helpful staff offer a complete range of travel agency services for both Nepal-based and international requirements. Located at the northern end of Thamel, they can book flights, treks, and tours to anywhere in the country including Chitwan, Pokhara, and the Everest region, book international flights and arrange onward train and bus travel in India from the Nepal border or internal Indian flights. Also, it has an on-site internet café.

ACCOMMODATION
Hotel Surya $

S.20/51, A-5 The Mall Road
Varuna Bridge
Varanasi
PIN 221 002

☎ (542) 343014/511012 **fax:** (542) 348330
email: Suria@lw1.vsnl.net.in

Although this popular and recommended travellers' hotel is not in the old town, it can prove to be a wise choice once you experience the manic life on the streets of Varanasi. Set around a large, peaceful garden—a great spot for afternoon tea—it offers a range of very good value accommodation, from standard economy rooms with basic en-suite facilities to spacious, air-conditioned, super deluxe rooms. The upper rooms have good views too. During quieter periods discounts may be available. There is piping hot water in the showers, a laundry service, steam bath, massage centre, a very good, hygienic restaurant, and a travel agency.

8 TALES FROM THE ORISSAN TRIBAL LANDS
➤ 84–93

GETTING THERE
FLIGHTS
Indian Airlines

See p. 261 for details.

Indian Airlines fly to Bhubaneshwar from several cities, including Delhi, Mumbai, and Calcutta. The 2-hour flight from Delhi operates daily. Book flights as far in advance as possible as they are popular. There is no direct flight at the time of writing from Varanasi to Bhubaneshwar, and Indian Airlines' flights to Nepal were suspended indefinitely following the hijacking incident at Kathmandu airport in late-December 1999—enquire for the latest information.

TRAINS
Indian Railways

website: www.indianrailway.com

Any visit to India would not be complete without taking at least one train trip. The 8476 *Neelanchal Express*, which starts from New Delhi and terminates in Puri, leaves Varanasi in the evening on Tuesdays, Fridays, and Saturdays for the 22-hour journey to Bhubaneshwar in Orissa. The 2-tier A/C ticket the author bought cost 1,200 rupees. Second-class sleeper tickets are about one third that price, but it is a long journey! Basic but reasonable food, with vegetarian option, is available in 2-tier A/C class, as well as tea and coffee. Blankets and bed linen are also available though it is a good idea to mention this when booking your ticket. Indian Railways offer an Indrail Pass that varies in duration and type (for example, first class, 2-tier A/C). There are reservation offices at 400 locations throughout the country, open 8–1 and 2–8 Mon–Sat and 8–1 on Sundays.

OPERATORS
Gagan Surangi's Dove Tours

C/23 Saheed Nagar Market Building
Bhubaneshwar 7
Orissa

☎ (674) 500143 **fax:** (674) 500143
email: doveadventure@usa.net
website: www.orissaindia.com/DoveTours

Operating since 1994, this company offers small-group, tailor-made trips such as culture and trekking tours to Sikkim and wildlife trips and temple trips around Orissa. Gagan speaks good English and runs a very professional operation. You will get a wonderful insight on the Orissa tribal area tours (4–12 days), which usually include visits to the tribal markets and craft villages. Accommodation is in hotels and/or camping, the latter allowing more flexibility to get further into the tribal hills. A boat trip on Chilka Lake may be an option. Transport is normally by jeep or minibus. Permits and local arrangements take time to organize owing to the lack of telephones in many villages, so you need to book the tours as far in advance as possible, preferably at least a couple of weeks. Price varies greatly with your requirements and your group size, so enquire for an accurate quote.

9 TRAVELS IN TEMPLE LAND ▶ 94–103

OPERATORS
Clipper Holidays

14/1 Josier Steet
Nungambakkam
Chennai 600 034

☎ (44) 822 3109 **fax:** (44) 823 2645
email: clipper@chennai.wipro.net.in (Chennai; clipper@bangalore.wipro.net.in (Bangalore—head office); clipcok@md2.vsnl.net.in (Kerala);

Highly professional agency with friendly staff who can take care of all your travel needs throughout southern India, including flight and train bookings. Car hire with air conditioning, and with driver if required.

OTHER OPERATORS
Tamil Nadu Tourism

4 EVR Salai
Park Town
Chennai 600 003

☎ (44) 582916 **fax:** (44) 561385
email: ttdc@md3.vsnl.net.in
website: www.tamilnadutourism.com

The government-run tourism organization offers very good value day-long city tours and 6–8 day trips around Tamil Nadu's main sights. Transport is in minibuses (air conditioned if you pay more) seating around 35 and you'll likely be travelling with many locals. The itineraries are gruelling, and the accommodation generally basic in the tourism department's own hotels.

Window to the World

106 West Perumal Maistry Street
Madurai 625 001

☎ (452) 745711 **fax:** (452) 747784
email: windowtotheworld@vsnl.com
website: www.windowtotheworld.com.au
Australian office: email: jsevern@acr.net.au
New Zealand office:
email: jhawley@clear.net.nz

Offers a range of lengthy guided tours (typically 2–3 weeks), with an emphasis on exploring the spiritual side of India. In the south, itineraries include the main temple towns of Tamil Nadu, wildlife, and eco tours, yoga and ayurvedic tours in Tamil Nadu, Karnataka, and Kerala. Inexpensive personalized tours, including a driver, car, and medium-range accommodation, are available.

INFORMATION
The Government of India Tourist Office
154 Anna Salai
Chennai
☎ (44) 852 4295 **fax:** (44) 852 2193
The best place for information. Has brochures on the state's main towns and sights. The monthly *Hallo! Madras* booklet, available from bookstalls for 5 rupees, is also very useful for local details, including air, bus, and train times. Open Mon–Sat 9:15–5:45.

Madurai Tourist Office
180 West Veli Street
Madurai
☎ (452) 734757
Staff are helpful and keen to warn about scams and fake tourist offices around town. There are also information counters at the railway station and the airport. Open Mon–Fri 10–5:45 and Sat 10–2.

Pondicherry Tourist Office
Goubert Ave (facing the sea)
☎ (413) 39497
You can get city maps here and book sightseeing tours. Open daily 8–1 and 2–6.

ACCOMMODATION
CHENNAI
Ambassador Pallava $$
53 Monteith Road
Chennai 600 008
☎ (44) 855 4476 **fax:** (44) 855 4492
email: pallav@vsnl.com
Conveniently located, old-style hotel with a touch of Raj style. The rooms are large, the service attentive and the food at the Salt & Pepper coffee shop reliable. Also has an outdoor pool.

GRT Grand Days $$
120 Sir Thyagaraya Road
Pondy Bazaar
Chennai 600 017
☎ (44) 822 0500 **fax:** (44) 823 0778
email: grtgranddays@vsnl.com
Modern business hotel with smart atrium lobby, non-smoking rooms, and 2 restaurants. Has indoor pool, gym, and friendly service.

New Woodlands Hotel $$
See Food and drink, below, for details. Advance bookings are essential for this highly recommended hotel.

Taj Coromandel $$$
17 Nungambakkan High Road
Chennai 600 034
☎ (44) 827 2827 **fax:** (44) 827 0070
Chennai's finest, with all the luxury you'd expect from the Taj group—even a palm reader three times a week in the business centre. The Taj also run the historic **Conomara Hotel** (Binny Road, Off Mount Road, ☎ (44) 852 0123 **fax:** (44) 852 3361)), parts of which were undergoing renovation at the time of research.

Y.W.C.A. International Guest House $
1086 EVR Periyar Salai
Chennai
☎ (44) 532 4234 **fax:** (44) 532 4263
Highly recommended budget option in a quiet off-road location near the Egmore railway station. The rooms are basic but clean. There are rules to follow, though, such as ordering meals in advance from the restaurant.

KANCHIPURAM
Hotel Tamil Nadu $
Railway Road
Kanchipuram
☎ (4112) 23428 **fax:** (4112) 22552
Standard government-run hotel in a quiet spot, with air conditioning and fan rooms and a reliable restaurant.

MAMALLAPURAM
Hotel Sea Breeze $
Ottawadai Street
Mamallapuram 603 104
☎/**fax:** (4114) 43035
New, upmarket hotel with sea views. The rooms are spacious with comfortable beds, en-suite bathrooms and fans or air-conditioning. Outdoor pool and restaurant.

Ideal Beach Resort $–$$
Mamallapuram 603 104
☎ (4114) 42240 **fax:** (4114) 42243
email: ideal@idealresort.com
website: www.idealresort.com
Pleasant resort complex, a few kilometres north of the town. Has swimming pools, a recommended restaurant.

PONDICHERRY
Anandha Inn $–$$
SV Patel Road
Pondicherry 605 001
☎ (413) 330711 **fax:** (413) 331241

This business hotel lacks character and is a bit distant from the more interesting end of town. In its favour are spacious, air-conditioned rooms with en-suite bathrooms and satellite T.V., and a decent restaurant.

Friend's House $–$$

6-B Labourdonnais Street
Pondicherry 605 001
☎ (413) 339745 **fax:** (413) 330057
Just 6 charmingly decorated rooms at this secluded colonial residence in the heart of the French quarter. Shared bathroom.

CHIDAMBARAM
Hotel Saradha Ram $

19 VGP Street
Chidambaram
☎ (4144) 21336 **fax:** (4144) 22656
The rackety old elevator and bus station across the way create a lot of noise, but this is about the best that the town can offer. Rooms have air conditioning and T.V. Try the vegetarian restaurant at the front or the non-vegetarian, air-conditioned restaurant at the back, both of which are excellent.

THANJAVUR
Hotel Sangam $$

Trichy Road
Thanjavur 613 007
☎ (4362) 39451 **fax:** (4362) 36695
email: hotelsangam@vsnl.com
website: www.hotelsangam.com
The town's most upmarket hotel, in a quiet location, has comfortable air-conditioned rooms, a good restaurant, and a swimming pool.

Ideal River View Resort $

Vennar Bank
Pallizgraharam
Thanjavur 613 003
☎ (4362) 24533 **fax:** (4362) 34933
email: ideal@idealresort.com
website: www.idealresort.com
A relaxing retreat beside the Vennar River, 3km (2 miles) outside of Thanjavur. Both the rooms and food are excellent value for money.

TIRUCHIRAPALLI (TRICHY)
Hotel Sangam $$

Collector's Office Road
Tiruchirapalli 620 001
☎ (431) 441 4700 **fax:** (431) 415779
email: hotelsangam@vsnl.com
website: www.hotelsangam.com

Undergoing renovation at the time of research, the Sangam promises to be Trichy's best hotel. The staff are very helpful and facilities include a pool, gym, restaurant, and 24-hour coffee shop.

MADURAI
Germanus Days Inn $$

28 By-Pass Road
Madurai 625 010
☎ (452) 610011 **fax:** (452) 603478
New, business-class hotel, 2km from the centre. Good air-conditioned rooms with satellite T.V. and 24-room service. The complex's Restaurant Utsav is worth checking out, although service can be a bit over the top.

Hotel Aarathy $

9 Perumal Koil
West Mada Street
Madurai 625 001
☎ (452) 731571 **fax:** (452) 733345
Convenient for the train and bus stations, the roof of this clean, friendly budget hotel provides a spectacular view across the neighbouring temple. Drop by the courtyard café around 6am and 4pm to meet the temple elephant.

Taj Garden Retreat $$$

Pasumalai 40
TPK Road
Madurai 625004
☎ (452) 601020 **fax:** (452) 604004
email: retreat.madurai@tajhotels.com
Rooms so big you can get lost in them at this hill top luxury resort, spread over 62 manicured acres, 4km (2½ miles) south of the town centre. Those in the original colonial villa are best. The restaurant's terrace is the place to dine.

FOOD AND DRINK
CHENNAI
New Woodlands Hotel

72-75 Dr Radhakrishnan Salai
Chennai
☎ (44) 827 5222 **fax:** (44) 826 0214
The food just keeps coming at this sparkling clean, air-conditioned restaurant specializing in cheap *thali*, tandoori dishes and *dosa*.

Raintree Restaurant

Hotel Connemara
Binny Road
Off Mount Road
Alfresco dining in this leafy courtyard. Fine Indian cuisine accompanied by live classical music and dancing.

PONDICHERRY
Hotel Aristo
Nehru Street
Between Mission Street and Mahatma Gandhi Road
This rooftop restaurant/café is one of the best places for Indian food in "Pondy," and a convivial spot to while away the afternoon.

Le Club
38 Rue Duma
Pondicherry
☎ (413) 339745
Collection of fine restaurants in a colonial building, serving French and Vietnamese food in the leafy courtyard, and Spanish *tapas* inside. Expensive, but worth indulging in for the atmosphere.

MADURAI
Arya Bhavan
Corner of West Masi Street & Dindigul Road
Madurai
The enormous, special *dosas* at this local favourite will feed the hungriest appetite. There's an air-conditioned room, behind the chaotic front section.

Surya Restaurant
Hotel Supreme
110 West Perumal Maistry Street
Madurai
On the hotel roof, with a grand view of the Meenakshi Temple, this place, serving a wide range of dishes, is always busy in the evenings, so expect slow service.

---

10 SAILING THROUGH THE SPICE KINGDOM ► 104–113

OPERATORS
Clipper Holidays
40/6531 Convent Road
Cochin 682 035
☎ (484) 364453 **fax:** (484) 381453
email: clipckok@md2.vsnl.net.in
Can arrange all holiday options in Kerala, from overnight houseboat cruises around Alappuzha coast to elephant safaris in plantations near Cochin. These are the best people to approach to sort out permits for trekking in tribal areas around Munnar. Trekking prices include covering tents, sleeping bags, rucksacks, and guide.

Tourist Desk Information Counter
Main Boat Jetty, opp. Corporation of Cochin Offices
Ernakulam
☎ (484) 371716 or (9847) 044688
email: raiyaan@vsnl.com
Book their half-day cruises (daily 9–1:30 or 2–6:30) directly at the Tourist Desk office (it costs more via an agent). These backwater cruises in wooden punt boats are excellent, but be prepared for the tedious 1-hour road journey from Cochin. Can also arrange houseboat cruises.

OTHER OPERATORS
Indo World Tours & Travel
39/4155 Heera House
Opp Deepa Theatre
Ravipuram, MG Road
Cochin 682016
☎ (484) 370127 **fax:** (484) 370127
Half-day and full-day backwater cruises. Houseboats and hill station tours of 3 days/2 nights from Cochin to Munnar and Thekkady.

Kerala Travels
Mangala Saundham
Vellayambalam
Thiruvananthapuram 695010
☎ (471) 324158 **fax:** (471) 323154
email: keralt@md2.vsnl.net.in
Contact to make bookings for the 3 day/2 night Thekkady Tiger Trail camping tours, around Periyar Lake. Cost varies with number on tour. All food, tent, sleeping bag, and leech socks are included. Also offer 1-night treks.

Tourindia
PB No 163
MG Road
Thiruvananthapuram 695 001
Kerala
☎ (471) 330437 **fax:** (471) 331407
email: turindia@giasmd01.vsnl.net.in
website: www.richsoft.com/tourindia
Can arrange *kettuvallam* houseboat trips. Also has an eco-lodge, the Green Magic Nature Resortr, at Vythiri, 65km (40 miles) east of Calicut, with full board accommodation in tree houses in the midst of the forest. Treks into the Wayanad Wildlife Sanctuary can be arranged here.

INFORMATION
The Government of India Tourist Office
Willingdon Island
☎ (484) 668352
Next to the Taj Malabar Hotel. Open Mon–Sat, 9–5:30.

Kerala Tourism
Park View
Thiruvananthapuram
☎ (471) 321132 **fax:** (471) 322279
email: deptour@md2.vsnl.net.in
website: www.keralatourism.org

Kerala Tourist Development Corporation (KTDC)
Shanmugham Road
Ernakulam
☎ (484) 353234
You can arrange accommodation at their hotels across the state from here. Open daily 8–7.

Tourist Desk Information Counter
Ernakulam
☎ (484) 371716 or (9847) 044688
email: raiyaan@vsnl.com
Beside the main boat jetty. The staff are most helpful. You can pick up their South India travel information guidebook here. Open daily 8–7.

ACCOMMODATION
KOCHI (COCHIN)
The Brunton Boat Yard $$–$$$
Fort Cochin 682001
☎ (484) 222557 **fax:** (484) 222562
email: casino@giasmd01.vsnl.net.in
An airy, well-designed modern hotel built in 17th-century Dutch style, on the site of an old boat yard. Rooms are tastefully furnished with high, four-poster beds and retro fittings; ask for the ones overlooking the water. Large pool, fine restaurant and café. Rates include breakfast.

Fort Heritage $$
1/283 Napier Street
Elphinstone Road
Fort Cochin 682001
☎/fax: (484) 225333/221455
email: hapynest@satyam.net.in
This 10-room hotel is set in a modestly renovated 17th-century Dutch palace. The simply furnished rooms have cable T.V. and en-suite bathrooms. The restaurant on the lawn in the back courtyard is a lovely spot for dinner.

The Fort House $
11/6A Calvathy Road
Fort Cochin 682001
☎ (484) 226103 **fax:** (484) 222066
Staff are very friendly at this inexpensive, small hotel. Has clean and spacious, fan-cooled rooms with attached bathrooms, set in a quiet courtyard littered with weathered statues, beside the water. The restaurant also serves fine curries and fish dishes, but there's no alcohol. Rates include breakfast.

Malabar House Residency $$$
1/268-269 Parade Rd
Fort Cochin 682001
☎/fax: (484) 221199
email: malabar@giasmd01.vsnl.net.in
website: www.malabarhouse.com
Wallow in luxury at this boutique hotel, decorated to the glossiest of magazine standards. Has a small pool and 2 restaurants: The Malabar Junction, serving a menu of gourmet Mediterranean and South Indian food, and The Tandoor Terrace, for Indian barbecue meals. Rates include breakfast.

KUMARAKOM
Coconut Lagoon $$$
Kumarakom
Kottayam
☎ (481) 524491 **fax:** (481) 524495
email: casino@giasmd01.vsnl.net.in
By far the best of the backwater resort complexes on to Vembanad Lake. Original Keralan mansions have been relocated and converted into the airy restaurant, bar, reception, and ayurvedic massage centre, and a few tastefully furnished guest rooms (the rest are concrete chalets). All have open-air courtyard bathrooms and are set in landscaped grounds, cut through by narrow canals.

Taj Garden Retreat $$$
1/404 Kumarakom
Kottayam
☎ (481) 524377 **fax:** (481) 524371
This elegant, quiet complex has 10 spacious concrete cottages with waterside verandahs and a couple of moored houseboats. The restaurant and bar are in a restored colonial mansion. Offers a range of water sports activities as well as ayurvedic massage and traditional arts demonstrations.

PERIYAR
Aranya Nivas $
Thekkady
☎ (4863) 22023 **fax:** (4863) 22282
email: ktdc@giasmd01.vsnl.net.in
KDTC-run colonial-style hotel overlooking
Thekkady boat jetty. A bit shabby in places, but
still has charm. There's a pool, good restaurant,
and the rooms have telephones and satellite
T.V. channels. Packages, including all meals,
and boat trips are available. (A preferable
option to Periyar House, ☎ (4863) 22026 **fax:**
(4863) 22526, the cheapest of the KTDC-run
hotels in Periyar, where the rooms are damp
and dingy.)

Lake Palace $$–$$$
Thekkady
☎ (4863) 22023 **fax:** (4863) 22282
email: ktdc@giasmd01.vsnl.net.in
Also run by the KTDC, and more a luxury cottage than a palace, this 6-room hotel is the best
within the sanctuary. Kitsch touches, such as
fake tiger print sofas, mar the total Raj effect,
but otherwise a delightful hideaway. Offers 3-
day, 2-night packages including all meals and
boat transfers.

Spice Village $$–$$$
Kumily Road
Thekkady
☎ (4863) 22315 **fax:** (4863) 22317
email: casino@giasmd01.vsnl.net.in
Set in landscaped gardens, planted with spice
trees and bushes, this is a lovely complex of
thoughtfully designed cottages with excellent
facilities, including a pool, ayurvedic centre,
restaurant, and wildlife interpretation centre.
Activities offered include boat cruises, jungle
treks, and plantation tours.

FOOD AND DRINK
Periyar Wildlife Sanctuary
The **Spice Village** has an excellent buffet in its
restaurant, where you can try the best of Kerala
cuisine and drink alcohol. There are early
evening cooking demonstrations and live classical music later in the evening.
While visiting the sanctuary, you could try the
Aranya Nivas (see above, under
Accommodation) for lunch or dinner. The
pleasantly old-fashioned dining room serves a
range of Western and Indian dishes.

Muckumakal Tourist Hotel
Kumily
The Family Restaurant at the back of this budget hotel near the bus station is worth checking
out for its cheap *thalis.*

Hotel Ambadi
Kumily
☎ (4863) 22193
A good range of standard Indian and Chinese
dishes, with lots of vegetarian options, at this
inexpensive restaurant, just down the road
from the Spice Village.

KOCHI (COCHIN)
The best location to dine in Kochi is Fort
Cochin, where each of **Fort Heritage**,
Malabar House Residency, **The Brunton
Boat Yard** and **The Fort House** (all listed
above, under Accommodation) has an excel-
lent restaurant. You can also buy fresh fish and
have it cooked up by one of the stalls around
Vasco Da Gama Square.

Kashi Art Café
Burgher Street
Fort Cochin
Appealing café and contemporary art gallery,
with lovely courtyard at back, serving Western
food and coffee. Open Mon–Sat 8:30–6:30 and
Sun 8:30–2:30.

11 A PASSAGE TO OOTY
► 114–121

OPERATORS
Clipper Holidays
Suite 406 Regency Enclave
4 Magrath Road
Bangalore
☎ (80) 559 9032/559 2023 **fax:** (80) 559 9833
email: clipper@bangalore.wipro.net.in
Professional agency with friendly staff who can
take care of all your travel needs throughout
southern India. Apart from organizing hiking
trips in the Nilgiris and wildlife safaris around
Mudumalai, they recommend Kabini River
Lodge in the Nagarhole Sanctuary, Karnataka,
as the best-run wildlife resort in South India.
Also has branches in Chennai and Cochin.

Jungle Retreat
Bokkapuram
Masinaguddi
P.O. Box 643 223
Nilgiris

Tamil Nadu
☎ (423) 56470 **fax:** (423) 56469
email: jungleretreat@yahoo.com
website: www.jungleretreat.com
Organize treks around Mudumalai Wildlife Sanctuary and up into the Nilgiris from their extensive property in Bokkapuram.

S Rajan
No 5, 1st floor Bharathiyar Complex
Charring Cross
Ootacamund
☎ (423) 41297 **fax:** (423) 45453
Local travel agent who can make bookings for trains, accommodation, and buses and arrange trekking programmes. Works in association with Clipper Holidays.

OTHER OPERATORS
Albatross Flying Systems
Catwalk
35 Cash Bazaar
Ootacamund
Nilgiris
Tamil Nadu
☎/**fax:** (423) 42313
email: fly_albatross@yahoo.com
Also at:

The South Indian Aerosports Co
11 Y-Crofft
Llansaint
Carmarthenshire SA17 5JQ
U.K.
☎/**fax:** (01267) 267 688
email: south.india@virgin.net
website: freespace.virgin.net/south.india
The chief flying instructor for both these operations is John Penry-Evans, who has been flying gliders since 1975 and lives in Ooty from around September to May each year. Javad Hassan is his Ooty-based partner. Offers a 4-day course learning how to paraglide or hang glide. Also, 2-week programmes starting from Chennai, with price depending on the type of accommodation you go for.

INFORMATION
Tourist Office
Lord Wenlock Road
☎ (423) 43977
Directly behind Breeks Memorial School at Charing Cross. The staff here are helpful and can provide basic maps and leaflets on the area, as well as rental camping gear. Open Mon–Fri 10–5:45.

Nilgiri Wildlife & Environment Association
District Forest Office Building
☎ (423) 43968
They publish the Tahr newsletter and a photographic guide to South Indian butterflies.

ACCOMMODATION
Black Thunder Resort $-$$
Ooty Main Road
Mettupalayam
☎ (4254) 26632 **fax:** (4254) 25740
website: www.blackthunderpark.com
Next to a tumultuous water theme park, this is the best hotel within easy shooting distance 3km (2 miles) of Mettupalayam station, if you want to sleep over before catching the early morning train.

Green Park Resorts $
Singara Road
Masinagudi
Nilgiris
☎ (423) 56351/56485 **fax:** (423) 56446
email: greenpark@india.com
website: www.karnatakatourism.com/grnpark
Eco-friendliness is stressed at this otherwise regular, small, concrete resort with some chalets made from bamboo and mud, and food grown in their own allotments. Worth booking a night in one of their ingenious treehouses, which are great for bird and wildlife watching.

Hotel Khems $
Shoreham Palace Road
off Ettines Road
Ootacamund, Nilgiris
Tamil Nadu
☎ (423) 44188/41264 **fax:** (423) 42461
Reasonably comfortable and less damp rooms than other similar cheap hotels in Ooty. Hot water is available and the service is friendly.

Jungle Retreat $
Bokkapuram
Masinaguddi
Nilgiris
Tamil Nadu
☎ (423) 56470 **fax:** (423) 56469
email: jungleretreat@yahoo.com
website: www.jungleretreat.com
Small, impeccably run eco-resort on the edge of the Mudumalai Wildlife Sanctuary. Well-designed cottages (no T.V., no telephone) and an excellent restaurant. Also offers trekking programmes—see Operators.

Ratan Tata Officers' Holiday Home $

Ootacamund
Nilgiris
Tamil Nadu
☎ (423) 42216
Around 10 minutes' walk north from the station towards the Ooty Club, this colonial villa, now owned by the army, is set in lovingly tended gardens and is open to the public, if rooms are available. Plenty of old-world charm, and incredibly good value.

Regency Villa Hotel $–$$

Fernhill
Ootacamund
Nilgiris
Tamil Nadu
☎ (423) 42555/43098 **fax:** (423) 43097
email: regency@md3
Part of the Maharaja of Mysore's estate, the best rooms—like museum pieces from the Raj—are in the main cottage (the rest are damp and shabby). Worth visiting for tea or lunch on their neatly clipped lawn if nothing else. Ask to see the nearby Fernhill Palace, still undergoing renovation.

Savoy Hotel $$–$$$

77 Sylks Rd
Ootacamund
Nilgiris
Tamil Nadu
☎ (423) 44142 **fax:** (423) 43318
Ooty's grandest hotel has high quality, modern rooms with wooden floors, fireplaces, T.V., and telephone. Rates are usually full board.

FOOD AND DRINK
Shinkows

38 Commissioners Road
Ootacamund
☎ (423) 42811
Fine Chinese restaurant, with a wide range of dishes. Has two sections, the Zodiac Room being the more upmarket.

Tandoori Mahal

Commercial Road
Ootacamund
Inexpensive and reliable Indian restaurant with a cosy ambience.

The Willow Hill

58/1 Havelock Road
Ootacamund

☎ (423) 42686
The restaurant here is a better bet than the accommodation. There's a lawn with a view across Ooty, where you can take afternoon tea.

12 ADRIFT IN THE ANDAMANS ➤ 122–129

OPERATORS
Andaman Divers

Peerless Resort
Corbyn's Cove
Port Blair 744101
☎ (3192) 33461 **fax:** (3192) 33463
A European dive master runs the operation at one of the two reliable dive centres in Port Blair. Groups of 4 or more people get a 10 percent discount.

Clipper Holidays

See p. 268 for details.
Can arrange flights to the Andamans and book accommodation and dives around Port Blair, with Andaman Divers at the Peerless Resort.

Jungle Resort

Beach 7, Havelock
Bookings via:
Travel World
Port Blair
☎ (3192) 37656 **fax:** (3192) 37657
Swiss instructors Willi Failer and Marcus Kommer run the only dive centre on Havelock Island. Single dives and P.A.D.I. courses.

Samudra

Sinclairs Bay View Hotel
South Point
Port Blair
☎ (3192) 33159/32937 **fax**: (3192) 31824
Mumbai office:
6th floor Sitakunj 164 Maharishi Karve
MargMantralaya
Mumbai 400021
☎ (22) 287 0729 **fax**: (22) 285 2037
email: manavi_tha@hotmail.com
website: www.welcometoindia.com/samudra
Female instructor and oceanographer Manavi Thakkar is P.A.D.I.-qualified and has over 10 years' experience diving in the Andamans.

South East Asia Liveaboards

225 Rat-U-Thit 200 Year Road
Patong
Phuket 83150
Thailand

☎ (76) 340406 **fax:** (76) 292561
email: info@sealiveaboards.com
website: www.sealiveaboards.com
For real diving enthusiasts, these liveaboard
cruises departing from Phuket are a must.
You'll dive at sites that are not easily arranged
or possible if you're based on the islands themselves. Also offer surfing trips to the southern
most islands of the Andamans.

INFORMATION
Andaman & Nicobar Tourist Office
☎ (3192) 32747/32694 **fax:** (3192)
30933/30234
Diagonally opposite the Indian Airlines office,
up the hill south of Aberdeen Bazaar. This is
the best place to go, though not wholly reliable.
Come here to book the government-managed
accommodation around the islands and to
check on ferry details. Open Mon–Fri 8:30–5.

The Government of India Tourist Office
189 Junglighat Main Road (above a shop)
☎ (3192) 33006
Open Mon–Fri 8:30–5.

ACCOMMODATION
PORT BLAIR
Bay Island Hotel $$
Marine Hill
Port Blair
☎ (3192) 32123/32112 **fax:** (3192) 31555
Friendly service and a lovely hilltop location
are pluses for the most upmarket of Port Blair's
hotel, where the rates are for full-board.
Spacious guest rooms have wooden floors and
satellite T.V., but not all have balconies. Has a
very small museum on environmental themes
and a seawater-filled pool.

Chief Wildlife Warden
Van Sadan
Haddo, Port Blair
☎ (3192) 33549
Smart forest guest houses at Chidiya Tapu,
Wandoor, and Mt Harriet can be booked here.

The Director of Tourism
Port Blair
☎ (3192) 32747/32694 **fax:** (3192)
30933/20234
Contact for accommodation in government
guesthouses in Port Blair and around the
islands.

Megapode Nest $-$$
Haddo
Port Blair
☎ (3192) 32380/32207
Run by a local government body, this pleasant
complex of concrete cabins, set in the hills
overlooking Phoenix Bay, is very popular. Book
well in advance. Their *thali* lunches are worth a
visit even if you're not staying.

Peerless Resort $$
Corbyn's Cove
Port Blair 744101
☎ (3192) 33461 **fax:** (3192) 33463
Quiet location for this low-key complex beside
the closest beach to Port Blair. Rooms are clean
and spacious with T.V. and air conditioning. Has
a dive centre (see Operators). The restaurant is
good, although service can be erratic.

HAVELOCK
Dolphin Yatri Niwas $–$$
Beach 5, Havelock Island
☎/**fax:** (3192) 82411
These blue and white concrete cabins offer the
best accommodation on the island, with direct
access to a fine beach. The restaurant is adequate, and it's often full for dinner, so book well
in advance with the Andaman & Nicobar
Tourist Office in Port Blair.

Jungle Resort $–$$
See Operators, above, for details.
Hidden in the forest at the north end of the
beach are simple huts with mosquito nets, mattresses, and bucket showers. Also, spacious
cottages with en-suite bathrooms.

Maya Bayview/Sea View Tourist Complex $
Havelock Town
☎ (3192) 82367/82442
Pretty row of simply furnished cabins with
attached bathrooms and a veranda facing the
ocean. Just beyond the central square, on the
way to the MS Guest House (which is mosquito-
ridden and not as pleasant).

FOOD AND DRINK
Annapurna Cafeteria
Aberdeen Bazaar
Port Blair
Behind the cake shop, at the hilltop end of
Aberdeen Bazaar. This packed joint serves a
fine range of cheap Indian and Chinese dishes,
including huge *dosas* and *thalis* at lunch.

China Room

Dignabad
Port Blair
☎ (3192) 30759

On a hill around 5 minutes' walk north of Aberdeen Bazaar, this excellent restaurant is worth searching out. Has an opium-den, decadent atmosphere, and specializes in fresh fish and seafood dishes, such as sardines in lemon sauce and tuna fillet with ginger. Open daily for lunch 12–2 and dinner 6–late.

Harmony Restaurant

Beach 7, Havelock Island
It might not look much, but this roadside shack on the way to the beach, run by the genial Ashok, is the best restaurant in the Andamans. You need to order the very reasonably priced 3-course dinner by noon since the fish—huge chunks of it—is bought fresh from the market. Don't miss out on the delicious *sandesh* milk sweets either.

Mandalay

Bay Island Hotel
Marine Hill
Port Blair
☎ (3192) 20881

Pricey, especially for drinks, but good food and a gorgeous view of the islands from the restaurant's veranda. Sometimes has buffet meals which are better value.

Waves

Corbyn's Cove
Port Blair
Has a nice view of the beach and one of the few places you can get a beer without busting your budget. Snack food available.

---

13 A RARE ANNAPURNA
TREKKING SANCTUARY
► 132–141

GETTING THERE
Qatar Airways

10 Conduit Street
London W1R 0QR
U.K.
☎ (020) 7896 3636 **fax:** (020) 7896 3610
website: http://qatarairways.com
Qatar Airways offer an excellent daily service on modern A320 Airbus jets, with friendly and helpful staff, from London to Kathmandu—although you change planes in Doha in Qatar, the stopover is so brief that it is virtually a direct service. The airline also operates an Adventure Club that is free to join and allows trekkers, whether travelling independently or with a group, to benefit from priority service at check-in, an extra 10kg (22lb) of luggage allowance, and information and discounts on services and products in Kathmandu.

OPERATOR
Specialist Trekking

Chapel House
Low Cotehill
Carlisle
Cumbria CA4 0EL
U.K.
☎ (01228) 562358 **fax:** (01228) 562368
email: trekstc@aol.com
website: www.specialisttrekking.com
Owned and run by legendary Himalayan mountaineer Doug Scott and his Nepalese wife Sharu, the company aims to operate treks that give a fair deal to the communities and working people of the areas they visit. They operate as a non-profit organization, with excess money going to their charitable organization, Community Action Nepal. Their range of treks suits most levels of ability. The trek the author took to Siklis is part of a 15-day package they offer from the U.K., which includes flights, accommodation with breakfast and full board on the trek itself, camping equipment (not including sleeping bags), guide, cook, and porters, and trekking permits. For trip extensions to visit the Royal Chitwan National Park see p. 276.

OTHER INFORMATION
Shona's Rentals

Jyatha
Thamel
Kathmandu
☎ (1) 265120 **fax:** (1) 265120
Shona's place is legendary in Kathmandu, though you wouldn't think it from peering into the small and gear-laden interior. In a city renowned for its tricky dealers, Shona provides a breath of honest and straightforward air to getting kitted out for a trek. The Nepalese-made equipment she sells and rents, which includes down jackets and sleeping bags, is amongst the best and most reliable on offer and the price is fair but most certainly not negotiable! Her down jackets are a particularly good bargain. There is also an array of original, imported equipment, both new and second-hand, for those who cannot make do with the

local gear. Prices for the imported gear are very similar to U.K. prices and more expensive than in the U.S.A. Amongst many things, Shona sells backpacks, fleece jackets, thermal underwear, hats, gloves, trekking poles, and ice axes. Shona's Australian husband, Andy, has plenty of mountain experience and is usually on hand to help out with advice on gear and potential trekking routes.

Accommodation
Acme Guest House $

P.O. Box 10506
Thamel
Kathmandu
☎ (1) 425326/414811 **fax:** (1) 414811
email: acme@mos.com.np

Thamel is a busy and frantic place, so the author was amazed to discover this lovely little sanctuary right in its heart. At the end of an alley near the Tom and Jerry Pub, the Acme Guest House has a large garden and restaurant on site and some rooms have south facing balconies to catch the warm afternoon sun. Although there is a disco bar nearby, the hotel is generally very peaceful and has excellent, helpful staff. All the rooms have en-suite facilities and hot water most of the time. The rooms are clean and spacious and there is a same-day laundry service available. There is also a safe luggage store. There are 3 types of room: economy; standard; and garden-facing. Weekly and monthly rates available; discounts for youth hostel members. Visa, Mastercard and traveller's cheques are accepted.

---

14 HIMALAYAN HIGH RIDERS
► 142–149

Getting There
Qatar Airways

See p. 274.

Operator
Himalayan Mountain Bikes

P.O. Box 12673
Kathmandu
☎ Thamel office (1) 437437 **fax:** (1) 419237
Director's ☎/**fax:** (1) 355739
Pokhara office, Lakeside (61) 22219;
email: bike@hmb.wlink.com.np
website: www.visitnepal.com/hmb

HMB has been at the forefront of pioneering mountainbiking in the Himalaya and has operated tours there since 1988. Based in the Adventure Centre at the entrance to the North

Field Café, next to the Kathmandu Guest House in Thamel. Scheduled and tailor-made biking trips to suit all, from the fit-but-inexperienced to gnarly trail experts. They use excellent, English-speaking local guides. Their tailor-made tour prices include a good-quality, imported, front-suspension mountain bike, services of a guide, bag drops at the overnight stops, and accommodation on a bed and breakfast basis. In addition to Nepalese mountain tours they offer trips down to the southern Terai region and Tibet.

The Borderlands Adventure Centre

See Accommodation, below, for details. There are numerous adventure activities to try, including rafting on the Bhote Koshi, trekking and canyoning, though the biking to the Tibet border can be a bit testing, especially when it is dry and vehicles kick up clouds of choking dust. Longer, multi-sport packages are also available.

Accommodation
Acme Guest House $

See above.

Peaceful Cottage $

(Nagarkot)
P.O. Box 37
Bhaktapur
☎ (1) 680077 **fax:** (1) 680127

One of the best accommodation options in Nagarkot, on clear days Peaceful Cottage offers superb views from its huge garden porch area of the Himalayan peaks, including 8 of the 10 highest in the world. Very spacious and comfortable rooms have en-suite facilities with piping hot water. A good restaurant in the round-house on the top level includes an à la carte menu. They even wake you up, if required, when there is a good sunrise. There are 3 types of rooms—budget (separate, shared bathroom); standard; and deluxe rooms —all good value.

The Borderlands Adventure Centre $

P.O. Box 13558
Thamel
Kathmandu
☎ (1) 425836 **fax:** (1) 435207
email: info@borderlands.net
website: www.borderlands.net

This wonderful, eco-friendly adventure resort is located right on the banks of the Bhote Koshi

River in a gorgeous, steep-sided valley near the Nepal-Tibet border. Accommodation is in spacious luxury tents with comfortable beds. There is a toilet block and the most refreshing showers you will ever have, as the water is diverted straight out of the glacier-fed river! In the landscaped gardens there is a thatched bar/restaurant area, which is perfect for relaxing in. At night the whole place is lit with lanterns. The food is very tasty and plentiful, and served buffet style.

FOOD AND DRINK
Kilroy's of Kathmandu
P.O. Box 10542
Jyatha
Thamel
Kathmandu
☎ (1) 250 441 **fax:** (1) 250 440
email: atcon@wlink.com.np
website: www.viewnepal.com/kilroy
If you want to sample the best cuisine in the city then Kilroy's is the place (although some travellers have reported contracting food poisoning here). With the kitchen staff trained by an ex-head chef from the Savoy Hotel in London, the excellent food is superbly presented. There is a range of dishes with international influences and you can enjoy it in a lovely fountain garden setting, or indoors on chilly evenings. It is expensive for Kathmandu but really not more than you would pay at an average restaurant in the U.K. or U.S.A.

15 TERAI TRUNK ROUTE
► 150–159

OPERATOR
Specialist Trekking
See p. 274 for details.
Specialist Trekking offer tours to the Royal Chitwan National Park as extensions on their trekking trips, or independently. The author took their 3-day trip to the Gaida Wildlife Camp; they also offer 4- and 5-day options.

GETTING THERE
FLIGHTS
Qatar Airways
See p. 274.

Gorkha Airlines
☎ (1) 472989 **fax:** (1) 471136
One of Nepal's private airlines, they fly daily from Kathmandu to Bharatpur, a 20-minute flight. Book ahead as flights fill up quickly.

Departures can be affected by fog in the Terai region.

BUSES
Greenline
P.O. Box 3904
Tridevi Marg
Kathmandu
☎ (1) 257544/253885 **fax:** (1) 241177
email: greenline@unlimit.com
Nepal's premier tourist bus company, Greenline offer comfortable and efficient daily services to Chitwan departing at 8am from their own depot in Thamel. Book ahead as they do fill up.

ACCOMMODATION
Gaida Wildlife Camp $–$$
Royal Chitwan National Park
P.O. Box 2056
Durbar Marg
Kathmandu
☎ (1) 220940/227425 **fax:** (1) 227292
email: gaida@mos.com.np
website: www.visitnepal.com/gaida
Situated inside the national park, this is a lovely place to relax and enjoy the wildlife and landscape. It has excellent camp staff and guides, including wildlife experts to guide you on the elephant tours, hikes, and canoe rides or answer questions at anytime. There are 30 twin-share rustic bungalows with front porches, built in an arc around the lush garden. There is no electricity—lighting is provided by lanterns. Hot water is heated by solar power (so it may not be available during cloudy periods). There is a good restaurant and a cosy bar with an open fire for cooler evenings. You buy accommodation as part of a package. It is well worth taking the short trip out to the Tharu village, and for really getting into the thick of things, you can opt to stay at the Jungle Camp tented accommodation. Good value for money.

16 RUNNING THE BHOTE KOSHI
► 160–167

OPERATORS
Equator Expeditions
P.O. Box 8404
Thamel
Kathmandu
☎ (1) 424944/425800 **fax:** (1) 425801
email: equator@mos.com.np
website: http://www.equatornepal.com
Rafting, tours and travel, mountaineering and trekking. This company does an excellent job:

the guides are professional, and ensure a good time with plenty of thrills.

GETTING THERE

The tour company takes care of all travel arrangements to get to the Bhote Koshi. The trip takes around 3 hours by bus to their comfortable camping base on the banks of the river.

ACCOMMODATION

Accommodation on the river is run by Equator Expeditions.

Dwarika Hotel $$$

Battisputali
Kathmandu
☎ (1) 470770/472328 **fax:** (1) 225131
A beautifully crafted, family-run hotel featuring many Nepalese antique features and the best Nepalese restaurant in town.

---

17 ON HORSEBACK TO THE KINGDOM OF LO ➤ 168–177

OPERATORS
Eco Trek

P.O. Box 6438
Thamel
Kathmandu
☎ (1) 420490/424113 **fax:** (1) 413118
email: info@ecotreknepal.com
website: www.ecotreknepal.com
A growing company that organizes treks and travel around Nepal.

Shambhala Trekking Agency

P.O. Box 7611
Kantipath
Kathmandu
☎ (1) 256670 **fax:** (1) 268093
email: amrit@kesh.wlink.com.np
A small, friendly and competent company specializing in Mustang, Tibet, Bhutan, Ladakh, and Zanskar. Trekking, mountaineering, and rock climbing available. English- and French-speaking guides.

Kailas Himalaya Trek Pvt Ltd

P.O. Box 4781
Bag Bazaar
Kathmandu
☎ (1) 241249/240980 **fax:** (1) 246571
email: himtravel@wlink.com.np or kailastk@vishnu.ccsl.com.np
website: www.nepalonline.net/himtravel

Kailas Himalaya Trek, established in 1991, specializes in adventure travel and climbing in the Himalaya. Its expertise includes arrangement and management of special cultural tours, filming, exploration, and climbing in Nepal. The company is registered at the Department of Tourism, recognized by His Majesty's Government of Nepal, and a member of 3 professional bodies: Trekking Agents Association of Nepal (T.A.A.N.); Nepal Mountaineering Association (N.M.A.); and Himalayan Rescue Association (H.R.A.).

GETTING THERE

Getting to Mustang requires a flight or bus trip to Pokhara on one day, and the next morning an early flight to Jomson. As this Mustang trip can only be done on a tour, all these travel arrangements are included in each operator's price.

ACCOMMODATION
KATHMANDU
Sidharta Garden Hotel $

Jyatha
Thamel
Kathmandu
☎**/fax:** (1) 222253
email: sidharta@htp.com.np
One of the nicest in the budget range, this small hotel is French-managed, with a pleasant ambience, good rooftop breakfasts, fresh baguettes, French filter coffee, and a courtyard with two pomelo trees.

POKHARA
Hotel Saino $

P.O. Box 299
Lakeside
Pokhara
☎ (1) 22868
Quite close to the post office. Pleasant and clean with mountain views and friendly, helpful staff. Nice garden and restaurant. Special discounts for volunteers of NGOs and expatriates working in Nepal.

LO MANTHANG
Mystique Himalayan Resort $$

Lo Manthang
Contact via:
P.O. Box 3488
Kathmandu
☎ (1) 427150 **fax:** (1) 427084
email: soi@wlink.com.np
website: www:south-asia.com/soi
Mustang's only hotel, under the direct

patronage of the king; it is quite well run and makes a welcome change from sleeping in a tent. Hot water showers in the rooms are total luxury. It is usually possible to get a room there for a negotiated rate rather than booking from Kathmandu.

FOOD AND DRINK
Pilgrim Restaurant
Thamel

An adjunct to the excellent Pilgrim Book Store, this sunny courtyard restaurant offers a wide range of Western, Nepalese, and Tibetan favourites in a relaxed setting. A pleasant place to while away the afternoon for those with abundant leisure time.

Rum Doodle Bar &Restaurant
Thamel

☎ 414336

One of the "must do"s whilst in Kathmandu, Rum Doodle offers excellent food and a great night out. A favourite with both mountaineers and tourists.

Yin Yang Restaurant
Thamel

Kathmandu

☎ (1) 425510

The best Thai restaurant in Thamel (and arguably in all of Nepal)—excellent quality food and a Western menu for those who prefer. One of my dining companions chose a very non-Thai pumpkin soup and mashed potato and pronounced it delicious!

18 IN AND OUT OF THE LOCKED CITY
► 180–189

The tourist hub of Thamel in Kathmandu is crammed with tourist agencies offering treks and trips in Tibet, so it's easy to shop around.

Eco Trek
See p. 277.
Organize Everest Base Camp treks, Ganden to Samye trek, tours of Lhasa, and eastern Tibet.

Explore Nepal Richa Tours and Travel (P) Ltd
Namche Bazaar Building

First Floor

Thamel

P.O. Box 1657

Kathmandu

☎ (1) 423064/420710 **fax:** (1) 421573

email: explore@enrtt.mos.com.np

Offer 12-day fly-in/overland tour from Kathmandu to Lhasa, including Everest Base Camp.

Himalayan Envpro Adventures Pvt. Ltd
P.O. Box 7217

Lainchaur

Thamel

Kathmandu

☎ (1) 410722/411746 **fax:** (1) 418918

email: hea@ccsl.com.np

Expeditions and treks in the Himalaya, including Tibet and tours to Lhasa.

Himalayan Kingdoms
20 The Mall

Clifton

Bristol BS8 4DR

U.K.

☎ (0117) 923 7163 **fax:** (0117) 974 4993

email: 101460.2022@compuserve.com

website: www.himalayankingdoms.com

Journeys International
107 Aprill Dr, Suite 3

Ann Arbor

MI 48103

U.S.A.

☎ (734) 665 4407 **fax:** (734) 665 2945

email: info@journeys-intl.com

website: www.journeys-intl.com

Organize cultural tours of Lhasa.

INFORMATION
Tibet Information Network (TIN)
City Cloisters

188–196 Old Street

London EC1V 9FR

U.K.

☎ (020) 7814 9011 **fax:** (020) 7814 9015

email: tin@tibetinfo.net

website: http://www.tibetinfo.net

U.S.A. office:

☎ (307) 733 4670/739 2501

email: tinusa@wyoming.com

Charitable organization with an independent news and research service, set up in 1987 to collect and distribute information on what is happening in Tibet. Especially useful travel pages offer visa advice and warn against putting Tibetans into danger unwittingly.

ACCOMMODATION
Amdo Guest House $
(On Everest Base Camp trek)

Tingri

Tibetan-run, friendly owners. Small, basic dormitory rooms, candlelit. Meals and jasmine/butter tea available in the owner's living room. Beds cost a few dollars a night depending on your bargaining.

Hotel Centre Point $
P.O. Box 12284

Thamel

Kathmandu

☎ (1) 424522/423789 **fax:** (1) 426320

email: cenpoint@wlink.com.np

Clean, nicely furnished rooms with T.V., phone, shower, or bath. Located in the heart of Kathmandu's tourist area, among adventure tour agencies, restaurants, and shops.

Pentoc Guesthouse $
Barkhor

Lhasa

☎ (891) 6326686

email: pentoc@public.east.cn.net

Refurbished to offer a welcoming reception where video evenings with Swiss coffee, tea, and cookies take place. Dormitory and single rooms. Showers, sauna, steam room, Jacuzzis available to both guests and non-residents.

Snowlands Hotel $
Barkhor

Lhasa

☎ (891) 6323687

Dormitories are cosy but not spotlessly clean. Single rooms in the new, refurbished hotel opposite the dorms. Restaurant next door serving a range of local and international dishes.

FOOD AND DRINK
In and around the Barkhor, in Lhasa's Tibetan quarter, are a number of popular restaurants frequented by travellers, and these are a good source of cheap meals, drinks, and also information about what to see and do. For example: **Makye Ame Restaurant** for *lhassi* yoghurt drinks, pastas, *thugpa*, coffees, and beers (it also has an internet café on the roof terrace); **Barkhor Café**, set to the right of the Jokhang and with great views of the Barkhor; **Tashi I Restaurant** for *momos*, yak burgers, cheesecake, and sweet milk tea; and **Snowlands Restaurant** for more upmarket, Tibetan, Chinese, and Western dishes.

19 OVERLAND TO THE SACRED MOUNTAIN ► 190–197

OPERATORS
Arun Treks and Expeditions (U.S.A.) Inc
301 East 33rd Street No 3

Austin

Texas 78705

U.S.A.

☎ (888) 495-TREK **fax:** (512) 495 9037

email: info@aruntrekexpedition.com

website: www.aruntrekexpedition.com

Organize treks to Mount Kailash.

Himalayan Envpro Adventures Pvt. Ltd
See p. 278 for details.

Organize overland trips to Mount Kailash.

Himalayan Expeditions Inc.
S.A.A.R.C. Secretariat Corner

Kanti Path

Sundhara P.O. Box 105

Kathmandu

☎ (1) 221394/226622 **fax:** (1) 228890

email: himalayan_guys@himalayas.org

website: www.himalayas.org

Journeys International
See p. 278 for details.

Organize pilgrimages and adventure treks to Mount Kailash.

INFORMATION
Tibet Information Network (TIN)
See p. 278 for details.

Zara Fleming
Freelance Tibetologist

Denbighshire

U.K.

☎ (0182) 4705429 **fax:** (0182) 4704745

Specialist in Tibetan and Central Asian art, culture, and affairs. Offer advice on treks and issues that can help you before you travel.

ACCOMMODATION
Hotel Utse $
Jyatha

Thamel

Kathmandu

☎ (1) 257614, 228952 **fax:** (1) 257615

email: utse@wlink.com.np

website: www.catmando.com/utse
A perfect start to a trip. The hotel is Tibetan-run and styled, extremely friendly with clean rooms with showers. Laundry, fax, and email. Restaurant serving Tibetan meals.

Accommodation on the road is very basic, usually with no running water or showers. Sometimes there is electricity, a thermos of hot water, blankets, and quilts. Toilets are dire, squat places, and unclean.

Tashi Guest House $
Zhongba
☎ None
Small, cosy dormitory rooms, no shower but an open-air toilet block. Meals prepared by the Tibetan lady owner.

Yak Hotel $
Paryang
☎ None
Beds are basic but swept clean.

Zhang Mu Hotel $
Zhangmu
☎ None
(just across the Friendship Bridge, on the left). Tatty entrance and reception, but has running water and showers, and a restaurant.

ON THE KAILASH *KORA*
Around the *kora* are 3 monasteries that offer very basic rooms (sometimes sleeping 6 to a room) but you can bargain them down. No meals, occasionally hot drinks, so you have to bring along your own food.

LAKE MANASAROVAR
If the weather is fine, you can camp on the beach to the right of Chiu Monastery, or take shelter in one of the 3 guesthouses behind the monastery, and enjoy the hot sulphur springs.

FOOD AND DRINK
Many guests houses en route prepare *thugpa*, a noodle soup with vegetables or meat, plus basic food. Booking an overland camping trip through an agency means full board is provided.

OPERATORS
Walji's Adventure Pakistan/ Walji's Travel Bureau
Walji's Building
10 Khayaban-E-Suhrawardy
P.O. Box 1088
Islamabad
Pakistan
☎ (51) 820908/270745/48
fax: (51) 270753/828264
email: walji@twlisb.sdnpk.undp.org or waljis@comsats.net.pk
website: http://www.waljis.com
The biggest operator of trekking and adventure tours in Pakistan, offering a full range of services. There are two divisions: Walji's Travel Bureau, a general travel agency, which handles everything from domestic and worldwide tours to conferences, and Walji's Adventure Pakistan, which specializes in trekking and adventure travel; it is also a licensee for Avis car rental. A professional company with very reliable and experienced guides, drivers, and trekking staff.

INFORMATION
Islamabad P.T.D.C. Tourist Information Centre
See p. 281 for details.

Gilgit P.T.D.C. Tourist Information Centre
c/o Sargin Travel
19 JSR Plaza
Airport Road
☎ (572) 3939
Limited information available.

ACCOMMODATION
ISLAMABAD
Hotel Ambassador $$
Khayaaban-e-Suharwardy
Islamabad
Pakistan
☎ (51) 824011/14 **fax:** (51) 812320
A pleasant, middle-range hotel with comfortable en-suite rooms. Good restaurant. Handy for Aabpara Market and central Islamabad. Book for late spring and summer.

Citi Lodge Guest House $
H 16, Street 56
Sector F-6/4

Islamabad

☎ (51) 275203/279347/815355

fax: (51) 273276

Comfortable guesthouse in quiet area, yet close to the main shopping area, known as Super Market. Meals can be supplied.

CHILAS
Panorama $

Karakoram Highway

Chilas

☎ (572) 340

Pleasant, lodge-style hotel with reasonable doubles with good air conditioning and shower. Excellent restaurant. Hotel shop sells local artefacts, books, maps, and postcards.

FAIRY MEADOWS
Green Land Camping Site $

Fairy Meadows

Post Office

Gonar Farm

Diamer

Northern Areas

☎ (572) 382

Pleasant, grassy location amidst tall pines. Tents and some chalet beds available. Shared squat toilets and basic washing facilities. Good food available.

Fairy Meadows Cottage $

c/o Fazal Medical Store

Gonar Farm

Diamar

Northern Areas

Most secluded of Fairy Meadows' campsites and in a beautiful location. Tents and some timber chalets. Shared squat toilets and basic washing facilities. Dining area and well-cooked meals available.

Raikot Sarai Camping Resort $

Fairy Meadows

Post Office

Gonar Farm

Diamer

Northern Areas

Reservations:

Centre One H-1 Street 15

F. 7/2 Islamabad

☎ (51) 276113/4/5/6/7/8

Longest-established, main campsite at Fairy Meadows. Tents and sleeping mats for hire. Some chalet beds available. Shared squat toilets and basic washing facilities. Good dining hut with excellent food. Reservations advised.

GILGIT
Mir's Lodge $

Domyal Link Road

Gilgit

☎ (572) 2875

Very pleasant hotel away from bustle of bazaars. Comfortable rooms with shower, fan, telephone, and some with T.V. First-class restaurant with sizzling hot meat dishes and big breakfasts. Popular with trekking groups and foreigners.

---

21 A LONG DRIVE TO THE HINDU KUSH
► 210–217

OPERATORS
Baltistan Tours

P.O. Box 604

Satellite Town Skardu

Northern Areas

Pakistan

☎ (575) 2626/2108 **fax:** (575) 2108

Branch office:

P.O. Box 1285

Islamabad

Pakistan

☎ (51) 270338 **fax:** (51) 278620

This well-established and helpful local company has a range of contacts throughout the area, and can organize most types of trek as well as being liaison for European trekking companies organizing major treks.

Walji's Adventure Pakistan/
Walji's Travel Bureau

See p. 280 for details.

Gilgit office:

P.O. Box 515

Airport Road

Gilgit

Northern Areas

Pakistan

☎ (572) 2665 **fax:** (572) 4129

A number of very experienced drivers and a well-maintained fleet of jeeps available.

INFORMATION
Islamabad PTDC Tourist
Information Centre

Room 6

Ministry of Tourism Building

13 College Road

Markaz F-7

Islamabad

☎ (51) 920 2766 **fax:** (51) 294540

Skardu P.T.D.C. Tourist Information Centre

P.T.D.C. K2 Motel

☎ (575) 2946 **fax:** (575) 270753

Limited information, but helpful with flights in and out of Skardu. Can arrange jeep hire.

ACCOMMODATION
P.T.D.C. K2 Motel $$

Hameed Garh Road

Skardu

☎ (575) 2946 **fax:** (575) 3322

Big, comfortable, but quite pricey hotel favoured by trekking and mountaineering groups. Wonderful garden overlooks the Indus. Good restaurant where you can even indulge in chicken and chips as well as standard local fare.

Kamran Hotel $

Rama Road

Astor

☎ (572) 140

Small, well-kept hotel at the heart of Astor and the best accommodation around. Very friendly service. Rooms with or without shower. Restaurant serves good local food.

Park Hotel $

Airport Road

Gilgit

☎ (572) 2379/3379/2479 **fax:** (572) 572/3796

Large hotel in own complex at southern entrance to Gilgit. Rooms near the front entrance on Airport Road can be affected by noise. Quiet rooms farther back surround a lovely central garden, but expect an early morning call from nearby mosques. Rooms are en suite, and have fan, telephone and T.V. Good laundry service and restaurant.

N.A.P.W.D. Inspection Bungalow (Gupis & Phandur) $

Administrative Officer

Office of Chief Engineer

N.A.P.W.D.

Khazana Road

☎ (572) 3375

These two nicely old-fashioned bungalows make excellent overnight stops. Squat toilets and cold running water. There is a *chowkidar* (caretaker) in charge who will often cook basic meals if you are not with a driver and cook. You should consider bringing food with you otherwise. Officials have precedence and it is always wise to book ahead. This will be taken care of by your operator.

22 ON HORSEBACK TO THE KALASH VALLEYS
► 218–227

OPERATOR
Hindukush Trails

37 Street 28

F-6/1

Islamabad

☎ (51) 821576 **fax:** (51) 275031

email: Culture@trails.sdnpk.undp.org

Chitral office:

Mountain Inn

Chitral

North West Frontier Province

☎ (933) 412581/412781/412800

fax: (933) 412663/412668

You can expect excellent sevice from this highly reputable agency which specializes in tailor-made treks and tours, meticulously planned and covering diverse themes. Also arranges all types of trek, including trips to the annual polo tournament at the Shandur Pass.

INFORMATION
Chitral P.T.D.C. Tourist Information Centre

P.T.D.C. Chitral Motel

New Bazaar

☎ (933) 412683 **fax:** (933) 412722

ACCOMMODATION
Mountain Inn $$

Chitral

North West Frontier Province

☎ (933) 412581/412781/412800

fax: (933) 412663/412668

email: mountain@inn.sdnpk.undp.org

Long-established and delightful hotel, set round a peaceful and colourful garden. All rooms are ensuite and very comfortable. Friendly, courteous service. The Mountain Inn is noted for being a great source of advice. Some good books on sale that give a rare insight into local culture and history. Good restaurant.

BUMBURET
Jinnah Kalash Inn $

Anish

Bumbaret

Kalash Valleys

Chitral

North West Frontier Province

Very simple and basic, but charming little hotel at the heart of Bumbaret. Squat toilet, cold tap. Simple but good food available.

23 RIVER RAFTING IN THE KARAKORAM
➤ 228–237

OPERATOR
Walji's Adventure Pakistan/Travel Walji's
See p. 280 for details.
Half day rafting on Gilgit River can be arranged here as well as extended multi-day trips.

INFORMATION
Gilgit P.T.D.C. Tourist Information Centre
See p. 280 for details.

ACCOMMODATION
PASSU
Passu Tourist Lodge $
Passu
Hunza District
Gilgit
Northern Areas
No ☎
In a good location on the KKH to the north of Passu village, with Batura Glacier close by. Chalet-style, en-suite rooms are reasonable, but not too special. Expect water to be dense grey in colour from hill supply. Expect electricity supply to be erratic—inevitable with most hotels this far north. Adjoining restaurant provides good meals.

SUST
P.T.D.C. Motel $
Sust
Gojal
Northern Areas
☎ (572) 46240
Custom-built, comfortable hotel at quieter north end of Sust and the best bet in the area. En-suite rooms with hot water showers and fan. Pleasant restaurant with good menu.

GULMIT
Marco Polo Inn $–$$
P.O. Gulmit Gojal
Hunza District
Gilgit
Northern Areas
☎ (572) 46107
A delightful setting for this charming hotel which has en-suite rooms with veranda overlooking flower-filled garden and with unbeatable views of surrounding mountains. Comfortable dining room and good menu.

Village Guest House $
Gulmit
Hunza District
Gilgit
Northern Areas
Pakistan
☎ (572) 46112
Located in a leafy orchard at the far end of the Gulmit's polo ground. Full of character. Range of rooms at differing prices. Camping.

24 SRI LANKA ON WHEELS
➤ 240–247

OPERATORS
Travelbag Adventures
15 Turk Street
Alton
Hampshire
U.K.
☎ (01420) 541007 **fax:** (01420) 541022
email: mail@travelbag-adventures.com
website: www.travelbag-adventures.co.uk
Have a 17-day tour using coach, jeep, train, boat, bicycle, and foot and takes in the beach, Negombo, cycling around villages, Kandy, climb up Adam's Peak, and optional elephant safari.

Pan-Lanka Travels and Tours (Pvt) Ltd
No. 6
Palmyrah Avenue
Colombo 3
☎ (74) 518888 **fax:** (74) 518881
email: info@panlanka.com
website: www.panlanka.com
Can organize tours and travel around Sri Lanka, including sightseeing.

Naturetrek
The Cadcam Centre
Bighton
Nr Alresford
Hampshire SO24 9RE
U.K.
☎ (01962) 733051 **fax:** (01962) 736426
email: sales@naturetrek.co.uk
website: www.naturetrek.co.uk
Run a 17-day birdwatching and wildlife tour with visits to Sigiriya and Anuradhapura, coinciding with the visit of Sri Lanka's large numbers of wintering birds; these include waders from Siberia and passerines from the Himalaya.

INFORMATION
Ceylon Tourist Board
80 Galle Road
Colombo 03
☎ (1) 437571 **fax:** (1) 437953/440001
website: www.lanka.net/ctb

Travel Information Centre
Headmans' Lodge
3 Dewa Veediya
Kandy
☎ (8) 222661

International Airport (Colombo)
☎ (1) 252411

Uda Walawe National Park
☎/**fax:** (47) 33201
Cars are not allowed because the track dips in parts and can be flooded after bad rain. A jeep safari with guide lasts up to 3 hours. All prices seem to have a service charge added. Although the park is open from 6am to 6pm, early morning and late afternoon are best for seeing animals as they come out of the shade and down to the watering holes.

ACCOMMODATION
There are plenty of places to stay whilst on the road. Some boast "Recommended by the Ceylon Tourist Board" signs, although your best bet is to check out the rooms yourself. There are guesthouses along Medilla Road in Tangalla, fronting the beach.

Ulpotha $$$
c/o 14/3 Ward Place
Colombo 7
☎ (1) 688409/347651 **fax:** (1) 688409/347650

Book through:
Neal's Yard Agency
BCM Neal's Yard
London
WC1N 3XX
U.K.
☎ (0870) 444 2702
email: info@ulpotha.com
website: www.ulpotha.com
Organize stays of 1 week or more at the sanctuary. Income derived from visitors (prices range from £950–£1,450 for two weeks) is contributed in its entirety to fund the village. Ulpotha is also funded by the East Pole Foundation, a non-profit organization whose primary interests include sponsoring the rehabilitation of ancient irrigation systems, promoting biodiverse organic farming practices, locals crafts, and revitalizing watersheds through reforestation.

Uda Walawe National Park
Bungalows in a wild setting. Service charges add considerable weight to the basic price. There is also a campsite. There are leopards, though snakes are the main threat, particularly cobras, vipers, and pythons.

FOOD AND DRINK
Uda Walawe Safari Village and Restaurant
Uda Walawe Road
Uda Walawe
☎ (74) 591223 (head office in Colombo)
Five minutes' drive from the entrance to the park. Chinese menu, rice, noodles, etc, all reasonably priced.

25 SKI, SURF, AND TURTLES AT THE OCEAN'S MOUTH ► 248–256

OPERATORS—GENERAL
Somak Holidays
Somak House
Harrovian Village
Bessborough Road
Harrow-on-the-Hill HA1 3EX
U.K.
☎ (020) 8423 3000 **fax:** (020) 8423 7700
email: holidays@somak.co.uk
website: www.somak.co.uk
Offer a 7-night B&B serendipity tour, taking in the major religious and historical sites, plus 6 nights at an all-inclusive beach hotel.

Sunset Watersports
Araliya Hotel
Galle Road
Kaluwamodara
Aluthgama
☎/**fax:** (34) 75385
Run by instructor Chandrasiri Silva, 1992 Sri Lankan Champion for waterskiing, mono and barefoot. Offer waterskiing (mono and barefoot), windsurfing, catamaran sailing, deep sea fishing for tuna and shark, snorkelling, jetskiing, and water scooter riding, and can arrange scuba diving. Also offer riverboat safaris, either 3 hours or a longer, 5- to 6-hour trip which includes a visit to the Galapota Temple,

believed to date back to the 12th century. To see it, you have to disembark and climb a hill.

Turtle Conservation

itoi International Projects
1 Cottage Road
Headingley
Leeds LS6 4DD
U.K.
☎ (113) 217 9800 **fax:** (113) 2179801
email: travel@i-to-i.com
website: www.i-to-i.com
Organises conservation work placements on Bentota and TCP turtle conservation schemes, from 1 to 3 months.

SCUBA DIVING
Divequest

Two Jays
Kemple End
Stonyhurst
Clitheroe BB7 9QY
U.K.
☎ (01254) 826322 **fax:** (01254) 826780
email: divers@divequest.co.uk
Offers liveaboard diving holidays in the Maldives, for experienced divers.

Lanka Sportsreizen-Confifi Marina

21 Paradise Island Hotel Complex
Bentota
☎ (1) 824500 **fax:** (1) 826125

Scuba Safaris Ltd

Coral Garden Hotel
Galle Road
Hikkaduwa
☎ (1) 694012 **fax:** (1) 694029

Underwater Safaris Ltd

25C Barnes Place
Colombo 7
☎ (1) 694012 **fax:** (1) 694029

INFORMATION

See p. 284 for details.

ACCOMMODATION
Araliya Hotel $

Galle Road
Kaluwamodara
Aluthgama
☎/**fax:** (34) 75385
Small and friendl hotel with 22 rooms (singles, doubles, and triples), bar, and restaurant

serving rice curries. No swimming pool but the hotel sits on the banks of the Bentota Ganga River and has its own watersports centre.

Blue Horizon Guest House $

Lakmal
Medilla Road
Tangalle
☎ (47) 40721
Opposite the beach, this family home is a bit scruffy and there are numerous cockroaches, but it is cheap.

A number of other guest houses, of varying standards, thrive along Medilla Road.

The Falado Guest House $

20 Beach Road
Mount Lavinia
☎/**fax:** (1) 716203
The friendly manager, Mervyn, speaks English and Dutch. Rooms have showers and mosquito nets. Good food, including curries, rice, pastas, and pizzas. The beach is a minute's stroll away.

FOOD AND DRINK
Flower Lounge Restaurant

18 Bagatalle Road
Colombo 03
☎ (1) 593032
Great Chinese fare at equally good prices. Smart restaurant—plenty of businessmen out to lunch—but excellent value. Crab and sweet-corn soup a speciality, as are chow meins.

Restaurant Refresh

384 Galle Road
Hikkaduwa
☎ (9) 77810/074 383089
Grade A, Ceylon Tourist Board-approved. Italian and Chinese food, lobster crabs, prawns, jumbo prawns, and vegetarian dishes such as stuffed eggplant.

ACTIVITIES A–Z

INTRODUCTION

This book has, we hope, whetted your appetite for adventure, and the Activities A–Z is intended to supply a useful, if not comprehensive, list of as many adventurous activities as the authors could discover within an area.

The activities vary from volunteer work, cultural, and language opportunities to really intrepid sports. Most of the experiences call for interaction with local people and many are directly connected to ecotourism—where strict controls are applied to guarantee the benefits to the environment and to minimize the damage caused by the impact of increasing numbers of visitors to sensitive areas.

We have supplied the names and addresses of organizations that can help the traveller to achieve these challenging pastimes, but they have not been inspected or vetted by us in any way. Even where the authors have used a company to organize their own trip, this is no guarantee that any company is still run by the same people or to the same degree of efficiency.

Bear in mind that many of the regions covered can be volatile both climatically and politically. Weigh up all the factors first, get a feel for your chosen destination, and let us guide you towards the outfits that can help.

BALLOONING

Ballooning is a great way to see the Himalaya without first having to climb them. Lift off as the dawn breaks, and from the wicker basket suspended below the balloon you will have an unrivalled 360-degree view of a landscape teeming with wildlife. With a telephoto lens you should be able to get some cracking animal photos. As you gain altitude the temperature will drop so make sure you're well wrapped up and to protect yourself from the harmful rays of the sun apply plenty of high factor block to exposed areas. Binoculars are useful, and for photography remember to take plenty of film and a set of spare batteries; for high altitude shooting you should use a UV filter.

INDIA

The main centre for ballooning here is at New Delhi's Safdarjang airport. The balloons generally hold from one to ten people and can rise over 244m (800ft).

Aero Club of India

Safdarjung Airport
Aurobindo Marg
New Delhi 110 003
☎ (11) 462 1341 **fax:** (11) 462 0191
The governing body for ballooning in India, and active member of the F.A.I. Can supply details of member clubs and general advice on safety.

NEPAL

Kathmandu, the starting point for many adventures, is the launching place for an aerial tour of the Himalaya. Your destination is Mount Everest but during the flight you will get some great views of other giants. Makalu, Kanchenjunga, Cho Oyu and Lhotse as well as the many hundreds of lesser peaks and pinnacles in this region.

Abercrombie and Kent

See Trekking.

Balloon Sunrise Nepal

P.O. Box 1273
Lazimpat
Kathmandu
☎ (1) 424131 **fax:** (1) 424157
email: balloon@sunrise.mos.com.np
website: www.view-nepal.com/balloon

Erco Travels

See Railway Tours.

Himalayan Treasures and Travel

3596 Ponderosa Trail
Pinole
California 94564
U.S.A.
☎ (510) 222 5307 or **toll free** ☎ 800 223 1813
fax: (510) 223 5309
email: govindsh@himtrek.com
website: www.himtrek.com
In business for over 28 years, this company

focuses on the Himalayan regions of Nepal, Tibet, India, and Bhutan. They also specialize in treks to some of the more remote areas.

Tiger Mountain Group

P.O. Box 242
Lazimpat
Kathmandu
☎ (1) 411225 **fax:** (1) 414075
email: info@tigermountain.com
website: www.tigermountain.com
Long-established company formed by the merger of Nepal's 2 original tour operators and now providing a wide range of trekking, rafting, ballooning, and cycling adventures.

BIRDWATCHING

One of the great delights for birdwatchers in the Himalayan region is the diversity of habitats and the bewildering variety of species which they support. National parks and bird sanctuaries throughout the region offer the best opportunities for the "go it alone" traveller, while several operators provide hiking, trekking, and boating trips for ornithologists. Binoculars are a must—7x magnification will be adequate. Photographers may have to pay for a camera permit in some parks. To keep the stinging and biting insects at bay, wear lightweight, long-sleeved clothing, and plenty of insect repellent. Colours that blend with the scenery will help you remain inconspicuous, and remember to take plenty of water, and, if you are alone, a map, and compass.

INDIA
KEOLADEO GHANA NATIONAL PARK

This is a World Heritage site and one of the best bird sanctuaries anywhere. The Siberian crane is an annual visitor and the magnificent Sarus crane, India's tallest bird, is here in large numbers. There are also ibises, pelicans, pink flamingos, spoonbills, and about 30 species of birds of prey.

Geographic Expeditions

See Trekking.

Naturetrek

See p. 283.

NEPAL
KOSHI TAPPU WILDLIFE RESERVE

This reserve on the floodplain of the Sapta Koshi river is almost completely surrounded by forest and is home to over 280 species of bird, including Bengal floricans, swamp partridges, storks, and ibisis.

ROYAL CHITWAN NATIONAL PARK

See Chapter 15.

SRI LANKA

Several reserves and sanctuaries provide the ornithologist with plenty of options. Bundala National Park, east of Hambantota is a wetland sanctuary, famous for its birdlife and, home to 149 species including the greater flamingo. Yala West National Park is where to see local birds like hornbills, orioles, and jungle fowl as well as migratory species including the white-winged black tern, while in the Hill Country, Sinharaja, the last significant area of virgin rainforest left in Sri Lanka, 18 of the country's 20 native species is represented along with another 120 other types.

Canda Tours Pvt Ltd

330 Galle Road
Colombo 4
☎ (1) 555828/591120 **fax:** (1) 589207
email: canda@eureka.lk
website: www.search.lk/canda
Canda Tours was born out of a desire by Chris Candappa to share and exchange notes with overseas birders about Sri Lanka's abundant birdlife. The company organizes birdwatching tours on foot or by horseback and also offers a range of trips to Sri Lanka's 2000-year-old heritage sites and the little-seen areas of the Cultural Triangle.

TIBET
JANGTANG NATURE RESERVE,

This is the second largest nature reserve in the world and the best place to go birding in Tibet.

Tribes Fair Trade Travel

7 The Business Centre
Earl Soham
Woodbridge
Suffolk IP13 7SA
U.K.
☎ (01728) 685971; **fax:** (01728) 685973
email: info@tribes.co.uk
website: www.tribes.co.uk
Tribes specialize in sustainable tourism,

offering a range of packages and tailor-made itineraries to India and Nepal and covering most activities from birdwatching to white-water rafting.

Wild Life and Nature Protection Society
Chaitiya Road
Marine Drive
Fort
Colombo
☎ (1) 325248; **fax:** (1) 580721
Offers a range of information on nature safaris, hiking, and birdwatching, plus advice on itineraries for the independent traveller.

BOTANICAL TOURS

India and the Himalayan region are a plant-lover's paradise—both amateurs and experienced botanists will find something of interest. Travelling into jungle, parks, and foothills, botanical tours offer an unrivalled opportunity to study the flowering plants, bulbs, bamboos, tree ferns, and orchids in their natural habitats as well as visiting botanical gardens to see cultivated specimens of many other plants. Tours are led by an experienced and knowledgeable botanist. Travel is by jeep and lunch is usually taken in a shady part of the forest. A botanical field guide makes a useful reference. Do not pick the plants or collect specimens unless you have written permission to do so and have ensured that you can legally import them to your country of origin.

INDIA
The Darjeeling and Sikkim Himalaya area is particularly good for palms, orchids, rhododendrons, and ferns. Tours are usually by coach, driving through the tea gardens of Darjeeling with great views of the Himalaya.

Situated 20km (12 miles) from Bhubaneshwar, Nandankanan is a combination of a botanical garden and a zoo. Set amid the vast expanse of the Chandaka forest with its abundance of flora growing in their natural habitat, the zoo is famous for its white tigers.

The countryside in the Kalimpong area has a vast range of forests around Lava and Loleygaon. The wild and protected Neora National Park reaches up to the 3,152m (10,341ft)-high Rachela tri-junction between Bhutan, Sikkim, and West Bengal. The meandering river valleys of Git, Rishi, Rilli, and the

mighty Teesta, and the enchanting Samthar Plateau make this a superb location for botanical adventures.

The Orchid Retreat
Ganesh Villa
Kalimpong 734303
West Bengal
☎ (3552) 57217 **fax:** (3552) 55389
email: thakro@cal2.vsnl.net.in
website: www.palms.org/ads/orchid.html
Organize tours for small groups, with a leader, or for individuals. Cater for trekkers wishing to camp out amongst the plants; otherwise trips are daily, returning to enjoy their delightful garden, complete with palms, orchids, and cycads, all set on a steep, south-facing slope with great views across the valley.

SRI LANKA
Sri Lanka has a wealth of plant species, most of which are endemic to the island, including many rare orchids, ferns, ayurvedic herbs and plants, and large trees. The only urban wildlife sanctuary is in the suburbs of Colombo at the Bellanwila-Attidya wetland marshes—all that remains of a once large and extensive network.

TIBET
On the Tibetan plateau conditions range from tropical to very cold, and from humid to arid, producing an extremely rich and varied selection of botanical specimens.

NEPAL
Nepal has about 6,500 species of flowering plant, of which more than 700 have medicinal properties.

Andrew Brock Travel Ltd
54 High Street East
Uppingham
Rutland LE15 9PZ
U.K.
☎ (01572) 821330 **fax:** (01572) 821072
email: abrock3650@aol.com
Organize a variety of botanical tours to India, Sri Lanka, and Bhutan—either in small group or individual itineraries.

CANOEING AND KAYAKING

If you're looking for some seriously strenuous watersports, look no further than the rivers of the Himalaya. Here you'll find some muscle-wrenching rides to test the stamina of the fittest and most experienced kayakers. Before you sign up for any of these hairy trips, make sure you're in peak physical condition, and are capable of the most demanding grades. Alternatively, there are many less challenging routes—some even suitable for novices—but they're no less thrilling and have the added bonus of giving you the chance to see (and photograph) the wonderful countryside and its plentiful wildlife. Operators should provide P.F.D.s (personal flotation devices), spray jackets, and helmets. If not, take your own, but you should question the professionalism of any operator who does not include basic safety equipment in their package. Sandals or trainers are best for foot protection and you should wear clothes made of synthetic, quick-drying fabric.

INDIA

Some of the finest white water in India can be found on the Ganges, near its source in Uttar Pradesh. Paddling through the Garhwal Himalayas you'll also see some of the country's most awesome scenery.

Global Adventures

P.O. Box 123
Delta
BC V4K 3N6
Canada
☎ (604) 940 2220 **toll free** ☎ 800 781 2269
fax: (604) 940 2233
email: global@portal.ca
website: www.netadssell.com/global/
Operating for 6 years throughout the Himalaya, their varied adventure travel programme aims to bring their customers face to face with local culture and natural history. They make extensive use of knowledgeable local guides, as well as having an experienced North American team leader on every trip.

India Outdoors

See Caving.

LADAKH

The Zanskar River flows from the "Roof of The World" through the Zanskar range of mountains and eventually joins the Indus. It's a remote area, ideal for wilderness trekking, rafting, and canoeing. Access is by a jeep road over a high mountain pass, only likely to be open from Jun to mid-Oct.

NEPAL

Opened to tourists only since 1995, the Marshyangdi ("raging") River is one of the world's top white-water rivers. Graded IV–V, it's not for the faint-hearted—if you are up to it, you'll get superb views of the Annapurnas. From the Sun Koshi River you'll have views of Mount Everest and the Himalayan range plus other spectacular scenery. Also graded IV–V, with superb white water, particularly just after the monsoon. It's also the longest river trip you can make here at present. At the other end of the scale is the Upper Sun Koshi, still very scenic but with a grading of II, ideal for the first-timer.

Bio Bio Expeditions World Wide

See Rafting.

David Allardice's Ultimate Descents

See Rafting.

Tribes Fair Trade Travel

See Birdwatching.

ROYAL CHITWAN NATIONAL PARK

See Chapter 15.

SRI LANKA

The Kilani River, running through the Kiyugala forest in the hill country 2 hours from Colombo, is one of the favourite sites for kayaking in Sri Lanka. Film buffs especially will enjoy this trip because it was here that David Lean shot *Bridge over the River Kwai*—trips start from the restaurant of that name. An easy Grade I rapid provides a warm up before the more strenuous, Grade III–IV stuff; towards the end of the run you can rest a bit and enjoy the view of the Yatiyantota mountain.

Adventure Sports Lanka

12A Simon Hewavitharana Road
Colombo 3
☎ (74) 713334 **fax:** (74) 577951
email: adventure@sri.lanka.net
Peter Black and Joel Kilgarriff own the only company operating white-water tours on the island, and they act as guides.

Equator U.S.A.

P.O. Box 10023
Ketchum
ID 83340
U.S.A.

☎ (208) 726 7427
email: info@equatorusa.com
website: www.equatorusa.com/about.html
A small, quality guide service that has specialised in multi-day white-water journeys, treks, and expeditions for 15 years. All trips also involve trekking and overlanding, but are centred on a major Himalayan river descent.

BHUTAN

Bhutan is a prime destination for a kayak trip. Fairy-tale river canyons surrounded by jungles and a myriad of bird and wildlife make it a photographer's paradise as well.

Adventure Whitewater

20 The Cobbins
Waltham Abbey
Essex EN9 1LH
U.K.
☎ (01992) 712006/242135
email: phil@adventure-whitewater.com
website: www.adventure-whitewater.com
Operating for 8 years, organize kayaking and rafting trips to Nepal and Bhutan.

Adrift (U.K.)

See Rafting for details. Allows experienced kayakers—capable of Grade IV rivers—to join their white-water rafting expeditions. They ask for a resumé of your kayaking experience before making a decision to let you join.

CAVING

In this region there are two types of cave: massive limestone systems extending for thousands of metres, and much smaller caves, used as dwellings or religious shrines. Stout footwear and a torch are essential for both, but in the latter the experience will be more of a cultural one as you gaze in wonder at ancient paintings and carvings. For the serious caver, there are many possibilities for exploring the dark underground caverns of stalactites, stalagmites, subterranean rivers, and lakes in some of the world's finest caving experiences. However you should not tackle these caves alone even if fully equipped and experienced—sign up with one of the operators, who will provide all the gear and a knowledgeable and experienced guide.

INDIA
Sanjay Gandhi National Park

In the heart of the national park, the Kanheri (or Mahakali) Caves consist of over 100 Buddhist caves that were in use up to the 9th century. Carved stone steps link the caves which contain carved pillars and Buddhist art.

India Outdoors

169/C Dr. Ambdekar Road
Dadar T.T.
Mumbai 400 014
☎ (22) 412 5897/416 4785/418 6360
fax: (22) 416 6944
email: info@indiaoutdoors.com
website: www.indiaoutdoors.com
Run weekend excursions to the caves at Kanheri as well as a full range of adventure trips, from parasailing to snowboarding.

MEGHALAYA

Meghalaya is one of the seven states of the northeastern region, sandwiched between Assam in the north and Bangladesh in the south. For caving enthusiasts there is no finer area in the Indian subcontinent—it boasts numerous natural caves including the longest in the region.

JAINTIA HILLS

Jowai, a picturesque town situated on the Shillong-Silchar national highway, is circled by the Myntdu river. Nearby are numerous thrilling caves and caverns used as hideouts during wartime between Jaintia kings and foreign intruders. The villages of Amlarem, Pdengshakap, Syndai, and Nongtalang are dotted with such caves and caverns. Krem Um-Lawan is a cave of the Eocene Age with an upper fossil passage and a lower active passage, numerous cataracts and waterfalls. It was the longest 6,381m (21,000ft) and deepest 107m (351ft) known cave in the Indian subcontinent until a link was discovered to Krem Kotsati, a neighbouring cave with 8 entrances, the main one through a deep pool. Portions of the river passage have to be traversed by swimming or by inflatable boat. At a little over 21km (13 miles), this is now the longest mainland system in Asia.

KHASI HILLS

Krem Dam is the largest sandstone cave in the Indian subcontinent, 1,297m (4,255ft) long, with a very large entrance and a stream running down its main passage. Krem Mawmluh is half a kilometre west of Cherrapunjee, adjacent to the small hamlet of Mawmluh. This cave has a fine river passage, and with a length of 4,503m (2,795ft) is currently the fourth longest in the Indian subcontinent.

GARO HILL

At 4,772m (2,965ft), Siju-Dobkhakol is the third longest cave in the Indian subcontinent. Situated on the bank of the Simsang River, just below the village of Siju, it contains the finest river passage to be found anywhere in the world. It is the most researched cave in India and is home to thousands of bats.

Meghalaya Adventurers Association

c/o Hotel Centrepoint Shillong
Meghalaya
☎ (364) 225210; **fax:** (364) 225293
This is the first point of contact for anyone wanting to go caving in Meghalaya (no email or website.) They can arrange accommodation, trips, guides, and equipment.

SRI LANKA

Dambulla Caves date back to the 1st century BC and were reputedly the refuge of King Valagam Bahu when he was driven into exile. When he was restored to the throne he converted the caves to a temple, containing 150 images of the Buddha.

CRUISING

India alone has 4,828km (3,000 miles) of coastline and numerous rivers. Her cultural and spiritual life is intertwined with the waters that flow through the land and lap the shores. Cruising is an ideal way to discover India. Whether on a long voyage round the coastline of the Indian Ocean and the Bay of Bengal, or simply a trip of a few days' duration along a short stretch of river, the operator will have taken care of your entire itinerary—just enjoy yourself and take plenty of photographs. Some land-based excursions may involve light trekking, so firm, comfortable footwear will be required. Protection against the sun is most important while on board as the cool breeze can disguise the early stages of sunburn.

INDIAN OCEAN

Many of the large cruise lines have itineraries including India and Sri Lanka. A mixture of land-based tours and cruising allow vast distances to be covered in a short period. Trips include some of the cultural and historical highlights of the Indian sub continent. The Taj Mahal and Agra, Jaipur, the deserted Mughal city of Fatehpur Sikri, and Delhi. Most cruises embark in Mumbai (Bombay) after a few days' touring then proceed via the ports in Goa, Kerala, and Sri Lanka to Madras. Transfers can be by air, coach, or even elephant back.

Swan Hellenic

77 New Oxford Street
London WC1A 1PP
U.K.
☎ (020) 7800 2200 **fax:** (020) 7800 2724
email: reservations@swanhellenic.com
website: www.swanhellenic.com
U.S.A. office:
12 West 37th Street
New York
NY 10018
☎ (212) 695 2053 **toll free** ☎ 877 219 4239
fax: (212) 268 8299
email: reservations@swanhellenic.com
website: www.swanhellenic.com

GOA

Cruise the Mandovi River from Old Goa then meander along the Cumburaja canal on an ancient fishing boat converted to a houseboat. Crocodiles sun themselves along the riverbank as local cockle fishermen search for shellfish. You can lie lazily on the deck, taking in the scenery as you pass, photograph the abundant birdlife in the mangrove swamps, or simply trawl a line and hook from the stern to see what you can catch. Overnight on board.

Abercrombie and Kent

See Trekking.

Concord Tours & Travels

See Rafting.

Crystal Holidays

See under Trekking for details. Offers several backwater trips by barge and scenic sailing on the River Ganges.

Solitair Exclusive Vacations

3 Woodside Avenue
North Finchley
London N12 8AN
U.K.
☎ 07071 881 204

email: enquiries@solitairhols.co.uk
website: www.solitairhols.co.uk/index.html
Arrange alternative breaks for groups up to 20
in Goa. Director Siân Jones is at hand to provide specialist knowledge of the local cuisine
and the many cultural aspects of Goa. They also
organize fishing, diving, and hiking holidays.

SRINAGAR, KASHMIR

Float along the Dal and Nagin Lakes on a traditional Kashmiri houseboat and you'll soon
discover why it's called "The Venice of the
East." They're grand constructions with rich
local carpets and hand-carved furniture.
Pedlars in boats sail round this fleet, stopping
at each in turn and trying to sell everything
from rice and saffron to papier maché souvenirs. *Shikaras*, Kashmiri gondolas, can be
hired to take you touring or to visit the vegetable markets on the shores of the lakes.

Indian Tribal Tours
See Trekking.

CULTURAL TOURS

Almost everywhere in this region has a palace,
shrine, fort, or monastery, but cultural touring
is much more than just visiting sites: you'll
learn about the history of the people who built
them, discover the great religions that had their
origins here, and meet people whose way of life
is little changed from that of their ancestors.
Transport will mostly be by coach with some
light walking, although some tours can involve
serious trekking. In either case, wear loose-
fitting, cotton clothes with long sleeves and
trousers. Take a wide-brimmed hat, sunglasses,
and a high factor sun block.

Many of the operators in this guide, listed
under other headings, include cultural tours of
the region as part of their range: **Abercrombie
and Kent** (see Trekking); **Concord Tours &
Travels** (Rafting); **Crystal Holidays**
(Trekking); **David Allardice's Ultimate
Descents** (Rafting); **Eastman Voyages**
(Horse Riding); **Erco Travels** (Railway
Tours); and **Euro Tours** (Safaris).

BHUTAN

The Chomolhari area of western Bhutan is ideal
for the serious hiker and cultural tourist. Here,
in one of the most pristine regions of the
country, bears, takin and feral sheep roam
undisturbed while the semi-nomadic people of

Tibeto-Burmese origin tend their yak herds in
high summer pastures.

Exotic Journeys
500 North Michigan Avenue
Suite 1405
Chicago
IL 60611
U.S.A.
toll free ☎ 800 554 6342
fax: (312) 832 9746
email: info@exoticjourneys.com
website: www.exoticjourneys.com
A one-stop agency for independent travellers,
offering custom made tours, air fares, hotel
bookings, and car rental.

Exotic Tours
B-64, Lower Ground Floor
Sarvodaya Enclave
New Delhi 110017
India
☎ (11) 685 0823/8361/8376 **fax:** (11) 685 9055
email: exotictr@del2.vsnl.net.in
website: www.exotic-tour.com/
Established in 1990 and specializing in cultural
tours of India, Nepal, Bhutan, and Tibet. Travel
is mainly by coach with some light walking.

Steppes East
Castle Eaton
Swindon
Wiltshire SN6 6JU
U.K.
☎ (01285) 810267 **fax:** (01285) 810693
email: sales@steppeseast.co.uk
website: www.steppeseast.co.uk
Founded in 1989, their range of fully guided
treks and cultural tours includes Tibet, Bhutan,
and Sri Lanka.

Other operators of cultural tours to Bhutan
include: **Explore Himalayas** (see Cycling);
Geographic Expeditions (Trekking);
Himalayan Treasures and Travel
(Ballooning); **Tiger Mountain Group**
(Ballooning); and **Tribes Fair Trade Travel**
(Birdwatching).

PAKISTAN
Explore Worldwide
See Trekking for details. Cultural tours world
wide, including Kalash valleys, Chitral.

Pakistan Guides
P.O. Box 1692
3rd Floor
62/2 Bank Road
Rawalpindi
☎ (51) 524808 **fax:** (51) 539497
All types of trekking and general tours, including cultural ones in southern Pakistan.

Pakistan Tours Ltd
24 Flashman's Hotel
The Mall
Rawalpindi
☎ (51) 563038 **fax:** (51) 565449
The company is connected with the Pakistan Tourist Department and so tends to work through P.T.D.C. hotels. Good operator for tailor-made treks and tours of all types.

Sitara International Inc.
102-3540 West 41st Avenue
Vancouver BC
V6N 3E6
Canada
☎ (604) 264 8747 **toll free** ☎ 800 888 7216;
fax: (604) 264 7774
email: sitara@sitara.com

Sitara Travel Consultants (Pvt) Ltd
Waheed Plaza, 3rd floor
52 West Jinnah Avenue, Blue Area
P.O. Box 1662
Islamabad
Pakistan
☎ (51) 813372/3/4/5
fax: (51) 279651/279676
email: sitarapk@isb.compol.com
Major Pakistan tour agency. Strong on conventional holidays in southern areas, but can arrange most adventure style holidays including jeep safaris, culture tours, and river boat tours.

CYCLING

Cycling is one of the best ways to explore India and the Himalaya, whether it's just a sedate morning trip or a multi-day expedition across very challenging terrain. Follow the quiet roads and secret trails of the Kathmandu Valley, the Nepalese national parks or go on an expedition deep into the Hindu Kush. Cycling is best in the early morning, taking a break when it gets too hot and resuming in the late afternoon. Cycles hired locally are heavy and often lack gears, but dismantling and bringing your own should present no problems (see p. 149). Remember to bring a comprehensive set of spares and a tool kit, elastic straps for attaching your belongings, and a strong chain and padlock. Try to avoid main roads with their obvious traffic hazards and head for the much quieter backroads. Always carry and drink plenty of water. Nepal caters for mountain biking from novice to descents of over 2,000m (6,560ft). From Kathmandu you can cycle to most places in the Kathmandu Valley.

Erco Travels
See Railway Tours.

Exodus Discovery Holidays
9 Weir Road
London
SW12 0LT
U.K.
☎ (020) 8673 0859 **fax:** (020) 8673 0779
email: sales@exodustravels.co.uk
website: www.exodustravels.co.uk

Explore Himalayas
P.O. Box 45
Main Bazar (opp. State Bank Of India)
Leh
Ladakh 194 101
☎ (1982) 52727 **fax:** (1982) 53354
email: wangchuks@hotmail.com and explore-himalayas@indiamart.com
Established in 1989, this leading specialist in the adventure tour market employs a team of highly experienced and trained guides with expertise in mountaineering, rock climbing, and river rafting, as well as cycling.

Gap Adventures
760 North Bedford Road
Suite #246
Bedford Hills
NY 10507
U.S.A.
☎ (914) 666 4417 **toll free** ☎ 800 692 5495
email: adventure@gap.ca
website: www.exodustravels.co.uk
Experts in discovery, hiking, biking, and overland holidays in India, Pakistan, Sri Lanka, Tibet, and Bhutan.

Tiger Mountain Group
See Ballooning.

Tribes Fair Trade Travel

See Birdwatching.

PAKISTAN
Mountain Movers

Head office:
P.O. Box 534
Gilgit
☎ (572) 2967 **fax:** (572) 2525
Liaison office: P.O. Box 985
Rawalpindi
☎ (51) 470519 **fax:** (51) 470518
Able to organize trekking, mountain biking, and culture trekking.

Adventure Centre Pakistan Ltd

468 Sir Aga Khan Road
Gilgit
14100 NA
☎ (572) 2409 **fax:** (572) 3695
email: ikram@acp-glt.sdnpak.undp.org
Locally based company for Northern Areas. Treks, jeep safaris, mountain biking.

KE Adventure Travel Ltd

32 Lake Road
Keswick
Cumbria CA12 5DQ
U.K.
☎ (017687) 73966 **fax:** (017687) 74693
email: keadventure@enterprise.net
Major U.K.-based trek organizers. Mainly set-piece, big group treks but also organize white-water rafting, mountain biking, jeep safaris, and culture tours, working with Pakistan agencies.

World Expeditions Ltd

4 Northfields Prospect
Putney Bridge Road
London SW18 1PE
U.K.
☎ (020) 8870 2600 **fax:** (020) 8870 2615
email: enquiries@worldexpeditions.co.uk
website: www.worldexpeditions.co.uk
Off-the-beaten-track adventures to some of the world's most spectacular wilderness destinations. Trekking in Bhutan, Nepal, and Tibet, and cycling in Pakistan and India, meeting local people along traditional mountain trails and picture-postcard backroads.

DRIVING

For the truly adventurous, the only way to get round some of the remote areas will be by car, but driving in this region is nothing like it is in Europe or America. India drives on the left, but rules of the road are seldom observed and vehicles will zip in and out of traffic, changing lanes and even direction without as much as a signal or indication. Add to that congestion in the major cities and rutted and potholed roads elsewhere, and you'll soon realize that a driving holiday should not be undertaken lightly. However there is a second option: hire a car with a driver. It's less expensive than you'd think and has the added bonus that the driver will also act as your tour guide. If you decide on self-drive, make sure the car is roadworthy before accepting it, check that you're fully insured, and always carry an international driving licence.

INDIA
AC Luxury Cars

Shirish and Reena Mhatre
Saraswati Niwas
Shop #1, Ground Floor
French Bridge
Mumbai 400 007
☎ (22) 3676634 **fax:** (22) 3674727
website:
www.indiatravels.com/carentals/autoquick/index.htm
One of the largest outfits in Mumbai, operating for over 15 years. Offers a 24-hour service from Bombay to any destination in India. All cars have English-speaking drivers.

Andrew Brock Travel Ltd

See Botanical Tours.

Budget Rent-a-Car

G3 Arunchal Building
Barakhamba Road
Delhi
☎ (1) 331 8600
Local branch of international company offering self drive hire and car with driver.

Connect Car Rental

Mayday House
Crescent Road
Luton LU2 0AR
U.K.
☎ (01582) 545403 **fax:** (01582) 736728
email: ksmith@travelextras.com

website: www.connectcarrental.com
Arrange car rental world-wide through an international network of hand-picked, independent car rental specialists, with an emphasis on high-quality vehicles and customer care. Bookings and quotes by internet or telephone.

Ramniranjan Kedia Tourism Services Pvt. Ltd

Suite 2, Kedia Apartments
29-F Dongershi Road
Malabar Hill
Mumbai 400 006
☎ (22) 364 9393 **fax:** (22) 363 5614
email: sales@rnk.com
website: www.rnk.com/
Another locally based outfit providing cars and drivers.

PAKISTAN

Most car hire is with driver but it is possible to pick up a self-drive in the major cities. In some regions jeeps are available through the larger hotels.

Avis

P.O. Box 1088
Waljis Building
10 Khayaban
Suhrawardy
Islamabad
☎ (51) 270751 **fax:** (51) 270753
Provide both chauffeu-driven and self-drive cars.

SRI LANKA

Roads, apart from the main highways, are narrow and full of potholes but generally speaking will be uncrowded. Driving here is much safer than in India. Driving, as in India, is on the left-hand side of the road and the maximum speed limit is 56kph (35mph). Self-drive cars are available but you will not be allowed to take them into the national parks or wildlife sanctuaries, or along unmade roads.

Mackinnons Travels

4 Leyden Bastian Road
Colombo 1
☎ (1) 448065 **fax:** (1) 44081
email: Avis@ens.lk
Local agent for Avis car rentals, providing self-drive cars.

FISHING

What could be more relaxing than a day spent on the banks of an idyllic river, casting your line back and forth until, eventually, you get a bite. It's a big one so you play it carefully. Gently pulling it in, then letting the line run out again until the fish tires and you can reel it in close enough to net it. Or alternatively sit strapped into a seat on the back of a powerful boat as you wrestle with one of the monsters of the deep, returning in the evening to have your photograph taken on the quayside with your catch. Whatever your taste in sportfishing you'll find it in this region. Bring your own gear or hire it locally. Many tour operators will supply equipment as part of the package. Don't forget the sunblock, dark glasses, and a hat to avoid sunburn and drink plenty of water during the day.

INDIA

Inland and sea fishing are available and abundant. Cast for shark, kakara, and gohol in the waters of the Indian Ocean or the Bay of Bengal. In the clear rivers of the north, trout, carp, and mahseer are the favoured catch. Tackle hire from local fishing authorities should be no problem and the tourist office at your preferred locality will advise on seasons and licences.

Classic Adventure PVT Ltd
See Motorcycling.

Tribes Fair Trade Travel
See Birdwatching.

HANG GLIDING/PARAGLIDING

Paragliding and hang-gliding are the next best things to being a bird. Anyone can do it. You don't have to be super fit, although there is a fair amount of uphill walking involved. The difference between the two sports is the equipment used although both work on the principle of seeking rising currents of hot air (thermals) to maintain altitude. All you really need to bring with you is a pair of stout boots as the various clubs and operators will supply the rest of the equipment. Taking some lessons before travelling is a good way to prepare but full courses, ranging from a day to several weeks, are available locally. Normally day one will be ground-based, covering equipment, technique, and safety. Initial flights will be of short duration and staying close to the launch point, while experienced pilots can plan on cross-country flights.

INDIA

Weather conditions coupled with a varied terrain make India an ideal location for this particular adventure sport. Although it is early days, there are a number of first-class sites and a handful of organizations offering everything from the full package to equipment hire only. Panchgani is a hill station situated about 6 hours from Mumbai (Bombay); its clear weather and plateau topography make it ideal for basic to advanced level flying. Kamshet, 4 hours from Mumbai, has great thermals and excellent ridge waves that will take you soaring over fields and mountains that dip down to a large lake. Virar East, Kopri Hill, near Mumbai, is unspoilt, clean, and green and offers a mesmerising view of the winding Vaitarana River.

Nirvana Adventures

2-A,Takshashila Apts
Tagore Rd
Santacruz (W)
Mumbai 400054
☎ (22) 649 3110/605 3724 **fax:** (22) 649 3110
email: srao@giasbm01.vsnl.net.in
website: www.takeoffindia.com/nirvana
Offers beginners, intermediate, and advanced courses, including cross country circuits, at different hill stations including Panchgani, Kodaikanal, Ooty, Goa, Nanital, Pushkar, and Manili.

The Western Paragliding Association

Laksh Aviation Pvt Ltd
14 Percy I.C. Colony
Borivli (W)
Mumbai 400103
☎ (22) 893 4803/6184
email: Admin@airandadventure.com
website: www.airandadventure.com

HORSE RIDING

There's something about horse riding that sets it apart from all other sports. Whether it is galloping along endless beaches, or fording rivers and cantering through forests, riding gives you a sense of freedom. Adventure holidays on horseback can take the form of day or part-day outings from an equestrian centre, or you could try your hand at a game of polo. Otherwise they involve lengthy treks, and often reaching high altitudes. Accommodation may be in local hotels but is more often in tents. Proper clothing is a good idea whereas a riding hat is essential, as is a high factor sunblock. If you're a novice or it's been a long while since you were on horseback, get a bit of practice at your local stables before the trip; otherwise limit yourself to a trek with very short daily stages—saddle sores are no fun at all. If you opt for a trek don't forget the camera and plenty of film as the chances of re-stocking en route will be non-existent.

INDIA

Ladakh, on the Tibetan plateau, is one of the most remote regions of India, lying on the vast and magnificent Tibetan plateau and bisected by the Indus. It is along this river, retracing former trade routes and riding to altitudes of 4,527m (14,850ft), that you will find some of the wildest and most attractive scenery in India. Dundlod Castle, a 17th-century Rajputana Fort in the Shekhawati region of Rajasthan, is the base for a recently renovated equestrian and polo centre. You can ride from here each day, returning in the evening to splendid architecture and elegant furniture.

KUMBAL GHAR

Ride through Rajasthan's rural villages, scarcely changed since the days of the British Raj. Castles, and palaces, each a day's ride apart, form the basis of an accommodation chain. As well as food and a bed, they will often offer performances of traditional dance and singing by locals. Here's a chance to ride Marwaris, formerly the prized war horses of India but these days enjoying a secondary career as polo ponies.

TIBET

If you can't get a yak, get on a horse and trek through the highlands of Tibet. Riding on top of the world, through an area still largely unknown to Westerners, you will feel as if you have been pulled back through time. At 3,353m (11,000ft) above sea-level are the grasslands of northern Kham, home to the "black tent" herders, Tibetans who graze their yaks, horses, and sheep on the side of the hills. Travel a route between the Yangtze and the Yellow rivers with nomads whose way of life has not altered one bit in the last millennium.

Canda Tours Pvt Ltd

See Birdwatching.

Eastman Voyages

42 Gautam Nagar
New Delhi 110049
☎ (11) 696 8494 **fax:** (11) 696 0484
email: info@eastmanvoyages.com
website: www.eastmanvoyages.com
Offering a range of packages, from pilgrimages to the most important Buddhist shrines to horse riding in the Himalaya and wildlife safaris.

Explore Himalayas

See Cycling.

Hidden Trails

5936 Inverness St
Vancouver
BC V5W 3P7
Canada
☎ (604) 23 1141 **toll free** ☎ 888-9-TRAILS;
fax: (604)23 1148
email: hiddentrails@hiddentrails.com
website: hiddentrails.com/asia
Owned and operated by nature enthusiasts who love horses and adventure activities, and have been involved with riding and outdoor activities for the last 15 years.

International Horseback and Polo Holidays

D383 Defence Colony
New Delhi 110024
☎ (11) 462 4879 **fax:** (11) 461 6137
email: inder.tigers@aworld.net
website: www.horsebackholidays.com
North American office:
8034 112B Street
Delta
BC V4C 5A7
Canada
☎ (604) 501 1652 **fax:** (604) 501 9213
email: info@horsebackholidays.com
website: www.horsebackholidays.com
Offers a wide variety of tours throughout India, the Himalaya and Nepal. Inder Jit Singh, the proprietor, personally leads many of the rides.

Regal Holidays & Expeditions

Maharajkumari Meenakshi Devi
105 /17, 8th cross
R.M.V. Extension
Bangalore 560 080
☎ (80) 331 4566 **fax:** (80) 331 4566

email: regalholidays@yahoo.com
website: www.regalholidays.com/hsafari.htm
Runs tours all over India, including wildlife, fishing, horse safaris, and cultural tours specialising in Nepal and Bhutan... and they really are "regal": the proprietor, Princess Maharajkumari Meenakshi Devi Urs, is the daughter of the late Maharaja of Mysore and sister of the current Maharaja. Regal run a series of treks ranging from 1–7 days, as well as residential riding holidays at the Princess Academy of Equitation, based in the Palace grounds in Bangalore.

Tiger Mountain Group

See Ballooning.

Tribes Fair Trade Travel

See Birdwatching.

PAKISTAN

Riding through northern Pakistan through areas like Hunza, the Shandur Pass, Chitral, and the Kalash valleys will give you a deep feeling for the scenery and way of life of remote rural communities. The terrain varies from narrow trails to wide valleys, ancient villages to grassy plains and some of the highest mountains in the world. You can even take a short ride through the Hindu Kush.

Adventure Foundation

Adventure Inn
Garden Avenue
P.O. Box 1807
Rawalpindi
☎ (51) 272 537 **fax:** (51) 274 625
Can organize all manner of alternatives to trekking, including horse riding, angling, paragliding, ballooning, mainly in the Islamabad area. Can also arrange trekking and jeep safaris.

Ride Worldwide

58 Fentiman Road
London SW8 1LF
U.K.
☎ (020) 7735 1144 **fax:** (020) 7735 3179
email: RideWW@aol.com
Specialist agency dealing with riding holidays. All inclusive packages offered as well as tailor-made itineraries.

BHUTAN

Horse riding holidays in Bhutan are in their infancy and very few tourists have ridden there. Being mounted on small local ponies and trekking through valleys and mountains covered in dense forest enhance the feeling of remoteness.

Equitour Peregrine Holidays Ltd

41 South Parade
Summertown
Oxford OX2 7JP
U.K.
☎ (01865) 51142 **fax:** (01865) 512583
email: 106357.1754@compuserve.com
Riding tours in Bhutan with optional visits to Chitwan National Park in Nepal. Equitour also organize riding trips in Rajastan on former polo ponies, visiting historical, and cultural sights and the famous Pushkar Camel Fair.

JUNGLE TOURS

This section will appeal to those who want to get close to nature without trekking for miles to do it. Most jungle tours take place within national parks and are led by experienced guides, but remember that there is still always a danger, so take sensible precautions: jungle boots, sleeves and trousers will provide some protection from biting and stinging bugs. A wide-brimmed hat, dark glasses, and sunblock will save you from the ravages of ultraviolet; listening to your guide and not wandering away on your own should prevent you getting eaten by the parks' larger inhabitants. If you are going it alone, make sure you have a trail map and compass. In some parks you are not allowed to walk about by yourself—or even walk at all—and if this is the case you should not feel tempted to break the rules. Wherever you go, it's also a good idea to carry a plentiful supply of water to avoid dehydration.

INDIA
CORBETT NATIONAL PARK

The first, and still one of the finest, of India's national parks, consisting of the valley of the Ramanga River and the forested slopes of the Himalayan foothills. It is particularly rich in bird and wildlife, being noted for its population of tigers and elephants. Walking, apart from in the immediate area around the entrance gate, is prohibited, and foreigners who bring their own cars must hire a guide. The best way to explore the park is by elephant—tours may be booked at reception, as can jeep safaris.

Corbett Trails India

114 Siddharth Enclave
New Delhi 110 014
☎ (11) 691 4308/684 9269/684 6857
fax: 981 0064 322
email: info@corbett-trails.com
website: www.corbett-trails.com
Specialize in adventure holidays, package tours, organized treks and safaris all over India.

KANHA NATIONAL PARK

This is the country so vividly described by Kipling in his *Jungle Book* stories. Although you won't spot Mowgli or Baloo the bear, there will be plenty of opportunities to see tigers, not to mention monkeys, squirrels, wild boars, and jackals.

Tiger Resorts

206 Rakesh Deep
11 Commercial Complex
Gulmohar Enclosure
North Delhi
☎ (11) 685 3760 **fax:** (11) 686 5212
Operate Kanha Jungle Lodge accommodation and run a variety of guided tours in the park.

PAKISTAN
HAZERGANJI CHILTAN NATIONAL PARK

A massive, 12,950ha (32,000-acre) area north of Quetta and close to the border with Afghanistan, Chiltan is a remote wilderness, teeming with wildlife, including scary creatures like cobras, pythons, leopards, and wolves, as well as the rare Chiltan Markhor goat and the Afghan tortoise. There are rangers to guide you round and tell you about the wildlife. Visitors need a permit, obtainable from the Forestry Department, who also run the guest house.

Forestry Department

Spinney Road
Quetta
☎ (81) 02240

SRI LANKA
BUNDALA NATIONAL PARK

A coastal strip, east of Hambantota, which is an important wetlands sanctuary and a prime spot for crocodile spotting. It's also home to a wide variety of other species, including leopards, bears, elephants, and four species of marine turtle.

Wildlife Department

Gregory's Road
Colombo 7
☎ (1) 694241 **fax:** (1) 698556

Gabo Holidays

11 Bagatella Road
Colombo 3
☎ (1) 581777 **fax:** (1) 589546
Local tour operator arranging trips to all the wildlife parks.

TIBET

DZITSA DEGU NATIONAL PARK

Some 30km (29 miles) of forested ravine make this one of the most spectacular park areas in Tibet. From the lakes, pools, and waterfalls of the river valley, to the high peaks of the Sema and Dega mountains, to the tiny monastery at Tsaru village, there is enough variety of scenery and terrain to satisfy most tastes.

Abercrombie and Kent

See Trekking.

Cox & Kings Travel

Gordon House
10 Greencoat Place
London SW1P 1PH
U.K.
☎ (020) 7873 5000 **fax:** (020) 7630 6038
email: cox.kings@coxandkings.co.uk
website: www.coxandkings.co.uk
U.S.A. office:
25 Davis Blvd
Tampa
FL 33606
toll free ☎ 800 999 1758
email: tours@coxandkings.com
website: www.coxandkings.com
The oldest travel company in the world specializes in providing a wide selection of cultural and natural history tours through India, Nepal, Pakistan, Tibet, Bhutan, and Sri Lanka.

Geographic Expeditions

See Trekking.

Jiuzhaigo International Travel Service

Room 207 Hualong Hotel
18 Yingmenkou Street
Chengdu
Tibet
☎ (28) 777 8699 **fax:** (28) 777 8696
Organize tours by bus to Dzitsa Degu.

Tribes Fair Trade Travel

See Birdwatching.

MOTORCYCLING

Imagine roaring up some of the highest mountain passes in the world on a motorcycle that has been out of production for over 40 years. Royal Enfield went out of business in the U.K. in the 1960s but the Indian Enfield Factory at Chennai (Madras), established in 1955, is still going strong and producing the original 350 Bullet, which Indians call the "Raja Gadi." Working to 40-year-old specifications, the Indian factory continues to build brand-new vintage bikes. Riding one of these classic bikes must be one of the best ways to experience the cultures, people and scenery of this region. Motorcycle touring in the high passes of the Himalaya is only possible during the months of Jul to Sep. Elsewhere the monsoons make wet-weather riding unavoidable. Temperatures and weather conditions can change daily. It is essential to bring professional quality riding gear with you as well as a crash helmet. You will also need sun glasses, sunblock, and clothes with long sleeves, trousers, and a wide-brimmed hat.

GOA AND SOUTH INDIA

South from the beaches of Goa, the coastal road follows the Arabic sea, passing through busy harbour towns into the mountainous landscape of the Nilgiris.

Classic Adventure PVT Ltd

Casa Tres Amigos
Assagoa 403 507
Goa
☎ (832) 254467 **mobile** ☎ 9810 162263 (New Delhi)
email: info@classic-bike-india.de
website: www.classic-bike-india.de/about.htm
Founded in 1994, this company grew out of a trip made by five German bikers in 1989 and is now one of the leading operators of motorbike tours and a member of the International Association of Motorcycle Tourism. They also run and organize river rafting, paragliding, sportfishing, trekking, and golf tours.

NEPAL

This is a biker's paradise with a network of country roads and "highways" that are little more than dirt tracks. Taking in hill forts and villages, palaces, parks, and nature reserves, trips can cover the country and climb high into mountain passes such as the 2,600m (9,920ft) Kulekhani Pass, before returning to the starting point at Kathmandu. Kathmandu and Pokhara are the only places where the independent traveller will be able to hire a motorcycle. An international driving licence is essential and a hefty deposit will be required. Don't forget to check that motorcycle touring is not excluded from your travel insurance policy.

RAJASTHAN

From the Yaj Mahal in Agra via the Palace of the Winds in Jaipur to the marble palace of the Maharajas of Udaipur, this is classic touring country, with so much to see and so little time to see it. Go deep into the Thar Desert to the golden city of Jaisalmer or search for wild tigers in the wildlife park at Ranthambhore, then complete the trip with a visit to a hill station.

Crystal Holidays
See Trekking.

Erco Travels
See Railway Tours.

MOUNTAINEERING

This is probably the most demanding of adventure sports and in the Indian subcontinent you will find the most challenging and demanding climbs on the planet. If you've never climbed before do not even think about starting in the Himalaya! Detailed planning and organization are essential here, as is a high degree of physical fitness, and you must be aware of the real risk of frostbite, altitude sickness, and hypothermia. Being properly equipped is vital, so ensure that all your gear is suitable for use at high altitudes and low temperatures. Sunglasses with a U.V. filter, snow glasses, lip salve, and sunblock are also important. Read up about mountaineering in the Himalaya before you go, and seek advice from a reputable tour operator.

Abercrombie and Kent
See Trekking.

KE Adventure Travel
32 Lake Road
Keswick
Cumbria CA12 5DQ
U.K.

☎ (017687) 73966 **fax:** (017687) 74693
email: keadventure@enterprise.net
website: www.keadventure.com
KE Adventure Travel was founded in 1984, when the first road link was opened to Skardu, in Northern Pakistan, running the first commercial treks into the high valleys of the Karakoram Mountains and along the Baltoro Glacier to K2. They now organize trekking, climbing, mountaineering, mountain biking, rafting, cultural trips, and safaris in the Himalayas, Karakoram, and the Hindu Kush.

INDIA
The Indian Mountaineering Federation
Anand Niketan
Benito Juarez Road
New Delhi 110021
India
☎ (11) 671211
Can provide advice and details of local mountaineering clubs.

NEPAL

Since Edmund Hillary conquered Everest in 1953, climbers have been flocking to Nepal in ever-increasing numbers. Expeditions to climb the high peaks must have a permit from the Nepal Mountaineering Association. Permits are expensive, and, as there are restrictions on the numbers attempting Everest, there is a long waiting list. Some lesser peaks, which nevertheless still call for a high degree of mountaineering skills, may be climbed without a permit.

Adventure Specialist Trekking (P) Ltd.
P.O. Box. 3500
Tangal
Kathmandu
☎ (1) 428914/428236 **fax:** (1) 428236
email: ast@ecomail.com.np
website: www.visitnepal.com/ast
Specialists in organizing tours, treks, and expeditions in Nepal, Tibet, Bhutan, and Sikkim.

Annapurna Mountaineering & Trekking (P) Ltd.
P.O. Box. 795
Durbarmarg
Kathmandu
☎ (1) 222999/221234/222329 **fax:** (1) 226153
email: amtk@ccsl.com.np
Established in 1970, AMTREK has since gained

a good deal of experience in operating trekking and mountaineering expeditions in the high Himalaya. They also organize white-water river rafting, wildlife safaris, and filming and photography treks.

Himalayan Sherpa Adventure (P) Ltd

P.O. Box. 4550
Chabahil
Kathmandu
Nepal
☎ (1) 471549 **fax:** (1) 480806
email: sherpadv@mos.com.np
website: www.himalayanadventure.com.np
Operated by sherpas from Solukhumbu, in the foothills of Mount Everest, this company offers a complete service for camping, treks, rafting, jungle safari, cultural tours, and climbing expeditions with renowned guides and high-altitude cooks.

Nepal Mountaineering Association

P.O. Box 1435
Kathmandu
☎: (1) 434525/435442 **fax:** (1) 434578
email: peaks@nma.wlink.com.np
website: www.view-nepal.com/nma
In its annual programmes, N.M.A. conducts a basic and advanced level mountaineering training for expedition-going sherpas and aspirant mountaineers, in addition to basic and advanced rock climbing training.

PAKISTAN

The Himalaya, Karkoram and the Hindu Kush, three of the world's great mountain ranges, meet in Pakistan. Five of the peaks are in excess of 8,000m (26,247ft), including K2, which, at 8,611m (28,251ft) is the second highest in the world. There are also 79 peaks over 7,000m (22,966ft) and hundreds above 6,000m (19,685ft). Mountaineers will find an unlimited range of challenges in this part of the Indian sub continent.

Nazir Sabir Expeditions

P.O. Box 1442
Islamabad
☎ (51) 853 672 **fax:** (51) 250 293
Long experience in trekking and mountaineering in the Northern Areas. Specialize in mountaineering but also run low-level trekking and jeep safaris.

PHOTOGRAPHIC TOURS

Most of the adventures listed in this section will provide great opportunities for taking photographs but that's really just a by-product of the original reason for the trip, be it trekking, cultural touring, or wildlife watching. Photographic trips, which are first and foremost for the purpose of taking photographs, are a different thing entirely. Most will involve touring wildlife parks and visiting the great cultural icons of the Indian sub continent but with the added advantage of having a professional photographer alongside to give superb technical advice to experienced as well as novice snappers. For the dedicated photographer this is the kind of trip to book. It will be carefully planned and timed so that you are in the right place at the right time to get the best light.

INDIA

Here you will find some of the best locations for wildlife in the world—Bandhavgarh, Kanha, and Kaziranga national parks. Combine this with ancient architecture, exploring the wonders of Old Delhi, and being there as the sun rises to photograph the Taj Mahal in the pink light of dawn.

Origins Travel Ltd

Bank Chambers
Royal Bank of Scotland
Main Road
Hathersage S32 1BB
U.K.
☎ (01433) 659331 **fax:** (01433) 659332
email: originsweb@dial.pipex.com
website: www.originstravel.com
Specialize in nature and adventure holidays, pioneering escorted trips to remote locations since 1970, when photographers Suzanne and Alfred Gregory first launched the company.

PAKISTAN

Like India, this country abounds with wildlife and cultural scenes and almost anywhere you go will be an ideal location for photography.

Culture Tours

36 National Square
Khayaban-e-Jami
Clifton
Karachi
☎ (21) 579289 **fax:** (21) 5832632

In the U.S.A.:
toll free ☎ (877) 243 6838; **fax:** (708) 575 6936/ (909) 257 7600
email: travel@cyber.net.pk
website: tours.hypermart.net/index.htm
This owner-managed company has over 10 years' experience in handling all kinds of tours in Pakistan and southeast Asia, including photographic tours and tailor-made itineraries. They have assisted many companies in the making of documentary films, including the English BBC.

Explore Himalayas
See Cycling.

Palanquin Travels
6 Palace Courtyard
Priory Road
Wells BA5 1SY
U.K.
☎ (01749) 671311 **fax:** (01749) 671310
and
98 Boston Place
Regents Park
London NW1 6EX
U.K.
☎ (020) 7724 6022 **fax:** (020) 7724 5749
email: sirdars@palanquin.co.uk
website: www.palanquin.co.uk
Run by the expeditioner who designed the feeding programmes for Richard Branson's world ballooning projects, the film maker who recreated Hillary and Tenzing's 1953 ascent of Everest, and the former Commandant of India's High Altitude Warfare School, Palanquin has an impeccable reputation for organizing all sorts of adventure and cultural tours of the Indian subcontinent, including some of the best photographic trips.

RAFTING

What could be more exhilarating than being part of a team guiding and paddling a raft along the great rivers of the Himalaya? On a 2-week combined trek and rafting trip you can sail all the way from the Himalaya to the Bay of Bengal, carrying all your equipment and food with you and camping by the banks of the river at night. The difficulty of the descent can be gauged by the international river grading. Grade I is slow-moving water—the best choice if you are inexperienced or lack the stamina for the rough stuff. Grade V is the ultimate in stomach-churning, white-knuckle rides. One thing is guaranteed: after a couple of weeks of this you'll be at peak fitness. Whatever company you organize your trip with, make sure they provide life jackets and helmets and that all their staff have completed a relevant safety course.

INDIA
The rivers running through Uttar Pradesh, Sikkim, Kashmir, and Himachal Pradesh provide some excellent white-water rafting, particularly when swollen by the snows melting on the surrounding mountain ranges. Every grade can be found here. Grades II and III runs on the Indus are suitable for amateurs and the inexperienced while the Rangit, Chenab, Tons, and Beas provide Grades IV and V for the experienced sensation-seekers. There's even the odd Grade VI, which is not considered safe for commercial use and should only be tackled by very experienced rafters who know what they're doing.

Abercrombie and Kent
See Trekking.

Adrift (U.K.)
Wessex House
127 High Street
Hungerford RG17 0DL
U.K.
☎ (01488) 684509 **fax:** (01488) 685055
email: raft@adrift.co.uk
website: www.adrift.co.nz
An established company employing a number of well-qualified and experienced guides (see website for profiles).

Adventure Whitewater
See Canoeing and Kayaking.

Concord Tours & Travels
56 Deepak Building
13 Nehru Place
New Delhi 110019
☎ (11) 622 1559/622 1560/648 7120
fax: (11) 622 1560
email:- concords@ndb.vsnl.net.in
website: www.indiamart.com/concord
Reputable travel agent and tour operator with head office in Delhi and a wide network of associate offices throughout India and Nepal. Offers a wide range of packages as well as tailor-made itineraries.

Crystal Holidays
See Trekking.

David Allardice's Ultimate Descents
P.O. Box 387
Motueka
New Zealand
☎ (3) 543 2301 **fax:** (3) 543 2302
email: ultimatenx@xtra.co.nz or
ultimate_descents@xtra.co.nz
website: www.ultimatedescents.com

Exotic Journeys
See Cultural Tours.

Explore Himalayas
See Cycling.

Tiger Mountain Group
See Ballooning.

Tribes Fair Trade Travel
See Birdwatching.

NEPAL

Nepal is a river runner's paradise, containing some of the world's best. The Marsayangdi (Grade IV–V) rises on the slopes of the Annapurna and flows east through Manang and then south to the Trisuli River. There are lots of rapids and white water which need fast manoeuvring. The Sun Koshi (Grade III–IV), or "River of Gold," flows east from Tibet through the Himalaya and into the Northern plains of India before flowing into the Ganges. Not surprising for a river draining water from the highest mountains in the world, the Sun Koshi just after the monsoon is a bit hairy and must rank as one of the great river experiences of the world. There are no roads or towns in this part of Nepal so expeditions have to be self-sufficient. The first few stages are relatively easy. Then come rapids with names like Meatgrinder, Jaws, and Roller Coaster. The Karnali (Grade IV), in the far west, is Nepal's longest river. Rising near Mount Kailash in Tibet, it descends from the Himalaya through a series of gorges and flows through the Royal Bardia Wildlife Park before eventually joining the Ganges.

Bio Bio Expeditions World Wide
P.O. Box 2028
Truckee
CA 96160
U.S.A.

toll free ☎ 800 2GO RAFT/800 246 7238
fax: (530) 582 6865
email: H20Marc@aol.com or
LarsAlvarez@compuserve.com
website: www.bbxrafting.com
Organize a variety of kayaking and rafting trips in Nepal using professional and experienced guides. Safety measures include safety-rescue kayakers. Bio Bio run all their own trips and do not contract out to local suppliers.

Ultimate
P.O. Box 14431
Kathmandu
Nepal
email: rivers@ultimate.wlink.com.np
Pioneers of raft descents on most of Nepal's Rivers, Ultimate has been operating in the region for 20 years. They also offer Himalayan treks, wildlife safaris and cultural tours, plus what they describe as "the ultimate bungee jump," leaping from a bridge over a 160m (525ft) tropical gorge on the Bhote Koshi, one of the world's wildest rivers.

PAKISTAN
Golden Bridge International
21/F Tak Woo House
17-19 D'Aguilar Street
Central
Hong Kong
☎ (2801) 5590 **fax:** (2523) 7293
email: info@goldenbridge.net
White-water rafting specialists and general trekking in Himalaya and China.

Himalayan Kingdoms
20 The Mall
Clifton
Bristol BS8 4DR
U.K.
☎ (0117) 923 7163 **fax:** (0117) 974 4993
email: 101460.2002@compuserve.com
website: www.himalayankingdoms.com
Long-established, major U.K.-based trek organizers, whose main speciality is multi-day treks for groups. Can organize white-water rafting, mountain biking, and other tours through Pakistan agencies.

Mountain Travel Sobek
6420 Fairmount Avenue
El Cerrito
CA 94530 3606
U.S.A.
☎ (510) 527 8105 **toll free** ☎ 800 282 8747

fax: (510) 525 7710
website: www.gordonsguide.com/whitewater-rafting/mountaintravelsobek
White-water rafting specialists world-wide. Also trekking and mountaineering.

RAILWAY TOURS

Some of the world's greatest railway journeys run through the Indian subcontinent. They offer the truly adventurous the best way to meet and interact with local people. For the tourist market, luxury trains, with air-conditioned sleeper berths, link most of the great cultural centres—they can cost as much as air travel but will certainly be comfortable. Indian trains have a whole array of classes, down to the cheapest hot, overcrowded and smelly carriages, in which it is often impossible to secure a seat (see also Train Tickets, p. 83). For security, always keep your money out of sight, preferably in a belt under your clothing, and padlock your bags to the seat or luggage rack—otherwise it might disappear.

INDIA
The Palace on Wheels

The last word in luxury travel in an Edwardian-style train with all the comforts of a high class hotel—think *Orient Express* and you'll get the picture. It's not cheap, but when you consider that tours include accommodation, food, transport, and sightseeing, it's a great way to see India. The route is: Delhi–Jaipur–Chittorgarh–Udaipur–Sawai Madhopur (Ranthambore)–Jaisalmer–Jodhpur–Bharatpur–Agra–Delhi.

Rajasthan Tourism Development Corporation Ltd

Hotel Swagatam Campus
Near railway station
Jaipur 302 006
email: jaipur@palaceonwheels.net
website: www.palaceonwheels.net
Has information on *The Palace on Wheels*.

India Tourist Office

The Manager
Central Reservation Office
Bikaner House
Pandara Road
New Delhi 110003
☎ (11) 338387/3381884 **fax:** (11) 33823
email: jaipur.rtdc@axcess.net.in
website: www.inetindia.com/rajasthan

Takes bookings—mark your letter "Reservation *Palace on Wheels*".

The Royal Orient

Like The Palace on Wheels, this is first-class travel, based on the luxurious salons of former Maharajas but modernized with air conditioning and 21st-century plumbing. Takes passengers from Delhi through the little explored state of Gujarat.

Tourism Corporation of Gujarat Ltd

Central Reservation Office
A-6, State Emporia Building
Baba Kharak Singh Marg
New Delhi 110001
☎ (11) 373 4015 **fax:** (11) 373 2487

The Toy Trains of India

These affectionately named trains run on narrow gauge rails in various locations. One of the classic rail journeys of all time is the last leg of the journey from Calcutta to Darjeeling, on a miniature train built in 1889—the 9-hour trip from Jalpaiguri is uphill all the way, passing through unbelievable scenery to the high pass at Jorebungalow, where the High Himalayan panorama comes into view. Following the old cart road, the railway rises to 2,135m (7,000ft) in 86km (53 miles). The station at Dhoom is the highest in India.

The Toy Train journey from Kalka to Shimla, the state capital of Himachal Pradesh, is entrancing, with 107 tunnels and lofty arched bridges. The dazzling view and the stops at the small stations along the way add to the experience. Shimla is connected to New Delhi by a broad-gauge line up to Kalka.

Ooty (Udhagamandalam) is connected by a narrow-gauge line to Mettupalayam, which serves as the railhead for main-line trains. At a maximum speed of 33kph (20mph), this Toy Train treks across plains, plantations, and forest clad hills. The 16 tunnels and tall girder bridges on the way, along with the breathtaking view, make it a trip not to be missed.

Darjeeling Himalayan Railway Society

c/o Marilyn Mertz (Secretary D.H.R.S.)
80 Ridge Road
London N8 9NR
U.K.
email: m.metz@pro-net.co.uk
website: www.dhrs.org

It is not surprising, given the British background in Darjeeling and their long-standing love affair with trains, that they have organized a society for the Toy Train. Devoted to promoting interest in, and support for, the Darjeeling Himalaya Railway and its surrounding area, the society publishes a quarterly magazine.

Indrail Pass

Indian Railways offers the Indrail Pass to tourists who wish to tour India by rail. These passes are sold only to foreign passport-holders and Indians who live abroad, and are payable in US dollars or pounds sterling. Indrail Pass holders are exempt from paying any extra charges such as reservation fees, sleeper charges, or charges for super fast trains. These passes are sold through general sales agents in New York and London (see **SD Enterprises** on p. 262), and at major railway stations all over India.

PAKISTAN
KHYBER PASS

There are two ways of visiting the legendary Khyber Pass: pay the cost of the permit and the hire of the compulsory armed guard, or take a trip on the equally legendary Khyber Railway. Built by the British in the 1920s, it is now run as a tourist attraction—the train is pushed and pulled along the track by two 1920s steam engines. The 42km (26-mile) journey takes 3 hours one way, the train threading its way through 34 tunnels, across 92 bridges and culverts and climbing 1,200m (4,000ft). On the Changai Spur section, which is shaped like a 'W', the track climbs 130m (427ft) in less than a mile. At Landikotal station the train waits for 2 hours before starting the return journey, which is just enough time to take a taxi 8km (5 miles) into Torkham and the Afghan border checkpost.

Alpine Trekkers & Tours Private Limited

Mailing address:
Post Box 2488 Islamabad
Head office:
21 AL-Amin Plaza
The Mall
Rawalpindi
☎ (51) 852496/519815/593160/593149
fax: (51) 260111/517330
email: alpine@meganet.com.pk
website: www.alpine.com.pk/khyber.html
Organize a variety of tours and treks including trips on the Khyber Railway.

Abercrombie and Kent
See Trekking.

Erco Travels
376-A, 3rd Floor
Sant Nagar
East of Kailash
New Delhi 110065
☎ (11) 640 5486/623 6817 **mobile** ☎ 981 000 5635 **fax:** (11) 623 6817
email: ravi.gusain@vsnl.com
website: www.ercotravels.com
Offer a wide variety of adventure and cultural packages throughout India and are adept at preparing tailor-made itineraries for all areas covered by this guide.

Exotic Journeys
See Cultural Tours.

Gateway to India
Gateway House
16 Jacks Lane
Marchington
Uttoxeter ST14 8LW
U.K.
☎ (01283) 821096 **fax:** (01283) 820467
email: specialist-travel@gateway-to-india.co.uk
website: www.gateway-to-india.co.uk
Supply a range of adventure holidays and tailor-made itineraries throughout the regions covered by this guide.

Geographic Expeditions
See Trekking.

Tribes Fair Trade Travel
See Birdwatching.

SAFARIS

A "safari" is a journey, and although the word still conjures up an image of hunting in the African bush from the back of a truck or landrover, the 21st-century safari is a different thing altogether. The mode of transport may still be a truck but more likely you will be astride a camel, elephant, horse, or even a yak. The pace of travel is slow, certainly no more than 16–24km (10–15 miles) a day, giving you the time to absorb and appreciate the country you are travelling through. For photographers and wildlife enthusiasts there can be no better way to travel. Wear loose-fitting cotton clothing with long sleeves, and long trousers, all preferably in "earthy" colours so you won't stand out. A wide-brimmed hat, sunglasses, and plenty of high factor sunblock are essential for avoiding sunburn and sunstroke, and an effective insect repellent will help keep the biting beasties at bay. Always carry and drink plenty of water to avoid dehydration.

INDIA

The heart of the Thar Desert is where you'll find the best camel safaris in India. travelling slowly through the Jodhpur, Jaisalmer, and Bikaner region and passing tiny villages and remote trading posts. Most organizers try to recreate the atmosphere of the caravan journeys of old, with evenings spent round the campfire eating traditional food and listening to local music.

NEPAL

Abercrombie and Kent
See Trekking.

Concord Tours & Travels
See Rafting.

Crystal Holidays
See Trekking.

David Allardice's Ultimate Descents
See Rafting.

Eastman Voyages
See Horse Riding.

Erco Travels
See Railway Tours.

Euro Tours
1012-A, Indra Prakash Building
21 Barakhamba Road
Connaught Place
New Delhi 110017
India
☎ (11) 3716448/9 **fax:** (11) 3716448
email: eurotours@usa.net
website: www.indiamart.com/eurotours
With a wide and well-established network, this operator organizes tours all over India, Nepal, Bhutan, and neighbouring countries, specializing in leisure and adventure tours based on different climatic conditions and major attractions.

Exotic Journeys
See Cultural Tours.

Geographic Expeditions
See Trekking.

Tiger Mountain Group
See Ballooning.

Travelbag Adventures
See p. 283.

Tribes Fair Trade Travel
See Birdwatching.

ROYAL CHITWAN NATIONAL PARK
See Chapter 15.

PAKISTAN
HIMALAYA AND KARAKORAM AIR SAFARI

Pakistan International Airlines (PIA) runs a mountain air safari to the heart of the Karakoram. Fly in a Boeing 737 past the peak of Nanga Parbat, then fly on to see dozens of other world-famous mountains, including K2. Other than physically climbing them, this is the only way you'll ever see these peaks and you won't even work up a decent sweat.

Trans Pakistan Adventure Services
P.O. Box 2103
Apt 8, 2nd Floor
Muzaffar Chambers
Fazl-e-Haq Road
Jinnah Avenue
Islamabad
☎ (51) 274796 **fax:** (51) 274838
Jeep safaris, culture, and special interest tours. in north and south Pakistan. Trekking and mountaineering.

SCUBA DIVING

You can enter the wonderful undersea world of Jacques Cousteau as soon as you strap on the aqualung, which he invented, and dive under the surface of the water. Scuba (self-contained underwater breathing apparatus) diving has been described as an adventure sport suitable for active grandmothers and indeed people of all ages, shapes, and sizes can do it after a period of basic training. Underwater you'll experience weightlessness and observe forms of undersea life you may not have seen before in their own habitat. The best way to learn to dive is to join your local diving club and progress slowly through the basic training and certification. Then take your certificates and log book on holiday and book dives through a local agency who will provide all the equipment, boat transfers and an experienced guide. If you're short of time you can sign up to do a course on holiday but make sure that tuition is by properly qualified P.A.D.I. (Professional Association of Diving Instructors) or B.S.A.C. (British Sub Aqua Club) instructors.

INDIA
ANDAMAN ISLANDS

Massive coral reefs and wonderful clear water make this a prime dive site with an abundance of marine life. Loggerhead turtles, manta rays, and reef sharks swim beside angel, parrot, and triggerfish. Equipment can be hired from the local dive centres, who also run courses from beginner to advanced.

Port Blair Underwater Dive Centre

Peerless Beach Resort
Corbyn's Bay
Port Blair
☎ (1392) 85389 **fax:** (40) 339 2718

Samudra

See p. 272.

GOA

Goa has a diving environment with marine life similar to the Maldives. Dives are shallow, with a maximum depth of 20m (66ft), and the absence of rip tides and strong currents make them very safe. Visibility on a good day can be as much as 12–15m (39–49ft), which is good enough to see the wide variety of fish. The presence of a few wrecks provides opportunities to try your hand at this exciting part of sports diving. The wrecks are magnets for fish and marine life.

Barracuda Diving

The Cidade de Goa Beach Resort
Dona Paula
Goa
☎ (832) 221133, extn 5706 **fax:** (832) 223303
email: barracuda@vsnl.com
website:
www.goenkar.com/barracuda/default.htm
Running everything from basic certification to

advanced open water courses, Barracuda Diving has three fully qualified P.A.D.I. instructors and membership of the P.A.D.I. International Resort Association.

Goa Diving Private Limited

House No. 145P Chapel Bhat
Chicalim
Goa 403 711
☎ (832) 555117
Bogmalo Beach office:
☎ (832) 555036
email: contact@goadiving.com
website: www.goadiving.com/middle.html
Run by a Scotsman, Willie Downie, and his wife Rajshree, they have been organizing trips since 1992. This was the first diving school on mainland India and the largest in Goa. Instructors are both P.A.D.I. and B.S.A.C. qualified.

LAKSHADWEEP ISLANDS

Situated some 225–400km (140–250 miles) west of the coast of Kerala, the "one hundred thousand islands" are a divers' Shangri La, but are difficult and expensive to get to. Entry is strictly controlled— everyone needs a permit, and you will only get there if you book through one of the companies offering a package tour. Great visibility; expect to see turtles, dolphins, and coral reefs teeming with fish.

Lacca Dives

E 20 Everest
Tardeo
Mumbai
☎ (22) 494 2023 **fax:** (22) 495 1644
email: gen@bom2.vsnl.net.in
Experienced operator with environmentally friendly policy.

Natural Mystic Adventure Travel

Suite 1-B, 56 Pondfield Rd West
Bronxville
NY 10708
U.S.A.
☎ (914) 771 6011
email: info@naturalmystic.com
website:
www.naturalmystic.com/tours/in1.html
The dive centre is run by professionally trained and certified C.-M.A.S. dive instructors and has obtained special permission to take foreign passport holders diving on the unexplored island of Kadmat.

SRI LANKA

There's a series of wrecks off the coast here that must rank amongst the star dive sites in Sri Lanka. The aircraft carrier *Hermes*, sunk in 1942, 32km (20 miles) off Batticaloa on the east coast, is probably too deep for all but the most experienced sports divers, but there are plenty more to chose from round Colombo. For dive sites from resorts, where dive centres and access to hire equipment and dive boats is assured, Hikkaduwa is probably best. Other decent sites can be found at Galle, Unawatuna, Trincomalee, and the Basses Reefs.

Scuba Safari (Pvt) Ltd

Resort Centre
Coral Gardens Hotel
Hikkaduwa
☎ (1) 694012 / 699756 **fax:** (1) 694029
website: www.lanka-business.com/scuba/
Partner Hector Ekanayake founded this dive centre, together with the science fiction writer Sir Arthur C. Clarke, in the 1950s. It is a P.A.D.I. dive centre offering a full range of courses from beginner to advanced, equipment hire and sales, and boat dives.

SOARING (GLIDING)

Few experiences can compare with the moment you release the tow line from your glider and you're flying solo amidst the clouds. Apart from the sound of the airflow rushing over the wing surface you are in a silent world of your own. You'll soon be able to identify thermals, the upward currents of hot air which you'll use like a series of invisible elevators to gain altitude before moving off cross country. Vast distances can be covered by an experienced pilot with the right conditions but it can also be fun for beginners. Before booking a gliding holiday it would be a good idea to go to your nearest club and try a couple of experience flights just to get a feel for it. But beware—this is a seriously addictive activity.

INDIA

The British introduced soaring to the Indians and they have adapted it in their own inimitable manner. With variable terrain and plenty of hot weather to produce decent thermals, the prospects for cross country flights of long duration are good.

Government Gliding Centre

Hadapsar
Pune
Maharashtra
email: navair@giaspn01.vsnl.net.in
website:
www.geocities.com/CapeCanaveral/Hangar/2083/#GCP
Located on the Deccan Plateau amidst Sahyadri ranges= at the eastern end of Pune City, about 160km (100 miles) from Mumbai (Bombay). All instructors are government employees and fully qualified to international standards. This should be the first port of call for anyone interested in soaring in India as they maintain a list of contacts with other clubs and know who is operating and which sites are open. They operate Sunday to Thursday each week with a modern and impressive fleet of gliders. There are about 10 further registered gliding clubs in India, but as they form and disband on a regular basis, check here first for up-to-date information.

Deolali Gliding Club

Artillery Centre
Nashik Road
Nashik
Maharashtra

Ahmedabad Gliding and Flying Club

Ahmedabad Airport
Ahmedabad
Gujarat

Delhi Gliding Club

Safdarjung Airport
New Delhi 110 003

Birla Gliding Club

Pilani
Rajasthan

Jamshedpur Gliding Club

Sonari Aerodrome
Sonari
Jamshedpur
Bihar

Ranchi Gliding Club

Ranchi Airport
Ranchi
Bihar

Gliding and Soaring Centre

Indian Institute of Technology
Kalyanpur
Kanpur

Hissar Aviation Club

Civil Airport
Hisar
Haryana

Pinjore Aviation Club

Civil Airport
Pinjore
Kalka
Haryana

Ludhiana Aviation Club

Sanehwal Airport
Ludhiana
Punjab

TREKKING

With or without a backpack there is nothing to beat trekking as a means of travel and getting to grips with a country. Few places on earth are more suited to trekking than the Himalaya. Anyone who is fit enough to walk for 5 or 6 hours a day can go trekking. For your first Himalayan trek it is best to book an all-inclusive package through a tour operator. If you're experienced and want to go it alone, remember that you will be travelling through some very remote areas and will need to carry all your food, clothing, and accommodation with you. You should be aware of the hazards of altitude sickness and how to deal with them. Carry a first aid kit, make sure you drink plenty of fluids, and that you protect yourself from the harmful effects of ultraviolet radiation.

INDIA

ZANSKAR

Between the Zanskar range and the Himalaya, the Zanskar River flows from Padum to Zangla. For many months of the year, the river is the only access to the area, when it is cut off by the snow. Zanskaris use the frozen river as a highway and now a unique trek has been devised along its length. Travelling by jeep from Leh, the trek itself is a very strenuous 14 days with overnight stops in caves and small houses along the river.

Crystal Holidays

B 601, Ansal Chambers 1
3 Bhikaji Cama Place
New Delhi 110066
☎ (11) 618 6909/618 2772/616 1252/616 3107
fax: (11) 618 6122
email: trekking@crystalholidays.com, safari@crystalholidays.com, tours@crystalholidays.com
website: www.indiamart.com/crystalholidays
At the forefront of promoting adventure holidays to India since its creation in 1990, and approved by the Department of Tourism, Government of India and recognized by the Indian Mountaineering Foundation, New Delhi.

Geographic Expeditions

2627 Lombard Street
San Francisco
California 94123
U.S.A.
☎ (415) 922 0448 **fax:** (415) 346 5535
email: info@geoex.com
website: www.geoex.com
One of the pioneers of adventure travel, operating world-wide with an exceptionally varied list of overland tours, hiking trips, treks, and voyages. They also offer tailor-made itineraries to some of the world's "impossible to reach on one's own" places.

Tribes Fair Trade Travel

See Birdwatching.

NEPAL

THE ANNAPURNA CIRCUIT

Nepal's most popular trek, but it requires a high degree of fitness. Altitude sickness is a risk on the northern part of the circuit (trekking up to 5,410m (17,750ft)). The southern section passes through the world's deepest gorge, west of Annapurna, but still hits the dizzy heights of 3,710m (12,172ft). From Suikhet on the southern section you have the option of a 9-day trek to Annapurna Base Camp.

THE ROYAL TREK

Not as much energy or time is required for this 4-day circular jaunt from Pokhara, but you will still get some great views of Annapurna. There's nothing higher than 1,500m (4,921ft) to climb either. English Prince Charles was the royal who took a stroll along this route, thereby giving it a new name.

EVEREST BASE CAMP TREK

Another very popular Nepalese trek, again requiring considerable fitness to cope with ascents and descents across the grain of valleys on the 3-week journey from Jiri. Progressing from the Hindu Middle Hills to the Tibetan Buddist High Himalaya, the route goes through the Sagarmartha National Park which is a World Heritage Site with awesome views of Everest.

PAKISTAN
BALTORO GLACIER, CONCORDIA AND K2

Pakistan's most popular trek requires a permit and a registered guide because it's in a restricted zone. The only way to get there is to book through a recognized operator. It's a long and arduous trek just to get onto the Baltoro Glacier so you must be very fit to consider it. Once there, in the very heart of the Karkoram mountains, the views of some of the highest peaks in world make the effort worthwhile. There are many operators in this guide, listed under other headings, who operate treks in Pakistan: **Concord Tours & Travels** (see Rafting); **David Allardice's Ultimate Descents** (Rafting); **Eastman Voyages** (Horse Riding); **Erco Travels** (Railway Tours); **Explore Himalayas** (Cycling); **Euro Tours** (Safaris); **Concord Tours & Travels** (Rafting); **Exotic Journeys** (Cultural Tours); and **Tiger Mountain Group** (Ballooning).

Abercrombie and Kent

Sloane Square House
Holbein Place
London SW1W 8NS
U.K.
☎ (020) 7730 9600 **fax:** (020) 7730 9376
email: info@abercrombiekent.co.uk
website: www.abercrombiekent.com
U.S.A. office:
1520 Kensington Road
Oak Brook
Illinois 60523
☎ (630) 954 2944 **fax:** (630) 954 3324
email: info@abercrombiekent.com
website: www.abercrombiekent.com
Abercrombie and Kent has grown from a small family safari business to an award-winning global travel company. They offer a full range of activities including skiing, rafting, and trekking and use modes of transport ranging from train, plane, jeep and balloon to camel, elephant, and foot.

Backroads

801 Cedar Street
Berkeley
CA 94710 1800
U.S.A.
toll free ☎ 800 GO ACTIVE/800 462 2848
fax: (510) 527 1444
email: goactive@backroads.com
website: www.backroads.com
Established operator, founded in 1979, offering over 1,200 scheduled departures for cyclists, hikers and multi-sports enthusiasts.

Classic Nepal Ltd

33 Metro Avenue
Newton
Alfreton
Derbyshire DE55 5UF
U.K.
☎ (01773) 873497 **fax:** (01773) 590243
email: classicnepal@himalaya.co.uk
website: www.himalaya.co.uk
Established in 1986, this company is now one of the U.K.'s leading specialist operators for trekking, climbing, and adventure holidays in India, Nepal, and Tibet.

Concordia Expeditions, Inc.

P.O. Box 4159
Buena Vista
CO 81211
U.S.A.
☎ (719) 395 9191 **fax:** (719) 395 4868
email: infoaconcordiaexpeditions.com
website: concordiaexpeditions.com
Long-established company that prides itself on low-impact, environmentally aware treks for groups of 8 or fewer. Can arrange most types of trek, including foot trek, jeep safaris, and culture treks.

Guerba Expeditions Ltd

Wessex House
40 Station Road
Westbury
Wiltshire BA13 3JN
U.K.
☎ (01373) 826611 **fax:** (01373) 858351
email: info@guerba.demon.co.uk
website: www.guerba.com
Specialists in safaris and overland expeditions to Nepal, Tibet, Bhutan, India, and Sikkim. They cover everything from the gently paced adventure holiday with a variety of activities to serious trekking and climbing.

Shambhala Trekking Agency (P) Ltd.

P.O. Box 7611
Kantipath
Kathmandu
☎ (1) 268092 **fax:** (1) 268093
email: amrit@kesh.wlink.com.np
Specialize in interesting tours to Tibet and remote areas of Nepal.

Travel Plus

A-1 Madina Super Market
Gilgit
☎ (572) 2613/55278
Liaison office:
P.O. Box 417
Islamabad
☎ (51) 212452 **fax:** (51) 212451
email: trvlplus@isb.comsats.net.pk
Locally based agency that will arrange all types of treks, including mountain biking, jeep safaris, culture, trekking, and mountaineering.

TRIBAL TOURS

Tribal tours are a way of catching a glimpse of the simple yet interesting lifestyle of indigenous people. Their houses, clothes, food, crafts, languages, dances, and culture are strikingly different and their way of life may have remained static for centuries. There are many tribal groupings throughout this region and some are becoming dependent on tourism for a living—this, in itself, is altering the very thing you have come to see, so choose your operator carefully. Ask about their commitment to sustainable travel and try to ensure that what you are going to see is not a performance specially manufactured for tourists which bears no relation to the culture of the people. Respect the people you are visiting: don't take photographs without permission, or enter their homes without being invited.

INDIA
THE DROK-PA

The Drok-pa may be the purest survivors of the Aryan race, known as "Drookhpas." They live in the villages of Dunkhar Tirit, Skurbuchan, Hanudo Biama, and Dha on the banks of the Indus. Tall, well-built with aquiline noses, they are believed to have migrated from central Asia 1,000 years ago. Both sexes and children wear heavy metallic earrings.

RAJASTHAN

Over 10 percent of the population is made up of tribal groups, principal amongst them being the Minas and the Bhils, with lesser groups including Lohars, Damariyas, Garasias, and Bhil-Minas. What separates their cultures are differences in dress, religious beliefs, and ceremonies.

Crystal Holidays

See Trekking.

Explore Worldwide

1 Frederick Street
Aldershot
Hants GU11 1LQ
U.K.
☎ (01252) 760 100 **fax:** (01252) 760 001
email: info@explore.co.uk
website: www.explore.co.uk
Leading operator for over 17 years, specializing in tours, treks, safaris, and expeditions throughout Nepal, India, Bhutan, Tibet, Pakistan, and Sri Lanka.

Geographic Expeditions

See Trekking.

Indian Tribal Tours

3/4, Windsor Mansion
Janpath Lane
New Delhi 110 001
☎ (11) 372 3353/335 3208 **fax:** (11) 332 3906
email: ittindia@nda.vsnl.net.in
website: www.indiamart.com/itt/
The Baktoo family have been operating this company for over 20 years and have a very good reputation.

Tribes Fair Trade Travel

See Birdwatching.

WILDLIFE WATCHING

Fortunately, the killing of game on safaris is now outlawed, but people continue to bag their favourite animals with the long lens and binoculars instead of a high-velocity rifle. Getting close to (and photographing) the local wildlife can be done while engaged in a host of other safaris and activities, but if the fauna of the region is what turns you on then sign up for a tour geared to that and nothing else. (See also the Photographic Tours section.) From a safety point of view it is vital to listen to, and heed the advice of (!), your tour leader or guide. Don't try to get too close to the animals. Some are positively lethal and even the small cuddly-looking ones may take a bite-sized chunk of your anatomy or have a very large mamma lurking nearby. Wear loose-fitting cotton clothing and a wide-brimmed hat, use plenty of sunscreen, and drink lots of water. As well as binoculars, a camera and plenty of film, a field guide to the animals of the country will also be useful.

INDIA

India has preserved vast expanses of forests and habitats in its 80 national parks and 441 wildlife sanctuaries. Whatever you want to see, the chances are you will.

Crystal Holidays

See Trekking.

Koshi Tappu Wildlife Reserve

See Birdwatching.

NEPAL
ROYAL BARDIA NATIONAL PARK

The largest wilderness area in the Nepalese Terai and the best place to see tigers. It's also home to a wide variety of animal life, including swamp deer, rhinos, the marsh mugger crocodile, and several hundred species of bird.

ROYAL CHITWAN NATIONAL PARK

Nepal's oldest and most popular national park is the perfect place for spotting Royal Bengal tigers, leopards, bears, barking deer, mongoose, and the Indian rhinoceros. Tours of the park can be made on foot, by jeep, or on the back of an elephant. It is also home to over 400 species of bird, including seasonal migrants. (See Chapter 15.)

There are several operators in this guide, listed under other headings, who operate wildlife watching trips: **Concord Tours & Travels** (see Rafting); **Eastman Voyages** (Horse Riding); **Euro Tours** (Safaris); **Exotic Journeys** (Cultural Tours); **Explore Himalayas** (Cycling); **Geographic Expeditions** (Trekking); **Himalayan Treasures and Travel** (Ballooning); **Naturetrek** (see p. 283);and **Tribes Fair Trade Travel** (Birdwatching).

Footprint Adventures

5 Malham Drive
Lincoln LN6 0XS
U.K.
☎ (01522) 804929
email: sales@footventure.co.uk
website: www.footventure.co.uk
Eleven years operating wildlife, birdwatching and trekking holidays in India and Nepal, trekking in Tibet and Bhutan, mountain-biking in Pakistan, and yak safaris on the Batura Glacier.

Wildlife Worldwide

170 Selsdon Road
South Croydon
Surrey CR2 6PJ
U.K.
email: sales@wildlife-ww.co.uk
website: www.wildlife-ww.co.uk
Working with local naturalist guides, this company provides hand-crafted itineraries and small group tours for wildlife enthusiasts from the national parks of India and Nepal to the wilderness areas of Bhutan.

GENERAL INDEX

GAZETTEER

ACKNOWLEDGEMENTS

Steve Watkins
Nepal: Peter Stewart at HMB, Sharu Scott at Specialist Trekking Co-operative, Gaida Wildlife Camp
India: Gagan at Dove Adventures, Himalayan Journeys

Des Hannigan
would like to thank for their expertise and good company all those he worked with in the Northern Areas and in the North West Frontier Province of Pakistan. Special thanks for help and advice to Abdul Aziz Awan in Islamabad, Naunihal Shah in Gilgit, Yousuf Wazir in Skardu, Muhammad Hussain in Khaplu, and Babu Mohammad in Chitral. Very special thanks for their kindness and hospitality to Shahzada K. A. Mulk in Ayun, to Maqsood ul Mulk in Islamabad, and to Shah Khan and Raja Hussain Khan in Gulmit. Thanks, as always, to Tim for being a good mate. And eternal gratitude to Dr. David Hillebrandt for making sure we knew how to stay fit and well.

Jill Gocher
would like to thank the fabulous people of India and Nepal who provided her with so many compelling moments and experiences.

Lee Karen Stow
Tibet: Zara Fleming; Tibet Information Network; Himalayan Envpro Adventures, Kathmandu; Hotel Utse; our Tibetan and Nepalese crew; and finally, my gutsy female travelling companions.
Sri Lanka: Deirdre and all at itoi International Projects; Viren and Tennakoon at the Ulpotha Sanctuary; Somak Holidays; Travel PR, London; Jake my motorbiking companion.

Simon Richmond
Clipper Holidays for all their assistance organizing my adventures in southern India; Sini for being an excellent guide in the Nilgiris.

Emma Stanford
would like to thank Manju Barua of Wild Grass in Guwahati, Ronesh Roy and his unfailingly cheerful and willing staff at the Wildgrass Resort Kaziranga, and my inestimable guide and fount of local knowledge, Rajan Dowerah.

Copy editors: Sue Gordon, Nick Reynolds **Paste-up:** Simon Buchanan **Proofreading:** Hilary Weston, Jackie Staddon **Indexer:** Marie Lorimer

Abbreviations for terms appearing below: (t) top; (b) bottom; (l) left: (r) right; (c) centre

Cover acknowledgements
Front Cover (t): **Planet Earth Pictures Ltd**
Front Cover main picture: **Bruce Coleman Collection**
Front Cover inset: **AA Photolibrary/S Richmond**
Spine: As Front Cover (t)
Back Cover (t); **AA Photolibrary/J Gocher**
Back Cover (c); **AA Photolibrary/J Gocher**
Back Cover (b); **AA Photolibrary/S Watkins**
Back Cover (br); **AA Photolibrary/D Corrance**
Inside flaps: (t) **AA Photolibrary/D Hannigan**; (ct) **AA Photolibrary/S Watkins**; (cb) **AA Photolibrary/S Watkins**; (b) **AA Photolibrary/S Watkins**

The Automobile Assocation wishes to thank the following photographers and libraries for their assistance in the preparation of this book.

Bruce Coleman Collection 30/1; **Emma Stanford** 8(br), 62(t), 62(c), 62(b), 66(t), 66(b), 67(t), 67(l), 67(r), 70, 71, 71(inset).

The remaining photographs are held in the Association's own photo library (AA PHOTOLIBRARY) and were taken by the following photographers.

Fredrik Arvidsson 55(r); **Douglas Corrance** 34(b); **Jill Gocher** 1(tc), 3, 8(bc), 14, 15, 18/19, 22/3, 22, 23, 26(t), 26(b), 27, 30, 31, 34(t), 38, 38/9, 42, 54/5, 55(l), 58/9, 59(t), 59(b), 131, 162/3, 163(t), 163(b), 166(t), 166(b), 167, 168, 170/1, 171, 174/5, 175(t), 175(c), 175(b); **Des Hannigan** 1(tr), 8(tr), 198/9, 199, 202, 202/3, 203, 206, 207(l), 207(r), 210, 210/1, 214, 215, 218, 219, 222, 223, 226(t), 226(b), 230, 231, 231(inset), 234, 235(l), 235(tr); **I Morejohn** 182(t), 187(b); **Simon Richmond** 8(b), 95, 95(inset), 98, 99(t), 99(b), 102(t), 102(c), 106/7, 106, 107, 110(l), 110(r), 111(t), 111(b), 114/5, 115(t), 115(b), 118, 118/9, 122, 123(t), 123(b), 126, 126(inset), 127(t), 127(b); **Lee Karen Stow** 1(bl), 6/7, 8(tc), 178/9, 179, 182(b), 183, 186, 187(t), 190, 191, 194, 195, 238/9, 242(l), 242(r), 243(t), 243(b), 246, 247, 250/1, 251, 254, 254/5, 255; **Steve Watkins** 1(t), 1(tl), 1(c), 2/3, 7, 8(tl), 46(t), 46(c), 46(c), 47, 50, 74, 75(t), 75(b), 78, 79(t), 79(b), 82(l), 82(r), 86(l), 86(r), 87(l), 87(r), 90/1, 91(t), 91(b), 130/1, 134/5, 135(t), 135(b), 138, 138(bl), 138(br), 139, 142, 143(t), 143(b), 146, 146/7, 150, 151, 154(t), 154(b), 155, 158, 159.